Mark Powell

SECOND EDITION

in company

UPPER-INTERMEDIATE STUDENT'S BOOK WITH CD-ROM

MACMILLAN

SECOND EDITION STUDENT'S BOOK:

▶ **13 SKILLS UNITS** focusing on everyday, functional business language

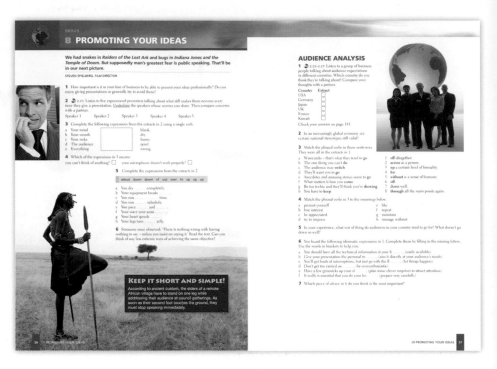

▶ **5 TOPIC DEBATES UNITS** focusing on topical business issues

▶ Phrase Bank for summary and revision

▶ **Discussion phrase bank**

I think we have to ask ourselves whether we really want ... or not.

These forecasts take absolutely no account of ...

The consequences of ... could be far-reaching – for example, ...

The real danger is that ...

I'm quite positive / sceptical about ...

But I really can't see us allowing ...

▶ 13 LANGUAGE LINKS consolidating grammar and extending vocabulary from the Skills Units

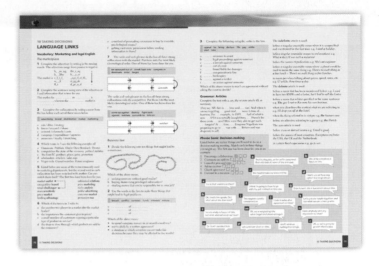

▶ 5 CASE STUDIES reflecting real-life business scenarios

▶ BACK-OF-BOOK MATERIAL:

● Listening Scripts with useful phrases from the Language Link Phrase Banks in bold

● Additional material for communicative activities

SELF-STUDY CD-ROM:

● Extra listening activities
● Interactive grammar and vocabulary activities
● Interactive glossary
● Downloadable Student's Book audio
● Downloadable Student's Book Phrase Banks

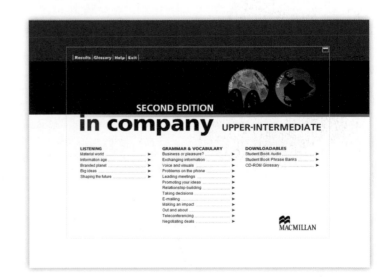

WEBSITE:

Course updates, regular e-lessons and supplementary material available at: **www.businessenglishonline.net**

CONTENTS

1 BUSINESS OR PLEASURE?

All things being equal, people will buy from a friend. All things being not quite so equal, people will still buy from a friend.

MARK McCORMACK, *WHAT THEY DON'T TEACH YOU AT HARVARD BUSINESS SCHOOL*

1 How important do you think it is to actually like the people you do business with?

2 Read these two short extracts from different business articles. Is the point they are making equally valid in your country?

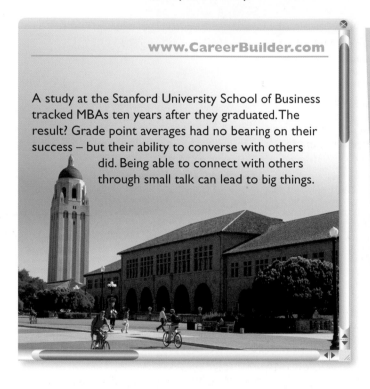

www.CareerBuilder.com

A study at the Stanford University School of Business tracked MBAs ten years after they graduated. The result? Grade point averages had no bearing on their success – but their ability to converse with others did. Being able to connect with others through small talk can lead to big things.

When Jack Welch gave a guest lecture at MIT's Sloan School of Management in 2005, someone in the crowd asked, 'What should we be learning in business school?' Welch's reply: 'Just concentrate on networking. Everything else you need to know, you can learn on the job.'

Fortune magazine

3 How good are you at small talk? You are going to practise networking with a business contact.

a First, briefly note down some information about yourself in the chart below. Omit or change any of the topics you want to.

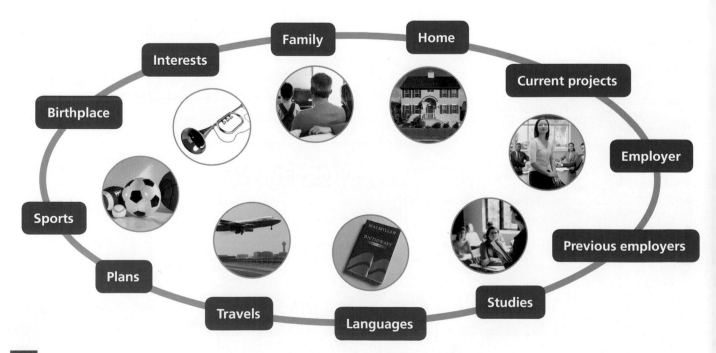

Interests   Family   Home   Current projects

Birthplace   Employer

Sports   Previous employers

Plans   Studies

Travels   Languages

b Work with a partner to set the scene of your conversation. Where are you – at a conference reception, a social event, in the coffee break at a training seminar? Are you enjoying yourself? How did you travel there? What's the weather been like? What's been happening in the news lately?

c Swap personal information with your partner and use this and the scene you built up in b as the basis for your conversation. How long can you keep the conversation going? The language in the conversation phrase bank may help you.

4 How did the conversation go? Which topics had the most mileage? Did you find anything in common?

> **Conversation phrase bank**
> So, how are you enjoying …?
> Isn't this weather …?
> I hear you … Is that right?
> I understand you used to …
> Am I right in thinking you …?
> Ah, I see. So, …?
> Oh, that's interesting, because I …
> Really? That's a coincidence!
> So, tell me more about …
> Is it true that …?
> Well, it's been nice talking to you.

CORPORATE ENTERTAINMENT

1 The Japanese economy has had its ups and downs, but Japanese firms continue to spend around $40 billion a year on corporate hospitality. Can that kind of money ever be considered well spent? Should it be the first thing to cut in a recession? How can entertaining clients and colleagues be good for business?

What better way to build and maintain (a)_____ with key (b)_____ and to reward star (c)_____ of your (d)_____ than to offer them a unique and unforgettable (e)_____ far away from the pressures and constraints of an (f)_____ environment? Whether it's front row (g)_____ at the Metropolitan Opera in New York, a VIP (h)_____ at the World Cup Final, a private (i)_____ at the Guggenheim Gallery in Bilbao or a champagne (j)_____ at the Paris Ritz, we can provide the ideal (k)_____ and first-class (l)_____ that will leave your guests simply saying 'Wow!'

2 Complete the extract from a corporate entertainment company's website using the words in the box. Are you persuaded by what it says?

box clients experience members
office reception relationships seats
service setting team viewing

3 🔊 1.01 A group of Russian business people, who are about to collaborate with you on a major international project, is visiting your London office. As part of the planning committee, it's your job to decide on a special event to celebrate their visit. Listen to some of the suggestions of the other committee members and take notes.

4 Work in two groups to find out about four different events you could take your Russian visitors to. Group A turn to page 138. Group B turn to page 147.

5 Pair up with someone from the other group and discuss the options. Prepare to briefly present your recommendations.

MAKING CONVERSATION

1 1.02–1.03 Listen to some business people chatting at two corporate events and answer the questions.

Conversation 1

a What's the connection between Helen Keating, James McRae and Alan Sullivan?

b When Helen asks James 'Mind if I join you?', how does he reply?
N............. a............. a............. . B............. m............. g............. .

c What excuse does Helen make for leaving the rest of the party?

d Two of the following mean 'That can't be true.' Which two?
You're joking! ☐
You're fooling! ☐
You're kidding! ☐

e Helen and James use several expressions to refer to memories. Can you remember the first three words of each expression? Contractions (*it's, you're* etc.) count as one word.

1 .... somewhere before?
2 .... me to forget a face.
3 .... recognised you.
4 .... back to me now.
5 .... remember spending most of the evening fighting off some creepy little guy called Alan.

Conversation 2

a How would you describe relations between Mr Ishida and Mr Thompson?
warm ☐ amicable ☐ cordial ☐ cool ☐ strained ☐ frosty ☐

b Mr Thompson uses the word 'so' five times during the conversation:

> *So, Mr Ishida, let me freshen your glass.*

> *So, how are you enjoying the match?*

> *So, tell me, have you been to one of these big tournaments before?*

> *So, shall we return to our seats?*

> *So, do you still play?*

Why does he need to use it so often? What's the equivalent word or expression in your own language?

c Mr Ishida says he's too old to play table tennis now. Mr Thompson replies 'Oh, I'm sure that's not true.' Is he:
paying Mr Ishida a compliment? ☐   calling him a liar? ☐

d Mr Thompson tries to use his background knowledge to keep the conversation going. Complete his remarks below.
1 I h............. you're quite a tennis fan.
2 I u............. the Japanese are world table tennis champions.
3 I s............. the Nikkei's looking strong. That m............. be good news for you.
4 I r............. somewhere that things were improving. Or a............. I mistaken?

e What word is Mr Ishida avoiding by saying the following?
Not at the moment, thank you.   Not really.   Not especially.
Not any more.   As a matter of fact, ...

2 Work with a partner. Practise avoiding saying 'no'.

THE NO-NO GAME

Prepare

Write down eight false (but believable) statements about yourself, your job, your family, your interests, your company or your country. When you are ready, swap lists with a partner.

Play

Imagine the two of you are chatting at a conference or corporate event. Take it in turns to make wrong assumptions about each other using the lists as a starting point but adding remarks of your own if you can.

> e.g. **I hear** you're based in Rotterdam.
>
> **I understand** you're a keen golfer.
>
> **I believe** your company's about to be involved in a merger.
>
> **I read somewhere** that Russia will be joining the EU soon.

Your objective is to get the other person to say 'no'. Their objective is the same. Use the expressions opposite to help you avoid saying 'no'.

Whoever says 'no' first loses.

▶ **Conversation phrase bank**

Not very.
Not really.
Not especially.
Not exactly.
Not yet.
Not any more.
Not at the moment.
Not as far as I know.
Actually, …
As a matter of fact, …

3 🔊 **1.04–1.05** Listen to some business people chatting at the other two corporate events you discussed and answer the questions.

Conversation 1

a What sort of people are the Hamiltons? Compare your impressions with a partner.

b Put the words in the following greetings and introductions in the correct order.
1 Dan call please me
2 meet last to both pleasure at a you
3 mentioned name Julian's course your of
4 Fiona calling me mind do don't you you you?

c It's common when someone joins a group at a party to tell them a bit about the conversation you've just been having. Complete the following:

discussing   saying   talking   trying   wondering

	a	.... what a marvellous party this is.
	b	.... these new tax laws they're bringing in.
We were just	c	.... about you – how are things?
	d	.... what this pile of dirty laundry was doing in an art gallery.
	e	.... to work out what this whole thing must have cost.

d Why does Dan say to Alistair 'I wonder if we could have a word?' when they're already talking?

e All the expressions below mean 'I'm going'. Which also mean 'but I'm coming back'? Some of them were in the conversation you just listened to.

It's been nice talking to you.	☐	Would you excuse me a moment?	☐
I'll have to be going.	☐	I'll be right back.	☐
If you'll excuse me.	☐	Is that the time?	☐
Don't go away.	☐	I'll catch you later.	☐

Conversation 2

a   Do Tom and Ricardo do a deal?

b   What expression does Tom use to switch from discussing motor racing to discussing business?
T............... o............... races, how's the South African bid going?

c   Complete the expressions below. They were all in the conversation you just listened to. Contractions (*I'd, wouldn't, who's* etc.) count as one word.

   1   Glad .... make it.
   2   I .... missed it for the world.
   3   There's .... like you to meet.
   4   Can't .... standing there with an empty glass.
   5   So, ... person you wanted me to meet?
   6   I .... two know each other already.
   7   I'll .... two to chat. See you later.

d   What do the following remarks tell you about Ricardo and Élise's relationship?

> Long time no see.

> You haven't changed a bit.

> Neither have you. Charming as ever.

> Ricardo and I go back a long way.

> I'll have whatever you're having.

4   Work with a partner. Practise paying and receiving compliments.

THE MUTUAL APPRECIATION GAME

Conversation phrase bank

You're looking well!

Hey, nice ...!

What (a) brilliant/fantastic/fabulous ...!

You know, that/those ... really suit(s) you!

I (really) like your ...! Where did you get it/them?

By the way, you did a great job in the meeting/presentation the other day.

Prepare

Spend a few minutes thinking of compliments you could pay your partner. Use the expressions opposite to help you.

Play

When you are ready, start exchanging compliments with your partner. Respond to each compliment you receive in an appreciative but modest way. See who can give the most compliments in under a minute!

5   They say 'Flattery will get you everywhere.' How important is it in your culture to

a   pay people personal compliments?

b   compliment them on their work?

Does it depend on how well you know each other or how senior you are? Is it different for men and women? Can it ever be risky?

6 According to Dale Carnegie, author of the all-time best-selling people skills book *How to Win Friends and Influence People*, 'You can make more friends in two months by becoming interested in other people than you can in two years by trying to get people interested in you.' Work with a partner to practise keeping up a conversation.

First choose just three 'hot buttons' from the list below – topics you are especially interested in talking about, but don't tell your partner what they are!

Then take turns to ask each other questions from the list. Whenever your partner asks you about one of your hot buttons, you should speak enthusiastically about the topic for a minute or so. If the topic is not hot, then just reply very briefly and ask your next question.

Whenever you or your partner hit a hot button, you score five points. When you miss, you lose one point.

The game ends after ten minutes or when one of you has hit all the other's hot buttons. Whoever has the most points at the end of the game is the winner.

THE HOT BUTTONS GAME

Topic	Conversation starters	Hot or not?
THE WEATHER	Isn't this weather ...? Apparently, the forecast is for ...	Hot/Not
WORK	How's business? I hear ...	Hot/Not
RECENT NEWS	Have you heard about ...? ... news, isn't it?	Hot/Not
THE ECONOMY	I see the stock markets are ... It's probably a good time to ...	Hot/Not
SPORT	Are you into sport at all? Did you see the game/match on ...?	Hot/Not
MUSIC	What kind of music are you into? Have you heard ...'s latest album?	Hot/Not
MUTUAL FRIENDS	Do you know ..., by the way? S/he's a bit/very ..., isn't s/he?	Hot/Not
MOVIES	Have you seen any good films lately? I quite liked ...	Hot/Not
BOOKS	Have you, by any chance, read ...? I read quite a lot of ...	Hot/Not
TRAVEL	Do you get to do much travelling? Have you ever been to ...?	Hot/Not
GADGETS	Have you seen those new ...? I wonder if they're any good? I heard ...	Hot/Not
CLOTHES/JEWELLERY	I like your ...Where did you get it/them? I suppose it/they must have cost you ...?	Hot/Not
HOLIDAYS	Have you been away this year? I was/We were planning to go to ...	Hot/Not
FOOD/DRINK	Shall we get ourselves ...? What would you like? How about ...?	Hot/Not

LANGUAGE LINKS

Vocabulary: Small talk

1 Put the conversation in the correct order.

[1] We were just talking about this new sports centre they're building. Do you play any sport at all, Kim?

☐ Not yet, no. Why, are you doing something?

☐ Against Real Madrid? No, I missed it. I had to go to a birthday party.

☐ No problem. Oh, before I forget. I've got two tickets to see them in Manchester if you're interested.

☐ No, me neither. Talking of football, did you see the match last night?

☐ Oh, right. Thanks for telling me. Incidentally, have you still got my Rolling Stones CD?

☐ Me? Well, not really. I used to play a bit of football.

☐ No, nothing special. By the way, sorry to talk business, but did you remember to send that estimate to Clive?

☐ Pity. It was a great game. On the subject of parties, have you made any plans for New Year's Eve yet?

☐ Did you? Me too. I was never any good, though.

☐ Oops! Yeah, sorry. I meant to give it back to you. I'll bring it in tomorrow. Thanks for lending it to me.

☐ Yeah, I sent it yesterday. Oh, that reminds me. Clive said to tell you he won't be able to make Thursday's meeting. He said he'd call you.

[13] Are you kidding? Of course I'm interested! I've never seen them live.

2 Find six expressions in 1 to guide the conversation or change the subject.

a I.............., ...
b T.............. of ...
c B.............. the w.............., ...
d B.............. I f.............., ...
e T.............. r.............. me, ...
f O.............. t.............. s.............. of ...

3 Which words and phrases in 1 could you replace with ...?

a Not so far.
b Not to worry.
c Nor me.
d Shame.
e So did I.
f Are you joking?

Grammar: Tense review

1 Try to complete the tense quiz in under five minutes.

1 *He **leaves** at five* means
   a today   b every day   c either
2 *We're **having** a meeting* means
   a now   b soon   c either
3 *Profits **went up**.* Are profits up now?
   a yes   b no   c maybe
4 *Profits **have gone up**.* Are profits up now?
   a yes   b no   c maybe
5 *He's **gone**.* Is he here?
   a yes   b no   c maybe

2 Read the e-mail and underline the best grammatical choice in each case.

From: Charles Wellcome
To: Deborah Newton, Stephen Clark, Willem Maes, Tatiana Korbutt
Subject: This year's client hospitality event

Dear all

As you (1) **know / are knowing**, the annual client hospitality event (2) **is fast approaching / will fast approach** and, as yet, we (3) **did not make / have not made** a final decision on where to hold it this year. One or two of you (4) **already came forward / have already come forward** with suggestions, which (5) **are currently considered / are currently being considered**, but, as we (6) **will have to / are having to** make the necessary arrangements quite soon, I'd like everybody's input on this asap.

What I particularly (7) **want / am wanting** to avoid is a repetition of the fiasco we (8) **had / have had** last year at the showjumping event. Apart from the fact that very few of our clients (9) **have / are having** even the remotest interest in the sport, the atrocious weather (10) **meant / was meaning** that we (11) **walked / were walking** backwards and forwards through the mud between the showring and the hospitality tent all day. The whole thing (12) **was / has been** a complete disaster. People (13) **still complained / were still complaining** about it six months later!

This year we (14) **have planned / had planned** to do something more cultural like go to the opera or even a musical, but (15) **I've wondered / I've been wondering** if this is a good idea. A musical event (16) **doesn't seem / isn't seeming** to be the best place to network. We can hardly ask the singers to keep the noise down while we all (17) **have / will have** a good chat!

I (18) **do think / am thinking**, however, that an indoor event (19) **makes / is making** most sense, so can I ask you to (20) **think / be thinking** along those lines over the next few days? (21) **I've scheduled / I'd scheduled** a meeting for next Friday to discuss the matter further. So, (22) **I'm speaking / I'll speak** to you all then.

Charles

6 *I've just **been**.* Am I back?
   a yes   b no   c maybe
7 *When I arrived he **was** just **leaving**.* Was he there when I arrived?
   a yes   b no   c we don't know
8 *When I arrived he'd just **left**.* Was he there when I arrived?
   a yes   b no   c we don't know
9 *I've **tried** to phone her.* Am I still trying?
   a probably   b probably not   c we don't know
10 *I've **been trying** to contact her all morning.* Am I still trying?
   a probably   b probably not   c we don't know

You use the **Present Simple** to talk about permanent facts (*I'm Spanish*), routines (*I get home at seven each evening*) and scheduled future (*The bus gets in at one*).

You use the **Present Continuous** to talk about current, perhaps temporary, activities and situations (*I'm staying at the Hilton*) or future arrangements (*I'm flying to Rome in the morning*).

You use the **Present Perfect** to talk about things that started in the past and continue up to the present (*It's rained for a fortnight*), personal experiences no matter when they happened (*I've only ever snowboarded once*) and things which have an immediate consequence (*I've lost my car keys*). Words like *already*, *yet* and *since* are often in the same sentence as a present perfect verb.

You use the **Present Perfect Continuous** to talk about things that started in the past and may be recently completed or not yet completed (*She's been rearranging her office*, *I've been working here since January 2002*).

You use the **Past Simple** to talk about finished past actions or states (*I studied engineering at Oxford*, *I was a happy child*). Phrases like *last week, a year ago, in 2006* etc. make the time reference clear.

You use the **Past Continuous** to talk about an action in progress in the past (*The company was losing money*). The Past Continuous gives the background to more important events which are in the Past Simple.

You use the **Past Perfect** to emphasise that one event happened before another in the past (*By the time I left college, I'd already decided I didn't want to be a lawyer*).

Some 'state' verbs like *think, know, understand* and *seem* are not generally used in the continuous form unless the meaning is different: *I think = I believe; I'm thinking = I'm considering something*.

will is a modal verb and, amongst its other uses, one of many ways of talking about the future (*I'll see you later*).

Phrase bank: Making conversation

Read the following tips on how to master the art of small talk. Match each of the tips to four things you might say. The first one has been done for you as an example.

The art of small talk

1 Use what you already know about people to start up a conversation.
[b][ ][ ][ ]

2 Try to bring people into conversation with others you know.
[ ][ ][ ][ ]

3 Show enthusiasm; pay people you know well the occasional compliment.
[ ][ ][ ][ ]

4 Be careful not to contradict people too directly.
[ ][ ][ ][ ]

5 Change the subject smoothly by referring to what others have said.
[ ][ ][ ][ ]

6 Don't break off the conversation too abruptly at the end.
[ ][ ][ ][ ]

a Oh, that reminds me: we're supposed to be meeting Leo at seven.

b I hear you speak Cantonese, is that right?

c Is that the time? I must be making tracks.

d Kenichi, there's someone I'd like you to meet.

e Erm, well, not exactly, no.

f Lisa, we were just talking about the property slump – you know a lot about this.

g Well, it's been really nice talking to you.

h I'm afraid I'll have to be going. But let me give you my card.

i I understand you used to work for 3M.

j Hey, that's great news! You must be pleased.

k Talking of stock markets, how's the DAX doing these days?

l Funny you should say that, something very similar happened to me.

m Ingrid, come and join us. We were just talking about you!

n Congratulations on the promotion, by the way!

o As a matter of fact, I don't – not really.

p You're looking well. Been on holiday?

q If you'll excuse me, I must rush. Catch you later.

r You're Mia, aren't you? Rachel asked me to say hello.

s Well, that's not entirely true, but I know what you mean.

t Nice watch! Is it new?

u On the subject of the merger, have you heard the latest?

v Let's see what Max thinks. Max, we've got a question for you.

w Actually, it's not as bad as you might think.

x I couldn't help noticing your accent. You must be from New Zealand.

2 EXCHANGING INFORMATION

If a problem causes many meetings, the meetings eventually become more important than the problem.

ARTHUR BLOCH, *MURPHY'S LAW*

1 Roughly how much of your working week do you spend in meetings?

2 Read the well-circulated web joke below. Is this anything like the meetings you take part in? What are some of the current 'buzzwords' in your line of business?

Lonely? Hate taking personal responsibility? Rather talk about it than do it?

Then why not **HOLD A MEETING!**

You can:
- catch up on the latest gossip
- bitch about work
- flirt
- take a nap during PowerPoint presentations
- share whatever's on your mind

- practise all the latest buzzwords
- offload nasty jobs onto absent colleagues
- reschedule missed deadlines
- postpone decisions
- feel important
- And all in work time!

MEETINGS *The practical alternative to work*

3 Native speakers (particularly those with MBAs!) tend to use a lot of buzzwords in meetings. It's not always helpful to use these yourself, but it can be useful to know the most common ones. With a partner, try to complete the buzzword dictionary definitions below by writing in the missing vowels.

a **BL M ST RM NG** is when a group meets to decide who's responsible for poor performance.
b You need to do a **R L TY CH CK** when you've lost touch with the real world.
c A change of **M NDS T** means completely rethinking your attitude and approach to something.
d To **SYN RG S** means to combine strengths and benefit from working together as a team.
e To be **PR CT V** is to make things happen rather than waiting for them to happen.
f To think **TS D TH B X** is to think in totally new and creative ways.
g A **P R D GM SH FT** is a fundamental change in the way something is done.
h **TH B TT M L N** is the essential point in a discussion.
i Looking at **TH B G P CT R** is looking at the situation as a whole.
j To **DR LL D WN** is to go into more detail.
k When you get **P SH-B CK** from someone it means they are resisting you or your ideas.
l Getting **B Y- N** from people means getting their support for a proposal or project.
m To **SC P T** the competition means to check what they are doing.
n A company's **C R C MP T NC S** are its strengths, the things it does particularly well.
o To **B NCHM RK** is to use a successful company's standards to measure and improve your own.
p The **L NG G M** is your objectives for the long-term future.
q To **PSK LL** workers means to train them to do things they cannot do at present.
r To **R MP P** production or sales is to increase them.
s A **C ST M R-C NTR C** company is one that bases its whole business on client needs.
t To take a business to **TH N XT L V L** means to expand it and make it more competitive.
u The **GR SSR TS** of an organisation are its workers, rather than its leaders.
v **EMP W RM NT** gives employees the confidence and authority to take control of their jobs.

4 🌐 1.06 You're going to play a game that's become popular with bored executives the world over – buzzword bingo! First, turn to page 139 to choose a bingo card. Then listen to a manager, fresh from a management training seminar, talking at a meeting and cross off the buzzwords as he uses them. The first person to cross them all off and shout 'Bingo!' wins the game.

5 Some of the things you might really want to discuss in an information-sharing meeting are listed below, but the second word in each collocation has been switched with another. Switch them back. The first two have been done for you.

production **margins** ◄
balance **appraisals**
market **channels**
staff **sheets**
profit **methods** ◄
distribution **trends**

quality **campaigns**
sales **chains**
advertising **control**
cost **development**
supply **projections**
product **cutting**

customer **budgets**
recruitment **setting**
salary **support**
training **relations**
price **procedures**
IT **reviews**

6 Work with a partner. Take turns to explain one of the terms in 5 and see if your partner can guess which one it is. How many can you get right in two minutes?

Example
It's predicting how many products you think you'll sell.
'Market trends'?
No.
Oh, you mean 'sales projections'?
Right.

MAKING THINGS CLEAR

1 How direct are people from your country when it comes to doing business? Complete the diagram below with the nationalities in the box. Then check your answers on page 159.

American   Brazilian   British   Chinese   French   German   Indian   Italian   Japanese   Russian

Direct | 1 | 2 | 4 | 3 | 5 | 6 | 7 | 8 | 9 | 10 | Indirect

Barry Tomalin and Mike Nicks, *The World's Business Cultures and How to Unlock Them*

2 In meetings, especially in indirect cultures, people are sometimes reluctant to say exactly what they mean – especially if they have bad news! Match the vague statements to their blunter equivalents.

Vague
a I'm sorry to report that the project has not been a complete success.
b Technically speaking, we have run into negative profit.
c I think there's a general lack of consumer confidence.
d You know we've always been a market-driven organisation.
e Now is not the time to expand, but to consolidate.
f There will have to be some restructuring of the department.
g We may also have to consider outsourcing production to cut costs.
h Of course, we won't be able to finalise anything today.

Blunt
1 Our assembly plant may be closed down too.
2 Sales are falling.
3 People are going to lose their jobs.
4 It's failed.
5 We'll have to hold another meeting!
6 We've made a loss.
7 Let's do nothing.
8 We've never had an original idea.

3 🔊 1.07 A computer games company has had problems with its latest product. Listen to an extract from their meeting and check your answers in 2.

4 Can you summarise the meeting you just listened to using the notes below? Listen again if you need to.

> ### Quasar Online Gaming System
>
> Considerable investment in design and marketing – project not a complete success – negative profit – disappointing sales – lack of consumer confidence – Sony and Nintendo innovate – we clone technology – do it cheaper – a market-driven organisation – market massively oversupplied – bad time to expand – good time to consolidate – departmental restructuring necessary – possibly outsource – cut costs – assembly plant closure likely – schedule another meeting – final decision

5 Work with a partner. Take turns to read out the vague statements below. The other person should paraphrase them in a more direct way using the expressions in the box and the words in brackets.

| In other words, ...   So what you're (really) saying is ...   What you (really) mean is ...   You mean ... |

a   The results so far have been rather disappointing. (disastrous)
b   We may currently be overstaffed in the customer relations department. (lay-offs)
c   Head office's reaction to the idea has not been as positive as we hoped. (hate)
d   Sales have not yet matched our original projections. (not selling)
e   The market doesn't seem to be as buoyant as it used to be. (dead)
f   The project is likely to cost rather more than we anticipated. (over-budget)

QUERIES AND COMMENTS

1 🔊 **1.08** Listen to short extracts from five meetings. Each contains one piece of information that doesn't make sense. When the conversation pauses, work with a partner and decide what the discrepancy is. Then listen to the rest of the extract and check.

2 Work with a partner to practise pointing out discrepancies. Speaker A see page 138. Speaker B see page 148.

3 🔊 **1.09** Listen to an extract from a meeting. A CEO is breaking some bad news to the board. When the conversation pauses, write the board members' queries and comments using the notes in brackets to help you. Then continue listening and check. The first one has been done for you as an example.
a   (say/fall short/projections again?)
    Are you saying they've fallen short of projections again?
b   (suggest/introduce/price cuts?)
c   (surely/not say/time/phase them out!)
d   (this mean/should/invest more/new technology?)
e   (tell us/could be layoffs?)
f   (mean some kind/job-share scheme?)
g   (so/say/should/spend more/R&D)
h   (this mean/think/centralise distribution?)
i   (hope/not suggest/situation/hopeless)

4 The following phrases and expressions were all in the meeting you just listened to. Can you reverse the meaning of each by changing the word or words in bold? The first one has been done for you as an example.

a **disappointing** figures
   encouraging figures
b **fall short of** projections
c 30% **down**
d **miss** our targets
e price **cuts**
f run at **a loss**
g phase them **out**
h keep costs **down**
i **major** restructuring
j the unions **oppose** it
k **slide into** debt
l **centralise** distribution
m **overseas** distributors
n an all-time **low**
o **inflated** prices
p **volatile** markets

5 Turn to page 164. Look at the script of the meeting you listened to in 3 and answer the questions.

a How many examples of conditional sentences and expressions are there?
b Apart from *if*, which three words are used to link the conditional to the main clause?
c Only one of the conditional sentences refers to the past. Which one?
d Why is the past tense used in the following example from the meeting?
   *Even if we **decided** to do that, and it's a big if, it would take time to implement.*
e *If only it was that simple* (line 24) means:
   I wish it was that simple. ☐   I doubt it's that simple. ☐
f *We're not really in a position to invest in anything, **even if** we wanted to* (lines 24–25) means:
   We don't want to invest in anything. ☐
   Wanting to invest would make no difference. ☐

THE LANGUAGE OF MEETINGS

1 Work with a partner. One word will complete each of the following extracts from meetings. Can you agree what it is? If you need help, turn to page 141.

a A scheduling meeting
A Right. Basically, the _____ is this: the contract is ours if we want it.
B But we're not in a _____ to take on another project right now, are we?
A I know. Jan, what's your _____ on this?

b An IT meeting
A Look, it's not just a _____ of software, Alessandro.
B Of course not. It's also a _____ of hardware. The entire system needs upgrading.
A But that's out of the _____ We can't afford that kind of capital outlay.

c A marketing meeting
A Sales are down. One _____ would obviously be to cut our prices.
B That's no longer an _____ for us. We're barely breaking even as it is.
A Well, then we've no _____ but to rethink our whole marketing strategy.

d An HR* meeting
A Well, there's no easy _____ to this, but how about voluntary redundancy?
B I don't think that's the _____ but maybe we could reduce people's hours.
A That might have been the _____ if we didn't already have a strike on our hands!

e A strategy meeting
A Now, let's not make a _____ out of this. What if we just pulled out of Sudan?
B Well, I've no _____ with that, but our partners won't be happy.
A No, but that's not our _____ is it? The political situation is just too unstable.

f A CRM** meeting
A I'll get straight to the _____ We're getting too many customer complaints.
B I agree with you. But the _____ is we don't have the staff to deal with them.
A That's beside the _____ We shouldn't be getting them in the first place!

g A crisis meeting
A I'm afraid the _____ is serious. And if the press get hold of the story, ...
B Look, we'll deal with that _____ if and when it arises. Let's not panic just yet.
A You're right. What this _____ calls for is calm and careful planning.

h A budget meeting
A The _____ is, we're simply not spending enough on R&D.
B As a matter of _____ we've doubled our R&D budget this year.
C That may be so, but the _____ remains we're losing our technological lead.

* Human Resources
** Customer Relationship Management

2 1.10 Listen to the meeting in 1 and check your answers.

3 Now decide which of the words in the box on page 141 will complete the following and match them to what they mean.

a That's a matter of ....   You're wrong!
b I think that raises a different ....   I disagree!
c Yes, but look at it from my point of ....   That's unimportant!
d Actually, that might not be a bad ....   That's irrelevant!
e That's not an ....   Good point!
f What gave you that ....?   What about me?

BREAKING THE BAD NEWS

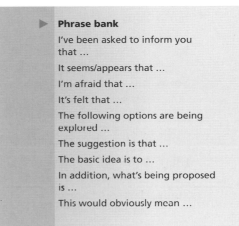

1 Your company was recently acquired by a former competitor in a hostile takeover. The new board of directors has decided it's time for a serious shake-up. Each of you has been chosen to announce at a special interdepartmental meeting some of the changes they would like to see implemented. Speaker A turn to page 139. Speaker B turn to page 148. Speaker C turn to page 152. The phrase bank may help you prepare.

> **Phrase bank**
> I've been asked to inform you that …
> It seems/appears that …
> I'm afraid that …
> It's felt that …
> The following options are being explored …
> The suggestion is that …
> The basic idea is to …
> In addition, what's being proposed is …
> This would obviously mean …

2 When you're ready, take turns in your group to present the proposals. They could be controversial, so:

• put them forward one step at a time and get reactions from the group before moving on to the next step
• invite discussion of each proposal and take notes on any comments or alternative suggestions
• even though you yourself may not be in favour of the proposal(s) you put forward, you should at least initially show loyalty to your new bosses by sounding positive.

3 Write a memo to the board outlining the reactions to the proposals you presented at your meeting.

LANGUAGE LINKS

Vocabulary: Meetings

Metaphor: discussion is a journey

A lot of the language of discussion refers to journeys. Read the conversation and <u>underline</u> the references to movement and travel. There are 20.

Ian returns to the boardroom to find the meeting in chaos ...

Ian   Sorry about that. Had to take a phone call from Bangkok. So, are we any nearer a decision?

Erik   Not yet, but we're getting there. I think we're more or less on the right track, anyway.

Sonia   Are we? I'd say we've got a long way to go yet. We just seem to be going round in circles.

Erik   Well, we were making good progress before we got sidetracked, Sonia. Now, returning to the question of logistics ...

Ella   Sorry, but could I just go back to what I was saying earlier about freight charges?

Sonia   Hang on, hang on. Aren't we getting ahead of ourselves here? We haven't got as far as discussing transportation yet, Ella ...

Erik   We don't seem to be getting very far at all!

Ian   The conversation seems to have drifted a little while I was away ... I can't quite see where all this is heading.

Erik   We've certainly wandered away from the main topic. Now, logistics ...

Sonia   I was just coming to that. In my opinion, this whole plan is totally impractical.

Ian   I don't think I like the direction this discussion is going in. OK, look, we've covered a lot of ground this morning, but I think that's about as far as we can go at the moment.

Erik   Now, just a minute! We haven't come this far to break off now, surely ...

Idiomatic expressions

1   In the fixed expressions below, delete the word you wouldn't expect to hear.

a   So, what do you **reckon/guess**?
b   I'd go **around/along** with that.
c   I wouldn't go quite as **far/much** as that.
d   Where do you **stand/sit** on this?
e   Well, that goes without **saying/speaking**.
f   I don't mind **either/each** way.
g   I'm afraid it's not **so/as** simple as that.
h   Any **responses/reactions**?
i   The way I **view/see** it is this.
j   I **wouldn't/couldn't** say that.
k   Yes and no/No and yes.
l   I **can't/couldn't** say, to be honest.
m   I'd like us to **share/spare** our views on this.
n   Oh, come **on/off** it!
o   Well, I haven't **given/taken** it much thought.
p   I'm **for/with** you there.
q   To my **meaning/mind**, it's like this.
r   To **a point/an extent** you're right.

2   Categorise the expressions in 1 according to their purpose.

1   asking for an opinion   ☐ ☐ ☐ ☐
2   giving an opinion   ☐ ☐ ☐
3   giving no opinion   ☐ ☐ ☐
4   agreeing   ☐ ☐
5   disagreeing   ☐ ☐
6   half-agreeing   ☐ ☐ ☐

Grammar: Conditionals

Put a cross next to the ending (1–4) which isn't grammatically possible and then correct it. The first one has been done for you.

a   As long as we're well prepared, ...
   1   we've got nothing to worry about. ✓
   2   we shouldn't have any problems. ✓
   3   we couldn't go wrong. ✗
   4   we'll be fine. ✓
   Correction
   .... *we can't go wrong.* ....

b   I'll send them an e-mail ...
   1   if you'll tell me what I should say.
   2   if you think it's worth it.
   3   unless you'd rather do it.
   4   provided I hadn't lost their address.

c   If you're going out, ...
   1   get me a newspaper, will you?
   2   you're going to miss the meeting.
   3   you'd better take an umbrella.
   4   I come with you.

d   Do that ...
   1   and you'll regret it.
   2   if it'll help.
   3   if you'll get the opportunity.
   4   – we'll lose business.

e   I'd stay and help you ...
   1   if I knew anything about computers.
   2   if I'm not going out this evening.
   3   if I hadn't promised Jo I'd meet her.
   4   if you asked me nicely.

f I'd be grateful …
   1 if you could sort this out for me.
   2 if you'd keep this to yourself.
   3 if you don't tell anyone about this.
   4 if you remembered that in future.

g If he actually said that to her, …
   1 she'd kill him.
   2 I'd have been very surprised.
   3 it was very stupid of him.
   4 he must have been mad.

h I wouldn't have asked you …
   1 if I didn't think you could do it.
   2 unless I trusted you.
   3 if I'd known this would happen.
   4 if you didn't say you wanted to do it.

i If it hadn't been for him, …
   1 I'd still be working at Burger King.
   2 I'd have got that job.
   3 we might never have found out.
   4 I hadn't had a chance.

You can use any tense in either half (clause) of a conditional sentence.

As well as *if, unless, as long as* and *providing/provided (that)*, you can also use *and* as a conjunction in a conditional (*Do that **and** we'll get complaints*) or no conjunction at all (*Do that – we'll get complaints*).

Conditional clauses can come either first or second in the sentence. However, with *and* or no conjunction, conditional clauses come first.

You can put *will* or *would* in the conditional clause (*If you'll wait here, I'll go and get her for you; I'd be grateful if you'd give this matter your serious attention*), but this is unusual.

The Past Simple in a conditional can refer to the past (*Even if I **did meet** her, I'm afraid I don't remember her*), to a future possibility (*If I **resigned** tomorrow, I could get another job within the week*) or to an unreal situation (*If I **spoke** Italian, I'd phone her myself, but I don't*).

Conditionals with the Past Perfect can refer to the effects of the past on the more recent past (*If you'd **made** a backup, we wouldn't have lost the whole document*) or on the present (*If I'd **got** that job, I could be earning a fortune now*).

Phrase bank: Debating issues

A small number of words account for quite a lot of the language of meetings and discussions. One noun (N) will complete each of the sets of expressions below:

a ....
I agree with you up to a N.
That's beside the N.
That's not the N.
That's just my N.
The N is…
OK, N taken.
I'll get straight to the N.
Good N.

b ....
That's out of the N.
Good N!
It's not a N of that.
It's not just a N of …
It's also a N of …
The (real) N is …

c ....
We're not in a N to …
What's your N on this?
This puts us in a very difficult N.
I'm in no N to …

d ....
The N is …
The N remains that …
As a matter of N, …
In actual N, …
Despite the N that …
In view of the N that …

e ....
We've no N.
That's not an N.
One N would be …
N two would be …
Another N would be …

f ....
There's no N.
What's the N?

3 DO THE RIGHT THING

Don't be evil.

OFFICIAL MANTRA AT GOOGLE

1 Can companies 'be evil'? Name an evil company. On what did you base your nomination?

2 What do you understand by the term 'corporate social responsibility' or 'CSR'? Make a short list of ways in which a company can demonstrate its social responsibility and compare with a partner. Can you give any specific examples?

3 Which is a greater corporate responsibility: to do well or to do good? Do priorities change when the economy is in recession and competition intensifies?

4 Work in groups of three to play 'devil's advocate'.

Each read one of the opinions on CSR opposite. Be prepared to summarise it to the rest of your group and defend the position, even if you disagree with it! The others should attack the position, even if they agree with it! Make as many opposing arguments as you can. The discussion phrase bank may help you.

5 🔘 **1.11–1.13** Listen to three international executives discussing the issues in 4 and answer the questions.

a The American takes a rather cynical view of regulations, CSR league tables, PR and the cost of CSR. Why?
b The Norwegian seems fairly modest about Scandinavia's exemplary CSR record. Why?
c Given what the Chinese says about cost-effectiveness, does the American's attitude make more sense?

> **Discussion phrase bank**
>
> The basic position … take(s) is …
>
> … make(s) a strong argument for …
>
> The way … put(s) it is…
>
> When it comes to …, I think … has/ have got a point.
>
> You really can't argue with the fact that …
>
> But surely you're not suggesting …?
>
> How can you say …, when …?
>
> Aren't you overlooking the fact that …?
>
> Surely, the real issue here is …
>
> Wait a minute, I'm not saying … What I'm saying is …
>
> The evidence is overwhelming …

ECO-SPEAK

1 How good is your eco-speak? With a partner, underline the terms being defined below:

a **Accountability / Transparency** is the term used to describe a company's acceptance of its responsibilities.
b **A shareholder / A stakeholder** is anyone who affects or is affected by a company's operations.
c **Recyclable / Renewable** means generated from natural resources which can be replaced.
d **Your carbon footprint / Carbon neutrality** is the impact you have on the environment by the emission of CO_2 gases.
e **Ethical trade / Fair trade** supports small producers in developing countries by offering favourable terms.
f **Diversity / Biodiversity** is the visible and non-visible differences between people, especially employees.
g **Green tech / Clean tech** refers to more energy-efficient, environmentally-friendly technological appliances.
h **Governance / Compliance** is the act of adhering to a prescribed legal code of conduct.
i **Social capital / Social entrepreneurship** is a measure of the ability of people to work together for a common purpose in groups and organisations.
j **Bottom line / Triple bottom line** is the simultaneous pursuit of economic prosperity, environmental quality and social equity.

2 Now write short definitions for the terms you didn't underline. Compare them with the ones on page 158.

Suzy and Jack Welch authors of *Winning,* former editor-in-chief of the *Harvard Business Review* and former CEO of General Electric respectively

In this enlightened day and age, whether times are good or bad, companies must be socially responsible. That's a given. But tough economic conditions underscore a blunt reality. A company's foremost responsibility is to do well. That may sound politically incorrect, but the reason is inexorable. Winning companies create jobs, pay taxes and strengthen the economy. Winning companies, in other words, enable social responsibility, not the other way around. Leaders today need to pin down, for themselves and their employees, CSR's place among the company's priorities.

CSR can play a powerful part in recruiting talent, retaining talent and keeping up morale. But how should companies think about CSR with margins narrowing, layoffs rampant and consumers embracing the 'new frugality?' Moreover, when you're letting people go with one hand, doling out checks to 'worthy causes' with the other is hard to rationalize. When most consumers have good, secure jobs, expecting them to pay more for an eco-friendly product makes sense. With bank accounts drained, it's a tough sell. That doesn't mean the era of 'socially responsible' products is over. It just means increasingly intense cost pressures on the companies selling them.

CSR belongs in every company. But every company must face reality. You have to make money first to give it away.

> **Glossary**
> **underscore** emphasise
> **foremost** main
> **inexorable** inescapable
> **margins narrowing** profits getting smaller
> **rampant** widespread
> **frugality** economising
> **doling out** distributing
> **drained** empty

We've had downturns in the last twenty-five to thirty years and corporate responsibility has not been thrown out of the window. When the upturn comes and you need to get people back, the best people, the most skilled people, are going to be looking at the companies that kept going, the companies who are consistent, who really said we care and followed through on that care.

If you come into a work environment that connects you with the world where you want to see solutions delivered, you're going to feel that this work environment is something that's about my whole person. Work is transformed from being the duty of the function I must perform into the opportunity to make a powerful difference in the wider world around me.

I think we have moved from corporate philanthropy and the giving of money towards a much more strategic approach, about understanding impact and the investing of time right through to big global dilemmas like climate change and environmental responsibility. And the next area that is being talked about in this rapid movement of corporate citizenship is the role of corporations in conflict resolution, in the investment that companies can make in troubled areas of the world to provide jobs and security. Politics needs more of the skills of business and business needs more of the sense of purpose of politics.

> **Glossary**
> **downturn** recession
> **upturn** recovery
> **followed through** continued
> **corporate citizenship** CSR
> **troubled** politically / economically unstable

Lord Michael Hastings
Global Head of Citizenship and Diversity, KPMG

Brendan May
Managing Director, Planet 2050

I think everybody agrees that by 2050 we're going to need at least another planet to sustain our current levels of consumption. The truth is that today we have not enough fish, not enough forest, not enough water, an unstable climate and we're six and a half billion people. Come 2050, we're going to be nine billion. So what are the prospects for businesses and organisations to thrive in that sort of environment?

If we're going to tackle these global challenges, whether it's health, whether it's poverty, whether it's HIV AIDS, whether it's malaria, whether it's climate change, whether it's deforestation, a very large part of the solution is going to be from business.

Now, it is wrong, I think, to completely hand all the accountability to business because you start to wonder, well, what is government for? But I think, if you look at NGOs, businesses and governments, it is, of course, business that has the greatest resources and know-how to be able to tackle these changes. And if you look at a company like Coca-Cola, they're the biggest employer in Africa, so clearly they have a huge amount to give to Africa issues, such as HIV AIDS. You know, if you're an oil company, you can either take a path that recognises climate change and addresses it or you can choose to effectively absolve yourself of responsibility.

> **Glossary**
> **sustain** support
> **thrive** do well
> **tackle** deal with
> **hand all the accountability** give all the responsibility
> **NGOs** non-governmental organisations
> **absolve yourself of responsibility** claim it's not your responsibility

THE STAKEHOLDER GAME

Work in teams of three. Congratulations! You have just been appointed chief executive officer, chief financial officer and chief marketing officer of Randall Inc., an international manufacturing company which is trying to clean up its image as an old-fashioned smokestack industry and honour a new commitment to its stakeholders: customers, employees, suppliers, the local community, NGOs and environmental pressure groups and, last but not least, its shareholders!

Your job is to steer the company through the next twelve months, keeping as many of your stakeholders happy as you can. Let's hope you have a job at the end of it! Listen to the problem raised at each monthly meeting, take notes and decide on a course of action. Then check your performance on page 156. Good luck!

January 1.14

a As a company committed to transparency, we must publish, but make sure we emphasise the action we're taking.
b We should get in touch with some local NGOs to get their input on how to tackle the problems.
c Let's keep this confidential until we've brought the situation under control.

Which stakeholders might support/oppose your decision?

February 1.15

a Yes, the first rule of CSR is being able to 'keep one's own house in order'. Let's implement the proposal immediately.
b OK, but let's make the tests voluntary and include senior personnel as well as first line and middle management.
c This is a breach of the trust we have in our workforce. Let's provide an education programme and support group instead.

Which stakeholders might support/oppose your decision?

March 1.16

a Yes, the PR advantages outweigh the financial considerations. Let's go ahead. I suggest a quota of 10%.
b Wait a minute. Let's not be hasty. I suggest we set up a study group to look into other ways of promoting diversity.
c This is nothing more than a trendy positive discrimination exercise to make the government look good. No!

Which stakeholders might support/oppose your decision?

April 1.17

a We need to offer employees a re-employment package and invest heavily in the regeneration of the region after closure.
b We don't want to make any commitments we can't honour, but clearly we must negotiate a rescue plan with local NGOs.
c We should offer good severance pay and some retraining, but we can't afford more in today's economic climate.

Which stakeholders might support/oppose your decision?

May 1.18

a We should encourage this kind of initiative. Offering it to all employees is also a way of attracting and retaining talent.
b This should only be a reward for outstanding performance or long service to the company and must have job relevance.
c We should allow career breaks, but not paid. As a donor to many charities we already fulfil our obligations in that area.

Which stakeholders might support/oppose your decision?

June 1.19

a Let's set up a quality circle to work out a plan for phasing out the existing procedures within eighteen months.
b We don't know exactly what form the legislation will take yet. Let's see what our competitors do first.
c We've had no complaints from the shop floor. Changes cost money and man-hours, so why do anything?

Which stakeholders might support/oppose your decision?

July 🌓 1.20

a   Winning the support of the local council is a separate issue. We should withdraw our bid on the site to help a local charity.
b   If we play our cards right, we can do ourselves a favour both in terms of PR and our factory expansion plans.
c   This is a preposterous idea and no way to do business! And we don't need to bribe councillors to get planning permission.

Which stakeholders might support/oppose your decision?

August 🌓 1.21

a   We're taking no risks with our employees' health and safety. Authorise a complete overhaul of the system.
b   Let's get a waste management consultant in to see if it's actually worth making any major changes.
c   If we got through the last health and safety check, things can't be too bad. But if we're losing money, that's a problem.

Which stakeholders might support/oppose your decision?

September 🌓 1.22

a   Our union rep is right. We can't call ourselves socially responsible unless we adjust our pension fund.
b   We obviously need specialist financial advice and any changes we make would have to be phased in gradually.
c   There's not much chance of workers agreeing to a strike when our current fund is doing so well. Why do anything?

Which stakeholders might support/oppose your decision?

October 🌓 1.23

a   We can't be seen to be condoning corruption in any part of our organisation. We know the distributor is guilty. Pull out.
b   It would be unethical to make a move until we're certain of the position. But, once we know, we must act immediately.
c   We need that distributor, so we stick with them until proven guilty. In fact, can't we use our influence to prevent that?

Which stakeholders might support/oppose your decision?

November 🌓 1.24

a   This is a straightforward ethical decision – we cease to be a supplier to Colbert as of now!
b   We are the victims here, not the criminals! We should sue Colbert for breach of contract, but continue to supply them.
c   Since none of this is public knowledge, we should negotiate with Colbert behind the scenes to get the deal we want.

Which stakeholders might support/oppose your decision?

December 🌓 1.25

a   Clear the area of TV crews, initiate a precautionary evacuation and set up an emergency press conference.
b   Let's stay calm and leave crowd control to the police, while we conduct our tests. We don't want to overreact.
c   Play for time while we sort out the environmental and legal implications of the accident. Admit nothing at this stage.

Which stakeholders might support/oppose your decision?

CASH OR CONSCIENCE?

1 Do you have any personal investments or savings plans? Do you know how your money is actually invested? Do you care or are you mostly just interested in getting a good return?

2 All things being equal, are there particular types of company you'd like to see your money help to finance? Are there certain sorts of company you'd be uncomfortable about being involved with, no matter how sound the investment? Compare views with the rest of your group.

3 *The Lion's Share* is a hugely popular American reality TV show. Read the television guide extract below to find out more and answer the following questions:

a Why is the programme called *The Lion's Share*?
b What kind of business people appear on the show?
c What are the best- and worst-case scenarios for the contestants?

Thursdays at 9 p.m. on MBC

The Lion's Share (21.00-21.45) MBC

Four teams of entrepreneurs from around the world are 'thrown to the lions' (an international panel of self-made billionaires) to pitch for the venture capital they need to hang on to their struggling high-risk businesses. They have just two minutes to make their case!

This week contestants from as far afield as Argentina, Libya, Russia and South Africa fight tooth and nail to win the life-saving injection of cash they need to stay in business.

A million dollars are up for grabs, but only one of the start-ups will get 'the lion's share' of half a million, leaving the others to fight over the other half. Did we mention that all the lions must agree on who gets what? Or everybody goes away empty-handed!

4 🔊 **1.26** After three series at the top of the television ratings, *The Lion's Share* is starting to lose some of its audience appeal. Malcolm Carter is programming director at MBC. Listen to part of a planning meeting between him and Ruth Straub, the executive-producer of the show, and complete the charts in the report extract below:

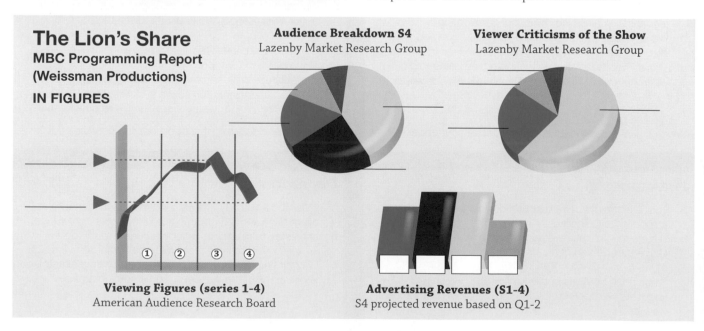

The Lion's Share
MBC Programming Report (Weissman Productions)

IN FIGURES

Viewing Figures (series 1-4)
American Audience Research Board

Audience Breakdown S4
Lazenby Market Research Group

Viewer Criticisms of the Show
Lazenby Market Research Group

Advertising Revenues (S1-4)
S4 projected revenue based on Q1-2

5 How far do you agree with Malcolm Carter's recommendations? Does it make sense for a more socially responsible agenda to be allowed to influence the judgement of the 'lions' on the show? Why (not)?

6 You are the lions. Pick a profile from the selection below and give yourself a suitable name.

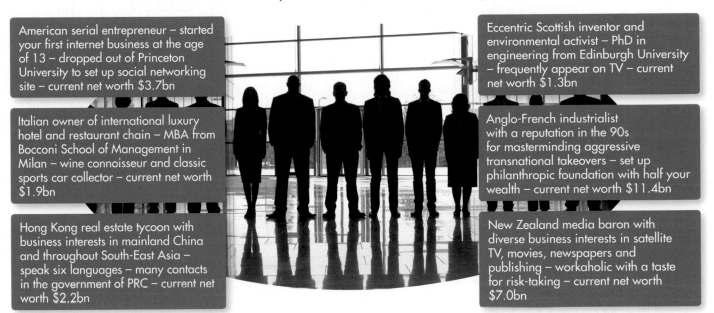

American serial entrepreneur – started your first internet business at the age of 13 – dropped out of Princeton University to set up social networking site – current net worth $3.7bn

Italian owner of international luxury hotel and restaurant chain – MBA from Bocconi School of Management in Milan – wine connoisseur and classic sports car collector – current net worth $1.9bn

Hong Kong real estate tycoon with business interests in mainland China and throughout South-East Asia – speak six languages – many contacts in the government of PRC – current net worth $2.2bn

Eccentric Scottish inventor and environmental activist – PhD in engineering from Edinburgh University – frequently appear on TV – current net worth $1.3bn

Anglo-French industrialist with a reputation in the 90s for masterminding aggressive transnational takeovers – set up philanthropic foundation with half your wealth – current net worth $11.4bn

New Zealand media baron with diverse business interests in satellite TV, movies, newspapers and publishing – workaholic with a taste for risk-taking – current net worth $7.0bn

7 1.27–1.30 Listen to the entrepreneurs' pitches and expand on the notes below. Then confer with your group.

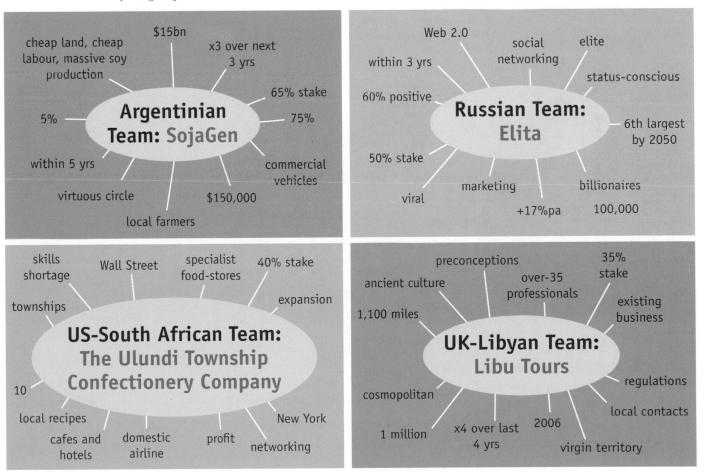

Argentinian Team: SojaGen
$15bn
cheap land, cheap labour, massive soy production
x3 over next 3 yrs
65% stake
75%
5%
within 5 yrs
commercial vehicles
virtuous circle
$150,000
local farmers

Russian Team: Elita
Web 2.0
social networking
elite
within 3 yrs
status-conscious
60% positive
6th largest by 2050
50% stake
marketing
billionaires
viral
+17%pa
100,000

US-South African Team: The Ulundi Township Confectionery Company
skills shortage
Wall Street
specialist food-stores
40% stake
townships
expansion
10
local recipes
New York
cafes and hotels
domestic airline
profit
networking

UK-Libyan Team: Libu Tours
preconceptions
35% stake
ancient culture
over-35 professionals
1,100 miles
existing business
cosmopolitan
regulations
local contacts
1 million
x4 over last 4 yrs
2006
virgin territory

8 You must now come to a decision as a group. Who, if anyone, gets the half million dollars and how do you divide up the other half? It's your money, but can you agree on how to invest it? Turn to page 155 for a checklist of criteria against which to evaluate each business.

9 Now turn to page 156 to see how your investments turned out.

4 VOICE AND VISUALS

I do not object to people looking at their watches when I am speaking. But I strongly object when they start shaking them to make certain they are still going.

LORD BIRKETT, BRITISH JUDGE

1 When you stand up to speak in public, what keeps an audience interested in what you're saying? Expertise or enthusiasm? Visual impact or vocal range? PowerPoint or natural presence?

2 You are going to read about power and public speaking. First test your communicative awareness below by <u>underlining</u> the correct information.

Test your communicative awareness

1 The attention span of the average audience member is **15 / 50** minutes.
2 People in an audience are distracted roughly every 12 **seconds / minutes**.
3 The best listeners are the **Germans and Swiss / Chinese and Japanese**.
4 Using visual aids makes your message **twice as / four times more** memorable.
5 It's been proved that presentations with visuals are **23% / 43%** more persuasive.
6 The brain processes images **40,000 / 400,000** times faster than text.
7 It's a **fact / myth** that only 7% of a presentation is what you actually say.
8 People generally prefer **lower / louder** voices.
9 Mrs Thatcher was trained to speak in a **lower, more authoritative / softer, friendlier** voice.
10 **Dutch / Spanish** women have the lowest female voices.
11 **Men's / Women's** voices are gradually getting deeper.
12 What people **see / hear** overrides what they **see / hear** every time.
13 Images and speech are processed by the **same / opposite** sides of the brain.
14 For over 100 years the US presidential election has been won by the taller candidate **70 / 90** % of the time.

3 Work with a partner to check your answers in 2. Each read a different web article opposite. Then share your information.

4 Do any of the points mentioned in the articles surprise you? If true, what are the implications for a business presenter?

5 Highlight in the article you read:
* three new words you'd like to remember
* three new phrases you'd like to remember
and explain why to your partner.

Voice lessons

Is anybody listening?

Long before it is born, a baby can recognise its mother's voice. And it is said that our sense of hearing is the last to fade before we die. As unique as our fingerprints, our voice is a key component of our personality. Indeed, the word 'personality' itself comes from the Latin 'persona', which literally means 'through sound'.

But, in our televisual age, we tend to shut out what we hear and be over-influenced by appearances. Maybe that's why in nearly 90% of US presidential elections since 1900, the taller, usually better-looking, candidate has been the winner! The attention span of the average audience member is just fifteen minutes. In the more self-disciplined and data-hungry cultures of Germany and Switzerland it might be half an hour. But even the most attentive listener is distracted roughly every twelve seconds.

How low can you go?

Is there anything we can do to hold their attention? There is some evidence to suggest that a low voice is preferred in both men and women. Former British Prime Minister Margaret Thatcher famously hired a voice coach to lower her voice. And, except in Japan, where higher female voices are preferred, it can be no coincidence that over the last 50 years, as women have risen to higher management positions in the workplace, their voices have measurably deepened – in the Netherlands, where women have achieved almost equal opportunity, especially so.

The new voice of America

The 2008 US presidential election was the classic case of the triumph of the charismatic voice with Barack Obama bringing the art of rhetoric back into the spotlight. His catchphrase 'Yes, we can' has passed into American history and he has already been described as the greatest orator of his generation. But New York professor Ekaterina Haskins has a theory about that. 'I've been going through his speeches textually,' she says. 'The text alone cannot tell us why they are so powerful. It is about delivery.' Philip Collins, who used to be Tony Blair's speech writer, agrees. It's 'the way he slides down some words and hits others – the intonation, the emphasis, the pauses and the silences.' To become leader of the western world Obama's only visual aid was himself. The rest was voice.

Visual impact

Sex, lies and visual aids

It's the oldest cliché in communication training: 55% of the message is how you look, 38% is how you sound and a mere 7% is what you say. But it's wrong! The original research on which this myth is based was carried out at UCLA in the 1970s. Involving just a handful of volunteers, the experiments actually focused on how people judge others' feelings and had nothing to do with creating impact in a talk. So if your suit, slides and winning smile fail to impress, take it easy. All is not lost.

What is true is that, if your body is saying one thing and your words another, people will believe what they see. When we're nervous or ill-prepared, our bodies tend to give us away.

PowerPointless?

Of course, good visual aids do powerfully reinforce your message. In fact, according to a study by 3M, audiences shown visuals are four times more likely to remember what you said and 43% more likely to be persuaded by it.

But it depends what you show them. The typical list of bullet points, for example, can actually compete with you. At one stage, this became such a problem at Sun Microsystems that CEO Scott McNealy banned the use of PowerPoint. Images, on the other hand, are mentally processed 400,000 times faster than text and appeal to the opposite side of the brain, making them the perfect accompaniment to speech.

A whole new image

No-one knows this better than ex-US vice-president Al Gore. Once the invisible man of American politics, after his presidential election defeat in 2000, Gore returned to his true passion and began an environmental lecture tour that literally took the world by storm. Ditching PowerPoint for Apple Keynote, he created a set of dramatic visuals, video clips and computer simulations that caused a sensation around the world. Speaking to a thousand different audiences, in what *Fast Company* magazine has called 'one of the most remarkable personal turnarounds of all time', Gore went on to become the champion of the green movement, the star of the Oscar-winning movie *An Inconvenient Truth* and winner of the Nobel Peace prize. He readily admits that he owes it all to a slide show.

GIVING FEEDBACK

1 Work with a partner to practise giving and receiving feedback on a presentation. Speaker A see page 140. Speaker B see page 162.

2 1.31 Listen to the voicemail from your Taiwanese client following the presentation in 1. Discuss his reaction with a partner.

VISUALS

1 When you give presentations, what visuals do you use?

flipchart   handouts   overhead   PowerPoint   slides
videos   websites

2 Read the book extract. Do you share the author's doubts?

Death by PowerPoint

Are you risking 'Death by PowerPoint'? This is when you inflict on your defenceless audience endless bullet-pointed slides, keywords and clipart that look pretty, yet cumulatively create a numbing effect and loss of impact. Beware of spending more time on the technology than on preparing yourself. Remember, you are the presentation.

Adapted from *The Ultimate Business Presentation Book* by Andrew Leigh

3 All the expressions below can be used to comment on a visual in a presentation. Complete them using the verbs in the box.

draw   give   have   learn   mention   notice   point   put   see   show

Introduction	.... a look at this. As you can ...., ...
Highlights	One thing you'll immediately .... is that ...
	I'd particularly like to .... your attention to ...
	I'd also like to .... out ...
	And perhaps I should ....
Context	Just to .... you some of the background to this ...
	To .... this into some kind of perspective ...
Conclusions	Clearly then, what these figures .... is ...
	The lesson we can .... from this is ...

4 Draw a simple graph or chart relating to an interesting aspect of the business you're in, or the company you work for or your country's economy. Use some of the expressions in 3 to present it to the class.

5 There's more to visual aids than just PowerPoint. Reorganise the words in bold to make correct sentences.

a   OK, **lights run dim the let's and** the video.
b   OK, **to live with a go link-up let's** our team in Dubai.
c   OK, **set short up we've product a demo** we'd like to show you.
d   OK, **minute samples in handing we'll a be out** for you to look at.
e   OK, **online let's and a go look closer take at** how the website works.

VOICE

1 How might pausing sometimes be the most effective thing a speaker can do? Read what communication expert Courtland Bovée has to say about the power of the pause.

> A pause is more than just a way to vary your speaking rate. It's also an important way to add emphasis and meaning to selected phrases and sentences. You can insert a pause to allow an audience a moment to think about an idea, to indicate a shift to a new idea or to a new section of your speech, or to heighten anticipation of your next idea.
>
> From *Contemporary Public Speaking* by Courtland L. Bovée

2 🔊 **1.32** Listen to three presenters speaking in different ways. Decide which presenter sounds
1 fluent and confident
2 fluent but boring
3 hesitant.

a There's a whole market in Eastern Europe just there for the taking.
b Quite frankly, the results we've been getting are absolutely incredible.
c Now, I'm sure I don't need to tell you just how crucial this is.
d Net profits are up ninety-seven per cent – yes, ninety-seven per cent.
e Would you believe that so far we've not been able to sell a single unit?
f Miss this deadline and we'll lose the biggest client this company's ever had.

3 Why does the boring presenter sound so monotonous?

4 What exactly is the hesitant presenter doing wrong?

5 🔊 **1.33** Work with a partner. Listen again to the fluent and confident versions. One of you should mark the pauses like this: | The other should <u>underline</u> the stressed words. Compare your results. What's the connection between where we pause and what we stress?

6 🔊 **1.34** Deliver all the sentences in 2 in a fluent and confident way. Experiment with longer pauses and stronger stresses. Then compare your version with the recording.

7 1.35 According to Swedish businessman Jan Carlzon, 'All business is show business.' Listen to an extract from a radio programme on how several training companies have taken his opinion literally, and discuss the questions.

a   Would William Freeman's advice help you face a business audience?
b   What does Michael Lame think classically trained actors can teach business people?
c   According to Richard Olivier, what makes someone a brilliant speaker?
d   Which of the trainees' opinions would be closest to your own?

8 Work with a partner to make your Shakespearian debut! Choose one of the Shakespeare speeches opposite and take turns to be the actor and director. Don't worry – the speeches have been slightly modernised!

* Decide where you are going to pause – mark short pauses like this: | , longer pauses like this: || and very long pauses like this: |||
* Underline the words you are going to stress: usually nouns and verbs, but sometimes, for dramatic effect, you can stress pronouns and conjunctions.
* Highlight in different colours parts of the text you really want to project, even shout, and parts you want to say quietly or perhaps whisper.
* Try the speech a few times, the actor speaking, the director giving advice and feedback. When you are ready, have fun performing it!

9 2.01–2.02 Listen to the speeches in 8. How does your performance compare with the recorded version?

10 Prepare a 90-second presentation on a work or business topic that is important to you. Try to keep some of the power and drama from your Shakespeare speech in your voice as you present.

Marlon Brando as Mark Antony in *Julius Caesar*

The story so far:

The Roman leader Julius Caesar has been assassinated by a group of senators led by Brutus, the man in whom he once placed his greatest trust. His body lies in the Capitol in Rome and the assassins have explained convincingly why it was necessary to murder him – because of his great ambition to be crowned king and absolute ruler of Rome. Then the general Mark Antony, who was not involved in the killing, gets up to speak. His aim is subtly to change the minds of the crowd from support for the assassins to pity for Caesar and a desire to avenge his death …

The persuasion speech:

Friends, Romans, countrymen, listen to me.
I come to bury Caesar, not to praise him.
The evil that men do lives after them;
The good is often buried with their bones.
So let it be with Caesar. The noble Brutus
Has told you Caesar was ambitious.
If it was so, it was a serious fault;
And seriously has Caesar answered it!
Here, with permission of Brutus and the rest –
For Brutus is an honourable man.
So are they all, all honourable men –
I come to speak at Caesar's funeral.
He was my friend, loyal and fair to me,
But Brutus says he was ambitious;
And Brutus is an honourable man.
He has brought many prisoners home to Rome,
Whose ransoms increased the wealth of all.
Did this in Caesar seem ambitious?
Whenever the poor have cried, Caesar has wept:
Ambition should be made of stronger stuff.
Yet Brutus says he was ambitious;
And Brutus is an honourable man.
You all saw on the Feast of Lupercal
I three times offered him a royal crown,
Which he three times refused: was this ambition?
Yet, Brutus says he was ambitious,
And, sure, he is an honourable man.
I do not contradict what Brutus said,
But here I am to say what I do know.
You all did love him once, not without reason.
What reason prevents you then from mourning him?
Have we turned into wild beasts
And men quite lost their minds? Bear with me.
My heart is in the coffin there with Caesar;
And I must pause till it comes back to me.

Kenneth Branagh as King Henry in *Henry V*

The story so far:

The English army has fought a long hard campaign in France and now they face their final battle at Agincourt. They are heavily outnumbered and the soldiers are exhausted and almost ready to surrender. Henry's generals, Bedford, Exeter, Warwick, Talbot, Salisbury and Gloucester, do not really believe they can win. Henry knows he must somehow build confidence and self-belief in his troops if they are to stand even the remotest chance of victory. And so he tells his men not to wish for a bigger army, since all the glory can now be theirs …

The motivation speech:

If we are going to die, we are enough
To cause our country loss; and if to live,
The fewer men, the greater share of honour.
This day is called the Feast of Crispian.
He who survives this day, comes safely home,
Will hold his head high when this day is named
And stand up at the name of Crispian.
He that shall live today and see old age
Will celebrate it yearly with his neighbours
And say: 'Tomorrow is Saint Crispian'.
Then he'll roll up his sleeve and show his scars
And say: 'These wounds I got on Crispian's Day'.
Old men forget; yes, all will be forgotten;
But he'll remember all too well
What he achieved that day. Then will our names:
Harry the king, Bedford and Exeter,
Warwick and Talbot, Salisbury and Gloucester,
Be between cups of wine newly remembered.
This story will the good man teach his son;
And Crispian will never go by,
From this day to the ending of the world,
But we shall be remembered for it –
We few, we fortunate few, we band of brothers;
For he today who sheds his blood with me
Will be my brother. However poor and humble,
This day will make of him a gentleman.
And gentlemen in England, now in bed,
Will curse the fact they were not here,
And question whether they are really men,
While anyone speaks who fought with us
Upon Saint Crispian's Day!

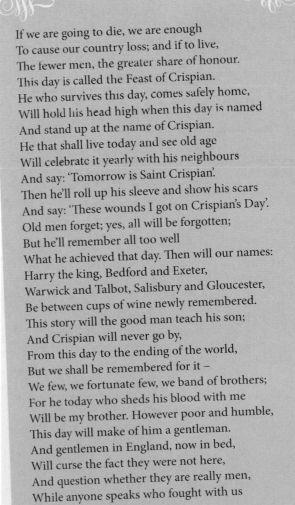

LANGUAGE LINKS

Vocabulary: Presentations

Commenting on statistics

1 Put the following verbs and verb phrases in order from the best news to the worst.

| almost halved   increased tenfold   more than tripled |
| nearly doubled   plateau'd   quadrupled |

Sales have

a ....
b ....
c ....
d ....
e ....
f ....

Which of the above means the same as *a fourfold increase*?

2 Pair up the adjectives with ones which have a similar meaning and put them in order from the biggest to the smallest.

| considerable   huge   massive   moderate   modest |
| reasonable   significant   slight |

a
a .... / ....
b .... / ....
c .... / ....   increase
d .... / ....

3 Describe the following success rates using suitable adjectives from the box.

| disappointing   disastrous   encouraging   miserable |
| phenomenal   promising   spectacular   unimpressive |

a(n)
a .... / 95%
b .... / .... 65%   success rate
c .... / 25%
d .... / 3%

Metaphor: trends and developments

1 Complete the joke by matching each noun or noun phrase on the left to a verb or verb phrase on the right. Use a dictionary to check the literal and metaphorical meaning of the verbs, if necessary.

And on the stock market today ...

mountaineering equipment — totally collapsed
military hardware — were up and down
lifts — went up sharply
kitchen knives — peaked
but the housing market — boomed

After a nervous start ...

rubber — quickly recovered
medical supplies — shot up
the automotive industry — bounced back
rifles — picked up after lunch
and vacuum cleaners also — rallied

In some of the fiercest trading seen in the City ...

swimwear — hit rock bottom
mining equipment — slumped
ice skates — plunged
alcoholic beverages — completely dried up
and the market for raisins — slipped a little

By close of trade ...

fireworks — remained unchanged
Prozac — fell dramatically
but paper products — were stationary
men's socks — reached an all-time high
and theatre curtains — skyrocketed

2 Mark the verbs and verb phrases in 1 according to the trend they describe: up (↗), down (↘), up and down (⋀), down then up (⋁) and no change (→).

Grammar: Modal verbs

1 In each of the sentences below, delete the modal verbs that are incorrect.

a We ... now, but we can if we want.
(mustn't pay/don't have to pay/haven't got to pay)

b I ... my laptop, so I left it at the office.
(needn't take/didn't need to take/needn't have taken)

c We ..., if we'd known he wasn't coming in today.
(didn't need to wait/mustn't wait/needn't have waited)

d When I was a student, I ... for hours on end.
('d study/would have studied/used to study)

e I ... quite left-wing, but I've become more conservative.
(used to be/would be/must have been)

f She ... by now – it's after twelve.
(should have left/'ll have left/won't have left)

g I took my driving test three times before I ... pass.
(could/was able to/managed to)

2 Complete the conversation using the modal verbs in the box.

> can't   can't   could have   could have   'll   'll   might
> must   must have   needn't have   shouldn't   won't
> would have   wouldn't

A Ivan, (1) .... Alexis be here by now? It's gone four!
B Yeah, she (2) .... got held up somewhere.
A But (3) .... she have phoned?
B Well, you (4) .... thought so.
A I mean, we're only having this meeting for her benefit.
   If she doesn't come soon, we (5) .... bothered.
B Quite, though I (6) .... think what (7) ....
   held her up. I (8) .... ring her and see what's
   going on. That's funny, I (9) .... find her number.
   I (10) .... sworn I put it in my diary. It (11) ....
   be in here somewhere!
A Well, if you ask me, she (12) .... be coming now,
   anyway
B Hang on. That (13) .... just be her now. I
   (14) .... go and check.

have to, have got to and *must* mean there's an obligation to do something.

don't have to and *haven't got to* mean there's no obligation to do something.

mustn't means there's an obligation *not* to do something.

I needn't have done means I did something but it wasn't necessary; *I didn't need to do* means it wasn't necessary so I didn't do it.

would do means *used to do* for repeated past actions.

She should have left means *I expect she's left* or *She's supposed to have left* or *It would have been a good idea if she'd left*.

You use *was able to* (not *could*) to talk about a specific past achievement.

That must be him is the opposite of *That can't be him*.

will is the most versatile modal verb and can be used for offers, spontaneous decisions, assumptions, predictions and to express willingness or determination.

Phrase bank: Describing and commenting on visuals

All the following phrases and expressions can be used to describe and comment on visual aids. Add them to the chart according to their function.

INTRODUCTION	HIGHLIGHTS
CONTEXT	**CONCLUSIONS**

a   Have a look at this. …
b   What these figures clearly show is …
c   I'd particularly like to draw your attention to …
d   As you can see, …
e   I think this demonstrates …
f   Just to give you the background to this. …
g   I'd like to point out …
h   I'll just talk you through it. …

i   To put this into perspective, …
j   What this means is …
k   The take-home message here is …
l   OK, let's take a look at …
m   One thing you'll notice is …
n   The lesson we can learn from this is …
o   Let's run the video. …
p   I'll just show you how this works. …

5 PROBLEMS ON THE PHONE

Most people spend more time and energy going around problems than in trying to solve them.

HENRY FORD, FOUNDER OF FORD MOTOR COMPANY

1 It's been said that 'When the phone rings, there's usually a problem on the other end of it.' What sort of problems do people phone you with at work? Share examples with a partner.

2 Complete the text below by underlining the correct words.

How to get rid of chatterboxes on the phone

We are living in the age of telephony. Over half the planet now has a mobile. In Finland, where they have more mobiles per person than anywhere else on earth, 40% of the country's exports are Nokia phones. Whenever we want, wherever we want, we can get in (a) **communication / touch**.

But when we do, it seems we can never get to the (b) **point / business**. Up to two hours in every working day are wasted in small talk on the phone. And great skill and determination are needed to escape the deadly game of social chit-chat – 'How are you? ... Settling (c) **in / down** to the new job? ... How's Ellen? ... And the kids? ... Hasn't your eldest just gone to college? ... How (d) **life / time** flies! ... Oh, I hear you're moving house as well. ... Did you have a nice holiday, by the way? ... I suppose you haven't heard the (e) **last / latest**, then? ... Well, I'm not supposed to say, but there's a (f) **rumour / gossip** going about ...'

Of course, what you really want to say in these circumstances is 'Look, I haven't got all (g) **year / day**. Either state your business or kindly get off the phone,' but professional courtesy forbids it. Here, then, is the definitive executive guide to getting rid of chatterboxes on the phone.

GETTING DOWN TO BUSINESS The most tactful way of bringing the conversation round to the subject of business is to ask in a slightly louder than normal voice 'What (h) **can / could** I do for you?' If you know the caller, you could try 'I (i) **expect / believe** you're calling about ...' and then mention anything you can think of. They, hopefully, will reply 'Er, no, actually, it's about something else' and you can finally (j) **pull / cut** the chat and get down to business. Should this strategy fail, you may have to resort to a firmer 'Was there (k) **nothing / something** you wanted to talk to me about?'

ENDING THE CONVERSATION This is more difficult. The trick is not to seem too abrupt. 'Anyway, ...', though a clear signal to most people that you want to end the call, is much too subtle for chatterboxes. Try instead 'Well, I mustn't (l) **hold / keep** you', 'I'll let you (m) **get / go** on' or the more insistent 'I'll have to let you (n) **go / leave** now.' If you feel that sounds a little too harsh, friendlier alternatives include 'Well, (o) **listen / see**, it's been great talking to you', 'We must (p) **come / get** together soon' or 'Oh, one last (q) **thing / point** and then I really must go.' Of course, with an incurable chatterbox this last alternative may be asking for trouble!

DRASTIC MEASURES In genuine emergencies the following may be used: 'Ah, someone's just this minute (r) **dropped / stepped** into the office. I'll have to ring (s) **off / out**.' Or 'I've got an international call just come (t) **in / over** on the other line. Can I call you back?' And, if all else fails, you can always try 'Hello? Hello? Are you still (u) **there / here**?' Of course the secret with this one is that when the caller says 'Yes, I'm still here,' resist the temptation to reply 'Well, I can't hear you!'

> **Glossary**
> **chatterbox** person who talks a lot about unimportant matters
> **24/7** 24 hours a day, 7 days a week

3 Do you agree with the writer of the article that small talk on the phone wastes time at work?

4 🔘 **2.03** Listen to someone trying unsuccessfully to get a caller off the phone. Raise your hand when you hear them use one of the 'getting rid' expressions mentioned in the article you just read.

5 Work with a partner to practise dealing with a chatterbox. Speaker A see page 140. Speaker B see page 147.

DEALING WITH COMPLAINTS

1 In 2009 American businessman Howard Schaffer got so fed up wasting time trying to get the phones in his office fixed, he worked out it had cost him $5,481.16, billed the phone company for it and was paid! Have you ever wanted to do that to a company that wasted your time?

2 When was the last time you made a formal complaint about something? Was it in person, in writing or on the phone? Were you satisfied with the way it was handled? Tell a partner about it.

3 Put the following stages of handling a customer complaint into the most likely order:

- suggest possible solutions
- get the details
- end on a positive note
- agree on a course of action
- greet and reassure the caller
- listen and empathise

1

2

3

4

5

6

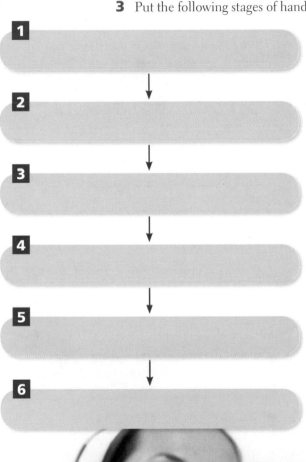

4 Which of the following expressions would be most inappropriate at each of the stages in 3? Delete one from each set of three below. Then <u>underline</u> which of the remaining two you prefer.

Stage 1 a How can I help you?
         b What can I do for you?
         c What's the matter, then?

Stage 2 a Can you tell me exactly what the problem is?
         b What exactly is your problem?
         c What seems to be the problem?

Stage 3 a Tell me about it! I know just how you feel.
         b I can understand exactly how you feel.
         c I can understand how upset you must be.

Stage 4 a Well, I suppose I could send you a new one, but I can't give you a refund. Sorry.
         b I can't give you a refund, I'm afraid, but I can certainly send you a new one. How's that?
         c Unfortunately, we're not authorised to give refunds, but what I can do is send you a brand new one. How would that be?

Stage 5 a Is that all OK for you?
         b Are you satisfied now?
         c Are you happy with that?

Stage 6 a I'm so pleased we've managed to sort this out. Was there anything else?
         b Glad to be of assistance. Is there anything else I can help you with?
         c Good. Anything else or is that it?

5 🔊 2.04 Listen to a customer services adviser at iDeals, a computer supplies retail chain, dealing with a complaint and compare what she says with your choices in 4.

6 A 'flame' is an angry or insulting e-mail. Have you ever received or been tempted to write one?

7 Work with a partner. Read the flames you and your partner wrote below and take turns to hold the telephone conversations that might have followed. Caller, be as direct as you like. Receiver, try to calm the caller down and deal with their complaint.

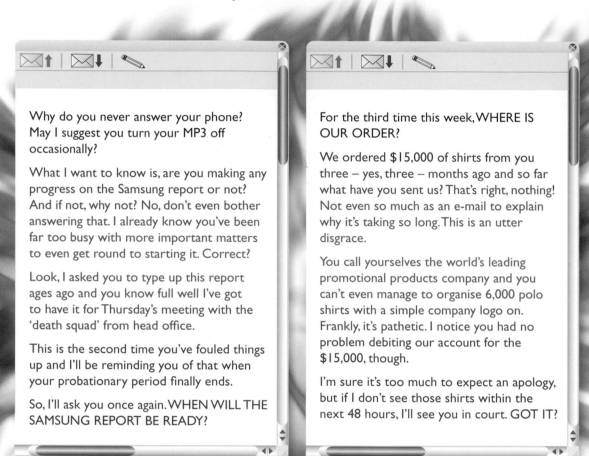

Why do you never answer your phone? May I suggest you turn your MP3 off occasionally?

What I want to know is, are you making any progress on the Samsung report or not? And if not, why not? No, don't even bother answering that. I already know you've been far too busy with more important matters to even get round to starting it. Correct?

Look, I asked you to type up this report ages ago and you know full well I've got to have it for Thursday's meeting with the 'death squad' from head office.

This is the second time you've fouled things up and I'll be reminding you of that when your probationary period finally ends.

So, I'll ask you once again. WHEN WILL THE SAMSUNG REPORT BE READY?

For the third time this week, WHERE IS OUR ORDER?

We ordered $15,000 of shirts from you three – yes, three – months ago and so far what have you sent us? That's right, nothing! Not even so much as an e-mail to explain why it's taking so long. This is an utter disgrace.

You call yourselves the world's leading promotional products company and you can't even manage to organise 6,000 polo shirts with a simple company logo on. Frankly, it's pathetic. I notice you had no problem debiting our account for the $15,000, though.

I'm sure it's too much to expect an apology, but if I don't see those shirts within the next 48 hours, I'll see you in court. GOT IT?

---

8 Rewrite the e-mail you sent in 7 to make it more polite but equally assertive. Use the prompts below to help you.

a Unfortunately / unable / reach / phone
Can / tell / managing / make / progress /
Samsung report? // having / problems / please
let / know / soon / possible // understand / been
preoccupied / other matters / may not / even /
made a start yet / although / hope / not / case
did ask / some time ago / this report / as you
know / do need / urgently / Thursday's meeting
/ people / head office
not / first time / let me down / consequently
/ shall have / discuss / matter / when /
probationary period ends
really must know today how / longer / going /
take

b again writing / regard / order / ref no 099X
records show / order / $15,000 / shirts / placed
three months / but so far / received anything //
Nor / sent / e-mail explaining / reason / delay //
afraid / quite unacceptable
You advertise / world's leading promotional
products company // therefore / find / inability
/ take care / simple order like this both
surprising / disappointing // notice / however /
were more efficient / debiting / account / sum /
$15,000
should like / delivery / 48 hours / together /
apology // Otherwise / no alternative / hand /
matter over / legal department // hope / made
myself clear

9 Exchange the rewritten e-mails with your partner and hold the two telephone conversations again. How do these calls compare with the ones you had in 7?

TACKLING PROBLEMS

1 2.05 Listen to an overheard telephone conversation. Take notes and, with a partner, try to work out what the problem is.

It sounds like ...
It seems as though ...
There's been some kind of ...,by the sound of it.
I'm not (exactly) sure whether ... or whether ...
It's definitely something to do with ...

2 2.06 Now listen to both sides of the conversation in 1 and check your ideas.

3 You heard the following idiomatic expressions in 2. Can you remember the missing words? The first two letters are given. Use the definitions in brackets to help you.

a I'm working fl................ out. (I'm working as quickly and as hard as possible.)
b It completely sl................ my mind. (I completely forgot to do it.)
c We're sn................ under at the moment. (We've got too much work to deal with.)

4 What would you do in Graham and Piotr's situation?

5 2.07 Listen to Graham and Piotr's second conversation and compare your solutions with theirs.

Ms. Paget

6 Match the halves of the following sentences. You heard them all in 5.

a Can you get hold   of sending someone else out here?
b I don't suppose   to have a phone number for the promotions people?
c Do you happen   getting some brochures to me in Polish?
d Is there any chance   of the organisers?
e I'll check   what I can do, but I can't promise anything.
f I'll see   with Liz and see if she can spare Kim for a few days.
g Would you mind   you remembered to put another CD player in?

h Is there any point   the minute I get off the phone.
i Are you absolutely   if we got a local Polish interpreter in?
j I'll look into it   to me.
k Could I ask you   in sending the ones we've got in Russian?
l Would it help   to that right away.
m I'll get on   to hurry that up a bit, please?
n Leave it   sure we didn't order a reprint of the Polish ones?

7 Work with a partner to practise solving problems on the phone. Speaker A see page 141. Speaker B see page 149.

LANGUAGE LINKS

Vocabulary: Phone, fax and e-mail

Complete the telephone conversation using the words in the box.

around	as	back	by	down	down	for	in
off	off	off	on	on	on	on	on	on
out	out	out	up	up	up	up	under

A design agency office is in chaos. The phone is ringing. Tina finally answers it.

A Hello? Tina Mallon.

B Tina. Thank goodness you're there!

A Hi, Geoff. What's (1) ....?

B Listen. I'm (2) .... a bit of a mess here.

A Where are you?

B I'm just (3) .... my way to see the people at FlexiPak and you'll never guess ... I've left the file with the visuals in it back at the office!

A Oh dear ... Well, can I fax them through to you at their office?

B No, I don't think they'd come (4) .... properly.

A Geoff, I'm (5) .... to my neck in it here. I can't access my e-mail because the server is (6) .... this morning and I'm rushed (7) .... my feet, running (8) .... trying to sort things (9) .... with IT and get those posters (10) .... to Milan by midday.

B Look, Tina, this is urgent. Could you go over the road to the print shop, scan the visuals and ask them to e-mail them to me (11) .... attachments? I'll give you FlexiPak's e-mail address.

A Geoff, I'm sorry, but I'm really snowed (12) .... here.

B Tina, I wouldn't ask you if I wasn't desperate. I haven't got time to come (13) .... and pick them (14) ....

A Well, maybe it would be easier just to send them (15) .... dispatch rider. Hang (16) .... Let me take (17) .... the details. Which visuals do you need exactly? Hello? Geoff?

B Tina?

A Geoff? You're breaking (18) .... Are you (19) .... your mobile? I can't hear you!

B Hello? Oh, what's going (20) .... with this phone? I can't be (21) .... of range. I must be running low (22) .... batteries. No, it's charged. Tina, can you hear me? I'll have to ring (23) .... and look (24) .... a payphone or something. Tina?

Tina hangs up, smiling.

A Now, maybe I can finally get (25) .... with some work!

Grammar: Complex question formation

Polite question forms

Rewrite the requests and offers to make them sound friendlier and more polite using the words in brackets to help you. Make any necessary changes to grammar.

a Can you turn the air conditioning up a bit? (think/could)

   Do you think you could turn the air conditioning up a bit?

b Can you help me? (wonder/could)

c Don't mention this to anyone else.(could/ask you)

d Can you do some overtime next week? (think/could/ask)

e Do you want me to put in a good word for you? (would/like me)

f Can you stop whistling while I'm trying to concentrate?(would/mind not)

g Is it OK to leave early today?(do/mind/if)

h Do you want me to give you a few days to think about it?(would/help/give)

i Can I ask you a personal question?(Would/mind/I)

j When is Mr Alvarez coming back?(happen/know)

k Can you lend me €50 until Friday? (don't suppose/could you?)

Being polite takes longer!

Modal verbs (*could, would*) soften a request that may be unwelcome.

'Type 1' conditionals (*Do you mind if I leave early?*) make requests more diplomatic.

'Type 2' conditionals (*Would you mind if I left early?*) make requests even more diplomatic.

Do you happen to know ...? is useful when you're not sure the other person knows the answer to your question.

I don't suppose you could ..., *could you?* is good way of asking people to do you a favour.

Phrase bank: Small talk on the phone

Put one word in each box below to make 30 things you could say to encourage a bit of small talk during a business call. Contractions (*You're*, *How's* etc.) count as one word.

a _____ life / business / the family / it going / the new job / your golf doing / your course going?

b _____ _____ _____ doing / keeping / enjoying Paris / getting on in Manila / settling down in Seville? / settling in at Goldman Sachs?

c _____ _____ the promotion / the new baby / winning the Dubai contract / finally getting your MBA!

d _____ _____ _____ moving house / getting married / about to visit Russia / about to sign a deal with Samsung, is that right?

e _____ _____ _____ been on holiday / come back from Buenos Aires / opened a new office in Cologne?

f _____ _____ _____ the news / the latest / from Ron lately / about the Asian situation?

g _____ job on the Siemens report / luck with presentation tomorrow, by the way!

Getting down to business on the phone

Complete the ways of switching from small talk to business. The initial letters are given.

a A_____, ...

b S_____, w_____ c_____ I d_____ f_____ y_____?

c I e_____ y_____ c_____ a_____ ...

d W_____ t_____ s_____ y_____ w_____ t_____ t_____ t_____ m_____ a_____?

Subtle

↓

Direct

Requesting assistance on the phone

Put the words in **bold** in the correct order.

a **mind you would** letting me know when they arrive?

b **hold you can of get** someone in accounts?

c **ask I could to you** arrange that for me?

d **chance there is any of** extending the deadline?

e **you suppose could don't I** speed things up a bit, could you?

f **have you happen do to** Alicia's mobile number?

g **sure can't absolutely you you are** do anything today?

Offering assistance on the phone

Complete the following using the pairs of verbs in the box.

check + see   help + give   leave + get   look + give   see + promise   worry + get

a I'll _____ what I can do, but I can't _____ anything.

b I'll _____ with IT and _____ if they can help.

c Don't _____, I'll _____ on to it right away.

d I'll _____ into it. _____ me an hour.

e Would it _____ if I got someone to _____ you a hand?

f Why don't you _____ it with me and I'll _____ back to you?

Ending a call

Each sentence ending in **bold** has been switched with another. Switch them back to make eight ways of ending a call.

a I mustn't **let you go now.**

b I'll let you **get together soon.**

c Someone's just **come in on the other line.**

d We must **get on.**

e It's been great **running a bit late.**

f I'll have to **keep you.**

g I've got a call just **stepped into the office.**

h Listen, I'm **talking to you.**

6 LEADING MEETINGS

Either lead, follow or get out of the way.

SIGN ON THE DESK OF TED TURNER, FOUNDER OF CNN

1 How much influence do you have at the meetings you participate in? When it comes to meetings, would you rather lead, follow or simply get out of the way?

2 Think about a regular meeting you attend and consider the following:

- Who is the most powerful person in the room? Does he/she actually lead the meeting?
- What are the seating arrangements – fixed or flexible?
- Does anyone tend to dominate the discussion? Is that ever a problem?
- Are there people who hardly speak at all? If so, why are they there?
- Who, if anyone, is the most 'dangerous' person in the room?

Explain to a partner how the meeting works. A simple diagram may help you.

3 Combine one word from each box to make ten common problems encountered in meetings. Do you have similar problems in your meetings?

communication communication group- hidden inadequate late over point- pulling time	+	agendas barriers breakdowns preparation rank runs scoring starts think wasting

1 ....
2 ....
3 ....
4 ....
5 ....

6 ....
7 ....
8 ....
9 ....
10 ....

Which of them mean:

a misunderstandings? ☐
b failing to finish on time? ☐
c competition between colleagues? ☐
d the need to agree at all costs? ☐
e secret intentions or objectives? ☐
f using your status to get what you want? ☐
g things which make people reluctant to talk? ☐

4 Read the suggestion below. Does it strike you as a good idea? Which of the problems in 3 might it help to solve? Which would it probably make worse?

The power table

Suppose you removed the table from your conference room and replaced the seats with armchairs. Suppose you turned it into a living room. How much would this affect your meetings?

That's how much your meetings are about power, not communication.

David Weinberger, *The Cluetrain Manifesto*

5 Five alternative approaches successful companies have taken to the problem of meetings are listed below. What do you think they might involve?

a the non-stop meeting   d the democratic meeting
b the mobile meeting   e the virtual meeting
c the recreational meeting

6 2.08 Listen to an extract from a business news programme and match the approaches in 5 to the companies that have adopted them.

Federal Express ☐
another.com ☐
Xerox Corporation ☐
Michaelides & Bednash Media ☐
St. Luke's Advertising ☐

7 Could any of the ideas in 6 work in your company? Would any be thought ridiculous?

CHAIRING SKILLS

1 Complete the following and compare with the other members of your group.

A meeting without a chairperson is like a .... without a ....

2 Complete the collocations by writing the nouns and noun phrases in the right-hand boxes. They are all things the leader of a meeting might do.

| the agenda   the final decision |
| the main goals   the meeting |
| the participants   points of view |

| an action plan   areas of conflict |
| follow-up tasks   the key issues |
| other speakers   troublemakers |

a	open / close	
b	welcome / introduce	
c	set / stick to	
d	ask for / summarise	
e	establish / define	
f	deliberate over / take	

g	bring in / shut out	
h	anticipate / avoid	
i	identify / discipline	
j	work out / draw up	
k	prioritise / assign	
l	explain / focus on	

Which of the skills above are mostly about managing

- the content of the meeting?
- the people present?

Write C or P.

3 What, in your opinion, is the single most important task of a chairperson? Read the article below. Does the author agree with you?

You have to start meeting like this!

We work, therefore we meet. But why do so few of our meetings meet our expectations?

Michael Begeman is a leading authority on one of the business world's most universal rituals: the meeting. An anthropologist and computer scientist by training, he is manager of the 3M Meeting Network.

So what's the most effective meeting that Begeman has seen lately? He says that it didn't take place in a high-rise office building or at a cutting-edge chip factory. In fact, it took place in a tepee – in a scene from *Dances with Wolves*, the Oscar-winning film featuring Kevin Costner. The scene takes place after a group of Native Americans discover Costner not far from their camp. Between 20 and 30 members of the tribe gather around for a meeting. There's one big question on their agenda: what should they do with this mysterious white man?

What follows, claims Begeman, is a masterclass in good meeting behaviour.

'People actually listen to one another,' he marvels. 'There are some genuine disagreements, but everyone recognises merit in everyone else's position and tries to incorporate it into his thinking. The chief spends most of his time listening. When the time comes to make a decision, he says something like "It's hard to know what to do. We should talk about this some more. That's all I have to say." And the meeting ends! He is honest enough to admit that he's not ready to make a decision.'

How does Begeman compare that with what takes place inside most conference rooms today? 'Do you want to know the truth?' he asks. 'Here's my mental image of what happens at most business meetings: you could take the people out and replace them with radios blaring at each other, and you would not have changed very much. That's what most meetings are like. People wait for the person who's speaking to take a breath, so they can jump into the empty space and talk. The quality of communication in most meetings is roughly comparable to the quality of the arguments that you used to have with your ten-year-old brother.'

Adapted from *Fast Company* magazine, www.fastcompany.com

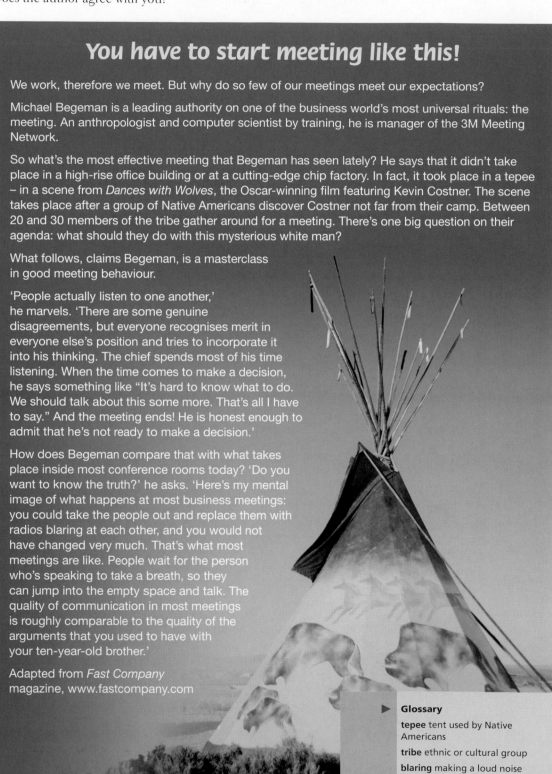

► **Glossary**

tepee tent used by Native Americans

tribe ethnic or cultural group

blaring making a loud noise

4 How do you think Michael Begeman would describe the ideal meeting? You may want to refer to some of the terms in the box.

authority consensus decisions diplomacy disagreement
listening patience respect teamwork

5 In the article, Begeman points out that although 'there are some genuine disagreements' in the meeting, 'Everyone recognises merit in everyone else's position and tries to incorporate it into his thinking.' How can you avoid upsetting people you disagree with? How important is it in your culture for people to 'save face'?

6 Match the examples on the right to the disagreement strategies they exemplify.

1 ☐ and ☐   2 ☐ and ☐   3 ☐ and ☐   4 ☐ and ☐   5 ☐ and ☐

Disagreement strategies	Examples
1 Show support before you disagree	a I think I'm going to go with Janine's idea, **but tell me more about your idea first**.
2 Disagree but ask for more detail	b That's not quite how I see it, **but how about looking at this a different way?**
3 Check you've understood correctly	c I'm not so sure, **but maybe I'm missing something here. Run me through it again.**
4 Be specific about your disagreement	d I'm not against your whole idea, **just the part about** pricing.
5 Disagree but offer an alternative	e **While I agree with a lot of what you say,** I think you may be exaggerating the problem.
	f I don't quite agree with you there. **However, you've given me another idea.**
	g I'm not so sure I'm going to agree with this. **I'd like to hear more about it, though.**
	h Before I answer that, **let me just check I understand what you're saying.**
	i **I can understand exactly how you feel,** but at the moment it's just not an option.
	j **It's not so much** your actual plan **I have a problem with as** how you intend to implement it.

7 In informal meetings with people you know well, you can use simpler expressions to show you disagree, but if there are problems, it is usually better to be more formal and explicit. Match the informal expressions below to the strategies in 6.

Go on. I'm listening. ☐
Yeah, but ... ☐
Hm, well, how about this instead? ☐
I'm not with you. ☐
OK, but just one thing. ☐

MANAGING MEETINGS

1 🔘 2.09–2.11 A venture capital firm is discussing the start-up company it had talks with last week. Listen to three extracts from their meeting and answer the questions.

Extract 1

a Who's absent from the meeting and why?
b What are the two main goals of the meeting?

Extract 2

a What's the main area of conflict in the meeting?
b Who do you think the main troublemaker is?
c Whose side is Tania on – Pieter's or Jack's?

Extract 3

a What follow-up tasks are assigned?
b Does timeofyourlife.com's business plan sound good to you?
c In your opinion, how effective was the chairman of the meeting?

2 You heard the following idiomatic expressions in 1. Complete them by filling in the missing letters. Use the words in brackets to help you.

a I wanted his in.................. on this one. (I wanted to hear his views)
b We're interested in taking things fu.................. (We'd like to progress with this deal)
c I don't want us ru.................. into anything. (We need to think about this carefully)
d We've been th.................. this. (We've discussed this in depth many times before)
e The fi.................. don't quite add up. (the financial part of a proposal is suspect)

3 The following expressions are all useful in chairing meetings. Complete them by filling in the missing vowels.

Opening the meeting

a ▢K, l▢t's g▢t st▢rt▢d, th▢n, sh▢ll w▢?
b Th▢nks f▢r c▢m▢ng, ▢v▢ryb▢dy.

Setting the agenda

c ▢s ▢s▢▢d ▢n my ▢-m▢▢l, th▢ p▢rp▢s▢ ▢f t▢d▢y's m▢▢t▢ng ▢s t▢ ...
d By th▢ ▢nd ▢f th▢s m▢▢t▢ng ▢'d l▢k▢ s▢m▢ k▢nd ▢f d▢c▢s▢▢n ▢n th▢s.

Managing the discussion

e P▢rh▢ps w▢ c▢n c▢m▢ b▢ck t▢ th▢s l▢t▢r.
f L▢t's m▢v▢ ▢n t▢ th▢ n▢xt ▢t▢m ▢n th▢ ▢g▢nd▢.
g W▢'s ▢m t▢ b▢ g▢tt▢ng s▢d▢-tr▢ck▢d h▢r▢.
h C▢n w▢ g▢ b▢ck t▢ wh▢t w▢ w▢r▢ d▢sc▢ss▢ng ▢▢rl▢▢r?
i P▢rh▢ps w▢ c▢▢ld sp▢▢d th▢ngs ▢p ▢ l▢ttl▢.
j ▢K, s▢ j▢st t▢ s▢mm▢r▢s▢ wh▢t w▢'v▢ s▢▢d s▢ f▢r.
k M▢yb▢ w▢ sh▢▢ld t▢k▢ ▢ sh▢rt br▢▢k ▢t th▢s p▢▢nt.

Managing other speakers

l Pieter ▢s g▢▢ng t▢ f▢ll ▢s ▢n ▢n th▢ b▢ckgr▢▢nd. Pieter?
m Jack, c▢▢ld Pieter j▢st f▢n▢sh wh▢t h▢ w▢s s▢y▢ng?
n H▢ld ▢n ▢ m▢m▢nt, Jack. Y▢▢'ll g▢t y▢▢r ch▢nc▢ ▢n ▢ m▢m▢nt.
o ▢K, ▢K! L▢t's ▢ll c▢lm d▢wn, sh▢ll w▢?
p D▢▢s ▢nyb▢dy h▢v▢ ▢nyth▢ng th▢y'd l▢k▢ t▢ ▢dd?
q Tania, wh▢t's y▢▢r p▢s▢t▢▢n ▢n th▢s?
r Pieter, ▢ th▢nk wh▢t Tania ▢s try▢ng t▢ s▢y ▢s ...

Assigning follow-up tasks

s Pieter, c▢n ▢ l▢▢v▢ th▢t ▢n▢ w▢th y▢▢?
t Tania, c▢n y▢▢ g▢t b▢ck t▢ m▢ ▢n th▢t?

Closing the meeting

u I th▢nk th▢t's ▢b▢▢t ▢s f▢r ▢s w▢ c▢n g▢ ▢t th▢s st▢g▢.
v ▢'m ▢fr▢▢d w▢'ll h▢v▢ t▢ st▢p ▢t th▢r▢.

4 Listen to the meeting in 1 again and tick the expressions as you hear them. Which two are not used?

5 Play the Chairperson's game in small groups. Flip a coin – heads move forward three spaces, tails move forward one space. Follow the instructions on the square you land on using appropriate chairing expressions. The first person to get through the meeting is the winner!

START	Open the meeting	Welcome the group to the meeting	Check that people got a copy of the agenda	Outline the aim of the meeting – to give a new project the go-ahead	PEOPLE LOOK CONFUSED. MISS A TURN	Say you need a final decision today
A FIGHT HAS BROKEN OUT! MISS A TURN	Suggest a short break	Resume the meeting	Give a follow-up task to Dan	Ask Amy to find something out by the next meeting	YOU'VE REACHED A DECISION! MOVE ON 3 SQUARES	Ask Mia to give the background to the project
Try to stop people all talking at the same time!					Comment that the meeting has been productive	Stop Amy interrupting Mia
Show support for James, but disagree					Find out if anyone has any last points to make	Check you've understood Monica
Move on to the next item on the agenda					Thank people for their contributions and close the meeting	YOU GOT A LAUGH! MOVE ON 2 SQUARES
Explain to Sanjay what Ivana means					FINISH	Find out what Philippe thinks
YOU'RE MAKING PROGRESS. MOVE ON 3 SQUARES						Ask if people have anything to add
Tell Frank he'll have a chance to speak later	Disagree with Dan but ask for more detail	Try to keep the meeting on track	Go back to an earlier point about production	EVERYONE'S ASLEEP. MISS A TURN	Find out if people agree with your summary	Sum up what's been said so far

IN THE CHAIR

Work in groups of three. Take it in turns to lead three short meetings. Prepare for each meeting separately by reading the information and related article at the back of the book. Speaker A see pages 141 and 149. Speaker B see pages 141 and 146. Speaker C see pages 141 and 154.

LANGUAGE LINKS

Vocabulary: Companies and capital

1 Group the verbs according to meaning.

> acquire   build up   buy into   buy up
> de-layer   establish   expand   found   grow
> liquidate   rationalise   sell off
> start up   streamline   wind up

set up ....
take over ....
restructure ....
develop ....
close down ....

2 A manager is comparing business in the past with business now. Complete what he says using the words in the boxes.

> 1–8   customer   economy   flatter   global   outsourced
> stakeholders   vision   value
>
> 9–16   effectiveness   empowered   flexibility   functional
> layers   learning   total   networked

'Well, the most important difference, obviously, is that nowadays we're all operating in a (1) .... market, rather than simply a national one – the so-called borderless (2) .... And the increased amount of competition means that this company, at any rate, has gone from being product-driven to much more (3) ....-oriented. And whereas we used to focus on price, now we focus on customer (4) .... And where we used to set goals, we now have something called a corporate (5) .... A lot of it is just a change in terminology but it certainly looks like we're doing something new!
'A company's chief responsibility used to be to its shareholders, but these days we prefer to talk about (6) .... – not just the people with a financial stake in the company, but everyone who has an interest in the way it's run. A big change in the organisation of this company is that we now have a much (7) .... structure, instead of the old hierarchy. Everything used to be kept in-house. Now a lot of work is (8) ....
So, we're a (9) .... company now, with fewer (10) .... of management. For the most part, we work in cross-(11) .... teams, which gives us much greater (12) .... And we aim to have an (13) .... rather than simply loyal workforce. That means we give training and development top priority. In fact, we like to think we're a (14) .... company. For us, now, (15) .... is a much more important concept than efficiency and we see product quality as just one part of a (16) .... quality mindset.'

The financial pages

1 Match the heads (a–h) and tails (1–8) of the following headlines.

a Disappointing pre-   ☐
b Venture   ☐
c $500m rights   ☐
d Kagumi plan ¥200b stock   ☐
e Fears of another rise in base   ☐
f Contex reject hostile takeover   ☐
g Government crackdown on offshore   ☐
h Record fourth-   ☐

1 rates hit housing market
2 investments
3 tax profits for Kovak
4 bid from Avalon
5 quarter earnings tipped to top €90m
6 capital dries up
7 market flotation
8 issue to finance acquisition

2 Find words and phrases in 1 which mean:

a attempted acquisition by predator company
b exceed
c rate of interest charged by banks
d predicted
e strict new laws or measures
f profits for the period October to December
g affect badly
h money invested in a foreign country with lower tax
i when a company goes public and issues shares
j runs out

3 Divide the following into good (✔) and bad (✗) news.

a deepening recession   ☐
b cash bonanza   ☐
c downturn in demand   ☐
d sales boom   ☐
e economic slowdown   ☐
f market meltdown   ☐
g windfall profits   ☐
h housing slump   ☐
i upswing in the economy   ☐
j major depression   ☐
k economic recovery   ☐
l rise in the cost of living   ☐
m rise in the standard of living   ☐
n stock market crash   ☐
o credit crunch   ☐
p lengthening dole queues   ☐
q economic surplus   ☐
r hyperinflation   ☐
s overheated economy   ☐
t a stabilised market   ☐

Grammar: Linking and contrasting ideas

Read the meeting extracts below. For each of the words or phrases in **bold**, underline the word or phrase in brackets that is similar in meaning. Don't change any grammar or punctuation.

a **A** Well, **in spite of** all these problems, I'd say we're still on target for a January launch. (despite/even though)

    B What, **even though** we've hardly completed phase one trials? (in spite of the fact that/despite)

    A Yes. **Although** obviously I'd have liked us to be further ahead by now, I'm confident we'll be ready in time. (However/Whilst)

    B Well, I admire your optimism, Sergio, but **nevertheless**, I think we should make some kind of contingency plan. (all the same/however)

b **A** I'm afraid that, **because of** the strong euro, exports are down again this quarter. (consequently/owing to)

    B And **as a result** our share price is falling. (consequently/owing to)

    A Quite. Now, **whereas** we've been able to sustain these losses so far, we clearly can't do so indefinitely. (despite/although)

c **A** Right, well, **as** nobody seems to be in favour of this proposal, I suggest we just scrap it! (due to/seeing as)

    B It's not that we're against it, Jakob, **although** it is an unusual idea. (though/whereas)

    C Yes, I'd like to support you on this one, Jakob, **but** I can't help feeling you're rushing things. (whilst/and yet)

    A Well, how much more time do you need? **In order to** put this before the board, I have to have your approval. (To/So that)

d **A** Now, I don't want to spend a lot of time on these new European guidelines. I do think we should go through them briefly, **however**. (though/although)

    B The guidelines do affect all of us, Renata.

    A **Even so**, we have more important things to discuss. (Whereas/Nevertheless)

e **A** Well, everybody, **thanks to** all your hard work, the campaign has got off to a great start. (as a result/as a result of)

    B And **while** it's too early to say exactly how successful it will be, it's looking very good indeed. (whilst/as)

    A Yes. **So as to** give you a clearer idea, I've prepared copies of our sales projections for year one. (so/in order to)

    B The figures are broken down by country **so that** you can get the full picture. (since/in order that)

    A And, **since** we're celebrating, I brought along some champagne! (seeing as/because of)

You can use the following words and phrases

- to make **contrasts and contradictions**:

all the same although and yet but despite in spite of (the fact that) even so even though however nevertheless though whereas while/whilst

- to express **purpose or intention**:

in order to/that to so as to so (that)

- to link **cause and effect**:

as as a result (of) because of consequently owing to seeing as since thanks to

Phrase bank: Chairing meetings

Complete the following chairing expressions.

a Bjorn, could you just fill us _____ _____ the background _____ the project?

b Janet, would you like to come _____ here or are you OK _____ that?

c We seem to be getting a little _____ the point. Can we come _____ this later?

d Going _____ what we were saying earlier, I'd just like to point _____ one thing.

e We need to speed things _____ a little. So, just to sum _____ what we've said so far.

f OK, if we're all _____ agreement, let's move _____ _____ the next item _____ the agenda.

g Let's break _____ here _____ a few minutes, shall we?

h OK, let's all calm _____ for a moment and go _____ _____ the main points we've discussed.

i Now, the Tokyo situation — Rashid, can you get _____ me _____ that?

j And then there's the training report – Suzanna, can I leave that one _____ you?

k OK, I think that about wraps things _____ for today. But we'll need to set _____ another meeting.

7 GAMES WITHOUT FRONTIERS

Talent wins games, but teamwork wins championships.

MICHAEL JORDAN, BASKETBALL LEGEND

1 How important is teamwork in your job and how much of a team player are you? Where would you place yourself on the scale below? Are you more of a 'me-person' or a 'we-person'?

ME ⟵―――――――――⟶ WE

2 What are the key ingredients of a high-performance team? Frame your opinion below and compare with a partner.

'In my experience, a good team is built on three main things – ...., ... and, above all, ... No matter what the project is, you need someone to ...., someone to .... and someone to .... But the one thing you don't want is ...., because that is the surest way to destroy a team.'

3 🔊 **2.12–2.17** Listen to an international group of project team leaders talking about what they have learned about how teams work. Take notes on some of the things they mention by completing the spidergrams below:

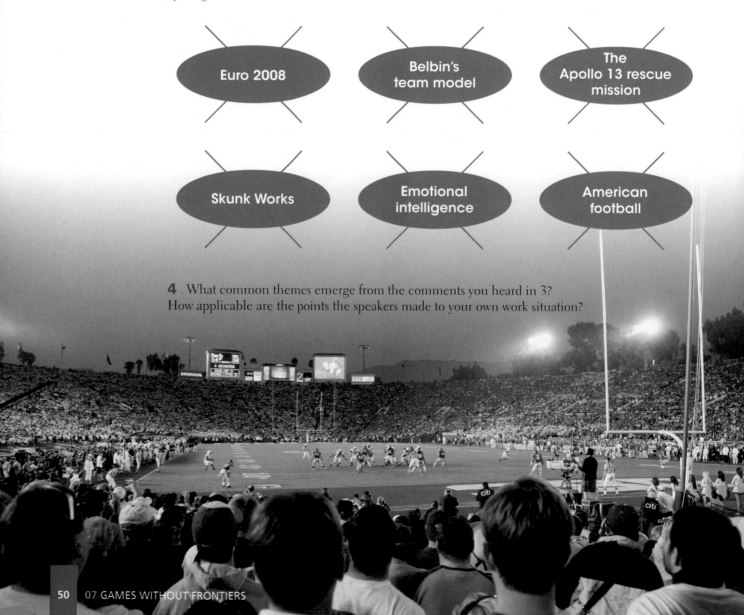

Euro 2008

Belbin's team model

The Apollo 13 rescue mission

Skunk Works

Emotional intelligence

American football

4 What common themes emerge from the comments you heard in 3? How applicable are the points the speakers made to your own work situation?

5 Match the following words and phrases you heard in 4 to what they mean:

a   team spirit
b   conflict resolution
c   in-fighting
d   can-do attitude
e   hotshots
f   the right chemistry
g   technical expertise
h   intellectual capital
i   buy-in
j   group effort

1   extremely successful, ambitious, usually young business people
2   support for an idea from other people e.g. bosses, customers
3   know-how; knowledge of one's job
4   a feeling of friendship and loyalty between members of a group
5   the effect of working together as a team
6   a number of methods for settling disputes between people
7   the combined knowledge and skills of employees
8   a willingness to try new things and make them successful
9   good compatibility between group members
10 disagreements between members of the same group or team

TRANSNATIONAL TEAMS

1 These days, 'virtual teams' communicating electronically across cultural boundaries and international time zones are becoming more and more common. What sort of problems do you think they face?

2 Different cultures tend to have different strengths and weaknesses when working in transnational teams. Label the chart below – what nationalities do you associate with the descriptions?

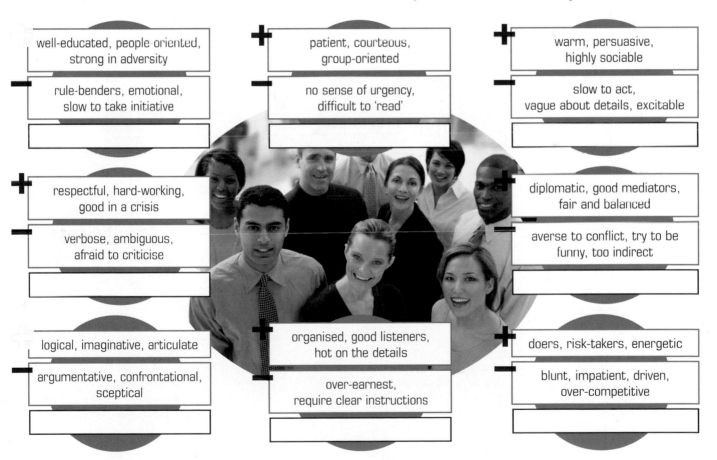

+ well-educated, people-oriented, strong in adversity

− rule-benders, emotional, slow to take initiative

+ patient, courteous, group-oriented

− no sense of urgency, difficult to 'read'

+ warm, persuasive, highly sociable

− slow to act, vague about details, excitable

+ respectful, hard-working, good in a crisis

− verbose, ambiguous, afraid to criticise

+ diplomatic, good mediators, fair and balanced

− averse to conflict, try to be funny, too indirect

+ logical, imaginative, articulate

− argumentative, confrontational, sceptical

+ organised, good listeners, hot on the details

over-earnest, require clear instructions

+ doers, risk-takers, energetic

blunt, impatient, driven, over-competitive

3 Pick two of the cultures above and discuss with a partner:
- how compatible they would be working in a team – what they'd have in common and how they might clash
- which culture could best act as a bridge between the two cultures you just chose
- which cultures might find it hardest to work in a virtual team without face-to-face contact

4 Share your ideas and any personal experiences you may have had with the rest of your group.

THERE ARE TWO SIDES TO EVERY STORY

1 2.18–2.20 Listen to team members from different countries giving their account of project meetings they've just come out of and take brief notes on the problems they had. What do these tell you about their cultures?

Meeting 1	a	Americans	b	Japanese
Meeting 2	a	British	b	Hungarians
Meeting 3	a	French	b	Germans

2 Which attitudes do you have most/least sympathy with?

3 The speakers mentioned the following stages of a project. Can you put them in chronological order?

the kick-off meeting ☐ we were ready to execute ☐

we were almost ready to sign off on this project ☐ we got the green light ☐

the last deliverables have been shipped ☐ the first milestone ☐

TEAMWORK

1 Work with a partner. Each read the executive summary of one of two popular books on teamwork. Then share information with each other, using the discussion phrase bank to help you. What are the most interesting ideas for you? How do the books agree and differ on how to work in teams?

The jazz process

'How can a group of jazz musicians that have never worked together before, immediately begin playing music as a collective and deliver a series of unique and great-sounding performances? And what does any of this have to do with the world of business?' Adrian Cho, musician, software developer and author of *The Jazz Process: Collaboration, Innovation and Agility*, thinks he has the answer.

All jazz bands are multi-disciplined teams. Each member is a strong soloist who must fit in with the other band members to form a cohesive unit that can deliver a smooth performance. But the direction that performance may take is unpredictable and here is the greatest parallel between jazz musicians and cross-functional project teams – their ability to improvise within constraints that are not always fixed.

To give a great performance, players must always be listening for and responding to change. Real-time innovations and sudden changes of direction cannot be planned. But, if the music is not to degenerate into noise and chaos, band members must be sufficiently tuned in to each other to pick up the subtlest of signals.

At different times different people will take the lead. Sometimes the lead player will simply emerge as the other musicians fade into the background. At other times a player will take a calculated risk, which might take the music in a completely different direction which the others must follow. As with management teams, it's all about synergy.

Whilst many artists are either lone geniuses working in isolation (painters, poets) or carefully rehearsed and directed professionals (actors, orchestras), in jazz the lines of leadership and responsibility are blurred. The end-result is co-managed and never quite the same twice.

Cho divides the 'jazz process' into fourteen golden rules, the first of which is: 'use just enough rules', but not too many! The others are: 'employ top talent, put the team first, build trust and respect, commit with passion, lead on demand, act openly and transparently, listen for change, make contributions count, stay healthy, reduce friction, maintain momentum, exchange ideas and take measured risks'.

Building trust and exchanging ideas are a given. But perhaps the best advice is: 'listen for change'. Mostly what this means is being aware of how others are deviating from the plan and responding to their initiatives. In jazz they call it 'having big ears'.

▶ **Discussion phrase bank**

The basic idea seems to be …

The author takes the view that …

Some of the examples he gives are …

He also makes out a case for …

I agree with the point about …

And I find the idea that … extremely interesting.

But I'm not sure I go along with the idea that …

I also have my doubts about …

For me, the most interesting point is …

In my own experience, what I've found is …

Overall, I think there's a parallel between … and … is …

BIOTEAMS

'How is it that, even with our vastly superior intelligence, nature's teams sometimes seem to work much better than ours – what do they know that we don't?' This is the question that Ken Thompson, expert in virtual professional communities and author of *Bioteams*, wants us to explore.

Even in today's technology-enabled environment with e-mail, videoconferencing and social networking, too many teams, says Thompson, are still managed according to the old command-and-control method with directives passed down through the corporate hierarchy. Add personality clashes and cross-cultural misunderstandings into the equation and you have a recipe for disaster. Could it be that millions of years of evolution have developed better communication channels for group collaboration?

Ant colonies, for example, are the masters of supply chain management. Ants solve route planning problems as fast as our most advanced computers. There seems to be no direct consultation within the group, and yet the smallest action of one member is picked up instantly by the network. But the intelligence of individual ants is not high. As Thompson puts it, 'exceptionally well coordinated morons can produce dazzling results!' And even in the most high-powered businesses today it's coordinate or die!

Higher up the food chain, geese, which can fly 70% further in flocks than they can alone, rotate leadership of their V-formation to optimise flight efficiency. There are no rules governing this and no status issues. Such teams are totally action-focused, working by continuous experimentation and feedback. Each team member is simultaneously in touch with both its environment and all the other members.

So what are the lessons for the world of business? Well, first, that in our knowledge-based economy, on-time, high-quality performance is more a matter of group trial and error, of collective intelligence, than of some individual stroke of genius. The team doesn't just consist of a group of people who may come up with the answer. The team is the answer.

Second, leadership should be on-demand with the leader's role moving from member to member to fit the task. And, third, messages between team members must be short and instant. With all other species this is always the case. What happened to us? Could Web 2.0 technology help us to achieve the same degree of connectivity?

According to Thompson, the most effective teams on the planet are not human. They are nerve cells, bees, wolves, dolphins, whole ecosystems. And they can teach us about success because the natural world consists of nothing but successes. As Thompson reminds us, in nature, if you fail, you're a fossil.

2 Teach your partner the words and phrases in the text you read which mean (the relevant paragraphs are in brackets):

The Jazz Process
a   an efficient tightly formed group (2)
b   limits or controls (2)
c   aware of (3)
d   the combined effectiveness of teams (4)
e   unclear (5)
f   disagreement or bad feeling between people (6)
g   the speed you've built up (6)

Bioteams
a   a leader who makes decisions and gives instructions (2)
b   problems with and arguments about seniority (4)
c   information that tells you how well you're doing (4)
d   in contact with (4)
e   trying different methods until you succeed (5)
f   sudden inspiration or good idea (5)
g   being in contact with others via the Internet (6)

3 You met several useful compound adjectives in the texts you just read. See how many you can make by combining one word from each of the boxes below:

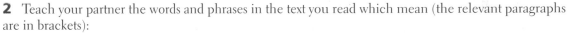

action- co- cost- cross- customer high- knowledge- market- multi- on- people- real- technology-	+	based centred conscious cultural demand disciplined driven effective enabled focused functional managed oriented powered quality tech time

4 Which combinations of the words in 3 mean:

a   helped by intellectual capital?
b   concentrating on what they do?
c   with many specialist areas of expertise?
d   receiving and reacting to information immediately?
e   from different departments within a company?
f   as, and only as, required?

5 Now think of nouns you could describe using some of the compound adjectives you made in 3.

6 Make an analogy of your own: 'A team is like…'. Present it briefly to the rest of your group.

A WINNING FORMULA

1 These days, sport is very much a business and business English is full of references to sport. What are the parallels, if any, between the corporate and sporting worlds? Discuss with a partner.

2 Sir Jackie Stewart is a former Triple World Driver's Champion and the founder and principal of Stewart Grand Prix. How relevant are his comments about Formula 1 to your own line of business?

> Formula 1 is entirely teamwork related. There's almost a dependency on teamwork. The people that work with us are not just employees. They're part of the family and you've got to build that family up.

3 Moretti Racing is a recent entrant into the world of Formula 1, but has quickly established itself as a serious competitor in the sport. At least, it had. But at the end of its second season, disaster struck. Read the article from *Winning Formula* magazine and answer the questions:

a How many examples of criticism and blame can you find in the article?
b How much confidence would you have in Moretti if asked to invest in his racing team?

MORETTI RACING: how it all went up in smoke for the new team on the track

Andy Martin reports from Abu Dhabi

Enrico Moretti must be wondering how the stars of his F1 dream-team have managed to go from heroes to zeroes in the space of just twelve months.

A remarkable debut

In its first season, the privately funded racing team of Modena-based sports car manufacturer Automobili Moretti could seemingly do no wrong, coming a creditable fourth in the Drivers' Championship and topping that with third place in the Constructors' behind Ferrari and McLaren.

Spectacular failure

But its second season ended in catastrophe yesterday at the Abu Dhabi grand prix when their top driver Mario di Angelo's car burst into flames on exiting the pit-lane. Di Angelo

narrowly escaped fatal injury, but sustained serious burns. The accident has put him out of racing for at least a year. If and when he does return, he vows it won't be for Moretti, who finished second-to-last in both championships this time round.

Technical problems

'What happened at the Yas Marina circuit was entirely the fault of the pit crew' said di Angelo from his hospital bed. 'They are rushing pit-stops and putting all our lives at risk in a desperate bid to win races. But it's the car that's at fault.'

Mixed motives

Chief of R&D, Oskar Rathenau, has a different theory: 'I wonder if Enrico really cares about winning races at all. For him what matters is getting publicity

for the Moretti brand, and the more drama, the more danger, the more fireworks, the better'.

Hiring and firing

The team has certainly attracted plenty of publicity of late. Sparks flew last month when chief designer Jean-Luc Bertrand was summarily dismissed and replaced with Moretti's son Giancarlo in a move many in the team have called 'pure nepotism'.

Then, with tension mounting between di Angelo and Moretti, the team started talks with Debora da Silva, the Harvard-educated Brazilian supermodel and Indy 500 motor racing sensation, who is bidding to be F1's only female driver. 'Debora's driving skills are unquestionable' admits Moretti's

technical director, Toivo Sukari, 'But to imagine she could be competitive in F1 is crazy.' Still, with di Angelo out of the picture, da Silva may soon find herself out on the grid alongside Moretti Racing's 20-year-old wunderkind, Roberto di Fiore.

And, now, the latest news is that Moretti himself is stepping down as team boss and on the lookout for his replacement. Firefighters only need apply!

The Moretti pits at Yas Marina

4 Amidst a blaze of publicity, Moretti finally hired F1 veteran François Basset as team boss and Debora da Silva as his new driver. But halfway through its third season Moretti Racing is still struggling, in spite of a couple of good races, and team morale is at an all-time low. Read the team member profiles opposite and decide what some of the interpersonal problems might be.

5 Turn to pages 142, 151 or 153 and each read about different rumours surrounding the team. Then compare notes.

6 As the major investors in Moretti Racing, it is up to you to decide what advice to give to the team and what action you'd like the senior directors to take. Remember, it's largely your money that is keeping the team afloat, so you can exercise a good deal of influence! The agenda for your meeting is on page 158.

Patriarchal chairman of Automobili Moretti, the family business started by his grandfather in 1917. Relies heavily on his managing director (a non-family member) to run the firm on a day-to-day basis. Has always wanted his own F1 team, but lacked the funds until he received backing from a small group of private financiers.

Personality: charismatic, but moody; very much a hands-on leader and a great motivator; has now reluctantly taken a backseat.

Enrico Moretti
Team Owner
56 years old, Italian

François Basset
Team Boss
62 years old,
French

40 years experience in F1 as driver, technical director and team boss. Never won a championship as a driver, but won the constructors' title three times for previous teams and has managed two world champions. Has been described as 'the great intellectual of the sport'.

Personality: quiet but firm leader; does not respond well to challenges to his authority; feels somewhat threatened by Sonia and Oskar; a private man who dislikes media attention.

Sonia Cassidy
Commercial Director
50 years old,
American

'A human dynamo' is what the press calls virtually the sport's only female senior executive. The deal-maker on the team, she's largely responsible for obtaining the financial backing that allowed Moretti to enter F1. Obtained $50m in sponsorship in Moretti's first season, but finding it harder now the team has slipped in the rankings.

Personality: single-minded magician with the figures; with a no-nonsense style, has no time for ego-battles at team meetings.

Toivo Sukari
Technical Director
51 years old,
Finnish

Likes to roll up his sleeves and get on with it rather than delegate. 'One of the boys', he has some slightly old-fashioned views about women in the business. Does not get on well with Sonia or Debora, but tolerates Nilda, whose expertise he respects. Upset about the di Angelo accident. Thinks drivers are too young and inexperienced. Team currently ninth in the constructors' championship.

Personality: slow, methodical perfectionist; loyal to Enrico.

Oskar Rathenau
Chief of R&D
48 years old,
German

MIT-educated automotive engineering genius. Has been responsible for many innovations in F1, not least the Moretti engine which did so well in its first season. Serious friction between him and Toivo, who, he claims, has 'wilfully misinterpreted' his engine designs. Still very angry about the firing of Jean-Luc Bertrand.

Personality: energetic ideas man; prides himself on finding solutions on schedule and within budget. Mistrusts Enrico.

Giancarlo Moretti
Chief Designer
29 years old,
Italian

A talented designer for Automobili Moretti, who also spent two years at Maserati, this is Giancarlo's first venture into F1. Is aware of the resentment caused by his appointment, but genuinely believes he can solve some of the problems with the layout of the Moretti car. Deeply admires François Basset. Eager to prove himself to the team.

Personality: calm and conscientious; works hard to break away from the playboy image associated with his father.

Nilda Carrió
Chief Aerodynamicist
34 years old,
Argentinian

Has had to put up with a lot of team politics at Moretti. Her appointment two years ago was initially opposed by Toivo Sukari, who has now grudgingly come to rely on her. Would like to work more closely with Oskar Rathenau on pushing forward innovations. Regrets the loss of Jean-Luc Bertrand, but gets on very well with Giancarlo.

Personality: an excellent communicator, able to connect with people at all levels both within and outside the team.

Roberto di Fiore
Driver
20 years old,
Italian

A racing prodigy who began his F1 career at the record-breaking age of 18. Has yet to win his first championship race, but stunned the world of motor sport by taking third place last season in the Hungarian grand prix. Recent performance has been affected by the departure of his racing partner and mentor, Mario di Angelo. Currently eleventh in the driver's championship.

Personality: a risk-taker who tends to crash too often; visibly jealous of Debora's celebrity.

Debora da Silva
Driver
27 years old,
Brazilian

A media celebrity in North and South America with a highly paid modelling career and a degree in physics from Harvard. Was not taken seriously on the American racing scene until she won two Indianapolis 500 races last season. Joined Moretti Racing this season for an undisclosed sum to launch her career in F1. Currently eighth in the drivers' championship.

Personality: focused; good with the media; easy-going manner hides her inner determination.

8 PROMOTING YOUR IDEAS

We had snakes in *Raiders of the Lost Ark* and bugs in *Indiana Jones and the Temple of Doom*. But supposedly man's greatest fear is public speaking. That'll be in our next picture.

STEVEN SPIELBERG, FILM DIRECTOR

1 How important is it in your line of business to be able to present your ideas professionally? Do you enjoy giving presentations or generally try to avoid them?

2 🔊 **2.21** Listen to five experienced presenters talking about what still makes them nervous every time they give a presentation. <u>Underline</u> the speakers whose worries you share. Then compare concerns with a partner.

Speaker 1   Speaker 2   Speaker 3   Speaker 4   Speaker 5

3 Complete the following expressions from the extracts in 2 using a single verb.

a   Your mind   blank.
b   Your mouth   dry.
c   Your mike   funny.
d   The audience   quiet.
e   Everything   wrong.

4 Which of the expressions in 3 means:

you can't think of anything? ☐   your microphone doesn't work properly? ☐

5 Complete the expressions from the extracts in 2.

about	down	down	of	out	over	to	up	up	up

a   You dry .... completely.
b   Your equipment breaks ....
c   You run .... time.
d   You run .... schedule.
e   You pace .... and ....
f   Your wave your arms ....
g   Your heart speeds ....
h   Your legs turn .... jelly.

6 Someone once observed: 'There is nothing wrong with having nothing to say – unless you insist on saying it.' Read the text. Can you think of any less extreme ways of achieving the same objective?

KEEP IT SHORT AND SIMPLE!

According to ancient custom, the elders of a remote African village have to stand on one leg while addressing their audience at council gatherings. As soon as their second foot touches the ground, they must stop speaking immediately.

AUDIENCE ANALYSIS

1 2.22–2.27 Listen to a group of business people talking about audience expectations in different countries. Which country do you think they're talking about? Compare your thoughts with a partner.

Country	Extract
USA	☐
Germany	☐
Japan	☐
UK	☐
France	☐
Kuwait	☐

Check your answers on page 141.

2 In an increasingly global economy are certain national stereotypes still valid?

3 Match the phrasal verbs in these sentences. They were all in the extracts in 1.

a Wisecracks – that's what they tend to **go**
b The one thing you can't **do**
c The audience may **switch**
d They'll want you to **go**
e Anecdotes and amusing stories seem to **go**
f What matters is how you **come**
g Be too techie and they'll think you're **showing**
h You have to **keep**

1 **off** altogether.
2 **across** as a person.
3 **up** a certain level of formality.
4 **for**.
5 **without** is a sense of humour.
6 **off**.
7 **down** well.
8 **through** all the main points again.

4 Match the phrasal verbs in 3 to the meanings below.

a present yourself
b lose interest
c be appreciated
d try to impress
e like
f repeat
g maintain
h manage without

5 In your experience, what sort of thing do audiences in your country tend to go for? What doesn't go down so well?

6 You heard the following idiomatic expressions in 1. Complete them by filling in the missing letters. Use the words in brackets to help you.

a You should have all the technical information at your fi............... (easily available)
b Give your presentation the personal to............... (aim it directly at your audience's needs)
c You'll get loads of interruptions, but just go with the fl............... (let things happen)
d Don't get too carried aw............... (be overenthusiastic)
e Have a few gimmicks up your sl............... (plan some clever surprises to attract attention)
f It really is essential that you do your ho............... (prepare very carefully)

7 Which piece of advice in 6 do you think is the most important?

INNOVATION

1 How much of your company's business depends on innovation? Give a few examples.

2 Look at the extract from a web page below. What do you think the title means? Now read the text. Does your company encourage this kind of initiative?

Intrapreneurs

Ideas are like insects – many are born, but few live to maturity. Because they closely resemble entrepreneurs, we call the people who turn ideas into realities inside an organisation 'intrapreneurs'. Intrapreneurs are the hands-on managers who make a new idea happen.

Texas Instruments, well known for intrapreneurial successes, studied fifty of their successful and unsuccessful new product efforts. In each of their successes there were one or more dedicated intrapreneurs who persisted despite great obstacles. Similarly, the common denominator of their failures was that every one of them lacked a champion, an intrapreneur. Innovations just don't happen unless someone takes on the intrapreneurial role.

Gifford and Elizabeth Pinchot, www.intrapreneur.com

3 Find the words and phrases in the text which mean:

a describing people who don't just talk about it, but do it

b giving a lot of time and energy to something

c kept on trying to do something

d things that make progress difficult

e the only thing in common

f someone who supports and fights for an idea

4 What new ideas within your company or department have you been closely involved with recently?

5 🔊 **2.28–2.31** Two managers for MaxOut, an American chain of fitness centres, are presenting a new business idea to their board of directors. Listen to four extracts from their presentation and answer the questions.

Extract 1

a Put the stages of the first part of the presentation in chronological order.

   quote statistics ☐   build up expectations ☐   pose a problem ☐   introduce themselves ☐
   thank the audience ☐   set a challenge ☐   share corporate vision ☐

b Are the presenters successful at arousing the curiosity of their audience? Why (not)?'

c The following figures were quoted. What do they refer to?

   1,000   250,000 $\frac{4}{10}$

   35              $\frac{7}{10}$ 61% (122m)

d On a scale of 1–5, how confident did the presenters sound?

e Is it more effective having two speakers instead of one?

f What advice would you give the speakers if they had to present in your country? Should there be more or less technical detail, humour, formality, audience involvement, 'hard sell'?

Extract 2

a What do these figures refer to? Do you find them surprising?

   a mere 13%
   a staggering 92%

b What do you think 'mere' and 'staggering' mean?

c Complete the following extract from the presentation.
   We did a nationwide su................. of people who had previously shown an in................. in joining a MaxOut club and then changed their mi................. Full de................. are in the re................. in front of you, but this chart hi................. our main fi.................

d Complete the chart, which shows the results of the survey referred to in c.

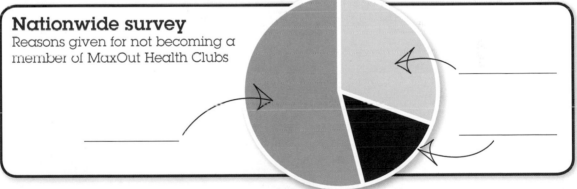

Nationwide survey
Reasons given for not becoming a member of MaxOut Health Clubs

e What product do you think the speakers are about to present?

Extract 3

a What is the product?

b How much of the project budget was spent on making the prototype?

c How long has it taken to develop?

d Complete the product features chart.

e What's the main selling point?

f In what ways do you think the product would benefit MaxOut's main business?

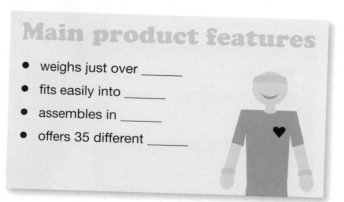

Main product features

- weighs just over _____
- fits easily into _____
- assembles in _____
- offers 35 different _____

Extract 4

a Complete the extract below using the verb phrases in the box. The first one has been done for you.

> are currently being considered   are all itemised   could be recorded
> ~~has been fully costed~~   has been suggested   is included   is still being carried out
> might easily be sold   would probably be priced

OK, to wrap things up. The Micro-GYM (1) ....*has been fully costed*........ – a complete breakdown (2) .... in the report. Estimated costs of manufacturing, packaging and advertising (3) .... Product testing (4) ...., but we would obviously need the go-ahead from you before we proceed much further with that. The Micro-GYM (5) .... at around $35: well within the reach of most people. It (6) .... that exercise demonstrations (7) .... on video and that the product (8) .... online. Both these suggestions would incur extra costs, but (9) ....

b If you were on the board of MaxOut, would you give the new product idea the go-ahead? If not, what other information would you need before you were persuaded?

6 Put the stages of the presentation you just listened to into the correct order.

> a gap in the market   interest   the key message   the main product features   the new product
> the objectives   the presentation   project approval   the Q&A session   some relevant statistics

1 Open _____

2 Outline _____

3 Arouse _____

4 Quote _____

5 Identify _____

6 Introduce _____

7 Describe _____

8 Sum up _____

9 Ask for _____

10 Lead into _____

7 An in-house team is presenting a new product idea it's been working on to senior management. Replace the words and phrases in **bold** with the nearest alternatives from the box.

address   advantage   breakdown   break into   competition   ~~confident~~   consensus   enthusiastic
fire away   golden   green light   major   obvious   optimal   players   possibilities   quote   research
selling points   seeking   staggering   stretch   to the next stage   tremendous   trust   universal

                                 confident

a   By the end of this presentation, we're **sure** you'll be as **positive** about this idea as we are.
b   As one of the **main competitors** in this industry, we are constantly **looking for** ways to stay ahead of the **field** and maintain our competitive **edge**.
c   Let me **show** you some figures … I'm sure you'll agree these are **amazing** statistics.
d   **Believe** me, we've really done our **homework** on this.
e   We think this product has **enormous potential**.
f   In focus groups, the **general opinion** was that the product will **meet** a real need.
g   The main **benefits** of the product are **clear**.
h   It is the **perfect** solution to a **common** problem.
i   It represents a **great** opportunity for us to **extend** our brand and **penetrate** a new market.
j   A full cost **analysis** is in the report in front of you.
k   What we need now is the **go-ahead** from you so we can take things **further**.
l   We'll take your questions now. So **over to you**!

PITCHING YOUR IDEA

Work with a partner to give a team presentation of a new product idea.

Step One: Prepare

You'll find information on real concept products in the additional material section. Team 1 turn to page 150, team 2 to page 154. Choose which product idea you want to pitch and decide what kind of company would be able to manufacture it. Find out or invent any supporting figures you'd like to refer to and create any simple visuals you'll need.

Step Two: Practise

Run through your pitch a couple of times. Use a similar presentation structure to the pitch you listened to. Some of the phrases and expressions in exercise 7 on this page and in the Phrase Bank in the Language Links may be helpful. Practise handing over to your partner after each phase of the talk.

Step Three: Perform

When you're ready, give your presentation. Make sure you invite questions at the end. Whose pitch was the most persuasive? Who gets the go-ahead?

LANGUAGE LINKS

Vocabulary: Phrasal verbs

1 The five most common verbs used in phrasal verbs are: *get, come, go, take* and *put*. Complete each set of sentences using one of these verbs in the Past Simple and a particle from the box. Use the definitions in brackets to help you.

> across around down for in into into off off
> on on on out out over over through through
> under up

a We .... too much work (accepted)
  .... a few details. (wrote)
  .... a bank loan. (obtained)
  .... the project. (got control of)

b They .... the recession. (survived)
  .... an accounting error. (discovered)
  .... a lot of money. (inherited)
  .... pressure to resign. (received)

c She .... to talk about training. (proceeded)
  .... the figures with us. (checked)
  .... the idea. (started to dislike)
  .... option B. (chose)

d We .... the problem in the end. (avoided)
  .... an argument. (became involved in)
  .... a ton of paperwork. (completed)
  .... well. (had a good relationship)

e They .... hours of work on it. (did)
  .... the meeting. (postponed)
  .... a press release. (issued)
  .... most of the cash. (provided)

2 Some phrasal verbs have three parts. Complete the sentences using the pairs of particles in the box.

> along with + in with   in for + back to   in for + down as
> on about + on with   out of + ahead with   round to + on
> to   up against + round to   up with + up for

a I'm afraid I haven't got .... doing that report yet, but I'll get .... it as soon as I've finished these spreadsheets.

b I know there's no point going .... it, but I really don't get .... this new boss of ours.

c I'm not putting .... this situation a moment longer – it's time I stood .... myself!

d I know it's too late to back .... it now, but I'm really sorry we went .... this agreement.

e I'm afraid I can't go .... this – it just doesn't fit .... our plans.

f We seem to be coming .... a lot of opposition from marketing at the moment, but hopefully they'll soon come .... our way of thinking.

g I put .... that promotion I was telling you about but they haven't got .... me about it.

h I hear Jon's come .... a lot of criticism from the board and may have to stand .... chairman.

Grammar: The passive

1 Make the following extracts from reports more formal by:

- using the passive
- replacing the words in bold with an adverb from the box
- deleting the subject.

> currently formally generally provisionally roughly
> tentatively thoroughly unanimously unofficially

a Our site engineers estimate that construction will take **about** eighteen months to complete.
  It is roughly estimated that construction will take eighteen months to complete.

b They've given us the go-ahead, but it's not official yet.
  We've ....

c We're considering several options at the moment.
  Several ....

d Almost everyone felt that the project was taking too long.
  It ....

e Everyone agreed that the proposal required further discussion.
  It ....

f We have tested every part of the new software.
  The ....

g The company will announce the plant closure at the official press conference next week.
  The ....

h They've OK'd the training budget at this stage, but they may change their minds.
  The ....

i They suggested that we could import the raw materials, but stressed that this was only a suggestion.
  It ....

2 Make the accusations below less personal by removing all references to 'we' and 'you' and making any necessary grammatical changes.

a But we understood that you'd agreed to this.
  But it was understood that this had been agreed.

b We assumed that you'd accept this.
  It ....

c We stated quite clearly in the contract that you must make your payments on the first of the month.
  It ....

d We presumed that you would comply with current health and safety regulations.
  It ....

3 Rewrite the impersonal e-mail below using only active verbs and replacing some of the more formal words and phrases with friendlier-sounding alternatives from the box.

> each other   exchange views   from now on
> get the chance   in this way   look forward   meet
> pencilled in   seeing you there   up to speed   various

From: Robert Masters
To: All departmental managers
Subject: Interdepartmental meeting

It has been decided that an interdepartmental meeting will henceforth be held every month. Heads of department will thus be able to network and generally be brought up to date on recent developments in other departments. Furthermore, they will be given the opportunity to have their voice heard on a number of matters relating to overall corporate strategy.

The first meeting is scheduled for next Thursday. Your attendance would be appreciated.

Robert Masters

You use the **passive** when you are more interested in actions, views and decisions than in the people who actually took them. The **passive** sounds more formal and objective than the **active**. For this reason it is frequently used in reports.

If the subject of the active sentence is *they, you, one, people, everyone* or *no one*, it is usually unnecessary to refer to it in the **passive** e.g. *No one can do it* becomes *It can't be done by anybody*.

When using reporting verbs in the **passive**, you need to insert the word *it* e.g. *They said 'There was absolutely no corruption'* becomes **It** *was strongly denied that there had been any corruption*.

The **active** generally sounds more personal than the **passive**. The danger is that in criticisms it can also sound more aggressive, and so in delicate negotiations the **passive** is often preferred to depersonalise potential conflict.

Phrase bank: Pitching an idea

Down

1 We are one of the major .... in our industry. (7)
2 We are constantly looking for ways to stay ahead of the .... (11)
3 We did a nationwide .... of our target customers. (6)
4 A complete .... of costs is included in the report. (9)
5 We set up special .... groups. (5)
6 What we need now is the green .... from you. (5)
9 The main .... of the product are clear. (8)
10 The .... so far has been overwhelmingly positive. (8)
12 We think this product has enormous .... (9)
13 Full .... are in the report in front of you. (7)
15 Believe me, we've really done our .... on this one. (8)

Across

1 As you know, we've been working on a .... of our own for some time now. (7)
7 We think this would be an excellent addition to our current .... of products. (5)
8 Let me quote you some interesting .... (7)
11 The product meets a real .... (4)
14 We need to maintain our competitive .... (9)
16 This is a great opportunity for us to stretch our .... (5)
17 I'm sure you'll agree this feature is a real selling .... (5)
18 This chart highlights our main .... (8)
19 OK, we'd like to throw this .... open now for questions and suggestions. (7)

9 RELATIONSHIP-BUILDING

Never do business with anybody you don't like. If you don't like somebody, there's a reason.

HENRY QUADRACCI, CEO OF QUAD/GRAPHICS

1 In business, have you ever:

a felt an instant rapport with someone you've only just met?

b taken an immediate dislike to someone you've just been introduced to?

c misjudged someone by taking too much notice of the way they looked or sounded?

Tell the story.

2 How good are your networking skills? Complete the questionnaire using the pairs of verbs in the boxes. Then circle your answers. Compare your answers with a partner and then read the analysis on page 143.

Questionnaire Are you an effective networker?

crack + break hover + wait look + say moan + bitch relax + let talk + catch	feel + mingle introduce + slip make + escape persevere + find stick + ignore try + draw	cut + get exchange + get get + mention give + keep go + make look + pretend

1 You meet a group of business people for the first time. Do you:

a _____ them in the eye, smile and _____ hello?

b _____ in the background and _____ to be introduced?

c _____ a joke to _____ the ice?

2 You meet up with some colleagues after work. Do you:

a _____ shop and _____ up on all the latest gossip?

b _____ about work and _____ about the boss?

c _____ and _____ your hair down?

3 You meet a fascinating person at a cocktail party. Do you:

a _____ to them like glue and _____ everyone else?

b _____ and _____ other people into the conversation?

c _____ obliged to go and _____ with other people?

4 You're stuck with a bore at a conference. Do you:

a _____ in the hope you'll _____ something in common?

b _____ some kind of excuse and _____?

c _____ them to someone else and _____ away?

5 You see someone you don't get on with at a function. Do you:

a _____ the other way and _____ you haven't seen them?

b _____ over and _____ the effort to speak to them?

c _____ them a polite nod, but _____ your distance?

6 You're introduced to a potential client. Time is short. Do you:

a _____ the preliminaries and _____ straight to the point?

b _____ to know them a bit before you _____ business?

c _____ business cards and say you'll _____ back to them?

3 Discuss the following points of view with a partner:

a   It's a cliché, but it's true: 'You never get a second chance to make a first impression'.
b   It's not how you start; it's how you finish. Last impressions are what really count.
c   They say 'humour is the shortest distance between two people'. But it can also be the furthest!
d   You don't have to be funny or clever. If you can tell a story, you can network.
e   As you travel round the world, you find that business and pleasure mix in very different ways.

4 🔘 **2.32** Now listen to some business people talking about the same points you discussed in 3 and make a note of anything you either find interesting or disagree with. Compare with a partner.

5 You heard the following phrases in 4. They're all connected. Can you remember what they were?

a   sm _ _ _ t _ _ _   b   soc _ _ _ chit- _ _ _ _   c   schm _ _ _ _ _ _
d   ming _ _ _ _   e   wor _ _ _ _ the r _ _ _

6 Work with a partner. For each of the situations below make a short list of things you could say.

a   The person standing next to you at the hotel bar is a good customer of your company. You've heard a lot about them from your new boss, who was about to introduce you, but was suddenly called to reception.
b   You're at a trade fair. The person on the stand hasn't met you before. A friend gave you their name, told you they might be able to help you make some business contacts and said they'd mention you'd be dropping by to say hello.
c   You unexpectedly bump into a very good friend at a conference who you haven't seen for ages. You've loads to talk about but unfortunately you were just on your way to a business appointment when you met them.
d   You meet your ex-boss at your children's school sports day. You used to get on quite well, but somehow lost touch after they took early retirement.
e   You're in the middle of a very interesting conversation with a potential client at a trade fair, but you suddenly notice the time and remember that your taxi will be arriving shortly to take you to the airport.

7 Compare lists with other people in your group.

8 🔘 **2.33–2.37** Listen to five short conversations. How quickly can you match them to the situations in 6?

Conversation 1 ☐   Conversation 2 ☐   Conversation 3 ☐   Conversation 4 ☐
Conversation 5 ☐

9 Listen again to the conversations. How similar is the language the speakers use to the lists you made in 6? Look at the listening scripts on page 174 and <u>underline</u> any expressions you'd like to remember to use yourself.

10 You're going to act out the situations in 6 with a partner. First, work together to build up the scenarios:

•   decide who's who
•   establish exactly where you are
•   agree on a few background details (names, shared acquaintances, past experiences, current business)
•   you may find some of the language in the phrase bank on page 71 useful.

If you prefer, base the scenarios on people and places you know.

11 When you're ready, take a couple of minutes to have each conversation. Try switching roles if you like. Which situations were the most challenging to deal with?

GETTING OUT OF THE OFFICE

1 Can the golf course, tennis court or pool hall be a good place to do business? Read the three short business articles below and think about the questions in the boxes. Then discuss them with a partner.

How to beat your boss at tennis and survive

Competing with the boss outside the workplace is an ancient ritual designed to test your thinking, competitiveness and ability to fit in. Once it involved weapons, but today it involves golf clubs, tennis rackets and pool cues. Your goal is to leave a good impression and that doesn't necessarily mean losing.

Before stepping onto the court, check two things: the boss's level of expertise and how much he cares about the game. It could be he's an A-tournament player so you'll have to sweat to survive. But if you judge your abilities superior, you'll have more decisions to make.

Even the game if possible. Play to win but not to kill. It's one thing to beat the boss. It's another to take the match in straight sets six-love. This doesn't mean deliberately missing shots. But you might consider scaling back your 160 kph serve, if only because you want everyone to have a good time.

www.ehow.com

a Is it easy to fit in where you work? Is there a competitive atmosphere?

b Are you a good loser or do you always play to win?

c Would you lose a match just to please the boss?

Golf and business

Not everyone can play tennis, but everyone thinks they can play golf. In an age of health and enlightenment, golf has replaced the three-martini lunch as the preferred vehicle for sealing deals. Sun Microsystems CEO Scott McNealy is a scratch golfer and Bill Gates is devoted to the game.

So why is golf the preferred sport of business? In a word, relationships. 'Four to five hours on the golf course, and you get to know the character of your golfing partners – honesty, humility, ability to handle success and failure, approach to risk, desire to have fun,' says Miller Bonner, a public relations veteran. 'That translates into a successful business relationship.'

Marketing director Derek Van Bronkhorst has his own test of character on the links. 'Do they cheat?' he asks. 'If they cheat in golf, would you want to do business with them?'

www.businessweek.com

d What's so wrong with the three-martini lunch for sealing deals?

e Are you a golf fan or do you agree with Mark Twain that 'golf is a good walk spoiled'?

f What else might your opponent do to reveal their character on the golf course?

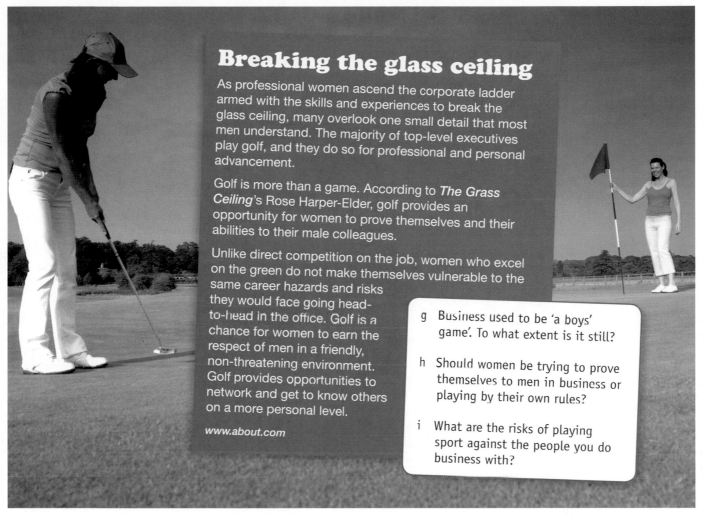

Breaking the glass ceiling

As professional women ascend the corporate ladder armed with the skills and experiences to break the glass ceiling, many overlook one small detail that most men understand. The majority of top-level executives play golf, and they do so for professional and personal advancement.

Golf is more than a game. According to *The Grass Ceiling*'s Rose Harper-Elder, golf provides an opportunity for women to prove themselves and their abilities to their male colleagues.

Unlike direct competition on the job, women who excel on the green do not make themselves vulnerable to the same career hazards and risks they would face going head-to-head in the office. Golf is a chance for women to earn the respect of men in a friendly, non-threatening environment. Golf provides opportunities to network and get to know others on a more personal level.

www.about.com

g Business used to be 'a boys' game'. To what extent is it still?

h Should women be trying to prove themselves to men in business or playing by their own rules?

i What are the risks of playing sport against the people you do business with?

2 🌐 **3.01–3.02** Listen to a group of oil company executives chatting during a game of golf and answer the questions.

Extract 1

a Why doesn't Stella immediately accept Craig's offer?
b Why are they only playing nine holes?
c How would you describe the men's attitude to the game?

Extract 2

a How's Craig playing today?
b What do Craig and Stella disagree on?
c What do you think Craig has to do if he wants the job?

3 Reorganise the words in bold to make correct sentences. They were all in the conversations in 2.

a We **be should thinking making probably of** a move quite soon.
b We **count staying can't weather fine the on** at this time of year.
c I **have have arranged lunch us to for** at the clubhouse.
d We **be get should able to around** the course in a couple of hours or so.
e You **be teamed been had must wishing you with up** Max.
f I **have have meaning been word you a with to about** this disposal operation.
g I **get would was mentioning wondering you when round to** that.

4 Work with a partner to practise mixing business and sport. Speaker A turn to page 142; speaker B turn to page 150.

VISITING SOMEONE'S HOME

1 What are the advantages and disadvantages of inviting a client or colleague to your home? Is it as common in your country as it is in Britain, Australia and the States?

2 🔘 3.03–3.06 Listen to some people entertaining at home and answer the questions.

Extract 1

a Did Magda have a problem finding Anne's house?
b What do you think 'Martin's still slaving away in the kitchen' means?
c What has Magda brought as a present?

Extract 2

a What do you think 'The whole place was an absolute wreck when we moved in' means?
b What does Magda have in her drink?
c What do you think Martin means by 'I had to rescue the starter'?

Extract 3

a What do you imagine Anne and Martin's apartment to be like?
comfortable ☐   dark and gloomy ☐   elegant ☐   full of antiques ☐
light and airy ☐   lived-in ☐   spacious ☐   tastefully furnished ☐
ultra-modern ☐
b When Magda sees the chairs, she says 'I could do with some of those for my place.' What does she mean?

Extract 4

a How does Magda describe the duck?
crispy ☐   juicy ☐   tasty ☐   tender ☐
b Who raises the subject of business? Complete the expression: I've been m............g to talk to you about this business in Poland.
c What excuse does Martin make to leave the two women to talk business?
d How many times does Magda indicate she's going to leave soon?

3 All the remarks below were in the conversation in 2. See who can remember the most in just three minutes!

Arrival

L__t me take your coat. —➤ You m_____d to find us OK, then? —➤ Oh, I b_____t you this. —➤ You shouldn't h__e. —➤ Come on t_____h. —➤ Oh, w__t a fabulous apartment! —➤ Now, what can I g__t you to drink? —➤ I'll be right b__k. —➤ Make y_____f at home.

The apartment

I was j__t looking at some of your oil paintings. —➤ You've got q___e a collection, haven't you? —➤ And I love the w__y you've done the fireplace. —➤ Was that here when you m___d in? —➤ Look at t____t view!

The meal

Dinner's r___y when you are. —➤ Sit w_____r you like. —➤ I thought we'd have a nice Spanish r_d. —➤ Now, there's more duck if you w__t it. —➤ And help y_____f to vegetables. —➤ Mm, this is a_____y delicious! —➤ I'm g___d you like it. —➤ You m___t let me have the recipe. —➤ A l____e more wine? —➤ I s_____t really. I'm driving. —➤ Oh, go on. You've o___y had one. —➤ Just a d___p, then.

Farewells

Well, I o___t to be making a move soon. —➤ You don't have to r___h off just yet, do you? —➤ How a___t some more coffee? —➤ OK, j___t half a cup. —➤ And then I really must be g___g. —➤ Thank you b___h for a lovely evening. —➤ Next time you must come to my p____e. —➤ T___e care now.

A DINNER INVITATION

Work with a partner. Act out the situation of a business person (the guest) visiting the home of a colleague (the host) from arrival to departure. The host is the guest's immediate boss. Before you start, establish:

- what company you work for (name, location and main business activity)
- exactly what your roles are at work
- how business is doing and what problems or opportunities your company currently has.

You both have an ulterior motive for the dinner. Guest see page 150. Host see page 143.

Step 1 This is the host's living room.

Guest, make some positive comments, ask questions, show interest in the answers and try to keep the conversation going. Host, make up any information you like about your house to answer your guest's questions.

Step 2 This is the view from the host's apartment.

Guest, comment on what you see. Host, make up any information you have to.

Step 3 This is the dinner.

Host, explain what the food is. Guest, compliment your host on the meal.

Step 4 Guest, take your leave, thank your host. Host, say goodbye to your guest and thank them for coming. Conclude any business you discussed during the evening or arrange to meet to discuss it again.

LANGUAGE LINKS

Vocabulary: Social English

1 Complete the conversation extracts from a dinner party using the pairs of verbs in the boxes.

> got + joking   is + accept   looking + ask   makes + think
> mean + talking   reckon + is   's + be   see + doing
> tells + going   think + happen

A So, what do you (1) .... is going to .... with this Ukrainian contract then?

B Good question. You know, something (2) .... me we're not .... to get it.

A Oh, really? What (3) .... you .... that? It (4) .... not like you to .... so pessimistic.

B Well, for one thing, we've gone in way too high. My guess (5) .... they'll .... a lower tender.

A Mm. By the way, have some more meat – there's plenty of it. You know, I don't (6) .... price .... really the issue.

B No?

A No. I (7) ...., we're .... long-term here. This is a seven-year project, maybe longer.

B So?

A So, reliability is what they'll be (8) .... for, if you .... me. They'll pay more for that.

B You've (9) .... to be .... This is one of the most price-sensitive markets in Eastern Europe. The way I (10) .... it, we'll be .... well just to get part of the contract. They'll probably get a local firm in to do the main work.

A Hm, well, that's bad news ...

> can't + say   had + would   hear + going   is + getting
> knew + coming   might + known   's + help
> shouldn't + saying   stop + get   suppose + heard

A I (11) .... you've .... the news about Alex?

B About her leaving to join HP? Well, we (12) .... that was ...., didn't we?

A I suppose so. The word (13) .... that Eduardo's .... her job now. You know, I (14) .... a feeling he ....

B Mm. I (15) .... really .... I'm surprised. He's had his eye on it for a while. And, anyway, if you get engaged to the executive vice-president's daughter, it (16) .... bound to .... your career prospects, isn't it?

A He's what? I (17) .... have ....! He'll (18) .... at nothing to .... a promotion.

B Well, you didn't (19) .... this from me, right, but there's a rumour .... around that ... well, maybe I (20) .... be .... this, but ...

A No, no, go on! I'll go and open another bottle of wine ...

2 Underline eight new expressions in 1 that you could use yourself.

Grammar: Multi-verb sentences

1 Decide which of the verbs below precede the infinitive with *to*, the *-ing* form or both and tick the appropriate boxes. The first one has been done for you.

	to do	doing		to do	doing
agree	✔	☐	manage	☐	☐
admit	☐	☐	enjoy	☐	☐
suggest	☐	☐	hope	☐	☐
try	☐	☐	miss	☐	☐
put off	☐	☐	avoid	☐	☐
aim	☐	☐	expect	☐	☐
stop	☐	☐	promise	☐	☐
refuse	☐	☐	go on	☐	☐
carry on	☐	☐	fail	☐	☐
remember	☐	☐	dislike	☐	☐

2 Complete the conversation using the correct form of the verbs in brackets.

A Hi, James. Client meeting overran a bit, did it?

B Mm. And Lucy and I stopped (1) .... (have) a coffee on the way back.

A Oh, right.

B By the way, did you remember (2) .... (send) those invoices off?

A What invoices?

B Stuart! I distinctly remember (3) .... (ask) you to deal with the invoices. They should have gone last week.

A Well, I've been a bit busy trying (4) .... (fix) this wretched computer!

B OK, look, stop (5) .... (do) whatever you're doing and deal with them now, would you? And what's wrong with the computer?

A No idea. It keeps crashing.

B Well, have you tried (6) .... (ask) Callum about it?

A Of course I have. I've been trying (7) .... (get) through to him all morning. But he's like you, isn't he? He's never in!

3 Complete the conversation using an appropriate preposition and *-ing* form from the boxes below.

> about   about   of   of   in   on   for

> being   changing   having   making   putting
> telling   wanting

A Of course, Tim succeeded .... a complete fool of himself at the drinks party.

B Did he?

A Oh, yes. Well, he will insist .... those tasteless jokes, won't he? The president's wife was not amused.

B Well, he can forget .... in for that promotion, then, can't he?

A Hm, not much chance of that here, anyway. You know I complained .... us .... to work another weekend?

B Mm, I hear Angela went mad about it.

A Yeah, she practically accused me .... disloyal to the company! Can you believe it?

B Sounds like her.

A Did I tell you I was thinking .... jobs?

B No, but I can't say I blame you .... to get out of this place!

Some verbs can precede both the infinitive and the *-ing* form, but the meaning usually changes (*I like to work out twice a week* = I think it's a good idea; *I like working out* = I enjoy it).

Some verbs normally followed by the *-ing* form change when there's an indirect object (*I suggest stopping* now → *I suggest we stop* now).

When a verb is followed by a preposition other than *to*, the *-ing* form is usually used (*They apologised for not getting back to us sooner*).

Modal verbs always precede the other verbs in a sentence and are followed by the infinitive without *to* (*You must be wishing you'd never come to work here!*).

Certain expressions always precede the *-ing* form: **It's no good** complaining; **There's no point (in)** complaining; **What's the use of** complaining?

A number of expressions take the past form: **I'd rather** you **didn't**; **It's time we went**.

A number of expressions of intention take the infinitive with *to*: **I'm planning to** do it later; **I've been meaning to** have a word with you.

Phrase bank: Networking

Complete the phrases using the words in the box. Then match each to two things you might say.

| asking breaking bumping catching looking meeting offering paying |
| raising referring saying taking |

1 .... people for the first time
2 .... into old friends
3 .... compliments
4 .... about a journey
5 .... up with old friends
6 .... an important subject
7 .... to help someone out
8 .... to third parties
9 .... off a conversation
10 .... your leave
11 .... forward to future contact
12 .... goodbye

a You managed to find us OK?
b You're looking very well!
c Bye now!
d I don't think we've met.
e It's been great talking to you.
f Long time no see.
g I could put in a word for you if you like.
h Fancy meeting you here!
i Is that the time? I must be going soon.
j I wonder if I could have a word with you.
k Married life obviously suits you!
l We must get together soon.
m Give my regards to Theo when you see him.
n Take care.
o I didn't expect to see you here!
p I could put you in touch with someone I know.
q How's life treating you?
r I've really enjoyed our conversation.
s Fiona mentioned you might be dropping by.
t I don't think we've been introduced.
u I should be making a move.
v Did you have any trouble finding us?
w Let's not leave it so long next time.
x There's something I've been meaning to talk to you about.

1 ☐☐ 2 ☐☐ 3 ☐☐ 4 ☐☐ 5 ☐☐ 6 ☐☐
7 ☐☐ 8 ☐☐ 9 ☐☐ 10 ☐☐ 11 ☐☐ 12 ☐☐

10 TAKING DECISIONS

Standing in the middle of the road is very dangerous – you get knocked down by the traffic from both sides.

MARGARET THATCHER

1 When was the last time you were faced with a difficult decision and were unable to make up your mind? How did you decide in the end, or was the decision made for you?

2 You may be a cool-headed decision maker in the office, but would you know what to do in a real life-and-death situation? Read the following extract from an unusual website and discuss the questions.

Worst-case scenarios

The principle behind this site is a simple one: you just never know.

You never really know what nasty surprises life has in store for you – what is lurking around the corner, what is hovering over your head, what is swimming beneath the surface. You never know when you might be called on to perform an act of extreme bravery and to choose life or death by your own actions.

But when you are called, we want to be sure that you know how to react. We want you to know what to do when the pilot passes out and you have to land the plane. We want you to know what to do when you see that shark fin heading toward you ...

www.worstcasescenarios.com

a What kind of things 'lurking around the corner', 'hovering over your head' or 'swimming beneath the surface' do you think the website is referring to?

b Have you ever found yourself in a really dangerous situation where you needed to act quickly? Tell the story.

c What worst-case scenario would you least like to face:
1 at work 2 in life?

3 Work in two groups. Hold an emergency meeting to decide what decisions you'd make in real life-and-death situations. There are four items on your 'agenda' and you have just five minutes to decide what action to take. Group A your worst case scenarios are below. Group B turn to page 143.

On a driving holiday in India you lose control of your hire-car travelling downhill at 70 mph on a mountain road. You've no brakes and there's a 300m drop to the valley below. Do you:

a   try to jump out of the car and roll to safety?
b   steer away from the cliff edge and into the mountainside to stop the car?
c   steer into the crash barriers on the cliff edge to slow the car down?

On a trek in the Chilean Andes you get cut off from the rest of your group and become hopelessly lost. As you try to work out which direction to take, you are confronted by a hungry mountain lion. Do you:

a   lie down and play dead?
b   shout and flap your coat at the animal?
c   run and hide (maybe find a tree to climb)?

Whilst walking over a frozen lake in Norway, which you were assured was perfectly safe, you fall through the ice and are in danger of drowning. Do you:

a   attempt to pull yourself out?
b   move about in the water to generate body heat?
c   stay calm, conserve energy and cry for help?

Good luck!

During a flight over the Grand Canyon in a private plane, your pilot collapses unconscious and you have to land it yourself. You manage to reach the airfield. Do you:

a   keep the nose of the plane pointing above the horizon as you descend to the runway?
b   slow down to about 95 kph as you touch down and then hit the brakes hard?
c   keep the plane at a steady altitude of 150 metres as you approach the beginning of the runway?

4 Team up with someone from the other group. Briefly summarise the scenarios you faced and decisions you took.

5 🔊 3.07–3.14 Now listen to some advice on how to survive the situations in 3. How many lives did you lose? Which group did better?

6 Put the following expressions on the scale below according to how likely they are. Most of them were in the advice you just listened to. The first one has been done for you.

a You've a good chance.
b You don't stand a chance.
c There's a 50-50 chance.
d Your chances are slim.
e You're in with a chance.
f The chances are remote.

g You've blown your chances.
h There's a fair chance.
i There's an outside chance.
j It's a million-to-one chance.
k You haven't got a cat in hell's chance.

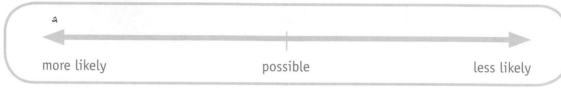

a

more likely   possible   less likely

7 Complete the following expressions using the nouns and verbs in the boxes. They were all in the advice in 5.

| bet circumstances idea mistake move point thing |

| do forget make put resist take think |

a Don't even .... about jumping from a moving vehicle.
b .... the temptation to run from a mountain lion.
c .... any ideas of playing dead out of your mind.
d Your best .... is to shout and flap your coat at the animal.
e Do not in any .... try to stand up on the ice.
f .... care to land on your back to avoid breaking it.
g There's not much .... trying to force the door open.
h .... about trapping air inside a sinking car.
i By far the most sensible .... to do is to open the car window.
j Just grabbing on to the nearest person with a parachute is not a smart ....
k It's a common .... to think the shark's nose is the best area to target.
l You'd .... much better to strike at the eyes or gills.
m .... sure that the nose of the plane is six inches below the horizon.
n It's a good .... to brake as soon as you've gained control of the steering.

8 Work with a partner. Practise using some of the expressions in 6 and 7 by advising them on how to handle one of the following situations. Don't worry if you can't give expert advice!

Worst-case scenarios

- on a round-the-world cruise the ocean liner you're on hits an iceberg and starts to sink
- during a bungee jump from the Golden Gate Bridge your cord snaps mid-jump
- a poisonous snake has crawled into your sleeping bag
- you've been abducted by aliens

Workplace dilemmas

- your boss is working you to death
- a colleague is taking the credit for all your ideas
- a computer virus is destroying your hard disk and you've had no time to back things up
- you've been passed over for promotion – again!
- there's a rumour your company is about to announce redundancies

THE DECISION-MAKING PROCESS

'Gentlemen, I take it we are all in complete agreement on the decision here.' Alfred P. Sloan, the head of General Motors, looked around the committee room table. His senior managers nodded in assent. 'Then,' continued Sloan, 'I propose we postpone further discussion of the matter until our next meeting to give ourselves time to develop disagreement and perhaps gain some understanding of what the decision is about.'

John Adair *Effective Decision-Making*

1 Read the anecdote about Alfred P. Sloan, the man who built General Motors into the biggest company in the world. What point is being made about group decisions?

2 🔊 3.15–3.17 Listen to extracts from three different decision-making meetings and answer the questions.

1 **An industrial dispute**
  a Why is Dan so concerned about a strike?
  b Who's the calmest person at the meeting?
2 **Political instabilities**
  a What's Hans's objection to the proposal?
  b What's Andrea worried about?
3 **A product recall**
  a Whose side is Laura on?
  b Do you think Simon has already made up his mind?

3 The following remarks were all in the meetings in 2. Replace the words and phrases in **bold** with similar ones from the box.

> advantages and disadvantages alternative come to complete support
> I don't think we should make a decision information intuition the main thing
> opinions plan pool our ideas serious thought stand by suggest undecided
> we need to take our time on this we're running out of time we unanimously agree

a Look, **time is short** .... So let's **put our heads together** .... and see what we can **come up with** ....

b OK, we've weighed up the various **pros and cons** .... Now it's time to **reach** .... a decision and **stick to** .... it.

c **I don't want us rushing into things** .... This whole issue requires **careful consideration** ....

d I take it **we're all in agreement** .... that **our first priority** .... is to safeguard the well-being of our personnel.

e Well, then, I don't see we have any **option** .... but to give this proposal our **full backing** ....

f I'd like your **input** .... on this before committing us to any definite **course** .... of action.

g I'm **in two minds** .... about it. At this stage **I think we should keep our options open** ....

h Well, in the absence of more reliable **data** .... , I think I'm going to have to go with my **gut instinct** .... on this one.

4 You also heard the following idiomatic expressions in 2. Can you remember the missing words? The first two letters are given. The meaning of the idioms in brackets may help you.

a the ball is in their co............... (we're waiting for someone else to make a decision)
b jump to co............... (decide too quickly without considering all the facts)
c when it comes to the cr............... (when a decision finally has to be made)
d sit on the fe............... (refuse to support either side in an argument)

CRISIS MANAGEMENT

1 What sort of crises can companies be faced with these days? Can you think of recent examples of any of the following?

> accusations of fraud   an anti-globalisation protest   a consumer boycott   an environmental disaster
> a hostile takeover bid   insider trading   an investigation by the monopolies commission   a lawsuit
> mass redundancies   a product recall   sabotage

2 Work in two groups. Group A read about a crisis at McDonald's; Group B at Mercedes. Twenty-five articles (*a, an* and *the*) are missing from each text. Write them in. If you do the exercise correctly, both groups should use *a, an* and *the* the same number of times.

McDonald's crying over spilled coffee

In 1994 Stella Liebeck, New Mexico grandmother, ordered coffee at McDonald's drive-through restaurant. Minutes later, sitting in her car in car park, she accidentally spilled coffee – heated, in response to customer preference, to scalding 180°F – and suffered severe burns requiring surgery. Crisis was about to unfold.

When McDonald's refused to take responsibility for paying woman's medical bills, she went to attorney and sued company. At trial jury found McDonald's liable and awarded $200,000 in compensatory damages (less $40,000 for negligence on Liebeck's part) and massive $2.7 million in punitive damages because of what they saw as McDonald's unacceptably dismissive attitude.

One might have expected bad publicity to ruin McDonald's, but instead newspapers leapt to company's defence, declaring what nonsense court's verdict was. 'America has victim complex,' announced *San Francisco Chronicle*. Punitive damages were later reduced by judge to $480,000 and, while awaiting appeal, parties made out-of-court settlement for undisclosed sum. But by then 'three million dollar coffee-spill' had already passed into corporate legend.

Mercedes on a roll

In automotive industry trend for many years has been towards smaller, more economical vehicle. So in autumn of 1997, Daimler-Benz introduced new economy model, Mercedes 'A Class'. It was car designed to compete with ever-popular Volkswagen Golf. But just before November launch, disaster struck.

Swedish auto magazine had conducted what they called 'elk test' on new car. Test is standard in Sweden to make sure cars can steer to avoid large deer crossing road. But at just 60 kph 'A Class' overturned, injuring both test drivers. Storm immediately blew up in press and on TV, as buyers waiting to take delivery cancelled their orders. For Mercedes it was not only financial but image crisis too.

Daimler responded quickly, adding wider tyres, electronic stability mechanism and stronger anti-rollbars – all at no extra cost to customer. Highly successful advertising campaign and public support from Niki Lauda, ex-formula one racing champion, helped to restore consumer confidence in 'A Class' but at cost of hundreds of millions of dollars.

3 Summarise the story you read in 2 to a member of the other group. What lessons can be learned from how the companies behaved?

4 What is the best thing a manager can do in a crisis? Match the following. Which do you think are good advice?

a	deny	someone	g	admit	honest
b	stay	time	h	take	data
c	delegate	calm	i	make	charge
d	buy	decisive	j	act	quickly
e	blame	everything	k	collect	nothing
f	be	responsibility	l	be	promises

5 Work in groups to act as crisis management consultants to the Coca-Cola Company. It is May 1999 and the world's most famous brand is in trouble ...

Step 1

🔊 **3.18** Listen to the first part of the case and answer the questions.

a How many Cokes are sold each day?
b How would you describe Coca-Cola's advertising strategy?
c What has just happened?
d Which markets are directly involved in the crisis?
e Calculate how much those markets are worth in annual sales.

Step 2

🔊 **3.19** Listen to the second part of the case and answer the questions.

a What do the following figures refer to?
   +25%   -13%
b What is the significance of these figures?
c What have the inspectors at the Belgian bottling plant found?
d What is the toxicologist's verdict?
e Who is benefiting from Coca-Cola's current problems?

Step 3

Hold a meeting to decide what recommendations to make to your client. As well as the information you have just heard, read the article and look at the agenda on page 144.

Coke products banned in Belgium

Associated Press 6/15/99

BRUSSELS, Belgium (AP) - Stores across Belgium removed all beverages of the Coca-Cola Co. from their shelves today, complying with a ban prompted by the hospitalizations of people who got sick after drinking Coke products.

For a second consecutive day, poison alert centers across Belgium received hundreds of phone calls from people seeking information. Some callers said they too had become nauseous after drinking Coke or Coca-Cola brands.

On Monday, Health Minister Luc Van den Bossche banned all sales of Coke and Coca-Cola brands such as Fanta, Sprite, Aquarius, Bonaqua and Minute Maid fruit juices.

'We are hard at work trying to find the cause of the problems,' said Maureen O'Sullivan, a spokeswoman for Coca-Cola in Belgium. 'We are also implementing a total recall of our products.'

The ban was imposed after nearly 50 people, most of them young people, were hospitalized on Monday suffering from nausea after drinking Coke products. Eight remained in the hospital today.

Step 4

Each group should present its recommendations to the class.

Step 5

🔊 **3.20** Listen to the final part of the case and find out what really happened. How do your recommendations compare with the action Coca-Cola actually took?

LANGUAGE LINKS

Vocabulary: Marketing and legal English

The marketplace

1 Complete the adjectives by writing in the missing vowels. The adjectives range from positive to negative.

The market is
b_ _m_ng	thr_v_ng
h_ _lthy	b_ _y_nt
v_l_t_l_	_npr_d_ct_bl_
w_ _k	sl_gg_sh
fl_t	d_pr_ss_d

+ (arrow pointing down) −

2 Complete the sentence using some of the adjectives in 1 and information that is true for you.

The market for .... in .... is
...................., whereas the .... market is
....

3 Complete the collocations by writing a noun from the box before each set of three nouns below.

| advertising   brand   distribution   market   marketing |

a mix / drive / strategy
b forces / research / share
c network / channels / costs
d campaign / expenditure / agencies
e awareness / loyalty / stretching

4 Which terms in 3 are the following examples of?
a Omnicom Publicis Doyle Dane Bernbach Dentsu
b competition / the state of the economy / political stability
c 'the four Ps': product, place, price, promotion
d wholesalers retailers sales reps
e Virgin cola Camel watches Ferrari sunglasses

5 Listed below are some of the terms commonly used in marketing departments, but the second word in each collocation has been switched with another. Can you switch them back? The first two have been done for you.

market **outlet**
competitive **brand**
retail **challenger**
mass **sensitivity**
price **market**
leading **advantage**

subliminal **relations**
price **marketing**
niche **analysis**
public **advertising**
consumer **market**
permission **war**

6 Which of the terms in 5 refer to:
a the number two player in a market after the market leader?
b the importance the customer gives to prices?
c a small number of customers requiring a particular type of product or service?
d the shop or store through which products are sold to the consumer?

e a method of persuading consumers to buy by invisible, psychological means?
f getting customers' permission before sending information to them?

7 The verbs and verb phrases in the box all form strong collocations with *the market*. Put them into the most likely chronological order. One of them has been done for you.

| be squeezed out of   break back into   compete in dominate   enter   target |

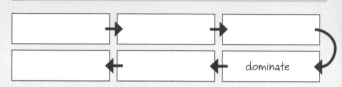

The verbs and verb phrases in the box all form strong collocations with *the competition*. Put them into the most likely chronological order. One of them has been done for you.

| come up against   destroy   fight back against outclass   succumb to   take on |

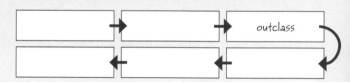

Business law

1 Divide the following into ten things that might lead to a court case.

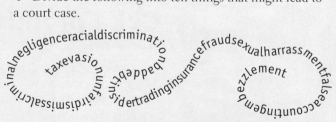

Which of the above mean:
a sacking someone without good reason?
b buying shares using privileged information?
c stealing money that you're responsible for in your job?

2 Use the words in the box to make three things that might lead to legal problems.

| breach   conflict   contract   funds   interests   misuse |

a .... of ....
b .... of ....
c .... of ....

Which of the above mean:
• to spend company money in an unauthorised way?
• not to abide by a written agreement?
• a situation in which someone cannot make fair decisions because they may be affected by the results?

3 Complete the following using the verbs in the box.

> appeal be bring declare file pay settle
> start take

a .... someone to court
b .... legal proceedings against someone
c .... a lawsuit against someone
d .... out of court
e .... found liable for damages
f .... compensation/a fine
g .... bankruptcy
h .... against a verdict
i .... an action against someone

Which of the above means to reach an agreement without asking the court to decide?

Grammar: Articles

Complete the text with *a, an, the* or zero article Ø, as necessary.

They say 'All's fair in ...... love and .... war.' And when it comes to getting .... good deal, ... same is true of .... business. For .... example, in 1803, ... half of what is now .... USA was actually bought from .... French for three cents .... acre! How were they able to get such .... bargain? At .... time, ... Emperor Napoleon was preparing to go to .... war with .... Britain and was desperate to sell.

Phrase bank: Decision-making

Listed below are six key things you'll need to do in a decision-making meeting. Match each to three things you might say. The first one has been done for you as an example.

1 Encourage collaboration b ☐ ☐
2 Comment on options ☐ ☐ ☐
3 Consider pros and cons ☐ ☐ ☐
4 Advise caution ☐ ☐ ☐
5 Check agreement ☐ ☐ ☐
6 Commit to a decision ☐ ☐ ☐

The **indefinite** article is used:

• before a singular countable noun when it is unspecified and mentioned for the first time e.g. *I need **a** holiday*.

• before singular countable nouns in exclamations e.g. *What **a** day!; It was such **a** nuisance!*

• before the names of professions e.g. *She's **an** engineer*.

• before a singular countable noun where a plural could be used to mean the same thing e.g. *There's no such thing as **a** free lunch = There's no such thing as free lunches*.

• to mean *per* when talking about prices, speed, rates, etc. e.g. *€3 **a** kilo; three times **a** day*.

The **definite** article is used:

• before a noun that has been mentioned before e.g. *I used to have two BMWs and a Lotus, but I had to sell **the** Lotus*.

• before a noun that is later specified in the same sentence e.g. ***The** guy I met in Rio runs his own business*.

• when it is clear from the context what we are referring to e.g. *I'll drop you off at **the** hotel*.

• when the thing referred to is unique e.g. ***the** human race*.

• before an adjective referring to a group e.g. ***the** Dutch*.

The **zero** article is used:

• before mass or abstract nouns e.g. *Greed is good*.

• before the names of most countries. Exceptions include: *the USA, the UK* and *the Netherlands*.

• in certain fixed expressions e.g. *go to war*.

a That's a big plus, as far as I'm concerned. But let's look at some of the minuses.

b OK; I'd like everybody's input on this.

c We need to take our time on this.

d I don't see we have any option but to go ahead.

e So is that unanimous then?

f I think I'm going to have to go with my gut instinct on this one.

g To be honest, I'm in two minds about this.

h OK, that's the upside. But what about the downside?

i This requires careful consideration.

j I take it we're all in agreement on this?

k Let's put our heads together and see what we can come up with.

l I'm not wholly in favour of this, but what alternative do we have?

m OK, we've weighed up the advantages and disadvantages.

n Does anybody have any objections to that?

o So that's decided then.

p Let's pool our ideas on this.

q I don't want us rushing into things.

r OK, so we're going to go with Marc's idea.

11 SIMPLY THE BEST

If winning isn't everything, why do they keep the score?

VINCE LOMBARDI, AMERICAN FOOTBALL COACH

I'm a PC.   I'm a Mac.

1 Are you a naturally competitive person? What really brings out your competitive spirit? Work? Sport? Something else?

2 Look at the advertisements. What are Apple and BMW saying about themselves in relation to their competitors? How effective do you think these ads are? Would they work in your culture?

3 How brand loyal are you? If forced to choose, which would you prefer:

a   a Mac or a PC?   e   Windows or Linux?
b   a Coke or a Pepsi?   f   Gap or Zara?
c   McDonald's or Burger King?   g   Nike or Adidas?
d   an Audi or a BMW?   h   Internet Explorer or Firefox?

Find someone who'd choose the opposite and defend your preferences.

Congratulations to Audi for winning
South African Car of the Year 2006.

From the Winner of
World Car of the Year 2006.

ALL IN THE GAME

1 Sports metaphors are common in business, especially when talking about competition. Read the headlines below and match the phrases in **bold** to what they mean.

a   Google's **game plan** for the next five years is to take over the mobile web.
b   Microsoft and Mozilla are still **the major players** in internet browsers.
c   US auto manufacturers need **a level playing field** in order to compete.
d   When it comes to protecting their patents, companies **play hardball**.
e   Steve Jobs: We haven't **hit our targets** for Q3, but we have come close.
f   As Steve Ballmer knows, when you're number one, you **call the shots**.

1   get tough
2   have the power
3   achieved our objectives
4   the most important companies
5   strategy
6   a fair situation

2 In business, competition is often compared to a race. Label the diagram below with the appropriate verbs:

| catch up with ...   fall behind ...   overtake ...   stay ahead of ...   THE COMPETITION |

3 Which verb or verb phrase in 2 could you replace with the following?

a   lose ground to …   b   match …   c   leave … behind

4 Discuss with a partner. Who are the major players in your line of business or the business you'd like to go into? Is there a level playing field? Who's the market leader? How has it been able to stay ahead of the competition? How could the other players catch up with or overtake it?

STRATEGY MEETING

1 A marketing team is holding a strategy meeting to discuss ways of becoming more competitive. Complete the suggestions in the yellow speech balloons below using the prepositions in the box.

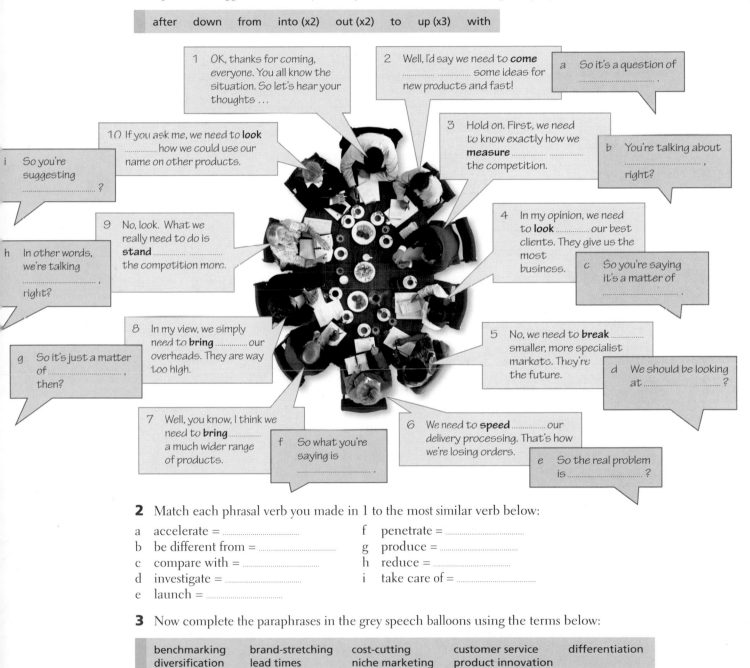

after   down   from   into (x2)   out (x2)   to   up (x3)   with

1   OK, thanks for coming, everyone. You all know the situation. So let's hear your thoughts …

2   Well, I'd say we need to **come** .... some ideas for new products and fast!

a   So it's a question of ....

10 If you ask me, we need to **look** .... how we could use our name on other products.

3   Hold on. First, we need to know exactly how we **measure** .... the competition.

b   You're talking about .... , right?

i   So you're suggesting .... ?

9   No, look. What we really need to do is **stand** .... the competition more.

4   In my opinion, we need to **look** .... our best clients. They give us the most business.

c   So you're saying it's a matter of ....

h   In other words, we're talking .... , right?

8   In my view, we simply need to **bring** .... our overheads. They are way too high.

5   No, we need to **break** .... smaller, more specialist markets. They're the future.

d   We should be looking at .... ?

g   So it's just a matter of .... , then?

7   Well, you know, I think we need to **bring** .... a much wider range of products.

f   So what you're saying is ....

6   We need to **speed** .... our delivery processing. That's how we're losing orders.

e   So the real problem is .... ?

2 Match each phrasal verb you made in 1 to the most similar verb below:

a   accelerate = ...
b   be different from = ...
c   compare with = ...
d   investigate = ...
e   launch = ...

f   penetrate = ...
g   produce = ...
h   reduce = ...
i   take care of = ...

3 Now complete the paraphrases in the grey speech balloons using the terms below:

benchmarking   brand-stretching   cost-cutting   customer service   differentiation
diversification   lead times   niche marketing   product innovation

4 3.21 Listen to extracts from the strategy meeting and check your answers to exercises 1 to 3.

5 Choose one of the suggestions in 1. Then, perhaps referring to your own company or a company you know well, prepare to support or oppose the idea for a minute or two.

COMPETITIVE ADVANTAGE

1 *Competitive Advantage* by Harvard professor Michael Porter is the classic study of competition in business. In it he claims that all companies face pressure to compete from five different directions:

The threat of new companies entering the market

The bargaining power of suppliers

The rivalry between industry competitors

The bargaining power of buyers

The threat of new products/services replacing yours

Discuss with a partner.

- Apart from your direct industry competitors, who exerts the greatest pressure on your company to remain competitive?
- How easy would it be for new companies to enter your market? What barriers are there to entry?
- Do some of your suppliers seem to have more power over you than you have over them?
- To what extent are your customers able to play you off against your competitors?
- Is it possible that totally new products or services could one day put you out of business?

2 Work with a partner. Each read the executive summary of one of two bestselling books on competition below. Then share information with each other, using the discussion phrase bank to help you. Which arguments do you agree with most? Where do the books agree and differ on how to compete successfully?

Blue Ocean Strategy

The big idea: 'The only way to beat the competition is to stop *trying* to beat the competition'. That's the controversial advice of authors W. Chan Kim and Renée Mauborgne. In fact, according to these two INSEAD business school professors, the ultimate objective of a business is 'to make the competition irrelevant'.

Most companies pursue what they call 'a red ocean strategy', fighting each other like frenzied sharks for a bigger share of the market. But there's only so much market to fight over and – guess what? – the biggest shark usually wins, leaving the water red with the blood of the tattered losers.

'Blue ocean strategy' companies behave in just the opposite way. Instead of competing in existing market space, they create uncontested market space. Rather than trying to beat the competition, they bypass it altogether and go after new business instead, as eBay did with its online auctions, Apple with its groundbreaking iPod and

Nintendo with its revolutionary Wii gaming console – indeed, as virtually every new industry has done from the automobile to the cell phone to biotech.

But what happens when competitors see what you have achieved, as they surely will, and try to copy your success? What happens when the sharks swim into your clear blue waters? At that point, you have no choice but to swim on and innovate again!

How to do it: The secret of Blue Ocean Strategy is to strongly differentiate your product or service and cut unnecessary costs at the same time, making yourself both unique and highly profitable. Kim and Mauborgne call this 'value innovation'. To do it you need to employ their 'Four-Action Framework'.

First, look at what your industry takes for granted, what it accepts as standard in its products or services. Then ask yourself what unnecessary features you could totally eliminate,

what you could significantly reduce, what you could inexpensively increase and, most importantly, what you could create that the market currently doesn't offer. Red oceans will always be a fact of business life, but set sail for blue oceans if you want to stay ahead.

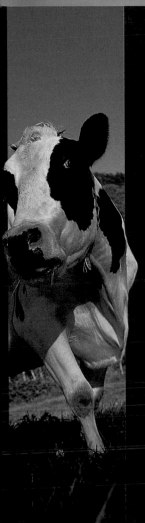

Purple Cow

The big idea: According to marketing guru and change agent Seth Godin, 'the old rule was this: create safe, ordinary products and combine them with great marketing. The new rule is: create remarkable products that the right people seek out'. In a world where mass media advertising is next to useless and nobody's listening any more, only by being remarkable will your marketing message spread by 'word of web', creating what Godin has famously called an 'Ideavirus'. So what's a Purple Cow?

Imagine ... you're driving down the road and see a herd of brown cows in a field. So what? If you'd seen a purple cow, now, that would be worth noticing! And this is Godin's point. Remarkable stuff gets noticed. 'It's a purple cow. Boring stuff is invisible. It's a brown cow'. The challenge to business is: 'be distinct or extinct'.

But here's the clever part: the opposite of 'remarkable' is not, as you might think, 'awful' or 'terrible'; it's 'very good'. As Godin puts it, 'if you travel on an airline and they get you there safely, you don't tell anyone. That's what's supposed to happen'. Nearly all products are quality products these days. 'Very good' is just average. Godin asks us to consider the question: 'Are *you* making very good stuff? If so, 'how soon can you stop?'

How to do it: Purple Cow is less a question of innovation than differentiation. But in a marketplace where 'all the obvious targets are gone', 'safe is risky', 'very good is bad' and the customer is spoilt for choice, just how are you supposed to stand out from the competition?

The first step is to stop spending millions marketing to the masses, who aren't paying attention, and concentrate on winning the loyalty of an influential few, who are. They'll share their enthusiasm with others, thereby doing much of the marketing for you. Great design, customer relations, creating a memorable experience are what matter and it is in these areas that you can become a market leader. But being first in is crucial. As Godin explains, 'The leader is the leader because he did something remarkable. And that remarkable thing is now taken – it's no longer remarkable when you do it'.

> **Discussion phrase bank**
> Basically, the theory is that ...
> According to the authors, ...
> I like the idea of ...
> Maybe they're oversimplifying ...
> And I'm not convinced that ...
> But the argument that ... makes a lot of sense.
> From a practical point of view, what they recommend is ...
> In a nutshell, the key take-away message seems to be ...
> If you applied it to the company I work for ...

BREAKING RULES

1 What sights, sounds and feelings do you associate with a night at the circus? How does the traditional circus compare with other more modern forms of family entertainment?

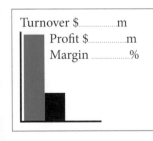

2 ⊙ **3.22** Have you heard of Cirque du Soleil? Listen to a podcast about their remarkable business model and complete the company profile. Then check your figures with a partner.

Turnover $..........m	Founder: Guy Laliberté Founded in: .... Employees: ....
Profit $..........m	Annual growth: ....% Based in: ....
Margin ....%	Global audience: .... people in .... countries
	Joint venture partners: ....
	Interbrand 2004 brands with most global impact, ranked: ....
	Value innovations: ....
	Target market: .... Cost structure: .... Pricing: ....

3 With your partner discuss the questions below.

a Why hasn't Cirque needed to benchmark itself against its competitors?
b How has the company successfully implemented a Blue Ocean Strategy?
c In what ways has it made itself a Purple Cow in the entertainment industry?

4 Work in small groups to decide what Cirque could do to maintain its competitive advantage. Things you could consider include: cost-cutting to reach a wider market, brand-stretching and merchandising, diversification into new media or themed service industries, alternative forms of advertising, collaboration with competitors to create innovative synergies. For further ideas see the Cirque du Soleil fact file on page 157.

5 ⊙ **3.23** Listen to what Cirque has in fact done to respond to ever-fiercer competition. Did it take any of your advice?

THE SKY'S THE LIMIT

1 Have you ever opposed an important decision at a meeting, lost the argument, but later been proved right? Have you ever been in a position to say 'I told you so'? Tell the story.

2 ⊕ 3.24 Gabrielle Bonnet is VP for marketing at NMI Group, a large Franco-Dutch conglomerate with diverse interests in media, beverages and sports goods. She's just come out of an all-day board meeting at which the controversial decision was taken to acquire a 49% stake in Indian low-cost airline Eastern Promise. Work with a partner. Listen to Gabrielle's conversation with CFO, Pieter De Vries. Each complete the key arguments of a different speaker. Then compare notes.

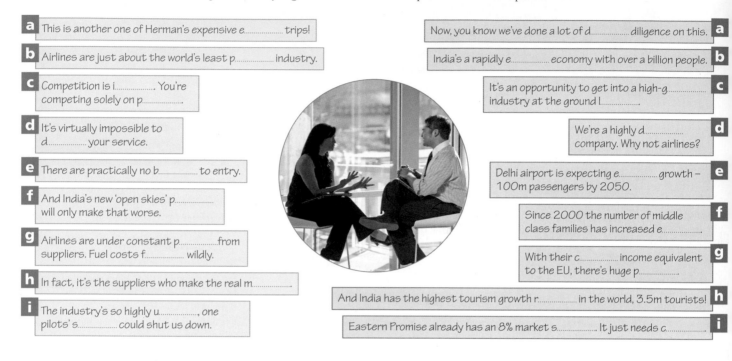

a This is another one of Herman's expensive e................ trips!

b Airlines are just about the world's least p................ industry.

c Competition is i................. You're competing solely on p.................

d It's virtually impossible to d................ your service.

e There are practically no b................ to entry.

f And India's new 'open skies' p................ will only make that worse.

g Airlines are under constant p................from suppliers. Fuel costs f................ wildly.

h In fact, it's the suppliers who make the real m................

i The industry's so highly u................, one pilots' s................ could shut us down.

a Now, you know we've done a lot of d................ diligence on this.

b India's a rapidly e................ economy with over a billion people.

c It's an opportunity to get into a high-g................ industry at the ground l................

d We're a highly d................ company. Why not airlines?

e Delhi airport is expecting e................ growth – 100m passengers by 2050.

f Since 2000 the number of middle class families has increased e................

g With their c................ income equivalent to the EU, there's huge p................

h And India has the highest tourism growth r................ in the world, 3.5m tourists!

i Eastern Promise already has an 8% market s................ It just needs c................

3 From what you've just heard, which way would you have voted at the meeting?

4 Sure enough, nine months after the decision was made, Eastern Promise is already in trouble. The following article has just appeared in *Skyways* magazine. How many of Gabrielle's original objections to the deal have proved justified?

Keeping its promise? Reena Damashakthu reports from New Delhi

The usual sunny disposition of serial entrepreneur and TV celebrity Suraj Kapoor is decidedly gloomy these days. The latest figures show that his much publicised budget airline, Eastern Promise, may soon be forced to slash the number of non-peak hour flights by up to 65% in response to mounting competition from cheaper low-cost carriers (LCCs). Substantial layoffs are likely, perhaps even closure if the struggling airline cannot turn itself around.

The launch of Eastern Promise three years ago was accompanied by a fanfare of publicity as the charismatic Mr Kapoor promised to 'open India's skies to the ordinary traveller'. Ironically, it is India's 'open skies' policy that has allowed bilateral agreements with foreign airlines to increase the number of players in an already overcrowded market. Competition for access to gates is now fierce and good pilots go to the highest bidder.

In 2003 there were just three main domestic airlines. Today there are around a dozen. With little to choose between them apart from the cost of a ticket, the pricing strategy of the main LCCs has rapidly become a race to the bottom.

LCCs operate on razor-thin margins at the best of times, but their overheads are not much lower than those of the premium-priced full-service carriers (FSCs). Aircraft leasing, maintenance and repair charges as well as salaries all cost the same and fluctuations in demand or in the price of fuel can push smaller operators to the brink of bankruptcy.

Kapoor is known to be in emergency talks with NMI, its partner in the airline. NMI came on board nine months ago when EP looked like a promising investment. It must now be wondering what happened to Eastern's promise?

Suraj Kapoor, the owner of Eastern Promise, declined to comment yesterday on renewed speculation that his airline may soon be squeezed out of the market by the current price war.

5 Which words and expressions in the article could be replaced by the following?

a   positive (paragraph 1)
b   negative (paragraph 1)
c   cut drastically (paragraph 1)
d   increasing (paragraph 1)
e   redundancies (paragraph 1)
f   a lot of media exposure (paragraph 2)
g   oversupplied (paragraph 2)
h   intense (paragraph 2)

i   payer (paragraph 2)
j   a price war (paragraph 3)
k   extremely narrow (paragraph 4)
l   expensive (paragraph 4)
m   edge (paragraph 4)
n   joined (paragraph 5)
o   potential (paragraph 5)

6 ☉ **3.25** The day after the article you've just read was published Gabrielle is not surprised to be called into the office of Herman Van der Poel, CEO of NMI Group. Listen and answer the questions.

a   What are the latest developments at Eastern Promise?
b   Why is the situation especially delicate?
c   Why has Herman chosen Gabrielle to fly out to New Delhi?

7 As members of Gabrielle's marketing team, you have accompanied her on her fact-finding mission to New Delhi. Work in three groups to research the market situation. Group A see page 153, group B page 159 and group C page 160.

8 Share your information with the rest of the team. Your job is to come up with a rescue plan for Eastern Promise. You can leave the financial details to the number-crunchers in the accounts department. What you need to do is decide the following:

EASTERN PROMISE

- Is there any future for Eastern Promise as a low-cost carrier?
- Is there a gap in the Indian domestic airline market that Eastern Promise could be filling?
- How could the company be successfully repositioned? Who should its target market be?
- How could NMI create synergies between its other businesses and Eastern Promise?
- Should NMI and Eastern Promise try to gain critical mass through acquisition of another airline?
- Is there a case for investing in infrastructure at some of the main Indian airports?
- Apply Blue Ocean Strategy to the problem. What do airline travellers typically expect? Are there any unnecessary features of flying you could eliminate or reduce? What could you offer more of without pushing up costs significantly? What innovations to airline travel could you introduce?
- Apply Purple Cow thinking to the problem. How could you make Eastern Promise 'remarkable'? How could you create marketing buzz amongst your target market without spending a fortune on mass advertising?

9 Now put together a short presentation outlining your recommendations to Gabrielle prior to her meeting with Kapoor. Use any of the data and graphics you studied in 7 to support your arguments and produce any other simple visuals you may need.

10 ☉ **3.26** Listen to the story of a real Indian airline that successfully implemented Blue Ocean Strategy. How does your business plan compare with theirs?

12 E-MAILING

The beautiful part of writing is that you don't have to get it right the first time, unlike, say, a brain surgeon. You can always do it better.

ROBERT CORMIER, AUTHOR

1 Read the following extracts from web and press articles and discuss the questions with a partner.

a How important is e-mail in your job? If you did what this businessman did, do you think you might find the same thing?

A friend of mine, a merchant banker, decided that for one month he would turn off his e-mails. When he switched back into gear he found that out of 753 e-mails, ten were really useful. Out of the ten, two were vital – so vital that the senders all took the precaution of ringing to confirm, just in case their e-mails were missed. *Business Life magazine*

b According to the Electronic Messaging Association, around seven trillion e-mails are sent annually. How many of them end up in your inbox? And how do you deal with the following problem?

When everybody has e-mail and anybody can send you e-mail, how do you decide whose messages you're going to read and respond to first and whose you're going to send to the trash unread? *Tom Peters in Fast Company magazine*

c Is e-mail a time-saver or does it distract you from more important business? Are you anything like the typical executives mentioned below?

As Clive Thompson pointed out in *The New York Times* magazine, after a worker has been interrupted with a message, it generally takes nearly half an hour for him to return to his original task. According to researchers, 40 per cent of workers moved on to completely new tasks after being interrupted, leaving their old task behind, neglected and unfinished. *SEND, The Essential Guide to Email for Office and Home*

d Do you send mass mailings? If so, do you get a similar response to the one described below? What do think is going on?

Patrick Lencioni, the author of *The Five Dysfunctions of a Team*, told us 'When I send an e-mail to one person, there's a 95 per cent chance I'll get a reply. When I send it to ten people, the response rate drops to 5 per cent.' *SEND, The Essential Guide to Email for Office and Home*

e Are you ignoring your e-mail more these days? Does this company's idea sound like it could work?

Signs are that the first rush of enthusiasm for e-mail may be waning. One big company in the computing industry is considering banning e-mails in the afternoon. It found that its people had stopped talking to one another. *Stuart Crainer in A Freethinker's A–Z of the New World of Business*

f Have you ever sent an angry e-mail or hidden behind an e-mail when you had bad news to deliver? How do you feel about the advice below?

Rule number one: never send an e-mail when you're mad. And if you want to know you're mad, just take two fingers, close your eyes, touch your eyelids, if they're hot, researchers say you're mad and you should put it in the draft pile, send it later. One of the things I've learned is that e-mail is for saying 'yes', e-mail is for answering or asking questions. If you say 'no', if you criticise, if you attack, please, do it in person – or, worst case, do it over the phone. *Tim Sanders, Better Life Media*

g The Institute of Management puts working with computers amongst 'The Top Ten Stress Factors at Work'. Have you ever resorted to any of the following?

A survey by Mori reveals that three quarters of computer users shout and swear at their machines. A similar study by IT support company Sosmatic shows that 43% of them have slapped, smacked and even kicked their computer. The mouse is the most abused piece of equipment, receiving 31.5% of the punishment, followed by the monitor, the printer, the hard drive and the keyboard. Over a year such outbursts of 'computer rage' can cost companies up to £25,000 in lost earnings and damaged hardware.

2 Make a list of your three top e-mail writing tips. Compare tips with the rest of your group.

WRITING E-MAIL

1 ⊙ **3.27** Listen to a podcast explaining what the kind of e-mail you send says about your career prospects. How do the pictures below relate to the research the podcast describes?

Bcc:

Aoccdrnig to rscheearch at Cmabrigde Uinervtisy, it deosn't mttaer in what oredr the ltteers in a wrod are. The olny iprmoetnt tihng is taht the frist and lsat ltteer are in the rghit pclae. The rset can be a toatl mses and you can still raed it wouthit porbelm. This is bcuseae the huamn mnid deos not raed ervey lteter by istlef, but the wrod as a wlohe.

2 If Professor Owens's research is right, are you writing the kind of e-mails that will get you promoted?

3 Look at the two e-mails below. From what Professor Owens said in the podcast you just listened to, which do you think was written by a junior manager?

4 Correct the grammar, spelling and punctuation mistakes in the first e-mail. There are 18. Break up the text into short paragraphs and add a suitable subject line.

5 Were the mistakes in the first e-mail mainly language errors or typos? Do e-mails like this create a bad impression or doesn't it matter as long as the message is clear and the tone friendly? Would you be more tolerant if you knew the writer was not a native-speaker?

6 Make the second e-mail shorter and simpler by deleting as many words as you can without changing the basic message or sounding too direct.

Steve

Can you udpate me on where you are with hte Rome Expo arrangements I was unable to open the attattchment you sent me, so i dont have a copy of the programme. As for as the Copenhagen conference is concerned I don't just have time for dealing with it myself. So please can you sort this out with the Danes asap? You'll need probably to contact Margrethe Rasmussen at there headquarters in helsingborg. Copy me in on any correspondance.

Thanks alot. Your a star!

Maxine

(BTW any news on Garys feasability study???)

Dear Stephen

I do realise that you must be very busy at the moment with all the arrangements for our exhibition stand at the Rome Expo in two weeks' time, but, if you have a spare moment sometime over the next few days, could you possibly just have a quick look at the first draft of my report on the ComTech feasibility study, which I've been working very hard on since we last spoke? As I'm sure Maxine has already told you, it was actually due last week and I know that she needs it quite urgently, but there are just a couple of points I need to check with you, if that's OK, before I submit the final report – see attachment.

FYI, I don't know if anyone has spoken to you about it yet, but it looks like I'm probably going to be coming to Copenhagen with you, Fiona and Michael in September after all. You'll remember from my CV when you interviewed me for this position that I studied German and Danish at university and, as a matter of fact, I still speak pretty good Danish, which might just come in handy in some of the bars ;-) although I'm quite sure most of the Danes we'll be meeting at the conference will have no problem whatsoever with English!

Many thanks, Gary

> **Glossary**
> **asap** /ˌeɪ es eɪ ˈpiː/ as soon as possible. In AmE, asap is often pronounced /æ s æ p/
> **BTW** abbrev by the way: used in e-mails and text messages for adding additional information
> **FYI** abbrev for your information: used in e-mails and text messages as a way of introducing a useful piece of information

7 Now make the shortened second e-mail friendlier by adding a few personal touches. Use some or all of the following information to personalise it in your own way.

Stephen Steele
- has just become a father for the first time
- has put in for a promotion
- is under a lot of pressure because three people in his department are off sick
- has never been to Denmark (Gary knows it well)
- is a keen squash player (so is Gary).

E-MAIL STYLE

1 How you write an e-mail largely depends on who you are writing to, but, in general, a friendly, neutral style will work best – neither too formal nor too familiar. Avoid unnecessary acronyms, abbreviations and slang which may confuse, date or sound silly. <u>Underline</u> the best option in each section of the e-mail below.

(1) Hi Tim / Dear Timothy / Yo! Timbo

(2) I trust you are well. / How's it hanging? / How's it going?

(3) You did a great job on the presentation. Well done! / My congratulations on a most effective presentation. / Way to go, man! Killer presentation! (4) The product demo just blew us away! / The product demonstration was extremely well received. / The product demo went down really well.

(5) The only thing is, I'm not too happy with the packaging design. / But – don't hate me for saying this – the packaging design really sucks! / The packaging design is, however, giving me some cause for concern. (6) I strongly recommend we review the situation. / Frankly, I'd scrap it. / I suggest we have a bit of a rethink. (7) Catch up with you sometime next week to chew over a few alternatives. / Let's get together next week and see what we can come up with. / I propose we schedule a brainstorming meeting for next week.

(8) BTW if you've a sec, run your eye over the Singapore report, would you? / Also, if you have time, could you have a look at the Singapore report? / If it's not too much trouble, your input on the Singapore report would also be much appreciated. (9) And please note: I require a complete cost breakdown for this project as soon as possible. / It's very important that I have your costing for this project just as soon as you can get it to me. / Need your costing for the project too – yesterday, if not sooner! (10) If you have any problems, give Sandra Taylor in accounts a call. / Any probs, give Sandra in accounts a buzz. / Should you have any problems, Sandra Taylor in accounts may be able to be of assistance.

(11) Best regards / Cheers / Ciao!
(12) Simon / Simon Allen (Director of Marketing) / Si

2 Write a short e-mail in reply to the one above using the prompts below.

glad / enjoyed / presentation / also pleased / response / product demo // disappointed / hear / not keen / design // thought / quite stylish // let / know / free / discuss / alternatives // around / most / next week // happy / go through / report // costing / ready / within / few days // may need / check / few things / Sandra // happen / have / extension number? / thanks

3 The following expressions are all useful in e-mails. Complete them using the prepositions in the boxes. Some of them have already appeared in this unit.

| at against out of to down through in back off off up up on on on |
| with with with with with with with |

| back + to   in + on   on + to   out + on   out + with   through + to   up + on   up + to |

a   Have a quick look .... these figures and get .... me asap.

b   Let me know if you need any help .... the Koreans. And copy me .... any correspondence .... them.

c   Could you get .... our suppliers and sort something .... them? I'll leave the details .... you, but keep me .... the loop.

d   BTW, you did a great job .... the presentation. It went .... really well .... the Belgians. We'll just have to wait and see what they come .... to us ....

e   Can you update me .... where we are .... the Expo arrangements? I'm a bit .... of touch. Can I leave it .... you to contact the speakers?

f   I'd like to sound you .... this new packaging idea. Let's meet .... to discuss it sometime next week. BTW, I still can't seem to get .... Monica.

g   I know you're .... to your neck in work at the moment and probably don't want to take .... any more, but could you take this Milan thing .... my hands? THNQ

h   I haven't had time to read .... the whole report and I'll probably need to check some of these figures .... the computer, but leave it .... me.

i   Thanks for your offer .... a beer. If I can finish this report .... by 7, I may just take you .... it! I could certainly do .... one!

THE BIGGEST E-MAIL BLUNDERS EVER MADE

1 Work with a partner and discuss the following questions.

a   There are an estimated 50,000 computer viruses out there in cyberspace. Have any of them found you yet?

b   What kind of things do people use their office computers for which are not strictly business? Have you ever been tempted to do any of these things yourself?

c   Have you ever sent an e-mail and later regretted it? How dangerous is it to send business e-mails (even internally) without considering the possible implications?

2 ⬤ 3.28 Listen to the story of some of the biggest e-mail blunders ever made and number the following in the order they are mentioned.

Netscape	☐	Merrill Lynch	☐
Dow Chemical	☐	Cerner	☐
the Love Bug	☐	Western Provident	☐
AOL	☐	Norwich Union	☐
Microsoft	☐	Norton Rose	☐

3 Work with a partner. Without listening again, can you remember:

a how much the Love Bug cost businesses worldwide?
b how much the two insurance companies settled out of court for?
c whose love life reflected badly on Norton Rose?
d how many people lost their jobs at Dow Chemical?
e whose stock fell by 28%?
f how much Merrill Lynch had to pay out because of Blodget's e-mail?
g who regretted sending e-mails in the Microsoft antitrust trial?

YOU'VE GOT MAIL!

1 Work with a partner to practise exchanging e-mails.

Stage 1

Write an e-mail (maximum 150 words) to a real colleague on one of the subjects below. Use the suggested phrases to help you, but change and add anything you need to.

Subject: Change of plan

I was/we were originally hoping to ..., but I'm afraid that won't be possible now because ..., so what I'm/we're planning to do is ...

Sorry it's a bit short notice, but do you think you'll be able to ... or is that going to be a problem? I'll wait to hear from you.

Subject: Update please

Sorry to be a pain about this, but I'm still waiting for ... Can you let me know how much longer it's likely to be? Do you think you'll have it finished by ... because ...?

If you anticipate any problems, let me know. I'll ... tomorrow to see how you're doing. Cheers!

Subject: Urgent request

I've got an important meeting/presentation coming up on ... and I'm going to need ... Can I leave it to you to ...? I expect I'll also be needing ...

I know you're probably up to your neck in work at the moment, but if you can get ... to me before next ..., it'll be a real help. Thanks.

Subject: Can you do me a favour?

I've had an e-mail/phone call from someone called ..., who wants ... Can I leave this one with you? I'm sure you'll know a lot more about it than I do. But keep me in the loop.

BTW a few of us may be ... on ... Are you going to be around? Fancy joining us? Should be fun.

Stage 2

Exchange e-mails with your partner. You are standing in for the person they e-mailed while that person is off sick / on holiday / on maternity/paternity leave / away on a long business trip (you decide which). Write a reply (maximum 100 words) explaining the situation and asking for clarification or any details you need. Mention that you are new to the department.

Stage 3

Exchange replies and continue the correspondence as long as necessary to complete your business.

2 Give your partner your impressions of the e-mails they wrote in 1.

- Do they sound friendly but businesslike?
- Is the style neutral?
- Have they kept their messages short and to-the-point?
- Have they made any important spelling, punctuation or grammar mistakes?

12 E-MAILING

LANGUAGE LINKS

Vocabulary: Prepositional phrases

1 In each box write the preposition that precedes the words and phrases below.

a   present   first   least   first glance
the very most   any rate   the latest
the same time   best

b   the whole   average   the contrary
second thoughts   reflection
the one hand   the other hand
no account

c   practice   other words   theory
no circumstances   general   short
particular   effect   some respects
any case

d   a result   a general rule
a matter of fact   a last resort

e   to now   to a point

f   the top of my head

2 Complete the meeting extracts using some of the phrases in 1.

a   **A**   Well, I haven't had time to study them in detail but, at ...., I'd say these figures were quite encouraging.
    B   Yes, on ...., they're pretty much in line with what we were expecting. In fact, in ....
...................., they're even better.

b   **A**   Have you been in touch with New York yet?
    B   As ...., I have.
    A   And are they in favour of this new initiative?
    B   One or two of them aren't, but in ...., yes.
    A   Well, that's something at ....

c   **A**   I'm going to authorise this budget increase, but on .... is this project to go over budget again.
    B   Yes, OK.
    A   By the way, how much are the admin costs on this?
    B   I couldn't tell you off ....
...................., but it shouldn't be more than 30% of the budget at ....
    A   30%! On ...., I think we'd better look at this whole budget again.

d   **A**   This idea of yours is fine in ...., but in ...., I don't think it'll work.
    B   But you were all for it when we spoke about it last time!
    A   On ...., I was as sceptical then as I am now. In ...., even if I supported you, this strategy would only save us a few thousand pounds at ....

3 <u>Underline</u> the other seven prepositional phrases in 2.

Grammar: Future forms

1 Present tenses for the future

Match the verbs in bold to their main function below.

Our train **leaves** (1) at six. So our taxi's **coming** (2) at quarter to.
I'm not working (3) this Saturday! **It's** (4) my wedding anniversary for goodness' sake!

an arrangement ☐   an indisputable fact ☐
a refusal ☐   a schedule or timetable ☐

2 *will*

Match the remarks on the left to the way they were later reported.

a   **I'll** help you.   He promised to be there.
b   **You'll** regret it.   He suddenly had an idea.
c   **I'll** be there.   He offered to help me.
d   **I'll** try it this way.   He refused to do it.
e   I **won't** do it!   He warned me about it.

3 *will be doing*

In each pair of sentences below tick the one you are more likely to hear.

a   We'll **land** at Heathrow in about fifteen minutes.
b   We'll **be landing** at Heathrow in about fifteen minutes.
c   **Will** you **go** past the chemist's this morning?
d   **Will** you **be going** past the chemist's this morning?
e   Give me five minutes and **I'll call** you back.
f   Give me five minutes and **I'll be calling** you back.
g   By the way, I **won't attend** the meeting.
h   By the way, I **won't be attending** the meeting.

4 Match the sentences a–d to what was said next.

a   I don't think I'll go. ☐
b   I don't think I'll be going. ☐
c   Will you go to the post office this afternoon? ☐
d   Will you be going to the post office this afternoon? ☐

1   At least that's what they've told me.
2   If you're not too busy, that is.
3   And if so, could you post this for me?
4   I certainly don't want to.

5 Lexical future

In English there are a lot of *be* (+ word) *to* expressions to talk about future intentions and expectations.

a   We're to
b   We're due to
c   We're about to
d   We're hoping to   meet them to
e   We're aiming to   discuss the matter.
f   We're planning to
g   We're intending to
h   We're going to

Which of the sentences above refer to:

1 something which will happen very soon? ☐
2 something which has been formally arranged? ☐
3 something which other people are expecting? ☐
4 something which has already been decided? ☐
5 something we'd like to happen, but it ☐ ☐ ☐ ☐
  may not?

6 Future in the past

Put the sentences into the past and match them to what
was said next.

a We're going to fly Lufthansa. ☐
b We're meeting at three. ☐
c I'm just about to leave. ☐
d I think we'll have problems. ☐

1 Can it wait till the morning?
2 But something's come up.
3 But there's been a change of plan.
4 But I never expected this!

7 Past in the future

Tick the sentences which refer to the future.

a They won't have heard the news.
b I'll have missed my chance by then.
c You'll have seen our advertisements, I suppose.
d Another month and I'll have been working here for ten
  years.

The **Present Continuous** and *be to* are frequently used to
talk about fixed arrangements.

The **Present Simple** is often used either to talk about
schedules and timetables or to refer to the future after
words like *if, when, as soon as, before*, etc.

There's a range of expressions including *be going to* and
be hoping to which are used to talk about plans and
intentions.

Both *will* and *going to* can be used to make predictions:
will for opinions and *going to* for more informed
predictions.

'll is frequently used to make offers, promises and take
initiatives.

The **Future Continuous**, *will be doing*, is used to talk
about something which will be in progress or which is part
of a routine.

The **Future Perfect**, *will have done* and *will have been
doing*, are used to talk about something which will already
be completed at a future time. The continuous form
usually emphasises the activity rather than its completion.

Phrase bank: E-mailing

Certain expressions are common in business e-mails. Match up the ones below. Then label them
according to their function using the labels in the box.

| Asking for advice Buying time Delegating tasks Requesting information |

a ....
Have   the details to you.
Can I leave   this off my hands?
Can you take   a quick look at this.
I'll leave   this with you?

b ....
Can I sound you   over this when you've a minute.
Cast your eye   check the figures for me?
Can you just cross-   what you think.
Let me know   out on something?

c ....
I'll just need to check this in a day or two?
Can I get back to you on what I can come up with.
Give me a week and I'll see something out.
Leave it with me. I'll sort this against the computer.

d ....
Can you update me   to me with the figures?
Can you get back   in the loop.
Copy me   on where we are with this?
Keep me   in on any correspondence.

13 MAKING AN IMPACT

Speech is power: speech is to persuade, to convert, to compel.

RALPH WALDO EMERSON, AMERICAN WRITER, PHILOSOPHER AND ORATOR

1 Look at the Emerson quote above. Can you see any techniques he's using to make his statement more powerful? Think about sounds, lists and repetition.

2 How important is it to make an impact right at the beginning of a presentation? Read the book extract. Do you agree with the author?

> **OPENING**
>
> The opener to any business presentation is nearly always important, establishing the tone for the rest of the event. It's that vital moment when you take charge, gaining people's close attention.
>
> People tend to remember openers more than any other part of a presentation, except perhaps for the closing remarks. You waste a wonderful opportunity if you resort to trivia like: 'Good evening, ladies and gentlemen, it's a great pleasure to be here today.'

Adapted from *The Ultimate Business Presentation Book* by Andrew Leigh

3 With a partner, make a list of ways you can attract people's attention when you start a presentation. Could any of them be risky?

4 🎵 3.29 Listen to the openings of six business presentations. Do the speakers use any of the techniques you listed in 3? What other techniques do they employ?

5 How effective are the speakers in 3 at capturing your attention?

6 The openers below were all used in 4. Can you remember the first three words of each? Contractions (*I'd, I'm, it's*, etc.) count as one word.

a .... that of the world's one hundred biggest economies only 49 are actually countries?

b .... favourite lawyer jokes is: this guy's having a quiet drink in a bar when a drunk starts shouting ...

c .... start off by thanking Dr Jensen, Dr Tan and Dr Martinez for inviting me to speak today.

d .... was Thomas Edison who said: 'I have not failed. I've just found 10,000 ways that don't work.'

e .... through the appointments pages the other day and came across this unusual job advertisement.

f .... about Total Quality, I think of the story of the American steel magnate, Andrew Carnegie.

charisma /kərɪzmə/
noun [U] a strong
personal quality
that makes other
people like you
and be attracted to
you: A man sadly
lacking in charisma

PRESENCE AND PERFORMANCE

1 For many people the magic ingredient great presenters have is charisma. What's the equivalent word in your language?

2 🔊 3.30–3.33 Listen to extracts from four famous political speeches. Rank them in order of how charismatic they sound. Compare with a partner.

Extract 1 ☐   Extract 2 ☐   Extract 3 ☐   Extract 4 ☐

3 The speakers in 2 used a number of rhetorical techniques. The main ones are listed below. Complete them using the words in the box.

language   opposites   points   questions   sounds   threes   words

The seven rules of rhetoric

1 **Repeat** _____
I still have a dream. It is a dream deeply rooted in the American dream.

2 **Repeat** _____
We are the people ... who persuaded others to buy British, not by begging them to do so, but because it was best.

3 **Use contrasts and** _____
Ask not what your country can do for you – ask what you can do for your country.

4 **Group key points in** _____
We must therefore act together as a united people, for national reconciliation, for nation building, for the birth of a new world.

5 **Ask rhetorical** _____
What are our chances of success? It depends on what kind of people we are.

6 **Accumulate supporting** _____
We are the people who, amongst other things, invented the computer, the refrigerator, the electric motor, the stethoscope, rayon, the steam turbine, stainless steel, the tank ...

7 **Use metaphorical** _____
To lead our country out of the valley of darkness.

4 Look at the extracts on page 96 and find more examples of the rhetorical techniques listed in 3.

John F Kennedy

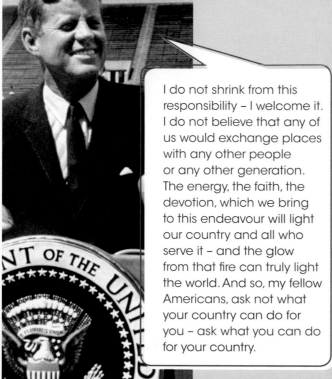

I do not shrink from this responsibility – I welcome it. I do not believe that any of us would exchange places with any other people or any other generation. The energy, the faith, the devotion, which we bring to this endeavour will light our country and all who serve it – and the glow from that fire can truly light the world. And so, my fellow Americans, ask not what your country can do for you – ask what you can do for your country.

I still have a dream. It is a dream deeply rooted in the American dream. I have a dream that one day this nation will rise up and live out the true meaning of its creed: 'We hold these truths to be self-evident; that all men are created equal.' I have a dream that one day on the red hills of Georgia the sons of former slaves and the sons of former slave owners will be able to sit down together at the table of brotherhood … I have a dream that my four little children will one day live in a nation where they will not be judged by the colour of their skin but by the content of their character. I have a dream today.

Martin Luther King

Nelson Mandela

What are our chances of success? It depends on what kind of people we are. What kind of people are we? We are the people that in the past made Great Britain the workshop of the world, the people who persuaded others to buy British, not by begging them to do so, but because it was best.

Margaret Thatcher

We understand it still that there is no easy road to freedom. We know it well that none of us acting alone can achieve success … Let each know that for each the body, the mind and the soul have been freed to fulfil themselves. Never, never and never again shall it be that this beautiful land will again experience the oppression of one by another …

5 🔊 **3.34** Look at the following extracts from ineffective business presentations and rephrase them to give them more impact. Then listen and check.

a Cash flow is the main problem we're facing.
What's the .... facing? The .... cash flow.

b It's critical to our success, even though it's so risky and problematic.
It's .... risky, ... problematic, ... yet .... critical to our success.

c It's faster, cheaper, more reliable – that's the most important thing – and easier to use.
It's ...., ... and .... But, above ...., it's more ....

d We can still be the best, but we can't ever be the biggest again.
Even .... we can .... again be the ...., we .... still ....

e Fewer jobs are being fought over by more graduates, that's the point.
The point ...., more and .... graduates .... over fewer ....

f We're number one in Latin America now, not just Brazil.
Not .... we number one in Brazil. We're .... in Latin America.

g There isn't a company that's ever outperformed us in this market.
In this ...., no .... has .... us, not .... – ....!

h We've had no complaints in over thirty years of business.
Not ...., in over ...., have .... had a complaint – not a ....!

6 Look carefully at word order and the order of clauses in the rephrased extracts in 5. What information tends to come last?

7 Practise delivering the rephrased extracts to make as big an impact as possible.

8 🔊 **3.35** The last few minutes of a presentation are your final chance to make a lasting impression. Listen to the closing remarks of four presentations and number the techniques in the order you hear them. Which is the most effective?

the sum up ☐   the call to action ☐   the famous quotation ☐   the emergency stop ☐

9 Choose one of the closes below and use it as the basis for closing a presentation you have given in the past or may give in the future.

a Ladies and gentlemen, we are on the brink/threshold of ... I'm reminded of the words of ..., who said... And I'd like this company/this department/us to be able to say ...

b Well, that just about brings me to the end of my presentation, except to say ... And if there's one central message I'd like to get across to you this morning/afternoon/evening, it's this ...

c So, how do you sum up ...? I could tell you that ..., that ... and that ... I could also mention ... But all that would fail to do it justice. For the fact is, that ... It is, quite simply, ...

THE LAST PARADISE ON EARTH?

1 If you wanted to escape from it all for a while, where would you go?

2 Read the article and information on Bhutan. Does it sound like your idea of paradise?

GROSS NATIONAL
HAPPINESS

Gross national happiness is more important than gross national product.' That's the official government policy of King Jigme Singye Wangchuck of Bhutan, ruler of what some have called 'the last paradise on earth'. Indeed, his programme of careful economic development and gradual change has so far
5 ensured that Bhutan, completely isolated from the rest of the world until 1961, has managed to balance the need to progress into the 21st century with the need to preserve its cultural heritage. But there's trouble in paradise.

10 Tiny Bhutan lies in the Himalayas, squeezed between the world's two most populous countries, China and India. Roughly the same size as Switzerland, Bhutan is a country of dense forest and breathtaking mountain ranges – at 6,895m, Gangkhar Puensum is the highest unclimbed peak in the world. This haven of peace
15 and natural beauty is home to a multitude of exotic wildlife, including the endangered red panda and almost mythical snow leopard. Brightly coloured prayer flags fly from every hillside. The people here follow the Buddhist Middle Way, a philosophy based on pacifism, paternalism and egalitarianism. Time itself is
20 measured differently in Bhutan – not in hours and minutes, but in kalpas, a unit of time equivalent to several million years.

At least, that's how it used to be. For now technology has finally come to this remote farming community. Foreign investment has helped build up the country's infrastructure, improve health and
25 education and create a growing tourist industry. Cybercafés have opened in the capital, Thimphu, and the television aerials rising from the rooftops may soon outnumber the prayer flags. But the traditional way of life, upon which so much of Bhutan's 'national happiness' has depended, is under threat.

30 In 1998 the king of Bhutan decentralised power and appointed a central cabinet. The country now has a seat at the UN. But the Bhutanese themselves seem divided over their country's future. Should they continue to reap the many benefits progress has already brought or try to regulate the accelerating pace of change
35 while there's still time?

- **Location** SE Asia
- **Area** 47,000 square km
- **Capital** Thimphu
- **Population** 657,000
- **Population density** 14.1 people per sq km
- **Industry** farming, forestry, timber, limestone, food processing, chemicals, cement, hydroelectric power, tourism
- **GDP** US$2.1bn
- **GDP per capita** US$1,060
- **Inflation** 9%
- **Economic growth** 7%
- **National languages** Dzongkha (official), Nepali, English
- **Currency** ngultrum (Nu) of 100 chetrums, US$1 = Nu50.63

3 Work in two groups. Group A is the Bhutanese Preservation Party (BPP) and Group B the Progress Party of Bhutan (PPB). Read the introduction to your party's manifesto opposite.

Bhutanese
PRESERVATION PARTY

To the outside world we are Bhutan, a tiny Himalayan kingdom of scenic beauty and scientific interest, but little economic importance. But in our own ancient language we are Druk Yul, 'the Land of the Thunder Dragon', a land steeped in history and legend.

We in the BPP have never stood in the way of progress, so long as it is in harmony with the natural order and cultural traditions of our country. But we believe it is essential to protect the unique way of life we have enjoyed for over a thousand years from the worst excesses of the 21st century.

Will you join us in our campaign to preserve those qualities the rest of the world most envies about Bhutan – its simplicity, its tranquillity and the contentment of its people? Vote BPP.

Progress Party of Bhutan

For over a thousand years Bhutan has stood still. But the rest of the world has not. King Jigme Singye Wangchuck himself has said: 'Change is coming' and there is nothing in the teachings of the Buddha that tells us to resist change – rather the reverse. Change is not to be resisted, but to be embraced. It is time to end centuries of isolation and poverty.

The PPB has no wish to damage either our environment or our rich cultural traditions. Indeed, these priceless treasures are the basis on which we seek to build a better future for Bhutan.

Support our programme of culturally sensitive and environmentally aware development, and provide your children and your children's children with the opportunity and prosperity they deserve. Vote PPB.

4 Work in your group to produce a ten-minute party political broadcast to the people of Bhutan. To help you prepare, Group A see page 144 and Group B see page 150. Use the rhetorical techniques you have studied to add impact to your speech. Your aim is to determine the future of what may well be 'the last paradise on earth'.

13 MAKING AN IMPACT

LANGUAGE LINKS

Vocabulary: Metaphor

1 Business English is full of metaphor (describing one thing in terms of another). Match the following expressions. Then match them to their metaphorical reference.

takeover	recovery	**war**
ballpark	debate	**fire**
heated	flow	**health**
economic	figure	**water**
cash	battle	**sport**

2 Complete the sentences using the words in the boxes.

> coming   growing   pooling   pouring   sowing   trickling

Money is liquid

a They're .... millions of dollars into R&D.

b A small amount of cash has started .... in.

c We should be .... our resources – together we'd have sufficient capital to fund new research.

Ideas are plants

d After years of work, our plans are finally .... to fruition.

e There's .... support for the project – most of the people we spoke to think it's a good idea.

f They're .... the seeds of doubt in the mind of the customer and, as a result, we're losing sales.

> attack   fight   goalposts   guns   idea   odds
> stakes   victory

Argument is war

g They shot down my .... before I'd even had a chance to explain it.

h We came under .... from the marketing team.

i He didn't put up much of a .... In fact, he just seemed to give in completely.

j She stuck to her .... and refused to move an inch.

Competition is sport

k We've scored a significant .... in the home market.

l The .... are high – we're risking the future of this company.

m The .... are against us, but there's still a chance we can succeed.

n We don't know what our objectives are supposed to be because they keep moving the ....

Grammar: Rhetorical techniques

1 Repetition

Decide which word in each statement could most effectively be repeated after a short pause and <u>underline</u> it. Read the statements aloud to check. The first one has been done for you.

a This is <u>very</u> important. ('*This is very … very important.*')

b This is a much better option.

c It's now or never.

d There'll always be a market for quality.

e It is here in Europe that the best opportunities lie.

f And today we start to turn this company around.

Rewrite **a** so that you can repeat the word *important*.

2 Sound repetition

Replace one word in each sentence with a word from the box that starts with the same sound as other words in the sentence.

> better   dynamism   past   promotion   simpler
> team   willing

better

a It's bigger. It's ~~superior~~. And it's British.

b I'm not interested in our history or in our present, but in our prospects for the future.

c We'll reach our targets together as a group.

d We need the right product at the right price with the right advertising.

e We have the drive, energy and determination to succeed.

f Are we prepared to work towards that goal?

g The new system is both more secure and significantly easier to install.

What sound is being repeated in each of the sentences above?

a ...... b ...... c ...... d ...... e ...... f ...... g ......

What do sentences a, b, d and e all have in common?

3 Contrasts and opposites

Complete the sentences using the idea of contrast to help you.

a It's not a question of time; it's a question of money.

b If we don't seize this opportunity, some............... el............... w...............

c Tackling a few minor problems now will save us a whole l............... of ma............... pr............... la...............

d Some people are saying we can't afford to advertise, but I s............... we c............... aff............... n............... to.

e I'm not saying we're certain to succeed: what I a............... s............... is we'll ne............... kn............... unt............... we tr...............

f Three years ago this company was going nowhere; to............... it's num............... o............... in the ind...............

4 Rhetorical questions

Rephrase the statements as negative questions and change the second person plural to the first person.

a This is what you need to be doing.
b You should be learning from your mistakes.
c Deep down, you all know this to be true.

5 Rhetorical questions + repetition

Complete the following using one word in both gaps.

advantages	answer	chances	point	problem	result

a So much for the disadvantages, but what about the _____? Well, the _____ are obvious.
b We're losing control of the company. So what's the _____? Clearly, the _____ is to centralise.
c What are our _____ of success? Well, frankly, our _____ are slim.
d So what's the _____ of offering an unprofitable service? The _____ is it makes us look good.
e So what's the basic _____ with this system? The basic _____ is it's far too complicated!
f Three years of R&D and what's the net _____? The net _____ is a product that doesn't work!

6 Inversion

Rephrase the statements below making any necessary changes in word order.

a This company is not only leaner, it's also greener.
 Not only _____
b We mustn't under any circumstances panic.
 Under no circumstances _____
c We've done better in Mexico than anywhere.
 Nowhere _____
d We'll only be ready to launch after exhaustive tests.
 Only after _____

In adverb + adjective phrases it is more effective to repeat the adverb (1).

If you want to repeat an adjective, it is more effective to use an adverb before repeating it (1).

It is more effective to repeat consonants than vowels (2).

Lists of three are especially memorable (2).

In a contrast it is more effective to make your main point second (3).

Asking questions (particularly negative questions) is a more effective way of getting audiences to think than making statements (4).

Talking about 'us' is a more effective way of building rapport than talking about 'you' (4).

Rhetorical questions sound more convincing when you answer them using some of the same words (5).

You can give weight and formality to what you say by sometimes reversing your word order (6).

Phrase bank: Opening and closing a presentation

Label the presentation openings and closes below according to the techniques the speaker is using:

Is anybody out there? Let me take you on a journey Now, here's a funny thing Oh, and one last thing... This is a true story, by the way To cut a long story short Wise words Would you believe it?

1 _____
 Did you know that...?
 In the time it takes you to ...
 Statistics / Studies show that...

2 _____
 One of my favourite stories / jokes about that is...
 Whenever I'm asked about ... I think of the story of ...

3 _____
 I'd like to start off by...
 My presentation this morning / afternoon is in three main parts...
 By the end of this morning's talk, ...

4 _____
 I think it was ... who said...
 Somebody once said...
 In closing, I'm reminded of the words of...

5 _____
 I was ... the other day and happened to / came across...
 I remember when I was working / living in...

6 _____
 Could you just raise your hand if you've ever...
 Have you ever been in the situation where...?

7 _____
 So how do you sum up...?
 So my central message today is this...

8 _____
 That just about brings me to the end of my presentation, except to say...
 If you take just one thing from today's talk, take this...

14 OUT AND ABOUT

Take a little of home with you, and leave a little of yourself at home.

MARK MCCORMACK, FOUNDER OF IMG SPORTS AGENCY

1 When packing to go on a business trip, apart from your travel documents, what are the absolute essentials? A good book? Swimming things? A decent hairdryer? An air pillow? Chargers? Adaptors? A travel alarm? Compare with a partner.

2 In the film *The Accidental Tourist*, travel guidebook writer Macon Leary gives advice on how to pack for a trip. Read the extract and discuss the questions.

The **business** traveller

'The business traveller should bring only what fits in a carry-on bag. Checking your luggage is asking for trouble. Add several travel-size packets of detergent, so you won't fall into the hands of unfamiliar laundries. There are very few necessities in this world which do not come in travel-size packets.

'One suit is plenty if you take along travel-size packets of spot remover. The suit should be medium-gray. Gray not only hides the dirt, but is handy for sudden funerals.

'Always bring a book as protection against strangers. Magazines don't last and newspapers from elsewhere remind you you don't belong. But don't take more than one book. It is a common mistake to overestimate one's potential free time and consequently overpack. In travel, as in most of life, less is invariably more.

'And most importantly, never take along anything on your journey so valuable or dear that its loss would devastate you.'

From *The Accidental Tourist*

a   Do you tend to travel light or do you bring along 'everything but the kitchen sink'?
b   Have you ever had any bad experiences with lost luggage or hotel laundries?
c   Is grey your colour? Do you dress for comfort or dress to impress?
d   What's the best way of avoiding unwanted conversations with strangers?
e   Is it important to allow yourself some free time on a business trip?
f   Have you ever lost something valuable on a journey? Tell the story.

3 What kind of person is Macon Leary? Tick the correct answers. Would you want to sit next to him on a flight?

a bit paranoid	☐	antisocial	☐	bitter	☐	dull	☐	fussy	☐
gloomy	☐	lonely	☐	outgoing	☐	overserious	☐	practical	☐
private	☐	sarcastic	☐	sociable	☐	well organised	☐	witty	☐

4 ◉ 4.01 Read and listen to an extract from *The Accidental Tourist*, where Macon Leary finds himself sitting next to an overweight man on a plane. What coincidence links the two men?

Traveller	I'm sorry I'm so fat. *Name's Lucas Loomis.*
Leary	Macon Leary.
Traveller	You a Baltimore man?
Leary	Yes.
Traveller	Me too. *Greatest city on the earth.* One of these seats is not really enough for me. And the stupid thing is, I travel for a living. I demonstrate software to computer stores. What do you do, Mr Leary?
Leary	I write travel guidebooks.
Traveller	Is that so? What kind?
Leary	Well, guides for businessmen – people just like you, I guess.
Traveller	'Accidental Tourist'!
Leary	Why, yes.
Traveller	Really? Am I right? Well, what do you know? Look at this. Gray suit – just what you recommend, appropriate for all occasions. *See my luggage?* Carry-on. Change of underwear. Clean shirt. Packet of detergent powder.
Leary	Oh, good.
Traveller	You're my hero. You've improved my trips a hundred per cent. I tell my wife, going with *The Accidental Tourist* is like going in a cocoon.
Leary	Well, this is very nice to hear.
Traveller	*Times I've flown clear to Oregon and hardly knew I'd left Baltimore.*
Leary	Excellent.
Traveller	I see you have your book for protection there. *Didn't work with me, though, did it?*

> **Glossary**
> **cocoon** warm, safe place
> **You're my hero** I really admire you/your work

5 Find expressions in the conversation which mean:

a That's interesting.
b I suppose.
c How did you know that?
d What a coincidence!

6 In natural conversation certain words are sometimes omitted. Look at the sentences in italics in 4 and decide which three types of word are missing.

7 The following things were said at different times during a business trip. Delete any unnecessary words to make them more conversational.

a **A** Is everything OK with your meal, sir?
  B It's delicious. It couldn't be better.
b **A** Do you need anything else, sir?
  B I don't think so, thanks.
c **A** I like your laptop. It's a Sony, isn't it?
  B Yeah. I haven't quite got used to it yet.
d **A** Are you ready to start?
  B Yeah, I'm just coming.
e **A** Do you mind if I switch the reading light on?
  B It doesn't bother me. I think I'll get another coffee. Do you want one?
f **A** I saw you earlier in the fitness centre. Have you been here long?
  B No, I just got here yesterday. Are you here on business too?
g **A** Have you got a light?
  B Sorry, I don't smoke.

8 What are the advantages of having someone to chat to on a long journey? Do you find it easy to start conversations with people you don't know?

9 The most common ways of starting a conversation with a stranger are:
a make an observation
b pay a compliment
c make a request
d ask for information
e offer assistance
f make an apology

Categorise the following conversation starters by writing a, b, c, d, e or f in the boxes.

1 **You couldn't** help me with my bag, **could you**? ☐
2 **Do you mind** swapping seats? ☐
3 **Looks like** we're in for a bit of turbulence, doesn't it? ☐
4 **Sorry about** my kids. **Let me know if** they're bothering you. ☐
5 **I couldn't help noticing** you speak Dutch. ☐
6 **Do you think I could** borrow your paper if you've finished with it? ☐
7 **Is this** row 17, **do you know**? ☐
8 **I like** your mobile. **Is that one of the new ones**? ☐
9 **Let me** help you with that. ☐
10 **I'll get someone to** come and help you. ☐
11 **I see you're** flying on to Caracas. ☐
12 **Nice** camera. **I used to have one like that**. ☐
13 **I'm sorry**, is that getting in your way? ☐
14 **Are you** from Lima, **by any chance**? ☐

10 Work with a partner to practise holding short conversations with fellow passengers on planes. Speaker A see page 144. Speaker B see page 151.

TRAVELLERS' TALES

1  4.02 Listen to four business people talking about their worst flying experiences and answer the questions.

a What was all the noise about on Emma's flight?
b How might Enrique's flight have ended in disaster?
c What surprised Joe on his flight to London?
d Who got lost on Joe's flight to Frankfurt?
e What was the strange request on Selina's flight in Asia?
f How did the Nigerian army solve the overbooking problem?

2 Read this extract from the first conversation and <u>underline</u> the best grammatical choice.

B After a while, some of the passengers (a) **were starting/had been starting** to get nervous, me included!

A I'm not surprised.

B Anyway, eventually, after (b) **we were sitting/we'd been sitting** there for about ten minutes with no announcement and the plane still not moving, (c) **I said/I'd said** something to one of the stewards and they (d) **went/were going** and (e) **opened/were opening** the door to see what (f) **went/was going** on.

A And what (g) **happened/had been happening**?

B The pilot (h) **got/had got** in!

A You're joking!

B No, (i) **they'd locked/they'd been locking** him out. Seems quite funny now, but it (j) **didn't/wasn't doing** at the time.

3 In the extract in 2 how many examples can you find of the:

past simple? ☐
past perfect simple? ☐
past continuous? ☐
past perfect continuous? ☐

4 According to publisher David Weinberger, 'most of our best conversations are about stories.' How useful is it in business to be able to tell a good story? Do you agree that the best ones are usually true?

5 Listed below are the typical stages in a story or anecdote. Add the expressions in the box to the correct place in the list. They were all in the conversations in 1.

> a And the strange thing was ...   b And then, to top it all, ...   c Anyway, to cut a long story short, ...
> d But that was nothing compared to ...   e Did I ever tell you about the time I was ...?   f I ended up ...
> g Seems quite funny now, but it didn't at the time.   h This was around the time of ...
> i Way back in (1985) it was.   j You should have heard/seen ...!

Opener
I'll never forget the time I was ... ☐
Context
It's quite a few years ago now, but I can still remember it. ☐ ☐
Emphasis
You're not going to believe this, but ... ☐ ☐ ☐ ☐
Close
Anyway, in the end ... ☐ ☐ ☐

6 Tick which one of the closes could also come straight after an opener.

7 Match the following to make ten things you might say while listening to someone telling a story. They were all in the conversations in 1.

a You're   god!   f I'm not   terrifying!
b I don't   earth for?   g I see   read about this.
c Oh, my   happened?   h Sounds   be serious!
d So, what   joking!   i Oh, yes, I   what you mean.
e What on   believe it!   j You can't   surprised.

8 Tell the story of your worst (or best) travel experience to the rest of the class.

THE BUSINESS LUNCH

1 What's the most expensive meal you've ever had? Was it worth the money? Who was paying? Was it on expenses? Tell a partner about it.

2 Read the information below. Does it shock or amuse you?

Out to lunch

In 1997 a London banker made the headlines when he was sacked for taking a five-hour lunch break – from 11.30am to 4.30pm!

He won back his job after an industrial tribunal ruled that he had been unfairly dismissed. The court decided that five hours is not an excessive amount of time to conduct business over a meal.

Do you agree with the court ruling?

This one's on me

The world record for the most expensive business lunch ever is held by six Barclay's Bank employees, who in July 2001 ate at the Pétrus restaurant in London.

The three bottles of vintage claret alone which they consumed during the meal set them back a staggering £33,410 (charged to expenses, of course), bringing the total bill to just under £44,000!

How could so huge a bill be justified?

3 🔊 **4.03** You are in a noisy restaurant with a group of colleagues and have to keep going outside to answer your mobile. Each time you come back in, the topic of conversation has changed. Listen and see how quickly you can guess what it is.

4 Listen again and note down key words and phrases that helped you decide. Compare with a partner and then check in the listening script on page 180.

5 Work in groups. Use the chart below to practise chatting over lunch with business contacts. Start off by talking about what you've just ordered and then keep changing the subject as indicated until your meal arrives – it seems to be taking a long time! Try not to interrupt each other too abruptly, but keep the conversation moving.

> Anyway, ... Before I forget, ... By the way, ... Incidentally, ... On the subject of ... So, ...
> Talking of ... That reminds me ... To change the subject for a moment ...

LANGUAGE LINKS

Vocabulary: Storytelling

Descriptive power

1 When describing things in a story or anecdote, try to avoid overusing (*not*) *very* + neutral adjective. Replace the dull descriptions in **bold** with more interesting alternatives from the box.

> absolutely ancient   absolutely delighted
> absolutely fabulous   absolutely filthy
> absolutely hilarious   drop-dead gorgeous
> quite inedible   really fascinating   totally pointless
> utterly astonished   utterly furious   utterly miserable

a The meeting was ~~not very useful~~. *totally pointless*
b It was a **very interesting** book.
c They were **very happy** about the idea.
d The food was **not very good**.
e The weather was **very bad**.
f Their boss was **very good-looking**.
g Her apartment was **very nice**.
h I was **very surprised**.
i The whole thing was **very funny**.
j The PCs they were using were **very old**.
k He looked **very angry**.
l The hotel was **not very clean**.

2 If you do use neutral adjectives, try using a more interesting adverb to describe them. Match the following pairs of adverbs to a suitable adjective from the box.

> beautiful   dangerous   difficult   disappointing
> enjoyable   expensive   funny   quiet

a hysterically/hilariously
b stunningly/breathtakingly
c outrageously/prohibitively
d immensely/thoroughly
e bitterly/terribly
f deathly/blissfully
g highly/downright
h exceedingly/fiendishly

The art of exaggeration

Complete the conversation below using the words and phrases in the boxes.

> 1–7   and that's putting it mildly   I'm telling you
> is literally   like something out of   me tell you
> ~~you'll never guess~~   you should have seen

> 8–13   believe me   I'm not exaggerating   let's just
> out of this world   talk about   you'll never believe

(in the bar)
A Did I tell you about my trip to Sweden?
B No, I don't think so. On business, were you?
A Yeah, but (1) *you'll never guess* the hotel the Swedes had booked us into.
B Somewhere posh, was it?
A No, not exactly. It's called The Ice Hotel. Have you heard of it?

B No, I don't think so.
A Well, (2) .... this place. (3) ...., it was (4) .... a James Bond movie! Right in the middle of nowhere. And completely built out of snow and ice!
B What? You mean the walls were made of ice!
A Walls, ceilings, doors, tables, beds, chandeliers, the lot! The whole thing (5) .... made of ice!
B But, hang on. That's not possible, is it? I mean, it would just melt!
A It does. They have to rebuild it from top to bottom every summer.
B You're joking.
A No, it's true. But in the winter it's minus nine or something.
B So how come you didn't freeze to death?
A We nearly did. Let (6) ...., it was like an igloo in there. (7) .... But (8) .... say we'd had plenty to warm us up in the bar before we went to bed!
B It's got a bar?
A Of course it has. (9) ...., you need a few vodkas in you if you're going to stay in a place like that!
B I can imagine.
A And they even make their cocktail glasses out of ice so you don't need any in your drink.
B Now, you're having me on.
A No, it's true. (10) .... All the glasses are made of ice.
B Amazing! But it doesn't sound like the sort of place I'd want to stay in.
A Actually, it wasn't that bad once you got used to it. And it was great at night, lying in bed under a reindeer skin, looking up at the Aurora Borealis lighting up the midnight sky. (11) .... spectacular; it really was (12) ....! And, (13) .... who we bumped into in the bar one night.
B Who?
A Naomi Campbell and Kate Moss!
B Oh, come on! You mean the models?
A Yeah, apparently, it's really popular with all the celebs. It's where the cool people go, you might say.
B Yeah, very funny! So, what are you having?
A Whisky and soda for me, thanks. No ice!

Grammar: Narrative tenses

Read the story about Pepsi A.M. and <u>underline</u> the best grammatical choices.

The Story of Pepsi A.M.

In the late 1980s Pepsi (1) **thought/was thinking** it (2) **identified/had identified** a lucrative gap in the highly competitive soft drinks market: breakfast cola.

Although it (3) **wasn't conducting/hadn't conducted** very thorough market research, it (4) **seemed/was seeming** that a lot of young consumers (5) **switched/were switching** from coffee to cola for breakfast. Pepsi's R&D department promptly (6) **went away/were going away** and (7) **came up with/had come up** with Pepsi A.M., a breakfast cola 'with all the sugar and twice the caffeine'!

But what the company (8) **wasn't realising/hadn't realised** was that the Pepsi drinkers (9) **were/were being** perfectly happy with the normal brand. Pepsi A.M., on the other hand, (10) **sounded/was sounding** like something you would only drink in the morning. Six months after its launch it obviously (11) **didn't sell/wasn't selling**.

Marketing experts (12) **were/had been** quick to point out the company's mistake. What (13) **had it thought of?/had it been thinking of?** At a cost of millions, it (14) **had developed/had been developing** a product nobody actually (15) **needed!/was needing!**

Pepsi A.M. (16) **was/had been** immediately withdrawn.

You use the **Past Simple** to talk about the main events in a story or to give factual information about the past.

You use the **Past Continuous** to talk about the things happening at the same time as these main events. Events in the **Past Continuous** are often interrupted by those in the **Past Simple**.

You use the **Past Perfect Simple** and the **Past Perfect Continuous** to look back from the time of the story to an earlier time, but the **Past Perfect Continuous** usually emphasises the activity rather than its completion. For this reason, it is not normally used with 'state' verbs like *be, know, seem, understand, mean* and *like*.

Phrase bank: Sharing anecdotes

All the following phrases and expressions can be used to share anecdotes. Add them to the chart according to their function.

OPENER	CONTEXT
EMPHASIS	**CLOSE**

a   You not going to believe this, but …
b   Anyway, to cut a long story short …
c   Did I ever tell you about the time I was …?
d   So, in the end, what happened was …
e   It's quite a few years ago now.
f   I'll never forget the time I was …
g   Talking of …, that reminds me of the time I …
h   You should have heard / seen …!
i   And then to top it all, …
j   This was around the time of …
k   And you'll never guess who / what / where …
l   Seems quite funny now, but it didn't at the time.
m   And the strange / funny / stupid thing was …

Reactions

Switch the endings in **bold** below to make 14 common reactions to anecdotes. The first one has been done for you.

a   I'm not **awful!** ◄
b   I can **blame you!**
c   How **serious!**
d   What a **god!**
e   You're **you!**
f   Sounds **surprised!** ◄
g   You can't be **odd!**
h   I don't **imagine!**
i   Wow, that's **really?**
j   Oh, I see what **happened?**
k   Were you **amazing!**
l   So, what **you mean!**
m   Oh, my **nightmare!**
n   Lucky **joking, right?**

Being powerful is like being a lady. If you have to tell people you are, you aren't.

MARGARET THATCHER, FORMER BRITISH PRIME MINISTER

1 It's the biggest question in management literature: what's the secret of leadership? Look at the following real and fictitious leaders of the past and present. What do you know about them?

2 They all have one vital thing in common. What is it?

3 Now think of a leader you personally admire. Do they have the same magic ingredient as the leaders above? Tell a partner about them.

4 🔘 4.04 Listen to a management trainer answering the question you answered in 2. Are you surprised by what he says?

5 In spite of all the fashionable talk about 'empowering' the workforce, we can't all be leaders. What do you think are the qualities of a great follower? Should there be courses in 'followship'?

The bottleneck is at the top of the bottle. Where are you likely to find people with the least diversity of experience, the largest investment in the past and the greatest reverence for industry dogma? At the top.

GARY HAMEL, STRATEGY AS REVOLUTION,
HARVARD BUSINESS REVIEW

THE ROLE OF LEADERSHIP

1 Not everyone is as enthusiastic about the importance of leaders in business. Read the short article extract. What point is Hamel making about leadership and change? Are any of your bosses like this?

2 Find out if you (would) make a better leader than the ones Hamel is talking about. Work with a partner to complete the quiz from *Fortune* magazine. Then check your leadership potential on page 160.

3 Try to work out the meaning of the words and phrases in italics.

Are you a good leader?

Think you have the skills it takes to succeed as a leader? Take our quiz and find out if a climb to the top is in your future.

1 **You have lots of training and experience managing people, but have trouble keeping up with the latest technology. You:**

a   Try to learn as much as you can about new advances in your spare time.

b   Sign up for extra training on how to motivate employees, evaluate their performance, and improve your public speaking skills.

c   Assume that, if there's anything you need to know about new office technology, the IT department will tell you about it.

2 **The CEO asks you for ideas for a new marketing campaign, even though advertising is not your area of expertise. You:**

a   Meet with people in the marketing department to get their views, brainstorm with *a mentor*, and research your competitors' marketing campaigns.

b   Explain to the CEO that you are the wrong person for this task, since you know nothing about marketing, and recommend someone with the right skills.

c   Put off dealing with the assignment until the CEO assigns it to someone else who is better qualified to handle it.

3 **You are so stressed about the *mountain of work* to be done over the next several weeks that you doubt whether you can finish it all. You:**

a   Resolve to *work around the clock*, including weekends, to get it all done.

b   Tell your boss that you think your workload is excessive and that you could do a better job if some of your deadlines were extended.

c   Slow down, leave the office at 6 p.m. each day, and maybe even consider a short vacation to *recharge your batteries*.

4 **You have several tasks to complete by the end of the week. The most efficient way of organizing your time is to:**

a   Do as many things at once as you can, since *multitasking* saves time.

b   Focus your attention on one thing at a time, moving on to the next task once you've finished with the one at hand.

c   Try to get everything done by *putting in longer hours* than usual.

5 **You are faced with an important decision that could *impact* your company's future strategy, but don't have enough facts to suggest which way it should go. You:**

a   Think carefully about what the information you have indicates, discuss the options with knowledgeable colleagues, and then make a decision.

b   Make no decision until you've done *exhaustive research* and analysed every possible outcome of every available option.

c   Delegate the decision to someone else with better intuition than you.

6 **Your department is not meeting its financial targets and key customers are less loyal than before. You need to *turn things around* fast. The best way to do this is:**

a   Cancel the Christmas party, ask people to take shorter lunch breaks, and get everyone to work longer and harder until the department gets *back on track*.

b   Take responsibility for the department's problems, since you're the one in charge, and do your best to fix them.

c   Inspire people by ordering free pizza at lunch, start a T-shirt slogan contest, and award free movie tickets or restaurant dinners for two to the person with the most creative solution to winning back a client.

7 **You have been assigned to lead a team of employees from different ethnic backgrounds and whose ages range from early 20s to late 50s. The best way to help the group *bond* is to:**

a   Encourage people to express different points of view based on their diverse backgrounds and experiences.

b   Ignore the differences among them since neither age nor ethnicity *has any bearing on* their abilities to do the job.

c   Take a course in managing diversity so that you're aware of the legal issues, but otherwise guide the team as if there were no differences among age or ethnicity.

8 **At the end of the year, your department has leftover money in the budget that you are free to spend how you choose. To help make the company more successful, you:**

a   Give the top five performers in your department a big *bonus*.

b   Ask employees for suggestions on which local charities need help, then come up with a project you can *sponsor* that will make a visible difference to the community.

c   *Throw a blowout bash* for the entire department and their families.

Quiz based on *Smarter, Faster, Better: Strategies for Effective, Enduring, and Fulfilled Leadership* by Karlin Sloan

CROSS-CULTURAL LEADERSHIP

1 Styles of leadership vary, often quite dramatically, from country to country. Match the metaphors below to the countries and regions whose leadership styles you think they best describe:

a   The Superstar   Argentina
b   The General   Germany
c   The Intellectual   China
d   The Expert   Japan
e   The Diplomat   USA
f   The Elder Statesman   France
g   The Warlord   UK

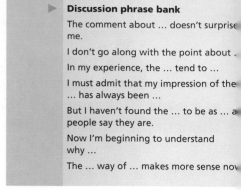

> **Discussion phrase bank**
>
> The comment about … doesn't surprise me.
>
> I don't go along with the point about …
>
> In my experience, the … tend to …
>
> I must admit that my impression of the … has always been …
>
> But I haven't found the … to be as … a people say they are.
>
> Now I'm beginning to understand why …
>
> The … way of … makes more sense now

2 🔊 **4.05–4.11** Now listen to executives from the different countries in 1 talking about the typical leadership style in the culture and check your answers in 1. Do you agree with the descriptions?

3 The speakers in 2 mentioned many different approaches to leadership. Some of these are listed below. Discuss the terms with a partner and decide which of them, for you, are helpful and which unhelpful in managing the workforce. Find the terms in the listening scripts if you need help working out their meaning.

> a lot of delegation   a powerful elite is in charge   analytical   autocratic   avoid conflict
> benevolent patriarchy   casual leadership   consensus   endless reports   expect to compromise
> fast implementation of proposals   feedback from subordinates   formalities   gentle persuasion
> important decisions already made   involve all levels of management
> leader motivates and fires up the team   little loyalty   meritocratic   opinions freely voiced
> paternalistic   plenty of debate and argument   put group needs first   rivalry   seek agreement
> slow decision-making   standardised procedures   suppress individual initiative   tight constraints
> top-down   use humour

Helpful	Unhelpful

4 How would you go about managing a multicultural workforce? Do you agree with intercultural guru Fons Trompenaars about the key competence of transcultural leaders?

What we have found in our research – and we interviewed many leaders – is that there is, in fact, only one competence that goes beyond culture. And that's the competence to reconcile differences created by cultural diversity. What we are trying to do is to give people insight: what are the types of dilemmas international leaders are facing? Global versus local? The individual versus the group? Do you have to show emotions or not? Do you go for an analytic approach or do you, rather, take things in a larger picture? Do you want to push your products or be pulled by the market? Etcetera, etcetera, etcetera…

http://www.youtube.com/user/THTconsulting

5 Which side of each dilemma Trompenaars mentions is the typical position of the culture you come from?

THE MYSTERY LEADER GAME

1 Following the sudden departure of your company's CEO, you are looking for a high-profile replacement with a lot of experience of running a multinational business and a superb track record. Complete and read the applicant profiles below. Each of them refers to a real business leader. Then, with a partner, decide which applicant could probably bring most to your company (or a company you know) and lead it into the future.

First applicant
Since 1994 this Princeton graduate and founder of an internet phenomenon has seen his company grow from an office in the garage into one of the world's leading e-tailers.

His leadership formula is:
1 .... a clear technological lead.
2 .... lean and efficient.
3 .... into new businesses.
4 .... close attention to logistics.
5 .... the industry trends.

stay   diversify
establish
ignore   pay

Second applicant
This ex-CEO of a major IT company has a reputation as a 'tough cookie' and master of mergers. Her no-nonsense management style has antagonised some, but she gets results.

Her leadership formula is:
1 .... from the front.
2 .... things up.
3 .... by acquisition.
4 .... criticism.
5 .... out the recession.

withstand   ride
lead   shake
grow

Third applicant
Stepping down after 10 years as CEO of a vast internet business, this Harvard MBA successfully navigated the dotcom bust and saw revenues increase by a factor of 88!

Her leadership formula is:
1 .... for the future.
2 .... early and often.
3 .... smart risks.
4 .... a sense of mission.
5 .... in training.

take
reorganise
invest   hire
have

Fourth applicant
President of his own manufacturing company in Brazil, an environmental activist and best-selling author, at his firm it's the workers who get to hire the boss and set their own salaries!

His leadership formula is:
1 .... up hierarchies.
2 .... employees in decisions.
3 .... conventional wisdom.
4 .... the company upside down.
5 .... exceptional talent.

reward   turn
break   ignore
involve

Fifth applicant
With an illustrious career in telecoms, automotive and oil companies, the firm of which this famous Finn was CEO for 14 years is now the clear market leader in its industry.

His leadership formula is:
1 .... on your core business.
2 .... off non-core operations.
3 .... on fierce competition.
4 .... one step ahead.
5 .... or die.

thrive
innovate
focus   sell
stay

Sixth applicant
This India-born Yale graduate is CEO of the world's fourth-largest food and beverages company. She has twice been voted the most powerful business woman in the world.

Her leadership formula is:
1 .... a diverse workforce.
2 .... a nurturing environment.
3 .... practical learning.
4 .... positive and affirming.
5 .... social responsibility.

create   be
demonstrate
emphasise
employ

Seventh applicant
One of China's handful of female CEOs and known as 'the iron lady', she heads the world's sixth-largest steel firm, overseeing 100,000 workers, rolling out 21m tons of steel a year.

Her leadership formula is:
1 .... operations.
2 .... performance.
3 .... joint ventures.
4 .... in developing economies.
5 .... unobtrusively but firmly.

invest
establish   lead
streamline
optimise

Eighth applicant
Chairman and CEO for 20 years of the world's biggest industrial conglomerate, this global warming sceptic made it his mission to eradicate inefficiency and get the job done.

His leadership formula is:
1 .... bureaucracy.
2 .... on the basics.
3 .... your market or get out.
4 .... about service and quality.
5 .... the future, forget the past.

obsess
concentrate
face   kill
dominate

2 Can you guess who the leaders are? Turn to page 161 to see who you've selected ... and who you've rejected!

1 Where do you stand on the following corporate issues? Tick the statements you agree with and be prepared to explain your position to a partner.

a A company is worth more than the price of its stock and assets – its people are its greatest asset.

b In the final analysis, leaders have a greater responsibility to their stockholders than to their employees.

c In a free-market economy there should be the minimum of state intervention and regulation.

d Governments should never rescue failing businesses. If a company cannot compete, let it fail.

e Taking over a company to acquire its expertise, gain critical mass, make economies of scale or even just to eliminate a competitor is ethical. Taking it over simply to sell off its assets and make a quick profit isn't.

2 How do you think business people from different countries would answer the questions in 1? What about Argentinians, Brazilians, Chinese, French, Germans, Italians, Japanese, Russians, Americans?

3 Chester Electrical Inc. is a medium-sized electrical, heating and plumbing company based in Chester, Pennsylvania in the United States. Read the business magazine extract below and answer the questions.

A *Spark* of Life at Chester Electrical?

Darren Lucas reports

The share price of struggling industrial wire and cable manufacturer Chester Electrical Inc. is finally showing a decided uptick after almost two years of steady decline.

CE's stock closed yesterday at $14.56, up $3.12 on last month's high. Newly elected CEO, Clark Brubaker, was quick to attribute the rise to talk of a possible government contract worth $15m over the next five years. Brubaker was appointed by the CE board to revive the company after his predecessor Lance Evans Jr. resigned at the end of last year.

Brubaker has a formidable reputation as a turnaround specialist, but he'll have his work cut out for him at CE. The firm has been hit hard by the recession. The collapse of the construction and automotive industries, in particular, has eaten into revenues. And the increasing use of wireless technology in IT also contributed to a $4.5m loss in its wire and cable division last year. If not for the success of CE's subsidiary heating and plumbing firms, both of which turned healthy profits, CE would have made an overall loss instead of a modest net income of $200,000.

At a press conference this morning, Brubaker remained buoyant. 'We're in great shape', he insisted. 'We're in the final stages of negotiations with the state transport department to supply all the cabling for their highway reconstruction program. And, as a result, our share price is recovering. We have zero debt and an impeccable environmental record, which, I can tell you, is really something to be proud of in this industry!'

Asked about the recent sharp rise in copper prices and the ongoing threat from Chinese competitors, Brubaker was dismissive. 'I'm not concerned. Chester Electrical is an American institution' he said. 'There were CE wires and cables in the US tanks that liberated Europe in World War 2 and in the bulldozers that cleared the debris after 9/11. And, thanks to our strength in R&D, we expect CE to continue to be a pioneer in this industry long into the future.' But does CE have a future? Time will tell.

a How significant do you think the recent upturn in CE's fortunes is?

b Why do you think there was a change of leadership last year?

c What possible dangers do you see on the horizon for CE?

d Are you convinced by Brubaker's arguments?

e Given that the government contract has yet to be finalised, do you think there could be another explanation for the sudden rise in CE's share price?

4 Two days after the press conference Clark Brubaker receives e-mails from two of his senior directors. Work in two groups. Group A see page 140. Group B see page 148. Then exchange information.

5 Report back on how the situation has changed.

6 At 11 p.m. that evening the light still burns in Clark Brubaker's office at the top of the Chester Electrical Building. Poring over the figures, he realises that the move by Black Investments might just make sense! Look at his charts and notes below and discuss as a group what problems Chester Electrical is facing.

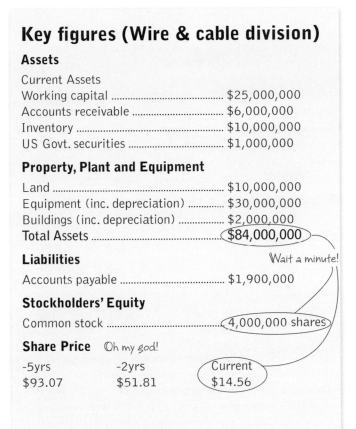

Key figures (Wire & cable division)

Assets

Current Assets

Working capital $25,000,000
Accounts receivable $6,000,000
Inventory $10,000,000
US Govt. securities $1,000,000

Property, Plant and Equipment

Land $10,000,000
Equipment (inc. depreciation) $30,000,000
Buildings (inc. depreciation) $2,000,000
Total Assets $84,000,000

Wait a minute!

Liabilities

Accounts payable $1,900,000

Stockholders' Equity

Common stock .... 4,000,000 shares

Share Price   *Oh my god!*

-5yrs	-2yrs	Current
$93.07	$51.81	$14.56

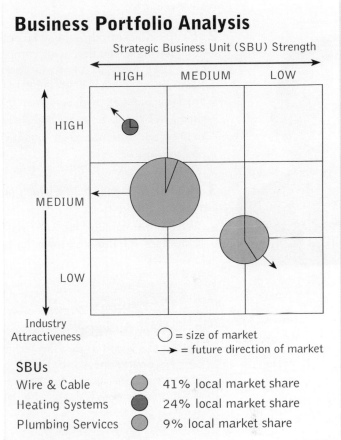

Business Portfolio Analysis

Strategic Business Unit (SBU) Strength

HIGH   MEDIUM   LOW

HIGH

MEDIUM

LOW

Industry Attractiveness

○ = size of market
→ = future direction of market

SBUs

Wire & Cable		41% local market share
Heating Systems		24% local market share
Plumbing Services		9% local market share

7 A week before the annual general meeting, Clark Brubaker receives a surprise e-mail from Sir Anthony Black himself. Turn to page 162 to read the e-mail and answer the questions.

a To what extent does Sir Anthony's interpretation of the figures in 6 agree with yours?
b What motion is he proposing to table at the AGM?
c How much support does he need at the AGM to have his motion passed?

8 In the run-up to the AGM of Chester Electrical's stockholders, the media are going crazy with the story. Turn to page 161 and take notes on points that may influence the meeting.

9 Work in two groups. Group A, you are the present management of Chester Electrical including CEO, Clark Brubaker. Turn to page 138 to prepare for your presentation at the annual general meeting. Group B, you are Sir Anthony Black and his team. Turn to page 143 to prepare for your presentation at the AGM.

10 It's time to go head to head at the AGM. Expect a hard fight with the other team! If you can, record or film your presentations, so that they can be shown to other classes, who'll take a vote on which proposal to support.

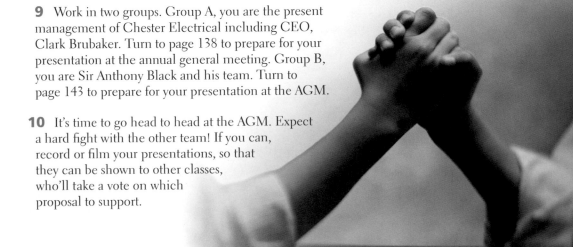

16 TELECONFERENCING

Teleconferencing is so rational, it will never succeed.

JOHN NAISBITT, MEGATRENDS

1 Is business travel a perk or a pain? With today's sophisticated telecommunications, how much of it is really necessary?

2 George Mackintosh is the serial entrepreneur who set up Geonconference, at one time Europe's fastest-growing teleconferencing company. Do you agree with what he says?

> Videoconferencing is never going to eliminate the need for at least one face-to-face meeting. If you are doing business with someone for the first time, I don't dispute the fact that you need to meet them, look them in the eye and shake their hand. After that it is likely you are going to be speaking to them on the phone or by e-mail. Videoconferencing allows you to have a more personalised relationship.

3 Read the web page below, which presents Cisco's TelePresence videoconferencing system, and answer the questions.

a What is the 'paradox' the web page describes?
b How does TelePresence solve this problem?

TELEPRESENCE
www.cisco.com

Business Benefits

We live in a world of paradox. Technology has allowed us to establish economically advantageous business operations worldwide. However, to excel in today's fast-moving business environment, you have to interact and collaborate with co-workers, partners, and customers all over the world at a moment's notice. You need to continuously innovate and transform your business model to maintain competitive edge. And you need to plan ahead to respond rapidly to unexpected issues that affect business continuity.

At the same time, much of business is still done based on the quality of your relationships with the people with whom you interact most often. To build and maintain these critical relationships, you often need to travel, which translates to lost time and reduced productivity, not to mention valuable time spent away from home and family.

All of this points to the need for a technological solution that allows the same type of face-to-face business interactions, without the constant need for global travel. That's where the concept of Cisco TelePresence comes in. It allows for real-time, face-to-face communication and collaboration over the network with colleagues, prospects, and partners, even if they're in opposite hemispheres.

4 Find two-word phrases in the text you just read which mean:

a how your business works
b an advantage you have over your competitors
c making sure your business can still operate even in a crisis.

5 ● **4.12** Now listen to a short commercial for TelePresence. Cisco recommends the system for the following kinds of meeting. Which do you think it would be best suited to? Would *you* use it?

design team meetings   consultations with vendors, suppliers and clients
in-company executive meetings   job interviews
product demonstrations   project meetings
sales presentations

TROUBLE AT THE PLANT

1 ● **4.13** Peter Devlin is CEO of the European division of Oriflamme, a manufacturer of candles and home fragrance products. Currently on a business trip to Vancouver with his marketing director Monica Brookes, Peter was woken at 2am by an unexpected phone call from his plant manager in Hamburg. Listen and answer the questions.

a What has happened at the Hamburg plant?
b Why didn't Max have any alternative?
c What happened last time there was a similar disaster?
d What does Peter suggest doing now?

2 Complete the phrasal verbs in the following sentences from 1 with the correct preposition. Use the synonyms in brackets to help you.

a We're going to have to shut .... the Hamburg plant immediately. (close)
b Otherwise, the whole thing could go ....! (explode)
c We'll have container lorries backed .... from Hamburg to Lübeck. (queueing)

3 You also heard the following idiomatic expressions in 1. Can you remember the missing words? The first two letters are given. Use the definitions in brackets to help you.

a Who on ea............... can that be? (I have no idea who this is.)
b All he...............'s broken loose here. (Everything's in chaos here.)
c Everything grinds to a ha............... . (Everything comes to a complete stop.)
d There's not a mo............... to lose. (We must act immediately.)
e I'm sorry to get you up at this unearthly ho............... . (I don't like to disturb you so late/early.)

4 Work with a partner. List the implications of a crisis like the one above.

5 Now match the following. Did you include them in your list in 4?

a a backlog of   bottleneck
b a production   hazard
c a safety   productivity
d a fall in   orders

e a damaged   manhours
f adverse   reputation
g lost   deliveries
h delayed   publicity

6 Work with a partner to discuss what immediate action Oriflamme should take to avoid the implications in 5.

7 🔊 **4.14–4.16** Listen to the emergency teleconference and answer the questions.

Extract 1

a Who hasn't been able to join the teleconference?
b Where are Peter and Monica?
c How long will it take to fix the problem at the plant?

Extract 2

a What state is the plant in?
b Why can't the orders be met completely?
c Describe Monica's response to Peter's suggestion that they buy product from their competitors to sell on to their customers 'to cover the shortfall'.
   enthusiastic ☐   positive ☐   lukewarm ☐   cool ☐   negative ☐   hostile ☐

Extract 3

a Why may Handelsmann be prepared to help?
b Is there still a safety hazard at the plant?
c What arrangement does Peter make with Otto?

8 The minutes on page 119 were taken by Françoise Fleurie directly after the teleconference. Complete them using the verbs in the boxes.

> **Points 1 and 2**
> assure authorised ~~confirmed~~ ensure estimated informed keep
>
> **Points 3 and 4**
> agreed follow mentioned OK'd opposed pointed proposed reach report smooth

Hamburg Plant Shutdown: Minutes of the Teleconference   **Date:**
Participants: Peter Devlin, Monica Brookes, Max Schiller, Otto Mendel, Françoise Fleurie Apologies: N/A
Next teleconference: 12pm ET

Point	Details	Action
1 Situation report	PD ....confirmed.... that a total shutdown of the H'burg plant has been officially .... OM .... us that the site had been evacuated in order to conduct safety checks, but was later able to .... us that the situation has now been brought under control.	OM to .... PD up to date on any changes in the situation
2 Repairs estimate	MS .... that repairs will probably take three days to carry out. The main reason given for the delay was the amount of time needed to obtain a replacement heat exchanger (48hrs).	MS to oversee and .... completion of repairs within three days
3 Production plan	PD .... rewriting the production plan to give priority to key customers, but OM .... out that we hold insufficient reserve stocks to fully meet current orders. It was generally .... that our European plants are too overstretched to transfer goods to H'burg.	OM to .... a compromise re main customers' orders and .... back to PD
4 Traded goods	PD's suggestion that traded goods be bought in from another supplier was initially .... by MB on the grounds that it would damage Oriflamme's reputation. FF .... the possibility of Handelsmann being able to help us out. This was provisionally .... by PD.	FF to .... up the Handelsmann offer and .... things over with key customers

9 Complete the puzzle using the extracts from the teleconference in 7 to help you.

a	OK, so we're just	_ _ _ t _ _ _	for Otto.
b	Let's go	_ _ e _ _	and get the meeting started.
c	Max, could you first of all just	_ _ l _	us in on what's going on?
d	Well, Pete, it's difficult to say at the	_ _ _ e _ _.	
e	I'll see what I	_ c _ _	do.
f	I'm already	_ o _ _ _ _ _	on that.
g	Monica, is there any	_ _ _ n _	in us buying in traded goods?
h	Pete, you know how I	f _ _ _	about buying from the competition.
i	Just for the time	_ e _ _ _.	
j	What	_ _ _ _ r _ _ _ _ _ _	do we have?
k	Can I	_ _ _ e	in on that?
l	I've already	_ _ _ n	on to Handelsmann.
m	OK, get back to them and see if we	c _ _	hurry things up a bit.
n	And get somebody in after-sales to	_ i _ _	round all our biggest customers.
o	OK, I'll see to it	n _ _.	
p	Otto, keep me posted if there's any	_ _ _ _ g _	in the situation.

DESERT ISLAND BLUES

The RJK Group is one of the world's leading advertising agencies with an impressive list of blue-chip clients. At the moment RJK (UK)'s top creatives are on location on the remote island of Oamu-Oamu in the South Pacific, filming a commercial for Vivacity, the new shower gel range from French cosmetics and toiletries giant Éternelle. But after eight days on the island, the film shoot is turning into a disaster.

Step 1

Work in groups of three. You are the senior management of RJK (UK). Add your names to the organigram below:

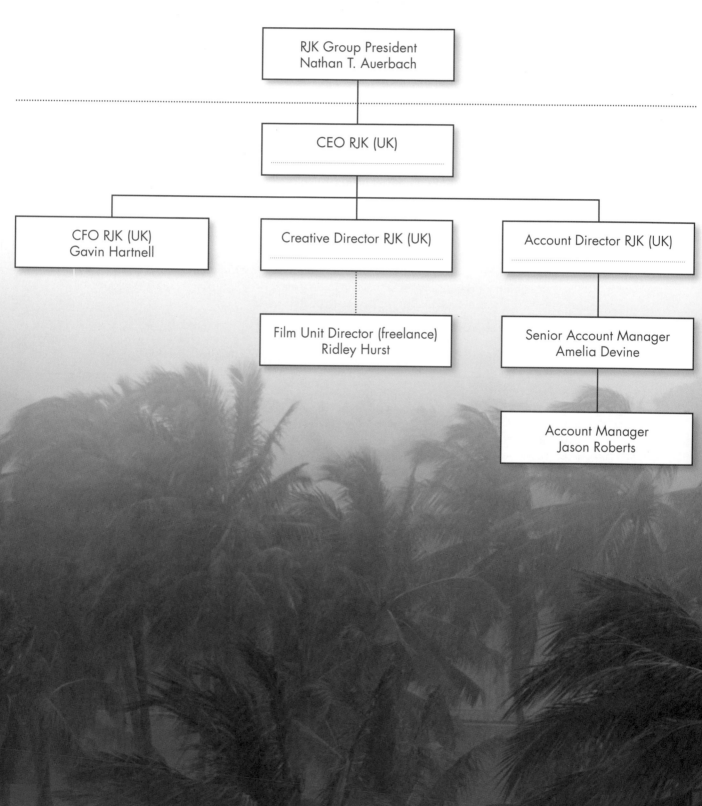

RJK Group President
Nathan T. Auerbach

CEO RJK (UK)

CFO RJK (UK)
Gavin Hartnell

Creative Director RJK (UK)

Account Director RJK (UK)

Film Unit Director (freelance)
Ridley Hurst

Senior Account Manager
Amelia Devine

Account Manager
Jason Roberts

Step 2

You are about to take part in a teleconference to decide what to do about the situation. First check your latest e-mail and make a note of any points you want to bring up.

Speaker A CEO of RJK (UK): You are currently attending an international conference in Milan. Read e-mails 1 and 2 on page 145.

Speaker B Creative Director, RJK (UK): You are currently in the middle of a pitch for the €15m Heineken account. Read e-mails 3 and 4 on page 152.

Speaker C Account Director, RJK (UK): You are currently on two weeks' holiday in Mauritius. Read e-mails 5 and 6 on page 155.

Step 3

Hold the teleconference using the agenda below. The CEO should chair the meeting. Report what you have learned from your e-mail and try to commit to a definite course of action on which you all agree. The final decision, however, is the CEO's.

Agenda: Éternelle Account – Vivacity Shoot

1 Situation report: Clarification of the situation on location

2 Financial considerations: Éternelle account – budgetary constraints

3 Action plan:
- Change of location? If so, where?
- Switch to studio filming? Implications?
- Change of actress? Contractual problems?
- How to present change of plan to client?
- Any other suggestions?

16 TELECONFERENCING
LANGUAGE LINKS

Vocabulary: Personnel and production

Organisational behaviour

Combine one word from the box on the left with one word from the box on the right to complete each sentence below.

human	prospects
incentive	burnout
promotion	benefits
appraisal	management
fringe	theory
track	scheme
leadership	record
executive	qualities
sickness	interview
selection	procedure
motivation	record
change	satisfaction
job	resources

a These days people talk about .... rather than personnel.

b Stress and overwork are both common causes of ....

c Rates of pay, recognition and opportunities for personal growth contribute to overall ....

d Demotivated employees tend to have a fairly poor .... and are prone to absenteeism.

e An .... is one way of monitoring employee performance and personal development.

f .... include health insurance, a company car and contributory pension plan.

g For hardworking and ambitious young managers there are excellent ....

h To get into Harvard Business School you have to go through a rigorous ....

i Essential .... include decisiveness and the ability to get the most out of employees.

j The successful applicant must have an MBA and an excellent .... in marketing.

k Many companies operate an .... – commissions, bonuses, and so on.

l According to one ...., giving people more autonomy is better than a higher salary.

m In a global market in which nothing stays the same, ... has a crucial role to play.

Operations management

1 Listed below are some of the terms commonly used in production departments, but the second word in each collocation has been switched with another. Can you switch them back? The first two have been done for you.

raw **goods** ◄   zero **regulations**
supply **shift**   quality **production**
assembly **control**   safety **defects**
stock **line**   carrying **time**
finished **materials** ◄   lead **costs**
night **chain**   batch **circle**

2 Which of the collocations in 1 refer to:

a unprocessed materials?

b the cost of storing and insuring stock?

c the time between planning something and putting it into action?

d manufacturing an article in groups rather than singly?

e where the factory workers put the products together?

f factory workers who start work at the end of the working day?

g a group of workers and managers who meet to discuss quality?

h a series of suppliers selling on raw materials and finished components to manufacturers?

Grammar: Reporting

1 Look at some silly things politicians have said and report each, making grammatical changes where necessary e.g. *have(n't)* → *had(n't)*, *did(n't)* → *had(n't) done*, *I* → *he*, *this* → *that*, etc.

a We have managed to distribute poverty equally. *Vietnamese Foreign Minister, Nguyen Co Thach* Mr Thach announced that ....

b I have opinions of my own, strong opinions, but I don't always agree with them. *US President George Bush Sr* President Bush affirmed that ....

c I will not tolerate intolerance. *US Senator Bob Dole* Senator Dole insisted that ....

d It isn't pollution that is harming the environment – it's the impurities in our air and water that are doing it. *US Vice President Dan Quayle* Vice-president Quayle pointed out that ....

e I haven't committed a crime – what I did is fail to comply with the law. *New York City mayor, David Dinkins* Mayor Dinkins denied that ....

f I can't believe that we are going to let a majority of the people decide what is best for this state. *US Representative John Travis* Mr Travis said that ....

2 Read the meeting extracts and write a summary of each using the words in brackets to help you.

Jon First of all, I'd like to hear your views on this.
(Jon/open/meeting/invite/comments/group)
Jon opened the meeting by inviting comments from the group.

Anna I don't think this training programme is necessary.

Niels Neither do I.
(Anna/question/need/training programme. Niels/be/same opinion)

Anna And what about the training budget for this?

Jon I haven't made up my mind about that yet.
(Anna/raise/issue/training budget. Jon/reply/not come/decision)

Niels So the board's OK about this?

Jon Absolutely.
(Jon/confirm/project/give/go-ahead)

Jon How about bringing in consultants?

Anna I don't think that's a good idea.
(Jon/wonder/if/be/good idea/bring in consultants. Anna/be/against)

Niels Anna and I think the situation should be reviewed.
(both Anna/Niels/recommend/review/situation)

Niels Well, I'm very much against these spending cuts.

Jon But they won't affect your department, Niels.

Anna Jon's right. These cuts won't affect us.
(there/be/some initial opposition/spending cuts)

Anna So, you see, Niels, the new system will actually be an improvement.

Niels Hm, well, on reflection, I suppose you're right.

Jon So do I take it we're now in agreement on this?
(issue/finally/resolve)

Jon I think this is an excellent proposal.

Anna So do I.

Niels Me too.
(there/be/unanimous agreement/proposal)

In reports

- it is more important to communicate the basic message than to repeat the exact words that were spoken
- we tend to use the passive when what was said is more important than who said it e.g. *It was suggested that ...*
- long conversations are often summed up in a simple noun phrase e.g. *There was some disagreement ...*

Phrase bank: Teleconferencing

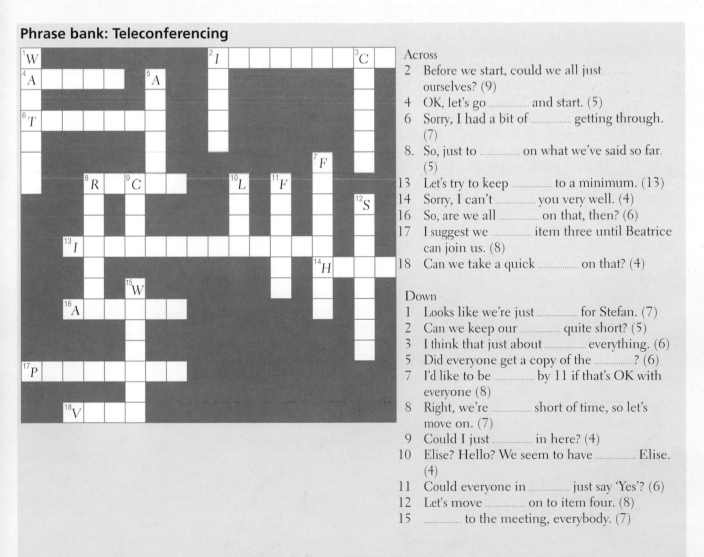

Across
2 Before we start, could we all just _____ ourselves? (9)
4 OK, let's go _____ and start. (5)
6 Sorry, I had a bit of _____ getting through. (7)
8. So, just to _____ on what we've said so far. (5)
13 Let's try to keep _____ to a minimum. (13)
14 Sorry, I can't _____ you very well. (4)
16 So, are we all _____ on that, then? (6)
17 I suggest we _____ item three until Beatrice can join us. (8)
18 Can we take a quick _____ on that? (4)

Down
1 Looks like we're just _____ for Stefan. (7)
2 Can we keep our _____ quite short? (5)
3 I think that just about _____ everything. (6)
5 Did everyone get a copy of the _____? (6)
7 I'd like to be _____ by 11 if that's OK with everyone (8)
8 Right, we're _____ short of time, so let's move on. (7)
9 Could I just _____ in here? (4)
10 Elise? Hello? We seem to have _____ Elise. (4)
11 Could everyone in _____ just say 'Yes'? (6)
12 Let's move _____ on to item four. (8)
15 _____ to the meeting, everybody. (7)

17 NEGOTIATING DEALS

Don't ever slam a door. You might want to go back in.

DON HEROLD, US NEGOTIATOR

1 Work in pairs and answer the questions.

a Are you a good negotiator? Work in groups of three to try out your negotiating skills. Speaker A see page 145. Speaker B see page 152. The third person in the group should observe and take notes on the kind of language the other two use.

b Speakers A and B, did you reach an agreement or did you get into an argument? What was the main problem you faced?

c Try the negotiation again, but this time read the extra information on page 142 first. The observer should again take notes.

d Was the negotiation easier this time? Did you manage to reach a compromise? Find out from the observer if the language used was different in the two negotiations.

2 🔘 **4.17** Listen to a management trainer giving feedback to some trainees who have just finished the negotiation in 1. Do you agree with the analysis?

3 Complete the collocations by matching the compound adjectives. Then match each adjective to its definition. You heard all the phrases in 2.

a a single-	sum game	one which is very direct
b a long-	win situation	one from which both sides feel they've gained
c a win-	issue negotiation	one that lasts
d a one-	term relationship	one where one side wins what the other side loses
e a zero-	on conflict	one that happens only once
f a head-	off deal	one where only one topic is being discussed

4 You also heard the following expressions in 2. Can you remember the missing words? The first few letters are given. The definitions in brackets may help you.

a There's little room for man................. (It's difficult to change your position.)

b win at all cos................. (do whatever you have to do to win)

c It simply wasn't worth the hass................. (It was too much trouble.)

d The negotiation ended in dead................. (Neither side was prepared to move.)

e resort to emotional black................. (make people feel guilty to get what you want)

f reach some kind of comp................. (an agreement that partially satisfies both sides)

NEGOTIATING STYLE

1 Work with a partner. Listed below are the ten most common high-pressure tactics negotiators use. One of you should match the first five to their description. The other should match the second five. Then compare notes.

Tactics

1 The shock opener
2 The vinegar and honey technique
3 The strictly off-limits ploy
4 The take-it-or-leave-it challenge
5 The I'll-have-to-check-with-head-office ploy

6 The sorry-about-my-English ploy
7 The good cop, bad cop approach
8 The once-in-a-lifetime offer
9 The salami technique
10 The last-minute demand

Description

a Make it look as though you are ready to leave the negotiating table if your demands are not met, that you are not prepared to move an inch further.

b Point out at the start that, though you are prepared to negotiate A, B and C; X, Y and Z are definitely not negotiable.

c Having obtained a concession from your opponent, inform them that you need your boss's approval before you can do what they ask in return.

d Make unreasonable demands early on in the negotiation. When you later 'see reason' and modify your demands, they'll be all the more welcome.

e Make a ridiculous initial demand (or offer), but keep a straight face as you make it. This works particularly well on inexperienced opponents.

f Don't make all your demands right at the start. Make a small demand and get agreement on it before you make the next, and the next …

g Pretend not to understand any proposal you don't like the sound of. You'll make your opponent uncomfortable by forcing them to repeat it.

h Pressurise your opponent by suggesting that the offer you're making is only for a limited period and if they don't act quickly, they'll miss it.

i After the deal has been done, make one modest extra demand in the hope that your opponent will not want to jeopardise the agreement for one small detail.

j One of your team is friendly and flexible, the other unpleasant and unreasonable. Your opponent will want to please Mr/Ms Nice to avoid Mr/Ms Nasty.

2 How might you respond to each of the tactics in 1? Can you see any risks in using them yourself?

3 ⊙ 4.18–4.19 Listen to extracts from two different negotiations. Which tactics in 1 are they trying to use? How successful are they?

Extract 1 ☐ ☐
Extract 2 ☐ ☐

4 Reconstruct the following sentences from the negotiation extracts in 3 by putting the words in bold in the correct order. Then listen again and check your answers.

a OK, so, do **take agreement we're in on I it** volume?
b Wouldn't it be a **idea before talk to good we prices go** any further?
c But in **happy principle taking about you're** forty cases, right?
d Look, **price back getting to a for** moment.
e Can you give us some **what idea of of kind figure were you** thinking of?
f There **seems slight a been have to** misunderstanding.
g With **prices respect simply are your not** competitive.
h I'm afraid that **absolute really bottom our is** line.
i Let's set the price **side moment the issue to one for**, shall we?
j I'll throw **free service 12 parts and months' as in** well.
k Now, **I can't fairer that say than**, now can I?
l What we'd really like to **movement see is more on bit a** price.
m A 6% discount **quite is had not what in we** mind.
n We were **closer hoping something for bit a** to 10%.
o I don't think **stretch far could I as as** that.
p Surely **sort we something out can** here.
q Would **meet willing be you to** us halfway?
r We might **position be a increase to in** our order.
s We'd need to **bit on flexibility see a more** terms of payment.
t I suppose **manoeuvre room there be may some for** there.

5 Look back at the expressions in 4 and answer the following questions.

a Find two phrases which mean 'bad news coming'.

b Explain the use of the word *seems* in f.

c If you change sentences e and n into the present tense, does this make them sound more or less negotiable?

d Do the question tags in i and k make it easier or more difficult to disagree?

e Does the negative question form in b make the suggestion
more persuasive? ☐   more diplomatic? ☐   both? ☐

f Why do you think the speakers use words like *slight*, *some*, *a bit* and *quite*?

g What is the overall effect of changing *wouldn't* to *isn't* in b, *can* to *will* in e, *could* to *can* in o, *would* to *are* in q, *might* to *are* in r and *may* to *is* in t?

6 The following expressions from the negotiations in 3 show strong disapproval, but think twice before using them yourself as they may cause offence. Complete them using the pairs of words in the box.

> joke + something   lot + that   other + time   way + earth

a Is this meant to be some kind of .... or ....?

b There's no .... on .... I'm paying you €4.

c Oh, come on! You'll have to do a .... better than ....

d Frankly, I think we're wasting each .... 's .... here.

7 🔊 4.20–4.24 Listen to five experienced negotiators talking about strategy and answer the questions.

Speaker 1   What does T.I.F. stand for?
Speaker 2   How can a friendly attitude be counter-productive?
Speaker 3   Why is silence more powerful than talking?
Speaker 4   How do you avoid pointless debates?
                What are the two most useful phrases in a negotiation?
Speaker 5   What did the Huthwaite Research Group discover?
                The speaker mentions three things it's better to phrase as questions. What are they?

8 Discuss the meaning of the following idioms with a partner. They were all in 7.

a Give them an inch and they'll take a mile.

b Play your cards close to your chest.

c Don't take 'no' for an answer.

NEGOTIATING A RECORDING CONTRACT

1 What kind of music are you into? Compare your tastes with a partner.

2 Work with a partner to answer the following questions. If you've no idea, just have a guess! Then check your answers in the article.

a Who are the world's wealthiest rock band?
b Who are the world's four most bankable solo performers?
c What is the bestselling album of all time?
d What are the two bestselling singles of all time?
e Which pop song has been recorded in over 2,000 versions?

Inside the music business

The world's biggest band

When Mick, Keith, Charlie and Ronnie come on stage at the Giants Stadium in New York to 40,000 adoring fans, they have the satisfaction of knowing that the Rolling Stones are easily the world's wealthiest rock band. Having generated more than $1.5 billion in gross revenues since 1989, two thirds of that earned on tour, they have made more money than even fellow megastars U2, Bruce Springsteen and Sting.

Financial acumen

Now firmly established rock legends, the Stones are also a rock-solid business. It was their chief financial advisor, London banker Prince Rupert zu Loewenstein, who was first to see that, whilst concerts make the most money, music rights provide the steadiest income stream. And though the Stones may never have produced a real blockbuster on the scale of Fleetwood Mac's *Rumours* or Pink Floyd's *Dark Side of the Moon*, Jagger and Richards have made over 40 albums and written more than 200 songs. Each time they get airplay, they collect 50 per cent of the royalties. According to *Fortune* magazine, that amounts to $56 million in the past decade. Microsoft alone paid them $4 million to use *Start Me Up* in the Windows 95 commercial.

Big business

The music business has come a long way since the Stones started out in the 60s. In those days record labels like Motown, Island and Elektra all had their own distinctive sound, and you could have a string of top ten hits but still barely be able to afford the bus fare home from your latest sell-out gig. These days just five major music companies – UMG, Sony, Warner, EMI and BMG – control 75 to 80 per cent of all commercially released recordings and the sums of money involved are huge.

Bankability

Today's most profitable solo performers remain Madonna, Elton John, Celine Dion and Garth Brooks. The back catalogues of Sinatra and Elvis also bring in millions. In fact, dead Elvis started out-earning live Elvis in 1988. The version of *Candle in the Wind* Elton John sang at the funeral of Princess Diana recently overtook Bing Crosby's *White Christmas* to become the world's bestselling single of all time and the most recorded pop song ever is The Beatles' *Yesterday*, which exists in over 2,000 different versions. But the real money has always been in albums, not singles. The top-seller is Michael Jackson's *Thriller*, which has sold over 100 million units worldwide, more than double the most successful albums of runners-up AC/DC, Eagles and Backstreet Boys.

Rights and rip-offs

With this kind of money at stake, it's not surprising that the relationship between artist and record company can be an uneasy one, with young up-and-coming bands often too dazzled by the prospect of stardom to look closely at the small print in their contracts. Even established performers like Prince and George Michael have had well-publicised clashes with their management. Courtney Love went so far as to file a lawsuit against Geffen Records to be released from her contract. And Mariah Carey found herself in the opposite situation, reputedly being paid off to the tune of £19.5 million when Virgin Records decided it didn't want to record her after all.

The future of music

But soon it may be the record companies themselves who start losing out. Piracy already costs the industry $4.3 billion a year, and with the arrival of MP3, only sound quality stands in the way of all music being burned onto CD on personal computers. Some 'Indie' music labels like Bombco produce albums exclusively on the Internet and artists as high-profile as David Bowie and Coldplay have experimented with website launches of their latest recordings. Of course, the major music companies have fought back by creating downloadable music services of their own, but with more direct access to the consumer, bands may yet be able to fulfil their dream of being immortalised without first having to sell their soul.

3 Find words and phrases in the article which mean:

a   money earned before tax and costs (paragraph 1)
b   the most regular source of money (paragraph 2)
c   highly successful album, book or film (paragraph 2)
d   money paid to artists each time their work is sold or performed (paragraph 2)
e   a series of bestselling records (paragraph 3)
f   a musical performance to which all the tickets are sold (paragraph 3)
g   earning more than (paragraph 4)
h   likely to become popular soon (paragraph 5)
i   excited at the chance of becoming stars (paragraph 5)
j   the details in a contract – often limiting your rights (paragraph 5)
k   angry disagreements (paragraph 5)
l   well-known (paragraph 6)
m   becoming famous (paragraph 6)
n   do anything to win fame (paragraph 6)

4 🔊 4.25 A major record label is considering signing a new band. Listen to an extract from a meeting between their A&R people (talent scouts) and senior management.

a   Why does Kate think they have to sign the band quickly?
b   What are the band's strengths?
c   Why isn't Ronnie as impressed as Kate?
d   Why does Ronnie sound more enthusiastic at the end of the meeting?

5 Work in two teams to negotiate a recording contract between the record company and the up-and-coming rock band you heard about in 4.

Team A you are representatives from the band The Penitents and their managers. The high-profile record company Starburst is interested in signing your band. See page 146 for your negotiating objectives.

Team B you are executives from the record company Starburst and their lawyers. You are interested in signing the promising new band The Penitents. See page 158 for your negotiating objectives.

17 NEGOTIATING DEALS

LANGUAGE LINKS

Vocabulary: Negotiations

Sounding out your opponent

Complete the questions using the prepositions in the box.

about	at	for	of	towards	with

What sort of ...
a figure were you thinking ....?
b terms would you be happy ....?
c discount were you hoping ....?
d delivery time are we talking ....?
e time-scale are we looking ....?
f deadline are we working ....?

Discussing terms

1 These are all key points you may want to discuss in a negotiation. Write in the missing vowels.

pr_c_
d_sc_ _nt
cr_d_t
v_l_m_
tr_nsp_rt_t_ _n
p_ck_g_ng
d_c_m_nt_t_ _n
g_ _r_nt_ _

c_ns_gnm_nts
m_ _nt_n_nc_
d_l_v_ry t_m_
p_ym_nt t_rms
sp_r_ p_rts
_xch_ng_ r_t_
_ft_r-s_l_s s_rv_c_
p_n_lty cl_ _s_s

2 Complete the negotiator's proposal using the words and phrases in 1. Which one is not needed?

'Well, on a repeat order of this (1) .... – 20,000 units – we'd be able to offer you what I think you'll agree is a very generous (2) .... of 17%. I think you'd also find our (3) .... extremely favourable – 120 days' (4) ...., of course – and we'd cover any fluctuations in the (5) .... between the dollar and the euro.
'We'd also be prepared to include in our quoted (6) .... all (7) .... costs. That is to say, we'd handle the shipping charges, insurance and all the necessary (8) .... to save you doing the paperwork yourself. We would have to use the same carrier for each delivery, however, which means the (9) .... would be 14 days. I hope that's acceptable to you.
'Now, all our products come with a three-year (10) .... which includes full (11) .... and (12) .... There's also a free 24-hour customer helpline, so your customers would be getting excellent (13) ....
'I think we could also be fairly flexible on (14) .... if you decided to increase or reduce your order from time to time.
'So, that just leaves the question of (15) .... We normally use styrofoam containers ...'

Negotiating procedure

Complete the phases of a negotiation using the nouns in the box. Two of them have been done for you.

atmosphere	breakthrough	champagne	concessions
deadlock	details	interests	options	phase	position
~~procedure~~	proposals	~~strategy~~	table	time-out

1 create a good	6 make counter	11 return to the negotiating ....
2 agree on a basic ~~procedure~~	7 trade	12 discuss the ....
3 state your opening	8 reach a	13 make the final ....
4 explore each other's	9 call for a	14 work out the ....
5 enter the bargaining	10 rethink your ~~strategy~~	15 crack open the ....

Grammar: Diplomacy and persuasion

Look at the negotiation extracts. Make the direct remarks more diplomatic and persuasive using the words in brackets to help you.

Negotiation 1
A This is still too expensive.
   (afraid/would still/a little out of/price range)
   I'm afraid that would still be a little out of our price range.
B Well, how much do you want to pay?
   (what sort/figure/did/in mind)
A $12 per unit.
   (were thinking/somewhere/the region of/$12 per unit)
B I can't go as low as that.
   (be honest/not a position/quite/low/this stage)

Negotiation 2

A You said we'd get 90 days' free credit.
(were promised/90 days' free credit)

B Yes, but you said you'd be placing a larger order.
(respect/was understood/rather larger)

A Look, this is getting us nowhere. We want free credit.
(doesn't seem/getting/very far/afraid/must insist/ free credit)

B Well, I can't offer you that unless you increase your order.
(unfortunately/unable/offer/you're prepared/slightly)

Negotiation 3

A We need a commitment from you today.
(had/hoping/some kind)

B Impossible! We're still unhappy about these service charges.
(this point/might/a bit difficult/not entirely/service charges)

A But you said you were OK about those!
(was assumed)

B Not at all. Look, I think we should go over these figures again.
(afraid/shouldn't we/figures/again)

Modal verbs (*would/might/could*, etc) are often used to soften the verb.

Modifiers are common (e.g. *a little difficult*).

Continuous forms keep your options open (e.g. *We were wondering*; *We had been hoping*).

Introductory softeners (e.g. *I'm afraid*) warn that bad news is coming!

Negative adjectives like *expensive* are often avoided.

seem is common (e.g. *We don't seem to agree.*)

There's a lot of approximation (e.g. *sort of*).

Qualifying phrases are common (e.g. *at the moment*).

Alternatives are preferred to *can't* and *won't*.

The passive sounds less like an accusation (not *You promised us ...*, but *We were promised ...*).

Suggestions are often phrased as negative questions (e.g. *Wouldn't it be better to ...?*).

Phrase bank: Negotiating

The following negotiation expressions are grouped according to their function. Alternate letters are missing from key words. Complete them. Then rearrange the headings.

BOPRING

a   Can you give us some i___e__ of delivery times?
b   What k__n__ of figure you were thinking of?
c   We were hoping for something a bit c_o__e_ to $3000.

MAGEERENT

d   So, in p_i_c__e, you're happy with the proposal, right?
e   So, do I take we're in a__r__e__t on payment in instalments?

PROCIMOSEM

f   Would you be w__l__i__g to meet us halfway?
g   Surely, we can s__r__ something out here.

TEXIFLIBLYI

h   I suppose there may be some room for m__n__e__v__e there.
i   I don't think I could s__r__t__h as far as that.
j   We might be in a p__s__t__o__ to increase our offer.
k   What we'd really like to see is a bit more m__v__m__n__ on price.
l   We'd need to see a little more f__e__i__i__y in terms of interest rates.

ESSONCONICS

m   OK, I'll t__r__w in free service and maintenance as well.
n   I can't say f__i__e__ than that, now can I?

EJECTORIN

o   3% is not quite what we had in m__n__.
p   I'm afraid that really is our absolute bottom l__n__.
q   With r__s__e__t, your terms are simply not competitive.

USINGFOREC

r   Look, g__t__i__g back to price for a moment.
s   Let's set the issue of discounts to one s__d__ for the moment.

COMMISUNIMIONCAT

t   There seems to have been a slight m__s__n__e__s__a__d__n__.
u   I think we may be talking at c__o__s-p__r__o__e__ here.

18 THE SHAPE OF THINGS TO COME

My interest is in the future because I'm going to spend the rest of my life there.

CHARLES E. KETTERING, ENGINEER AND INVENTOR

1 How much of your job involves planning for the future? What was the last planning meeting you attended? What was the outcome? Tell a partner about it.

2 In a time of rapid change, is there any point in trying to predict the future or do you agree with Dilbert creator, Scott Adams?

> " There are many methods for predicting the future. For example, you can read horoscopes, tea leaves, tarot cards or crystal balls. Collectively, these methods are known as 'nutty methods'.
>
> Or you can put well-researched facts into sophisticated computer models, more commonly referred to as 'a complete waste of time'. "

3 All the adjectives in the box can be used to talk about the future. Add them to the timeline below:

distant   foreseeable   immediate   near   not-too-distant

SOONER ◄─────────────────────────────────► LATER
In the .... future.

4 Complete the sentences below with words from the boxes. Then finish at least five of them with some predictions of your own concerning business, politics, the environment, health, energy, leisure time or just life in general:

era   future   indications   opportunities   possibility   way

a I think one industry that definitely has a bright .... is …
b Recent developments in … open up all kinds of exciting
....
c All the .... are that we're going to see …
d I think we're about to enter an .... of …
e As far as I can see, … is still a very long .... off.
f As far as … is concerned, we can't exclude the .... that
…

future   horizon   prospects   outlook   store   verge

g I think the long-term .... for … are …
h I think the … facing the bleakest .... is …
i I believe we may be on the .... of discovering …
j The .... for anyone involved in the … business is uncertain.
k There seems to be political change on the .... in …
l It's difficult to tell what lies in .... for …

5 Present your ideas to the rest of your group. Be prepared to support your views.

WELCOME TO THE MACHINE

1 Is there really such a thing as artificial intelligence? Surely, intelligence is more than memory and storage capacity. So are claims about computers becoming more intelligent than us anything more than media hype?

2 🔘 **4.26** Listen to a podcast about the future of intelligent computers. How do the pictures and figures below relate to the key point made?

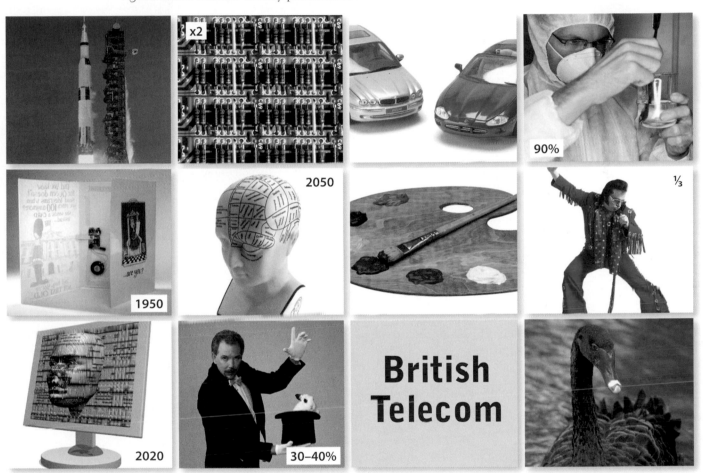

3 The podcast you just listened to takes a light-hearted look at computer technology and innovation, but do the developments it mentions have any serious implications:

- ethically?
- financially?
- politically?

Use the discussion phrase bank to help you.

4 The world of IT is full of acronyms. Are you familiar with the following key ones? Use the words in the box to write them out in full and then test a partner to see if they know what they mean. You can use several of the words more than once.

> **Discussion phrase bank**
>
> I think we have to ask ourselves whether we really want … or not.
>
> These forecasts take absolutely no account of …
>
> The consequences of … could be far-reaching – for example, …
>
> The real danger is that …
>
> I'm quite positive / sceptical about …
>
> But I really can't see us allowing …

aided	area	business	computer	consumer	customer	design	employee	enterprise
information	integrated	local	management	manufacturing	marketing	planning	network
relationship	resource	system	wide					

LAN   WAN   MIS   CRM   MRP   ERP   MRM   CIM   B2B   B2C   B2E   C2C   CAD/CAM

FAITH IN THE FUTURE

1 The unforgettably named Faith Popcorn is the founder and CEO of BrainReserve, a marketing consultancy whose clients include BMW, Avon, Campbell Soup Company, PepsiCo, Johnson & Johnson, Bacardi, Kodak and American Express.

One of the world's most talked-about Trend-analysts and futurists, widely known as 'the Nostradamus of marketing', her company's mantra is: *If you knew everything about tomorrow, what would you do differently today?*

Displayed on the right are sixteen of the key current social Trends in the BrainReserve TrendBank. Work with a partner. One of you should match the names to the even-numbered Trends and the other to the odd-numbered Trends.

Even-numbered Trends
Anchoring   Atmosfear   Being Alive   Down-aging   Egonomics
EVEolution   Fantasy Adventure   Pleasure Revenge

Odd-numbered Trends
99 Lives   Cashing Out   Clanning   Cocooning   Future Tense
Icon Toppling   S.O.S.   Vigilante Consumer

2 Now compare ideas with your partner, explaining why you chose the names you did.

3 Find phrases in the TrendBank which mean:
a   people who think like you
b   based on styles of the past
c   mentally and emotionally stable
d   contributing to society in some way
e   take a less well-paid but less pressured job
f   when customers get angry with companies
g   customers refusing to buy a product in protest
h   a secure place
i   employees are able to change when they work

4 Which of the Trends best describe your own attitudes and behaviour?

5 Take 10–15 minutes to think about which of the Trends might have most influence on the business you're in and prepare to give a short presentation on how the TrendBank could:
a   change one way in which you do business
b   lead to the development of a new product or service.

6 Field questions from the rest of your group.

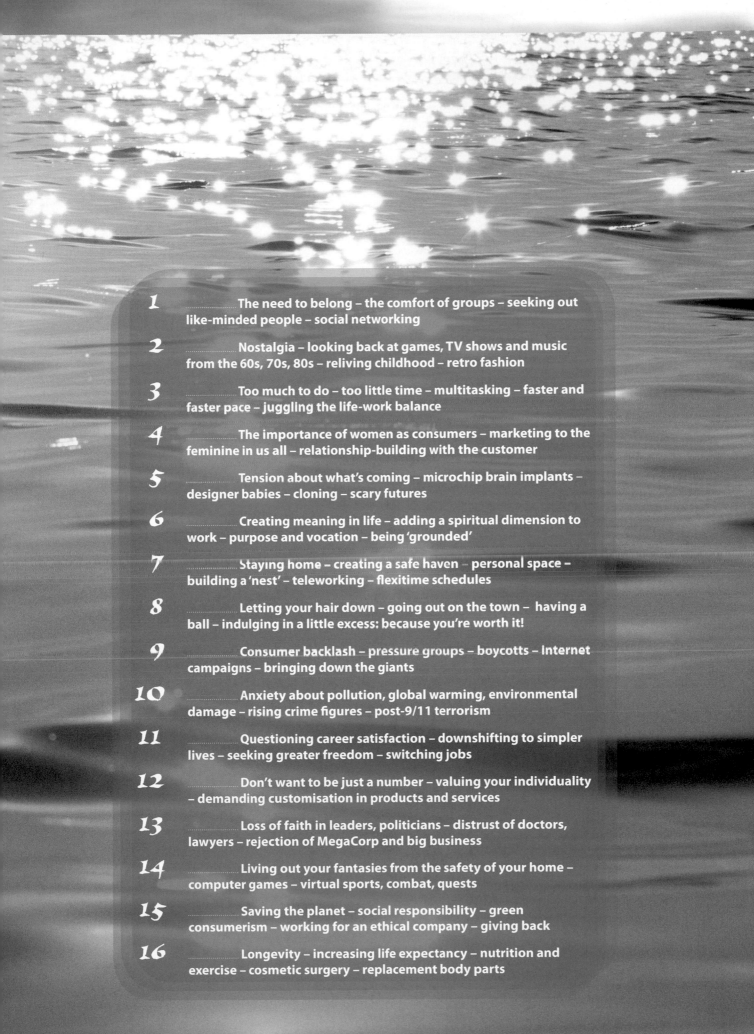

1 .... The need to belong – the comfort of groups – seeking out like-minded people – social networking

2 .... Nostalgia – looking back at games, TV shows and music from the 60s, 70s, 80s – reliving childhood – retro fashion

3 .... Too much to do – too little time – multitasking – faster and faster pace – juggling the life-work balance

4 .... The importance of women as consumers – marketing to the feminine in us all – relationship-building with the customer

5 .... Tension about what's coming – microchip brain implants – designer babies – cloning – scary futures

6 .... Creating meaning in life – adding a spiritual dimension to work – purpose and vocation – being 'grounded'

7 .... Staying home – creating a safe haven – personal space – building a 'nest' – teleworking – flexitime schedules

8 .... Letting your hair down – going out on the town – having a ball – indulging in a little excess: because you're worth it!

9 .... Consumer backlash – pressure groups – boycotts – Internet campaigns – bringing down the giants

10 .... Anxiety about pollution, global warming, environmental damage – rising crime figures – post-9/11 terrorism

11 .... Questioning career satisfaction – downshifting to simpler lives – seeking greater freedom – switching jobs

12 .... Don't want to be just a number – valuing your individuality – demanding customisation in products and services

13 .... Loss of faith in leaders, politicians – distrust of doctors, lawyers – rejection of MegaCorp and big business

14 .... Living out your fantasies from the safety of your home – computer games – virtual sports, combat, quests

15 .... Saving the planet – social responsibility – green consumerism – working for an ethical company – giving back

16 .... Longevity – increasing life expectancy – nutrition and exercise – cosmetic surgery – replacement body parts

THE FUTURE'S UNWRITTEN

1 Planning for the future isn't easy when we don't even know what industries will exist in ten to fifteen years' time! Look at the list of jobs below. How secure do you think they are? What future social changes and new technologies could potentially threaten them? Which have the best long-term prospects?

> high street bank manager   business lawyer   record company executive   surgeon   English teacher
> fast food restaurant franchisee   actor   video rental store manager   book publisher   priest   engineer
> advertising executive   comedian   production line worker   biochemist   police officer   web designer

2 Some cultures seem better able to take risks and live with uncertainty than others. Divide the following countries into risk-takers and risk-avoiders. Then check your answers on page 159. Are there any surprises?

> Japan   China   UK   Brazil   Italy   Denmark   USA   France   Germany   Poland   Turkey   Hong Kong

RISK-TAKERS	RISK-AVOIDERS

3 🔵 **4.27** Futurescape is a management consultancy that specialises in 'scenario planning', advising its clients on how to prepare for possible futures. You've just joined the company as new consultants. Listen to Alison Fielding, head of T&D, explaining how 'scenario planning' works and answer the questions:

a   Who pioneered scenario planning and with what success? Is it a short- or long-term strategy?
b   Explain two of the stages of a STEP analysis to a partner and let them explain the other two to you.
c   What kind of problems are 'long fuse, big bang' problems?

4 Alison mentions the importance of starting by 'taking an industry snapshot to get the big picture'. Take a snapshot of the industry you're in or one that you know well and compare with the rest of your group.

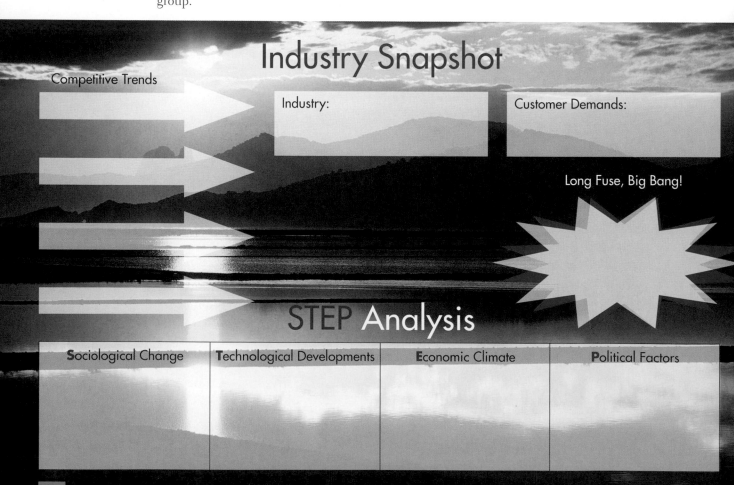

5 🔵 **4.28** Are you ready for your first assignment? Listen to a voicemail from the senior partner in the firm, Iván Ferreiro, and take notes on what you need to do.

6 Now, in your team, referring to your industry snapshots (where appropriate) and to the scenarios in the Futurescape database below, compile a short report for the client.

Scenario 1: Powershift World

In Powershift World women begin to take over in the small and medium-sized business sector as big businesses fail. Youth Culture is marginalized as marketers shift their attention to the growing number of adventure-seeking, computer-literate WOOPIES (well-off older persons).

Social services collapse under the burden of an ageing population and there is an influx of young immigrants from developing countries required to fill an undersupplied labor market. Racial tension mounts.

The BRIC economies of Brazil, Russia, India and China now dominate as the USA loses influence and fragments into separate trading blocs and the EU completely disintegrates. There are now three world languages: Chinese in the East, English in Europe and Spanish in the West. It is the end of globalization as we know it.

Scenario 2: Eco World

In Eco World communitarian values triumph in Europe and, in response to overwhelming scientific evidence, the environmental agenda gains a real foothold there. This leads to much stricter legislation on carbon emissions and the preservation and recycling of natural resources.

Slimmed-down, digitized governments now make major political decisions by means of public referenda. There is large investment in public services and a more even distribution of wealth. Dirty technologies are banned, forcing developing countries to adopt clean-tech solutions. Even China, in order to maintain its economic dominance, is forced to address its poor record on pollution.

Europe experiences a kind of renaissance, but the USA, still reeling from global recession, refuses to comply with environmental regulations and heads towards isolationism.

Scenario 3: Ego World

Ego World is populated by individualistic consumers rather than citizens. Now that technology can create unlimited customized choices, companies have to become incredibly agile just to survive. Trends change too fast to track. The customer is god.

In the developed world, singletons (people who live alone) represent 60% of all adults and forced leisure-time makes up 70% of the day. Almost all real business is now effectively outsourced, leaving only the creative industries, tourism and financial speculation as viable career choices.

Corporations rule supreme and take an active part in politics. Governments themselves operate virtually as corporations. Public services have all been privatized and businesses succeed only by being cheap (IKEA, Dell) or sexy (Gucci, BMW). Anything in between dies the death.

Scenario 4: Cyber World

Cyber World fragments into a community of flexi-time workers organized by job rather than geography. The Net is now the great de-centralizer with virtual workers and online education the norm. Nationality is meaningless.

In what will come to be known as 'the trans-human era' people become more like computers and computers more like people. Gene therapy and electronic implants create an affluent super-class. Offline life is seen to be boring by comparison with the many attractions of cyberspace.

India has the new Silicon Valley and Indian English takes over from Anglo-American English as a lingua franca, especially in IT. Almost all software has become so cheap it has made the leap to freeware. But a counter-reaction to too much technology creates a booming market for traditional, hand-made 'comfort' goods and retro classics.

01 BUSINESS OR PLEASURE?

Corporate entertainment
Group A

British Grand Prix, Silverstone

(100 km from central London)

Engines roar, tyres squeal and sparks fly as two-million-dollar supercars accelerate from 0 to 250 kph in under seven seconds. 200,000 spectators descend on Silverstone for this fabulous sporting occasion that attracts a worldwide TV audience of 350 million. From your trackside seat you'll soak up all the atmosphere of one of the most glamorous and spectacular events in the motor-racing calendar. VIP treatment; breathtaking action!

VIP box and hospitality tent: €1,000 per person

Banquet on board the Royal Yacht Britannia, Edinburgh

(600 km from London)

Dinner on board Britannia at her permanent berth in Scotland's capital is a once-in-a-lifetime experience – oysters and aperitifs, tables decorated with ice sculptures, waiters in white gloves and music played on the very piano Princess Diana used to practise on. You'll be seated in the state dining room where the Queen once entertained world leaders like Boris Yeltsin, Bill Clinton and Nelson Mandela. Why not really roll out the red carpet for your guests and make your corporate hospitality event a truly 'royal' occasion?

Five-course dinner, military band, fireworks: €500 per person

02 EXCHANGING INFORMATION

Queries and comments

Speaker A

1 Read out the following report to your partner. There are seven discrepancies in it (marked in **bold**). Can your partner spot them? If not, keep reading. Apologise for or justify any discrepancies your partner points out. If you lose your place in the text, ask your partner: 'Where was I?'

> Report: World trade fair
>
> Our exhibition stand at the World Trade Fair in Munich was very successful again this year, attracting visitors from all over **Munich**. Although this was **our first appearance** at the Fair, our people did a great job and handed out **nearly three** brochures.
>
> We met a group of Austrian business people at the **Frankfurt** Hilton, where we were staying, and arranged a formal meeting with them by the **pool**. They were very interested in our products and said they would e-mail us as soon as they got back to **Australia**.
>
> Apparently, next year the Fair is being held outside Europe for the first time – **Paris** here we come!

2 Now listen to your partner reading out a report. There are also seven discrepancies in it. Can you spot them? Remain polite no matter how confused your partner seems!

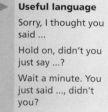

▶ **Useful language**
Sorry, I thought you said …

Hold on, didn't you just say …?

Wait a minute. You just said …, didn't you?

CASE STUDY: HEAD TO HEAD

Group A: The Board of Chester Electrical

Most of the important figures will already have been presented in detail in the company's annual report. Your job is to persuade the stockholders at the AGM that they should reject Black's motion to replace the board with his own people and sell off the firm.

Supporting arguments you could make: the company is at the beginning of a period of gradual but sustained recovery; selling off shares now would be premature; if Black's motion is defeated, there's a good chance CE can still win the DoT contract; a business is worth more than the price of its stock; people like Black are parasites who have no interest in businesses, but only want to make a quick killing; this area needs jobs and we have a responsibility to our employees to ride out the recession; CE is a true American company with a reputation for innovation.

Your team presentation should last no more than five minutes.

02 EXCHANGING INFORMATION

Choose a bingo card from the selection below.

04329

blame-storming	upskill	core competencies
customer-centric	empowerment	drill down
paradigm shift	the big picture	the long game
buy-in	scope out	outside the box

04330

scope out	grassroots	buy-in
ramp up	drill down	core competencies
the big picture	mindset	customer-centric
the long game	bottom line	blame-storming

04331

benchmark	ramp up	scope out
the long game	upskill	bottom line
proactive	drill down	the big picture
customer-centric	blame-storming	buy-in

04332

the next level	the big picture	benchmark
buy-in	blame-storming	the long game
scope out	customer-centric	paradigm shift
outside the box	drill down	ramp up

04333

mindset	customer-centric	push-back
drill down	reality check	the long game
grassroots	scope out	upskill
core competencies	the big picture	paradigm shift

04334

bottom line	ramp up	reality check
blame-storming	the long game	scope out
the big picture	core competencies	customer-centric
push-back	drill down	synergise

04335

synergise	reality check	scope out
drill down	customer-centric	benchmark
upskill	the next level	the big picture
bottom line	the long game	push-back

04336

empowerment	the long game	proactive
paradigm shift	the big picture	drill down
push-back	reality check	scope out
customer-centric	ramp up	benchmark

02 EXCHANGING INFORMATION

Speaker A

Proposal: Positive discrimination

- Board alarmed at low number of women in management positions
- Men currently outnumber women 13:1
- Plan to introduce policy of positive discrimination
- For eighteen-month trial period only women appointed to management positions
- No applications for promotion from male employees accepted
- Possible 'strategic demotion' of men to create more opportunities for women

Proposal: Work environment

- A lot of staff (35%) complaining about feeling tired and stressed
- Board thinks one of main causes may be poor work environment
- Feng shui expert called in – recommendations include radical changes to office layout
- Reception area to be turned into a water-garden to create positive 'chi' (energy)
- Internal walls to be removed to improve 'channels of communication'
- Desks ideally to be moved during the year to remain 'in harmony with the seasons'

04 VOICE AND VISUALS

Giving feedback

Speaker A: Boss

You are a senior partner in a major management consultancy. You have just attended a presentation by one of your best consultants to an important Taiwanese client. Unfortunately, the presentation was an absolute disaster from start to finish.

You forced a smile during the presentation but are now going to tell Speaker B exactly what you thought of their performance. Base your criticisms on the following information. Try to end on a positive note by making some suggestions for future presentations.

- Speaker B was wearing a T-shirt and jeans. The Taiwanese must have felt deeply insulted.
- You could hardly hear a word Speaker B said.
- They made no attempt to modify their English for a foreign audience.
- The PowerPoint slides were not working properly – it all looked very unprofessional.

> **Useful language**
>
> Why did/didn't you ...?
>
> You should(n't) have ...
>
> Couldn't you at least have ...?
>
> Don't you think it would have been a good idea to ...?
>
> Well, anyway, in future I suggest you ...
>
> And next time – if there is a next time – just make sure you ...

- The handouts were virtually illegible. There was no excuse for this: there was plenty of time to prepare.
- You have no idea what happened to the video you were expecting to see.
- You nearly died when they cracked a joke about China. The Taiwanese left the room in silence, clearly not amused.

05 PROBLEMS ON THE PHONE

Dealing with a chatterbox

Speaker A

If you don't know Speaker B well, swap lists of the following with them before you start your telephone conversation:

- your partner's name, job and main interest
- your children's names, ages and main interests
- when and where you went on your last holiday
- your own main interest
- your favourite sport (spectator or player?)
- the name of a close colleague
- a problem you've been having at work recently

You are director of the purchasing department for Mi Casa, a large chain of furniture stores in Mexico. You like to get in touch with your suppliers from time to time – not necessarily to do business, just to maintain the relationship. It's 10 a.m. on Friday morning, most of your week's work is done and the weekend is fast approaching. Phone Speaker B, the sales director of Möbelkunst, a designer furniture manufacturer in Berlin, for a little chat.

Keep the conversation going by asking lots of questions (using Speaker B's list as a starting point). You don't really want to do any business today, but Möbelkunst's stylish chairs, tables and lamps have been very popular with your customers who love the bright colours and modern designs. If the terms were right, you might want to increase your order – even double it – for a trial period.

CASE STUDY: HEAD TO HEAD

Group A

Read the following e-mail from Chester Electrical's chief financial officer, Susan Cameron, and summarise the main points to group B.

From: s.cameron@chesterelectrical.com
To: c.brubaker@chesterelectrical.com

Subject: Stock situation

Clark

Good news and bad.

The good news is that our stock price is continuing to rise – currently at $16.11 and, by the looks of it, still climbing sharply. But keep the champagne on ice.

The bad news is that, as I suspected, this is not entirely the result of the positive market sentiment surrounding our talks with the Penn Transport Dept., but of the recent acquisition of a considerable amount of CE stock by three different organisations going by the names of AWC, Drax Metals and the Orion Group.

But wait, it gets worse! My sources inform me that these three companies are actually buying on behalf of an anonymous investor. I say anonymous, but the word is it's Black Investments. If that name doesn't send a chill of horror through your veins, it should. It's owned by an ex-Brit turned naturalized American by the name of Sir Anthony Black. Still calls himself Sir Anthony, even though he switched nationalities to get round our foreign direct investment laws. Let's just say he specialises in viciously hostile takeover bids.

If this rumour turns out to be true, then Black now already owns 18% of CE stock – not enough to launch a takeover bid just yet, but enough to pose a real threat. As you know, the board jointly owns 29% of the stock. Employees own a further 3%. But that still leaves exactly half the stock in the hands of private investors. So we're certainly vulnerable.

Call me as soon as you get in, will you? We urgently need to talk.

Sue

05 PROBLEMS ON THE PHONE

Tackling problems

Speaker A

At the end of each conversation, give Speaker B a score out of ten for (a) helpfulness and (b) assertiveness.

1 You are having problems with your computer – it either won't do something you want it to or it's just done something you definitely didn't want it to (you decide which). Phone Speaker B and see if they can give you any advice. If not, ask them who you should phone instead.

2 Speaker B, your boss, will phone you with a problem. It's 6 p.m. and you are just on your way out of the office when the phone rings. You've arranged to go out with a few colleagues this evening (you decide when and where). This is the fifth time this month your boss has held you up right at the end of the day.

3 You have just been promoted and Speaker B is now your boss. You particularly like your great new office (you decide why), which is exactly what you need to do your new job (you decide why). Someone told you today that a colleague from an overseas division of your company may be coming to work at your division for a few months and you are waiting for your boss to phone and give you the details.

4 Speaker B is usually a star member of your team, but at the moment they are a month behind with an important report and you are under pressure from head office to get it completed on schedule (within the next two weeks). You think the best idea is to bring someone else in (you decide who) to help get the report finished in time and team present the final results to senior management with Speaker B. Phone and make your suggestion as tactfully but forcefully as you can.

06 LEADING MEETINGS

In the chair

Meeting 1

Should genetic tests decide job prospects?

What if you were faced, at a job interview, with a test that would tell whether you could expect to develop Alzheimer's or Parkinson's disease? What if you were turned down because of that tiny bit of your DNA?

This scary scenario is coming closer to reality with the development of a technology that will allow employers to carry out genetic tests and get the results in the time it takes to stroll to the canteen and have a cup of coffee.

Would it be ethical? Would it be legal? Would it be acceptable to recruiters, let alone society at large? The moral debate lags behind the scientific advances. A technology that will identify DNA electronically has been developed by Dr John Clarkson and his colleagues at the company Molecular Sensing. They plan to miniaturise it and build a hand-held device that will produce results in less than 30 minutes.

Adapted from *The Sunday Times*

Meeting 2

EMPLOYERS SPY ON WORKERS

Big Brother is watching. And it's increasingly likely to be your boss.

She might be recording the casual conversations between you and your co-worker, or tracking e-mails on your company computer, or watching the goings-on in the staff lounge.

Sounds like an invasion of your privacy? Think again. Most employee monitoring in the workplace is perfectly legal, and it happens more than most people realise.

Two-thirds of US businesses eavesdrop on their employees in some fashion – on the phone, via videotape and through e-mail and Internet files – according to a survey by the American Management Association International.

In fact, employers can trace everything from deleted e-mails and voice mails to the exact computer keys a worker strikes. Special software can follow employees' paths across the Internet and high tech employee badges even let bosses track their workers' movements within an office building.

Adapted from *Knight Ridder Newspapers*

Meeting 3

Creative way to better management

From Chopin to Schubert and jazz to jive, music, along with theatre, film, drawing and painting, is now widely used in UK business schools to help executives improve their management skills.

It may all be great fun, but does it work? Opinion is divided. Strongly against is David Norburn, director of Imperial College Management School, London. He says that after a few drinks he could probably make a case for any human activity having managerial relevance. 'Weber's clarinet concerto and emotion; jazz and chaos theory; sex and timing.'

His argument is that when executives and MBAs invest time in business school programmes they want rigorous and relevant training.

But staff at many of the UK's leading business schools, such as Patricia Hodgins at the London Business School, disagree. 'The key to creativity is being relaxed and being able to think laterally. Using arts, music and theatre helps us to find that.'

Adapted from *The Financial Times*

02 EXCHANGING INFORMATION

The language of meetings

Eight of these nouns will complete the conversations:

answer	fact	idea	issue	opinion	option	point
position	problem	question	situation	view		

08 PROMOTING YOUR IDEAS

Audience analysis

Exercise 1 answers

USA – Extract 3	UK – Extract 5
Germany – Extract 1	France – Extract 6
Japan – Extract 4	Kuwait – Extract 2

CASE STUDY: A WINNING FORMULA

1 Sources claim that Sonia Cassidy apparently had her sights set on the team boss position, in spite of her relative ignorance of the technical side of the business, and was furious when it went to François. Feels Enrico owed her a shot at the top job. Too shrewd a businesswoman to cause trouble, but will be looking for weaknesses in François's management strategy. Rumour reliability factor: 7/10.

2 Repeated complaints from female members of the team about Toivo and his generally sexist attitudes. Nothing in writing yet, but how long can it be before there's a formal harassment charge? Rumour reliability factor: 9/10.

3 Mutterings in the team that Giancarlo and Debora have been getting a little 'too close' off the track. The paparazzi have so far not caught up with them, but they have been seen frequenting nightclubs and bars together after races. Rumour reliability factor: 5/10.

4 Oskar may have been in talks with a rival team about a position as Technical and R&D Director. This would be a step up for him and a way of finally parting company with Toivo. If it's true, the team in question is quite low in the rankings, but has some promising drivers and a lot of money to spend. Rumour reliability factor: 7/10.

17 NEGOTIATING DEALS

The last one in the store

Extra information for second negotiation

You and the other speaker are ex-neighbours and very good friends. Your kids even used to play together. You both moved to different areas of the city about six months ago and meant to keep in touch, but, what with work and settling into new homes, you just haven't had the time.

09 RELATIONSHIP-BUILDING

Getting out of the office

Speaker A

Situation 1

Background: You're an IT security specialist. You're playing golf with Speaker B, the IT director of a major insurance company and one of your best customers. It's a beautiful spring morning.

Situation: You're playing really well today. Although Speaker B is a much better golfer than you, you were actually a shot ahead on the sixteenth hole, but you've just dropped two shots on the seventeenth. Damn! It was looking as though you might even beat them for a change.

Hidden Agenda: You've heard a rumour that Speaker B may be looking to engage another IT security consultancy. You've always got on well with them, but you know your company's fees are not the most competitive. When they invited you to play golf with them today, you saw it as your chance to find out what's going on.

Speaker B will start.

Situation 2

Background: You're a sales director for an international sports goods company. You're playing tennis with Speaker B, a new member of your sales team. When you started playing it was a warm summer afternoon, but it's just clouded over and looks like it might even rain.

Situation: You pride yourself on being an excellent tennis player, but Speaker B, who you haven't played before, is totally destroying you – 6-2 in the first set and 4-1 up in the second. This hasn't put you in a very good mood, especially as your company's marketing director, who's playing on the next court, seems to be thoroughly enjoying your humiliating defeat!

Hidden Agenda: Although Speaker B joined you with excellent qualifications and a good track record in sales, they don't seem to be fitting in very well. The other sales personnel complain that they're not much of a team-player and that they act superior to the rest of the staff. In fact, Speaker B is creating something of a morale problem. The only good thing about them is that, if they always play this well, you'll have no trouble beating marketing at the annual interdepartmental match!

You start: There's something I've been meaning to talk to you about …

09 RELATIONSHIP-BUILDING

Questionnaire analysis

How you network in specific situations will, of course, be influenced by many factors, but, in general, the most effective strategy will be: 1a, 2c, 3b, 4b, 5c and 6c.

1c, 2b, 5b and 6a could be risky.

3a and 4c might be unfair to other people.

1b, 3c, 4a and 5a may show a certain lack of assertiveness.

09 RELATIONSHIP-BUILDING

Host: Ulterior motive

You're considering promoting your guest to a more senior post (you decide what) at your company's subsidiary in Melbourne. You are very impressed with your guest's work record and general management ability, but you haven't made up your mind yet about the promotion. So, drop a few hints during the evening and see what the reaction is. Don't be too specific at this stage and be ready to change the subject if things don't go according to plan!

CASE STUDY: HEAD TO HEAD

Group B: Representatives of Black Investments

Most of the important figures will already have been presented in detail in the company's annual report. Your job is to persuade the stockholders at the AGM that they should accept Black's motion to replace the board with his own people and sell off the firm.

Supporting arguments you could make: the company has no future; two lucky acquisitions (the heating and plumbing businesses) have kept it afloat so far, but the prospects are bleak longer-term; too many factors count against CE – a decline in the industries it services, failing to keep pace with new technology; if not for Black Investments buying up stock, CE's share price would have continued to fall – it was only a sixth of what it was five years ago when Black first made his move; sell and invest the money elsewhere; there'll never be a better time than now to sell – the figures speak for themselves.

Your team presentation should last no more than five minutes.

10 TAKING DECISIONS

5 While staying in a hotel in Paris, you wake up to find the whole place is on fire. Your way down is blocked and you end up on the roof. Do you:

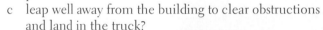

a take a long run-up and jump onto the next building (a distance of four and a half metres)?

b jump six floors down and land on your back in a truck packed with soft insulation materials?

c leap well away from the building to clear obstructions and land in the truck?

6 On a business trip to Amsterdam your taxi skids on a patch of oil and plunges off the road and into a canal. In seconds you are half-underwater. Do you:

a force open the door and swim to safety (taking the driver with you)?

b wind down the window fully to let the water in?

c wind the window up to trap air inside the car in case you sink?

7 You agree to do a parachute jump for charity with a group of friends. But as you free-fall from 4000m at 200 kph both your parachute and emergency chute fail to open. Do you:

a keep struggling with your emergency chute? It must work, damn it!

b grab hold of the nearest member of the group before they open their chute?

c take valuable time to attach yourself to the chest straps of another parachutist?

8 Whilst snorkelling off the Great Barrier Reef in North-Eastern Australia, you suddenly see a large shark swimming swiftly towards you from the depths. Do you:

a try to attack the shark's eyes?

b punch the shark on the nose?

c splash about and make a noise to frighten it away?

10 TAKING DECISIONS

Crisis management

Strategy Meeting

Client: Coca-Cola Co.

- Should there be an immediate product recall in spite of the lack of solid evidence?
- In the absence of any proof of contamination, should Coca-Cola appeal to the four European governments to lift their ban? Or even threaten legal action against them?
- Should any decision be postponed until the final results of the tests become available? Or will this just give the competition time to increase its market share?
- How should the company persuade the public that there's no real threat?
- Should there be an official apology? Or would that look like an admission of guilt?
- Should Coca-Cola put the blame firmly on its Belgian bottling plant and their shippers, whilst exporting Coke directly to Europe from the USA?
- What kind of public relations exercise would restore confidence in the world's number one brand?

13 MAKING AN IMPACT

The last paradise on earth?

Group A: Bhutanese Preservation Party

1 The success of our current gradual development programme
   - Since 1993 life expectancy has increased from 49 (for women) and 46 (for men) to 66 (for both).
   - In the same period infant mortality has halved.
   - 78% of the population now have access to safe drinking water.
   - Adult literacy has increased from 4% to 54%.
   - 95% of people who leave Bhutan to work or study abroad return.
2 The risks of overdevelopment
   - Alaska, Bali, Mongolia and Tahiti once enjoyed a lifestyle like that in Bhutan and have suffered irreparably from too-rapid development.
   - The arrival in Bhutan of the Internet and cable and satellite television stations like MTV is causing envy and dissatisfaction among Bhutan's young people.
3 The natural environment
   - The Bhutanese forests are home to many species of flora and fauna, which have as much right to be here as we have – 60% of Bhutan should remain virgin forest and 26% as parkland.
   - Many of Bhutan's indigenous species are on the endangered list: the red panda, snow leopard and tiger

(now the third most endangered animal on Earth).
   - The mountains are sacred and must be kept off-limits to tourists and climbers, who would disturb the spirits.
   - We welcome respectful tourists but their number must be restricted to the present quota of 7,000 a year.
4 Our religion
   - Our historic monasteries and temples are places of worship, not tourist attractions.
   - The teachings of the Buddha show that what matters is our long-term karma or spiritual development, not short-term gain and profit margins.

14 OUT AND ABOUT

In-flight conversations

Speaker A

Hold short conversations with a fellow passenger, Speaker B, on three different international flights.

Use the information below to get you started, but invent any extra information you need to keep the conversation going for a minute or two.

1 **Flight BA1311 from Dubai to London Heathrow, business class (9pm)**
   - You are an engineer travelling back from Dubai, where you have been working for Royal Dutch Shell (Emirates) for the last five years, to take up a senior position at head office in London.
   - Your three-year-old son is accompanying you on the flight, but your partner won't be joining you in the UK for another couple of weeks.
   - You're not looking forward to the flight much because your son is quite a hyperactive child and you can never sleep on planes anyway.
   - Try to start a conversation with the person sitting next to you, Speaker B. They seem to be playing with their hand-held computer at the moment.

2 **Flight AF6001 from Paris to Rio de Janeiro, economy class (3am)**
   - You are a product manager for Pfizer Pharmaceuticals on your way from a project meeting in Paris to another meeting in Rio.
   - You have an appointment with a group of Brazilian research chemists with whom you are collaborating on a new kind of miracle travel sickness pill, which, if all goes well, could be on the market in six months.
   - So far your journey has been a nightmare. Your original flight was cancelled due to bad weather and the only seat you could get was in economy class on the red-eye (a night flight, on which you do not get enough sleep) leaving at two-thirty in the morning.
   - To top it all, it looks like it's going to be a bumpy flight. You can't sleep, so you might as well try and read your book, a crime novel you picked up in the airport called *The Pentangle* by A. J. Bell. Seems quite good.

3 **Flight LH1706 from Los Angeles to Munich, first class (2pm)**
- You are a film producer for Touchstone Pictures flying from a meeting with Oscar-winning actor Al Pacino in Los Angeles to a casting meeting in Munich.
- You are looking for a German- and English-speaking actor to play the part of an environmental activist in your latest film and would prefer to choose an unknown rather than a big box-office star.
- You've just enjoyed your second glass of complimentary champagne, when you notice that the passenger sitting next to you looks perfect for the part! You can't believe your eyes, but remind yourself they are probably a business executive with no acting ability whatsoever.
- At the moment they are watching the in-flight movie on their headphones, but try to find an excuse to get talking to them.

16 TELECONFERENCING

Desert island blues

CEO of RJK (UK)

Here's your e-mail:

I'm becoming increasingly concerned about the costs we're running up on the Éternelle account. I think we're in serious danger of exceeding our budget.

As you know, the Éternelle marketing people were extremely unhappy when we came in €250,000 over budget last time, and it was for this reason that they insisted at the planning stage on a ceiling of €2.5m for the Vivacity campaign.

I've been looking at the figures and we're well past the €2m mark already. The main problem is this two-day film shoot on Oamu-Oamu which has already cost us €1m. The Hollywood actress the client insisted on using is costing us €100,000 a day! What on earth is going on there?

I estimate that with post-production costs, we could run €500,000–€700,000 over budget on this one.

We desperately need to talk.

Gavin Hartnell, Chief Financial Officer, RJK (UK)

I'm hearing rumours of a budget overrun on the Vivacity campaign. Please tell me I'm imagining things!

I had lunch with Éternelle's new head of marketing, Thierry DuPont, and he sounded pretty annoyed with what he called our 'endless production hold-ups'. He even said they may be forced to postpone the Vivacity launch.

I'm sure I don't need to remind you that Éternelle is by far this company's biggest European client (worth €10m annually) and that the loss of their account would have a drastic effect on both Group turnover and our reputation in the industry.

Your creative director must be in contact with our team on Oamu-Oamu. Are they still having weather problems or what?

I'm counting on you to sort this one out. Don't let me down.

Nathan T. Auerbach, RJK Group President

---

17 NEGOTIATING DEALS

The last one in the store

Speaker A

It's 6pm on Christmas Eve and you're still at the office. You've been so busy lately, you've hardly had a moment to spend with your family. You even had to miss your young son's first match for the school football team last week to attend an important meeting. Apparently, you were the only parent not there.

Fortunately, you have a chance to put things right. You know there's something kids are all going mad for this Christmas – the Z-Cube Gaming System. At $189, it's a little more than you were planning to spend, but it would be great to see the look on your son's face when he opens it. After phoning seven stores without success, you finally find one that has three left. You try to reserve one, but the shop assistant says 'Sorry, only my boss can do that and she's not here. But if you hurry, you should be OK. We're open till 6.30.'

You fly out of the office and into a taxi. You get to the store just before it closes. To your horror, you see there's only one Z-Cube left. It has a big label on the box saying 'LAST ONE'. But as you head for it, you see another person with the same idea (Speaker B) coming in the other direction. You both reach the box at the same time and grab opposite ends …

17 NEGOTIATING DEALS

The recording contract

Team A: The Penitents (band and management)

Obviously, you are delighted that a record company as high-profile as Starburst is interested in signing your band. If the deal goes through, you stand to make a lot of money. You are aware, however, that relatively unknown artists are vulnerable to exploitation by the big labels and should take this into account in your dealings with them.

Read your negotiating objectives below and then work with your team to plan your overall strategy. In particular, make sure you know which of your objectives are:

1 tradeables (things you'll concede to get what you really want in return)

2 ideals (things you'd really like to get, but not if it costs you the deal)

3 essentials (things you absolutely have to get or the deal's off)

1 Band line-up The four members of the band – the lead singer and rhythm guitarist, lead guitarist, bass guitarist and drummer – all met at college in Dublin and have played together through good times and bad for five years. You've heard a rumour that Starburst Records may want to make changes to the line-up – perhaps sacking the drummer, who is also the band's female backing vocalist.

2 Term You'd like a three-year commitment from Starburst. It can often take several albums before band members make a profit, so you'd like them to commission at least two albums during that time. If, after three years, the contract is terminated, you'd prefer to keep the rights to all the songs you have recorded – otherwise you would have to pay Starburst a fee to perform or re-record your old material.

3 Royalties You think a 15% royalty on net receipts from album sales would be fair. If the band's current popularity does not last, you'd like to make as much as money as possible before the bubble bursts.

4 Deductions You expect Starburst to cover all the costs of packaging and promotion, including any TV advertising. Accessing marketing power is one of the advantages of signing to a major label.

5 Advances You are more interested in a good long-term relationship with Starburst than instant cash. Nevertheless, a $200,000 non-repayable advance would allow band members to cover living costs, purchase of equipment and stage costumes, etc.

6 Territory You're happy for Starburst to have 'universal rights' to your material globally, provided the terms are right. Otherwise, you'd like to be able to approach other labels in the States and Asia.

7 Touring Touring is an essential part of building a band, especially in the early stages of its development. But some of the band members have other jobs and family commitments. They wouldn't want to take on more than 20 weeks' touring (not consecutively) in the first year unless the financial rewards were high – say, 50% of ticket sales.

8 Songwriting The lead singer, Rick Harlow, writes all the band's songs. He says he wants the usual 50:50 split with the music publisher on fees for airplay on radio and TV and other public performances.

06 LEADING MEETINGS

In the chair

Speaker B

Meeting 1: Genetic profiling (against)
You have heard a rumour that head office is planning to introduce genetic testing for future job applicants. You are about to attend a meeting to discuss the subject. At the moment you are strongly against the idea, but listen to what the other participants have to say before finally making up your mind. One thing you are fairly sure of is that genetic screening without consent would be illegal under civil law. You certainly consider it unethical. Also, since some of the conditions screened for (such as sickle cell disease) affect mostly black people, and others (such as breast and ovarian cancer) solely women, you are concerned that the tests could easily lead to racial and sexual discrimination.

Hidden agenda: There is a genetically inherited disease that runs in your family. Although you do not have the condition yourself, you are worried that it might show up in a genetic test and that you might be discriminated against if you applied for promotion.

Meeting 2: Employee surveillance (chair)
You have been asked by head office to chair a meeting on the possible introduction of surveillance and electronic security equipment to check up on employees of the company. In your business confidentiality is essential as many of your workers are dealing with highly classified information. Of course, a lot of your company files are encrypted, but leaks still happen. HQ is also concerned about the amount of time employees appear to be spending making personal phone calls and sending private e-mails. Details of what system to install have not yet been fully discussed, but suggestions include Internet monitoring software, random phone tapping and closed circuit television (CCTV) throughout the building.

You yourself are a little alarmed at the number of unnecessary e-mails sent back and forth over the company intranet and have overheard staff making international phone calls that were clearly not business. Monitoring Internet access and phone use is common practice in many companies these days and you don't see why anyone would object unless they had something to hide. CCTV seems a bit radical, however.

Leader's brief: Open the meeting, inform those present of HQ's proposal, make sure everyone gets a chance to speak and no one dominates. Try to avoid digressions and keep the meeting short. Give your own opinion only after everyone else has spoken and try to reach a decision on what recommendations to make to HQ.

Meeting 3: Alternative management training (in favour)
You have heard a rumour that head office is planning to introduce a series of alternative management training courses for all levels of staff. You are about to attend a meeting to discuss the subject. At the moment you are fairly enthusiastic about the idea, but listen to what the other participants have to say before finally making up your mind. You already have an MBA, but have never found what you learnt at business school much use in the real world of business. On the other hand, an ex-colleague of yours went on a course to learn about negotiating technique from an Olympic gold medal-winning judo player and says it was the best business training she's ever had.

Hidden agenda: You have a favourite cousin who runs a company that teaches business people creativity through song, poetry and drama workshops, stand-up comedy and exotic sports like Zen archery and rodeo riding. He's not doing too well at the moment and could do with more clients.

05 PROBLEMS ON THE PHONE

Dealing with a chatterbox

Speaker B

If you don't know Speaker A well, swap lists of the following with them before you start your telephone conversation:

- your partner's name, job and main interest
- your children's names, ages and main interests
- when and where you went on your last holiday
- your own main interest
- your favourite sport (spectator or player?)
- the name of a close colleague
- a problem you've been having at work recently

You are the sales director of Möbelkunst, a designer furniture manufacturer in Berlin. Your stylish products are getting rave reviews in the press, but business in Germany has not been good lately. Fortunately, you have recently won some very big overseas orders – one of them with Mi Casa, a large chain of furniture stores in Mexico. The only problem is Speaker A, Mi Casa's director of purchasing, who seems to like phoning you rather too often for no particular reason.

It's 5 p.m. on Friday afternoon. You would normally be getting ready to go home soon, but today there's been a crisis to deal with – your factory in Potsdam has just turned out 1,000 leather sofas in bright pink (rather than dark red) by mistake. You're still trying to sort a solution out with your plant manager. The last thing you need now is any interruptions.

01 BUSINESS OR PLEASURE?

Corporate entertainment
Group B

All England Lawn Tennis Championships, Wimbledon (11 km from central London)

Experience the nail-biting climax to the world's premier international tennis tournament as the true giants of the game clash in the men's Wimbledon final. All the tradition of vintage champagne and strawberries and cream combine with 225-km-an-hour serves and awesome cross-court shots to make what many consider to be the greatest sporting event on Earth. Game, set and match!

Men's final, lunch, champagne, music: €3,000 per person

London Eye and Private Tour of Tate Modern, central London

Your evening begins 130 metres above London in your very own capsule on the London Eye. A waiter serves champagne. On a clear day you can see for 25 miles – all the way to Windsor Castle. You are then transferred to the Tate Modern for a private tour of one of the world's most cutting-edge contemporary art galleries, followed by a superb dinner in the tasteful surroundings of the OXO Tower Restaurant overlooking the Thames. High altitude; high culture!

London Eye, tour of Tate Modern, dinner: €300 per person (minimum 20)

02 EXCHANGING INFORMATION
Queries and comments

Speaker B

> **Useful language**
> Sorry, I thought you said ...
> Hold on, didn't you just say ...?
> Wait a minute. You just said ..., didn't you?

1 Listen to your partner reading out a report. There are seven discrepancies in it. Can you spot them? Remain polite no matter how confused your partner seems!

2 Read out the following report to your partner. There are also seven discrepancies in it (marked in **bold**). Can *they* spot them? If not, keep reading. Apologise for or justify any discrepancies your partner points out. If you lose your place in the text, ask your partner: 'Where was I?'

> **Report: Korean negotiations**
>
> We held our first meeting with the Koreans two months ago at their headquarters in **Osaka**. Since then we've had **twelve weeks** of tough negotiations. There were some cultural difficulties at first. Of course, we've never done business in the **Middle East** before.
>
> They were very positive about our products, although they weren't happy with **the design, performance, price and maintenance costs**. Initially, they were demanding a discount on orders of over 10,000 units of 17%, but we finally managed to beat them down to **18**.
>
> We haven't heard anything from them so far, but the e-mail they sent **this morning** looks promising – an initial order of **a dozen units**.

02 EXCHANGING INFORMATION
Breaking the bad news

Speaker B

Proposal: Travel budget
- Board deeply concerned about cost of business travel (nearly $13m last year)
- Insist on 60% cut in travel budget
- Propose three main courses of action (see below)
- All flights from now on to be economy class or on low-budget carriers (no exceptions) – preferably on cheapest early morning and late night flights
- Motels and two-star hotels for everyone in future – room sharing wherever possible
- Meal allowance to be reduced to $20 a day (no alcoholic drinks)

Proposal: Performance management
- Board extremely dissatisfied with amount of customer complaints
- Complaints both about products themselves and general quality of service
- In future, board would like to see staff take more personal responsibility for their work
- Rewards for fault-free production and excellent service clearly not motivating staff
- New proposal to introduce a system of disincentives
- New (joke) awards for next year: Adminstrative Screw-up of the Month, Production Team Underachievement Award, Service with a Frown Award, Sick Leave Absentee of the Year

CASE STUDY: HEAD TO HEAD

Group B

Read the following e-mail from Chester Electrical's chief marketing officer, Jacob Gold, and summarise the main points to group A.

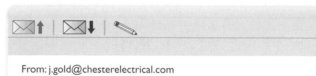

From: j.gold@chesterelectrical.com
To: c.brubaker@chesterelectrical.com
Subject: Status report on Pennsylvania Dept of Transport negotiations

Hi Clark

You sure are a hard guy to get hold of! Please get back to me asap. I've told Caitlin to expect your call and put you straight through to me the moment it comes in. We have to fix a meeting today to discuss this state highways project. I'm extremely concerned that the negotiations are about to stall.

Everything seemed to be going just fine until this morning. In fact, I thought we had the deal pretty much sewn up with only a few details to sort out. Then the DoT people drop a bomb. They've had a better bid. Won't say who or what it is – just that we'll have to improve our bid if we want to stay in the race! If your reaction is 'What the hell', that was my reaction precisely, expletives deleted!

At first, I thought they were bluffing. I mean, we know what the other tenders are for this contract and, frankly, they're nowhere near to matching ours. But if they are bluffing, they're damned good at it! As a matter of fact, they seem to have gone cold on us altogether, which makes me suspicious. Has someone been putting in a bad word for us? You know how dirty some of our competitors play, but I would have thought this was beneath even them!

I don't need to tell you how much we're relying on this government contract to break even in the wire & cable division by year-end, so let's try and find out what on earth is going on before we lose this one.

Jake

05 PROBLEMS ON THE PHONE

Speaker B

At the end of each conversation, give Speaker A a score out of ten for (a) helpfulness and (b) assertiveness.

1 Speaker A will phone you with a problem. You are very busy at the moment (you decide what you're doing) but try to give them some advice. If you can't, suggest someone they could phone who might be able to help.

2 You are Speaker A's boss. It's 6 p.m. and you still have a mountain of papers on your desk to go through before the morning (you decide what sort of papers they are). Phone Speaker A and ask them if they'd mind staying on for an hour or so to help you out. Be diplomatic but don't take no for an answer – unless they can suggest someone else.

3 Speaker A has just been promoted and you are now their boss. But a colleague from an overseas division of your company (you decide who) is going to spend the next three months working on an international project in your division and they need to be provided with a suitable office. Speaker A's office would be ideal (you decide why). Phone them and try to get their agreement without causing any bad feeling.

4 You have been working on an important report for nine months. Because of a lot of unforeseen difficulties and complications (you decide what) you are a month behind schedule and now need six, rather than two, more weeks to finish it. On completion of the report you are due to present your findings to senior management and you think they will be impressed. Much to your annoyance, however, you think your boss, Speaker A, is going to try to speed things up by bringing in someone else to help you finish the job and take half the credit for all your hard work.

06 LEADING MEETINGS

Speaker A

Meeting 1: Genetic profiling (chair)
You have been asked by head office to chair a meeting on the possible introduction of genetic testing for job applicants at all levels. Your company already insists on a medical when people apply for a job, as well as psychometric tests and checks on possible criminal records. Now they think a genetic profile would help to reduce the risk of employing or promoting people with potentially serious diseases and mental health problems. The test would probably be voluntary – this hasn't been fully discussed with the legal department yet – but refusal to undergo it may affect a candidate's chance of employment or promotion.

You have read that vulnerability to stress, alcoholism and strokes – the three main causes of people being off work for prolonged periods – are all to some extent genetically inherited, but the idea of genetic testing does seem quite drastic and is bound to provoke a certain amount of hostility.

Leader's brief: Open the meeting, inform those present of HQ's proposal, make sure everyone gets a chance to speak and no one dominates. Try to avoid digressions and keep the meeting short. Give your own opinion only after everyone else has spoken and try to reach a decision on what recommendations to make to HQ.

Meeting 2: Employee surveillance (in favour)
You have heard a rumour that head office is planning to introduce a system of checking up on employees using PC monitoring software and closed circuit television (CCTV). You are about to attend a meeting to discuss the subject. At the moment you are firmly in favour of the idea, but listen to what the other participants have to say before finally making up your mind. You are sure that huge amounts of company time and money are being wasted by employees accessing gaming and adult websites during working hours. You've even heard some of the male staff joking about it. An article you read in Business Week claims that employees who play computer games whilst at work cost US firms $100 billion a year – or 2% of GDP. You also remember the famous case of Chevron, who, by failing to monitor computer use, ended up being sued by four female employees who had suffered sexual harassment through the internal e-mail system. The company finally had to pay out $2.2 million in compensation.

Hidden agenda: You've heard that a junior manager in your department, who seems to have his sights set on your job, spends hours in private chatrooms on company time. In order to catch such people, you think the computer surveillance should be covert.

Meeting 3: Alternative management training (against)
You have heard a rumour that head office is planning to introduce a series of alternative management training courses for all levels of staff. You are about to attend a meeting to discuss the subject. At the moment you are not keen on the idea, but listen to what the other participants have to say before finally making up your mind. Frankly, you don't believe that 'fads' like this represent very good value for money. A friend of yours works for a firm that sent him and his colleagues to a Benedictine monastery to learn about 'Morality in the Workplace'. Predictably, it was thought to be a complete waste of time. You've also heard about weird courses offered by drama groups, orchestras, circuses, the army and even the prison service where executives spent a week in jail to build team spirit.

Hidden agenda: You have a close friend who is in charge of in-company training at a prestigious business school in the United States. If your company booked a course, you personally might get some kind of 'thank you'.

08 PROMOTING YOUR IDEAS

Pitching your idea

Team 1

PC Mug

A fully functioning PC built into a coffee cup? A couple of years ago it would have been sci-fi, but, thanks to new flexible screens and e-paper it's now technically possible, though very cutting-edge. Too expensive at this stage to retail to the consumer, its main market would be coffee shop chains like Starbucks who could offer an Internet café with a difference!

CabBoots™

Designed by Martin Frey, this 'guidance system for pedestrians' is currently at the prototype stage. A satellite navigation system is connected to electro-mechanics in the custom-made shoes that actually guide your feet in the direction you should be going. An ordinary mobile phone is sufficient to establish the satellite connection. Aimed at hikers, delivery personnel and the visually impaired.

09 RELATIONSHIP-BUILDING

A dinner invitation

Guest: Ulterior motive

You've secretly applied for and been shortlisted for a better job (you decide what) at another company in San Francisco. You've been fairly happy in your current job and you don't want to upset your host, so break the news gently at some point during the evening and try to see if they'll write you a good reference. Be careful what you say and be ready to change the subject if things don't go according to plan!

09 RELATIONSHIP-BUILDING

Getting out of the office

Speaker B

Situation 1
Background: You're playing golf with Speaker A, an IT security specialist. As IT director for a major insurance company, you frequently engage their services. It's a beautiful spring morning.

Situation: Your game is a bit off today. Although you're a better player than Speaker A and usually beat them, they were actually a shot ahead on the sixteenth hole. Then they were very unlucky to drop two shots on the seventeenth, putting you back in the lead.

Hidden Agenda: You've always got on well with Speaker A and rate them very highly as an IT expert. However, the consultancy they work for charges extremely high fees – higher than any of their competitors. You invited Speaker A to play golf because you've been considering offering them a permanent job within your company, but don't mention this straightaway. They seem to have something on their mind – or perhaps it's just that they don't like losing!

You start: Oh, bad luck! Looks like it's all down to the last hole…

Situation 2
Background: You work in the sales department of an international sports goods company. You're playing tennis with Speaker A, the sales director. When you started playing it was a warm summer afternoon, but it's just clouded over and looks like it might even rain.

Situation: You were warned that your boss takes tennis very seriously and doesn't like losing, but, even though you're not really trying very hard, you beat them 6-2 in the first set and you're 4-1 up in the second. Probably you should lose a few games to make them feel better, but you've noticed the head of marketing is watching you from the next court and you'd like to impress them.

Hidden Agenda: You've only been in the sales department for a few months, but already you hate it. Direct contact with customers all day is just not you and you don't get on with the rest of the team, who are all very competitive. You studied strategic marketing at university and that's what you really want to do, but there were no vacancies when you applied to the company, so you took the job in sales to gain experience. Big mistake. You keep meaning to talk to your boss about your problems, but now doesn't seem like a great moment!

13 MAKING AN IMPACT

The last paradise on earth?

Group B: Progress Party of Bhutan

1 The need to speed up the rate of progress
- 22% of the population still have no access to clean drinking water.
- 40% of children are malnourished.
- 33% of them are unable to attend school.
- Almost half the population remains illiterate.
2 Infrastructure and communications
- The 'last paradise on earth' image is counter-productive – Bhutan is exactly the kind of country that could benefit most from the Internet economy for both commercial and educational purposes.

- Until 1999 Bhutan was without TV and there was only one cinema. More needs to be spent on the Bhutan Broadcasting Service (BBS) and Sigma Cable Service.
- Bhutan's Internet ISP DrukNet, though popular, is still too expensive (seven cents per minute), but the use of websites and e-mail has reduced international phone bills by 90% and should be promoted.

3 Bhutan's enormous potential as a tourist resort
- Many of the current improvements in Bhutan are the result of foreign investment, principally from India and Singapore. Why shouldn't other countries be encouraged to invest as well?
- Bhutan's superb wildlife and fabulous mountain scenery would be ideal for ecological tourism and adventure holidays.
- Limiting the number of tourist visas to just 7,000 a year and insisting that 86% of the land area remain undeveloped is missing a huge opportunity.
- Druk Air, the world's smallest commercial carrier, consists of just two planes flying six or seven times a week.

4 The youth of Bhutan
- 45% of the population of Bhutan is under 15 years of age – it is time to respond to the needs of the younger generation instead of living in the past.

14 OUT AND ABOUT

In-flight conversations

Speaker B

Hold short conversations with a fellow passenger, Speaker A, on three different international flights.

Use the information below to get you started, but invent any extra information you need to keep the conversation going for a minute or two.

1 **Flight BA1311 from Dubai to London Heathrow, business class (9pm)**
- You are the senior partner in a small software company specialising in computer-assisted engineering applications for the oil industry.
- You are travelling back home from a series of meetings with potential clients in Dubai. It's been an exhausting trip and not as successful as you would have liked.
- Frankly, you'd just like to skip dinner and try and get some sleep. First, however, you think you'll order a martini while you update your client files on your Blackberry.
- You are not pleased to see that the person sitting next to you, Speaker A, has a young child with them. There goes your relaxing flight!

2 **Flight AF6001 from Paris to Rio de Janeiro, economy class (3am)**
- You are a financial speculator who specialises in medical, pharmaceutical and biotech stocks.

- You are coming back from a meeting in Paris to Rio where you live with your American partner, the crime novelist A. J. Bell.
- Due to the cancellation of your business class Varig flight, you've ended up in economy class on an early morning Air France flight instead. And you are already regretting this – there's barely room to move and the plane seems to be experiencing some turbulence. You've never been a great flyer and are starting to feel a bit sick.
- Perhaps talking to the person sitting next to you would take your mind off it. But they seem to be reading a book. Actually, the book looks quite familiar ...

3 **Flight LH1706 from Los Angeles to Munich, first class (2pm)**
- You are a highly paid German-English interpreter based in Munich and travelling back from LA, where you've been assisting at the American launch of the new BMW sports car.
- When you arrived for your business class flight this morning, you were delighted to find that it was overbooked and that you had been upgraded to first class.
- You've had quite an exciting, if stressful, week in LA and are now thoroughly enjoying the flight home. You've had an excellent lunch and have just tuned into the in-flight movie on your personal video screen.
- You've already seen the film, but don't mind seeing it again as it stars your favourite actor, Al Pacino. And anyway, the person sitting next to you looks like some big-shot multi-millionaire business type.

CASE STUDY: A WINNING FORMULA

1 It's no secret that Roberto is constantly being approached by other teams and he's known to be unhappy at Moretti at the moment. But the rumour is he's been visiting Mario in hospital and discussing plans to set up their own team with a mystery backer. Both Roberto and Mario are signed up for just one more season with Moretti. Rumour reliability factor: 6/10.

2 François has faith in Debora and is keen to develop her role as Moretti's top driver, but first he wants her to prove her commitment to the sport by giving up the modelling jobs, the photo-shoots and the appearances in Hello! magazine to concentrate on F1. Rumour reliability factor: 8/10.

3 Enrico is only going to give F1 one more season and if success still eludes the team, he'll pull out of the sport before paying off his backers' investment. He has confidence in François, but already misses the thrill of running the team himself. Rumour reliability factor: 6/10.

4 Toivo is about to go to the press with a story about how the di Angelo accident was in fact a conspiracy to get the 35-year-old driver out of the team and clear the way for a more glamorous and newsworthy replacement. Rumour reliability factor: 3/10.

16 TELECONFERENCING

Desert island blues

Creative Director of RJK (UK)

Here's your e-mail:

> Well, we've had eight days of incessant rain, two cameras damaged in transit and now the electricity generator's broken down. Whose idea was it to use a real desert island for the shoot?
>
> Flying Sandra in and out from Fiji every day is proving totally impractical. Didn't I say using a big Hollywood star was asking for trouble? She came down with some kind of tropical fever two days ago and hasn't come out of her hotel room since. So far we've only got about 15% of the commercial in the can.
>
> To keep costs down the crew are staying on Oamu-Oamu until we're finished. Today is the first fine day, but there's still no sign of Sandra, so we're just getting some footage of the island.
>
> I strongly suggest we either fly out a replacement or seriously consider filming the whole thing in a studio in Britain.
>
> Ridley Hurst, Film Unit Director

> No doubt you've already heard from Ridley. The good news is that Sandra's PA tells me she may be well enough for filming tomorrow. My suggestion is that we forget Oamu-Oamu and find a nice secluded spot here in Fiji. I'm sure that would suit Sandra much better if she's still not feeling too well. I've sent some of the team out scouting the beaches for possible locations.
>
> The bad news is that the animal handler's gone missing. You remember that we wanted to use real animals on this shoot instead of adding them digitally later? Well, now I'm left here with 36 African parrots and a rather lethal-looking python.
>
> Ridley seems to think we'd be better off doing the whole thing in a studio, but I think it would be a shame to pack up and leave now we're all here. Might be rather hard to explain the unnecessary expense to the client, too. Are we insured for this?
>
> Amelia Devine, Senior Account Manager, RJK (UK)

02 EXCHANGING INFORMATION

Breaking the bad news

Speaker C

Proposal: Language training
- Board keen to market products more internationally
- English now language of international business but many staff (65%) already speak it
- In board's view, Chinese is business language of the future
- Mandarin, however, is one of world's most difficult languages
- Therefore, compulsory Chinese lessons (in employees' own time) to start immediately
- All new managerial staff to be obliged to accept twelve-month transfer to new subsidiary in Beijing

Proposal: Team spirit
- Board strongly believes not enough team spirit
- Problem particularly noticeable at the production plant
- Obviously takes time to build a team, but certain things could be introduced right away
- Has been suggested a company song could be sung every morning
- The idea has proved very popular at big companies like IBM, General Electric and Mitsubishi
- Second idea is that all staff (including managers) wear a uniform in new company colours – orange and green

17 NEGOTIATING DEALS

The last one in the store

Speaker B

It's Christmas Eve and you and your family are placing the last few presents under the tree. Your partner turns to you and whispers how excited your young son is: 'Thank goodness you bought him that new gaming system back in November. Apparently, the stores have completely sold out, and it's all he's talked about for months. You remembered to get him the blue one, didn't you?'

You feel a sudden surge of panic. Oh, no ... the Z-Cube Gaming System! How could you have forgotten? You meant to get one months ago, but you've been so busy it completely slipped your mind. You mumble something to your partner about going out to get some better lights for the tree and spend the next three hours searching every store in town. But nobody has one. One shop offers to order it for you, but it will take at least a fortnight ...

In desperation, you try a tiny shop in a side street. It's just about to close as you walk in. To your relief, you see they have one Z-Cube left – and it's a blue one. You can't believe your luck. It has a big label on the box saying 'LAST ONE'. But as you head for it, you see another person with the same idea (Speaker A) coming in the other direction. You both reach the box at the same time and grab opposite ends ...

CASE STUDY: THE SKY'S THE LIMIT

Group A

Here are the results of your research into India's domestic airline market:

Market share (last five years)

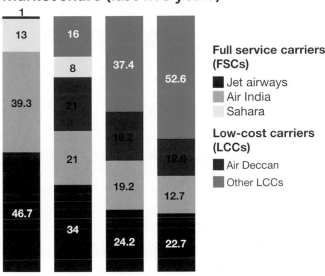

Full service carriers (FSCs)
- Jet airways
- Air India
- Sahara

Low-cost carriers (LCCs)
- Air Deccan
- Other LCCs

Service–price comparison

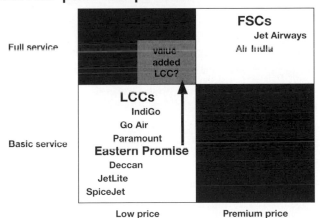

CASE STUDY: A WINNING FORMULA

1 Gordon Hayes, 33, a British ex-champion driver has shown an interest in joining the team if the remuneration package is right. Toivo and Sonia support the recruitment of a more mature and experienced driver. François and Enrico oppose it – François because he'd like to develop his young drivers; Enrico because he's happy with the publicity his current two drivers are attracting in the media. Rumour reliability factor: 7/10.

2 In the German grand prix last week Roberto deliberately refused to let Debora overtake him on the final lap to take second place and move up to sixth place in the championship. Assisting a team-mate in this way is officially illegal in F1, so he had a legitimate excuse, but in practice drivers usually follow the instructions of their team boss if it means advancing the position of their fellow driver at no points cost to themselves. Rumour reliability factor 9/10.

Airlines' annual performance

Indian airlines = €1bn loss

World airlines = €4.6bn loss

Conclusions and recommendations

- The two main FSCs do still lead the market, but have lost considerable ground to the LCCs. Jet Airways owes its continued success to its exceptional service and reliability. But the fact that, when Jet acquired FSC Sahara Airlines three years ago, it relaunched it as LCC JetLite, is a strong indication that value for money is now the critical factor in this market.

- The LCC sector has gone from just 1% of the market to a phenomenal 52.6% in the last 5yrs because of extreme price pressure and this trend looks set to continue. It is unlikely that Eastern Promise could succeed by increasing its prices and becoming an FSC. But if it could gain critical mass (through acquisition of another LCC?), it could offer more routes and would enjoy certain economies of scale.

- Competition in the LCC sector is now fierce and there is negative profit. Deccan, which pioneered the sector, still leads, but it is steadily losing market share to its many smaller competitors. This makes it ripe for takeover at a favourable price.

- Eastern Promise is in serious danger of getting 'stuck in the middle' – offering neither particularly excellent service nor the most competitive prices. To succeed it needs to be both bigger and more clearly differentiated.

- There seems to be a gap in the market for a 'value-added' LCC – an airline which, whilst reasonably priced, offers 'something special', perhaps to a particular type of customer, and has a distinctive brand identity.

3 The rivalry between Toivo and Oskar finally exploded into a full-blown argument a week ago with Oskar apparently yelling at the end of a technicians' meeting: 'That's it, you son of a b**ch. Either you go or I go!' and storming out of the room. It was especially shocking as Oskar is normally so calm and in control. The situation was made worse by Nilda and Giancarlo appearing to support Oskar. Rumour reliability factor: 7/10.

4 Sonia suspects that Toivo has some sort of hold over François. She's not sure what it is, but whenever the two disagree at a meeting, François seems to back down, which is certainly not in character, as he has no problem arguing to the bitter end with other members of the team – with her, especially! Some say Toivo worked with François a long time ago, but neither of them will talk about it. Rumour reliability factor: 4/10.

06 LEADING MEETINGS

In the chair

Speaker C

Meeting 1: Genetic profiling (in favour)

You have heard a rumour that head office is planning to introduce genetic testing for future job applicants. You are about to attend a meeting to discuss the subject. At the moment you are basically in favour of the idea, but listen to what the other participants have to say before finally making up your mind. You know that 350 million working days are lost each year in the EU alone through illness – stress being the cause of 41 million of those. UK companies lose £13 billion annually because of employees going off sick. If people with potential social problems (such as alcoholism or drug abuse) could be screened out at the job application stage, it would make for a healthier workforce and could save the firm millions.

Hidden agenda: Your department has been particularly affected by people taking sick leave. At the moment you are trying to cope without three of your key managers – one of them, you suspect, has a drink problem.

Meeting 2: Employee surveillance (against)

You have heard a rumour that head office is planning to introduce a system of checking up on employees using PC monitoring software and closed circuit television (CCTV). You are about to attend a meeting to discuss the subject. At the moment you are very much against the idea, but listen to what the other participants have to say before finally making up your mind. You firmly believe that a good work atmosphere is built on trust and that such security measures should only be taken when there is strong evidence to suggest that company facilities are being abused. Moreover, you suspect that phone taps, video cameras and PC monitoring may just be the thin end of the wedge. You've heard in some companies workers have also been videotaped in toilets and locker rooms and investigators have even been hired to follow them home. What next? Electronic tagging devices? Implants?

Hidden agenda: You often surf the Internet on your office PC during coffee and lunch breaks (never during working hours, however) and regularly log on to chatroom channels. You see this as valuable networking and not an abuse of company Internet access. Still, if Internet monitoring was introduced, you'd prefer the company to announce the fact and not investigate past use.

Meeting 3: Alternative management training (chair)

You have been asked by head office to chair a meeting on the possible introduction of a series of alternative management training courses. In the past, your firm has sent junior members of staff on practical office skills courses and middle and senior management on executive courses at several top business schools. But the feedback has sometimes been rather negative. As people at all levels in your company require a high degree of creativity, HQ is proposing to hire the services of a number of 'arts and business' companies to help employees 'think outside the box'.

Suggestions so far include: working with a renowned artist to produce a 5m x 30m company mural to be displayed at HQ; putting on a variety show with the help of professional actors with all members of staff taking part in song, dance and comedy routines; choreographing a modern ballet to dramatise the challenges facing the company; and music lessons from professional musicians leading to an end-of-year company jazz session. Many big-name companies have found similar training to be highly enjoyable and successful – why not your company too?

Leader's brief: Open the meeting, inform those present of HQ's proposal, make sure everyone gets a chance to speak and no one dominates. Try to avoid digressions and keep the meeting short. Give your own opinion only after everyone else has spoken and try to reach a decision on what recommendations to make to HQ.

08 PROMOTING YOUR IDEAS

Pitching your idea

Team 2

The Sauce-shooter

Load different sauces into the barrel of the sauce-shooter and 'shoot' flavour into your favourite dishes! More than just a gimmick, this kitchen appliance keeps sauces fresh and dispenses them in precisely measured amounts. The key market, obviously, is the young (probably male) single cook. 'Go ahead, punk, make my meal!'

Everglide™

Designed by Frag Woodall, an award-winning design student at the University of Sydney, the Everglide is 'an integrated solution for short distance travel'. It can be wheeled, cycled or worn as a backpack. Made of light and durable materials, it is aimed at both the young urban traveller and executive commuter.

CASE STUDY: CASH OR CONSCIENCE?

1 At the end of each pitch, record your initial impressions in the grid below. There's no need to complete every box. Just note down your main reactions.

2 Use your notes and evaluation grid to discuss the merits of each business.

Evaluation criteria	Pitch 1	Pitch 2	Pitch 3	Pitch 4
Name of business				
Does the business idea immediately appeal?				
How easy would it be for competitors to clone the idea?				
How big is the potential market?				
How profitable is the business likely to be?				
How much of the total capital needed does the business already have?				
Is the business already up and running?				
Do the business owners have the right background?				
Is the business socially responsible?				
Is there a well-developed exit strategy?				
Do you like and trust these people enough to do business with them?				
The lion's share? Yes/No				
Smaller share? Yes/No How much?				

16 TELECONFERENCING

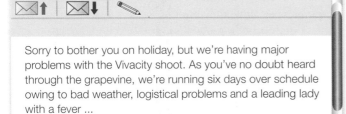

Desert island blues

Account Director of RJK (UK)

Assume that thorough due diligence would have to be done before any final investments are made. Your job today is to make a provisional decision on which business(es) to back. You must agree and you cannot change your minds later!

Here's your e-mail:

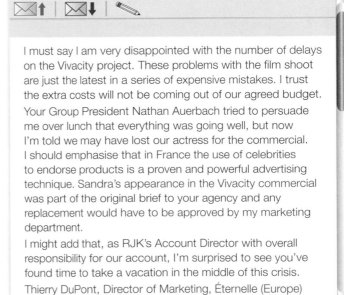

Sorry to bother you on holiday, but we're having major problems with the Vivacity shoot. As you've no doubt heard through the grapevine, we're running six days over schedule owing to bad weather, logistical problems and a leading lady with a fever ...

I've been asked to look into alternatives and have come up with the following, which I thought I'd better copy you in on:

1 If we fly the film crew home to do the commercial in a studio, with set building, studio hire and post-production, we could be looking at an extra €750,000. Plus we'd be unlikely to finish on schedule.

2 Finding an A-list actress to replace Sandra at such short notice would be extremely difficult, although there is provision for her replacement, if unable to perform, in the terms of our contract. I did speak to someone at a lookalike agency who said he had 'Sandra's twin' and could let us have her for €5,000 a day.

Jason Roberts, Account Manager, RJK (UK)

I must say I am very disappointed with the number of delays on the Vivacity project. These problems with the film shoot are just the latest in a series of expensive mistakes. I trust the extra costs will not be coming out of our agreed budget.

Your Group President Nathan Auerbach tried to persuade me over lunch that everything was going well, but now I'm told we may have lost our actress for the commercial. I should emphasise that in France the use of celebrities to endorse products is a proven and powerful advertising technique. Sandra's appearance in the Vivacity commercial was part of the original brief to your agency and any replacement would have to be approved by my marketing department.

I might add that, as RJK's Account Director with overall responsibility for our account, I'm surprised to see you've found time to take a vacation in the middle of this crisis.

Thierry DuPont, Director of Marketing, Éternelle (Europe)

CASE STUDY: CASH OR CONSCIENCE?

1 Epilogue: You invested in SojaGen, which seemed like both a wise and ethical investment at the time. But timing was your mistake. Soy production has increased by 500% in the last 35 years and many big conglomerates have already moved into the market making it difficult for you to compete even on a local level. To make matters worse, organisations like Greenpeace have actually criticised the biofuel industry for causing deforestation and droughts as they have cleared land to grow their crops, creating in the process a surplus of biofuel which has hit prices. Bad choice, ladies and gentlemen!

2 Epilogue: You invested in Elita mostly on the grounds that it could be grown quickly and sold to one of the major social networking websites. It was a high-risk decision, but the investment has massively exceeded your expectations. Status-oriented businesses have really taken off in Russia. A year or so ago a business magazine actually called *Snob* was very successfully launched onto the market and your website has done similarly well – so well, in fact, that you have been able to stretch the Elita brand and open a chain of cocktail bars and nightclubs in the Moscow area. You have had several bids for your successful networking business, but so far you're not selling!

3 Epilogue: You invested in The Ulundi Township Confectionery Company, which though a small-scale operation, seemed to have an excellent management team with an attractive and socially responsible business proposition. Your investment hasn't paid off spectacularly yet, but you are sure that it will. Small business is really booming in South Africa with techno-hubs springing up all over the country allowing business owners access to the internet and all its marketing possibilities. Ulundi is making a solid annual profit, has expanded by 400% and pushed through its first big export deal. You won't make a quick gain, but you do have a half-share in a business with real promise.

4 Epilogue: You invested in Libu Tours on the basis that it was an up-and-running company with a good track record in a new international market, namely, Libya. It was a brave decision, given the country's past, but you could see great potential. So far, the company is doing well, as is tourism in Libya, but you have been held back by a certain amount of bureaucracy and don't think the business is being as well managed by Andrew Collins as it might be. You'd like to replace him and alter the marketing strategy to attract younger more adventurous holiday-makers, but with just a 35% stake in the company, that won't be easy. It may be time to sell your share in the business and invest the money elsewhere.

3 DO THE RIGHT THING

The stakeholder game

January
a Your shareholders won't be happy, but it's your best option in the circumstances +3
b It's good to consult local experts, but you also need to take action +1
c This may seem like a good idea, but if the audit is leaked to the press, it will have a much more negative impact −3

February
a This will be a very unpopular decision with your employees, who may see it as divisive −3
b If you're going to introduce drug testing, you should at least be fair about who gets tested, but making it voluntary is only going to create problems −1
c This is by far the most socially responsible response to the problem, which is not widespread +3

March
a You will certainly get some good PR, but your shareholders, existing suppliers and purchasing department will be furious and positive discrimination helps no-one in the long-term −1
b This is a much more intelligent course of action +3
c You're right, of course, but you can't just ignore the diversity issue −1

April
a This is a noble gesture, but very costly and workers will still need to migrate to where there is work +2
b This looks like an indecisive move unless you really intend to do something after consultation +1
c By today's CSR standards, this is not very supportive – your shareholders will be pleased, but you may lose employees in other Latin American countries −2

May
a This will certainly set you apart as an employer in the manufacturing industry, but one out of every hundred employees off doing voluntary work is way too many −1
b A compromise (some will say you haven't gone far enough), but a good one, overall +3
c An understandable but not very community-conscious decision −1

June
a Safety is always a prime concern in manufacturing and going beyond compliance with existing regulations (on the recommendations of your quality circle) would win you a lot of support amongst opinion-formers +3
b Not exactly a proactive decision −1
c Receiving no formal complaints doesn't mean there isn't a problem – you seem a bit uncaring towards your workforce −3

July
a This is extremely honourable of you, but you may be missing a golden opportunity +1
b The factory expansion plan would seem to be more important than one storage facility – you can create a win-win situation here and assist abandoned and

maltreated animals at the same time (in the UK this is bound to get press coverage!) +3

c Who's talking about bribes? In business it's as much who you know as what you know. You're simply doing a good deed −1

August

a This may raise eyebrows at the shareholders' meeting if it turns out to be expensive, but ignoring safety issues is just creating bigger problems for the future +3

b You're just postponing the decision – you need to show more leadership −1

c You seem rather mercenary −3

September

a It's a serious oversight that your pension fund is not more socially responsible, but to change the fund's portfolio without expert advice is equally irresponsible −3

b The wisest choice for all concerned +3

c Avoiding strikes is not the issue here – you can't be an ethical company and invest unethically −3

October

a This might have serious financial ramifications, but mostly short-term – you'll find another distributor +3

b You're making excuses – if you know the distributor is guilty, you should act, regardless of the legal proceedings −1

c Not only are you condoning corruption, you're contemplating corrupting the justice system as well −6

November

a This will win you a huge number of fans in the anti-gun trafficking movement, but ruin your company −9

b In some ways this is a clever move – by suing Colbert (which you are legally entitled to do) you distance yourself from their arms business, but can continue to supply their non-arms business – but how long will Colbert want to do business with you if you take them to court? −1

c There's an element of risk here, but you can probably get a better (and more ethical) outcome for yourself by keeping the matter out of court +4

December

a A brave decision, but the golden rule in a crisis like this is to be seen to be taking firm action and putting the public interest first – so whether the situation turns out to be better or worse than expected, this is your best policy +9

b You're playing the fiddle while Rome burns −6

c You're adding gasoline to the flames −9

Score

If you scored in the minus numbers overall, bad luck! The board has voted you out of a job. Say goodbye to your corner-office on the top floor, the gym and club memberships, the five-star pension plan, your top-of-the-range Jaguar and private use of the company jet.

If you scored less than −23 there are those who will try to make sure you never work in senior management again!

If you scored between 0 and +10, you're also fired, but you leave with a golden parachute of $750,000 plus another $1m, if you want it, in stock options.

If you scored more than +10, well done, you get to keep your job!

But less than +20 means your position is far from secure.

More than +35 and you get a million dollar bonus. Of course, the ethical thing would be to donate that to charity!

11 SIMPLY THE BEST

CIRQUE DU SOLEIL

FACT FILE

Creative influences
Circus arts, gymnastics, ballet, contemporary dance, ethnic music, ice shows, water shows, extreme sports, martial arts, hip-hop culture, urban movements, street culture.

Customer profile
Educated, higher income, home-owner, frequent flier.

Target venues
The breakeven point for each series of shows is 100,000 tickets, so Cirque usually has to target big cities.

Research & development
70% of profits are reinvested in R&D.

Social responsibility
1% of turnover annually goes to community initiatives, helping the homeless and training street kids in circus arts to give them a 'trade'.

Possible future plans
Chief marketing officer Mario D'Amico has suggested that Cirque could stretch its brand to many other products and services.

CASE STUDY: A WINNING FORMULA

Moretti Racing Investor's Meeting

AGENDA

In attendance:

Apologies for absence: Enrico Moretti

Items	Points raised	Action
1 Situation report on the season so far *Are we happy with current performance? How safe is our investment?*		
2 Low morale: areas of conflict in the team *Have we got the right balance of skills and team roles? Have we even got a team or just a collection of high-achieving individuals?*		
3 How to capitalise on the team's strengths *Are we maximising the talents of the team members?*		
4 Rumours currently circulating *How, if at all, do these affect our decisions?*		
5 Changes that could be implemented *Who (if anyone) do we want to hire, fire or redeploy? Would training in team-building help? Do we want to address the team and/or talk to members individually?*		

3 DO THE RIGHT THING

Eco-speak

a   **transparency**: is the term used to describe a company's openness about its business practices and accounts

b   **shareholder**: an individual or organisation that owns stock in a company

c   **recyclable**: used goods that can be processed for reuse,

d   **carbon neutrality**: achieving a net zero carbon footprint by offsetting the effect of CO_2 emissions (eg. by paying into a tree planting fund)

e   **ethical trade**: commercial trade in compliance with non-financial, as well as financial, standards eg. labour conditions

f   **biodiversity**: the number and variety of plant and animal species in their natural environment

g   **green tech**: technological innovations with the objective of reducing our impact on the environment

h   **governance**: the activity of leading and administering a company

i   **social entrepreneurship**: change agents who use entrepreneurial skills and approaches to address social problems

j   **bottom line**: the amount of profit or loss after all the accounts have been calculated

17 NEGOTIATING DEALS

The recording contract

Team B: Starburst Records (executives and lawyers)

You are very excited about this band's prospects. The Penitents are musically exceptionally strong with proven song-writing abilities. What's more, they have already generated a lot of media interest. However, the risks with a new signing are always high. Fashions change quickly in your business and you should bear this in mind in your dealings with the band's management.

Read your negotiating objectives below and then work with your team to plan your overall strategy. In particular, make sure you know which of your objectives are:

1 tradeables (things you'll concede to get what you really want in return)

2 ideals (things you'd really like to get, but not if it costs you the deal)

3 essentials (things you absolutely have to get or the deal's off)

1   Band line-up Three of the four members of the band – the lead singer/rhythm guitarist, lead guitarist and bass guitarist are exceptionally talented, though the lead guitarist has a reputation for hitting members of the paparazzi and was recently involved in an unpleasant incident aboard an airliner that resulted in his being banned for life. The weak link is the drummer, who simply must be replaced.

2   Term You are prepared to offer a one-album deal, but would like to retain an option on at least two subsequent albums, if the first is successful. You'd also like to keep the performing and recording rights to all the songs – otherwise, if you don't renew their contract and they later become successful with a different label, you won't be able to profit from their backlist of songs.

3   Royalties You think a 10% royalty on net receipts from album sales would be fair. This might be renegotiable after the album, but you'd like to offset the initial risk of taking on the band by maximising profits in the early stages.

4   Deductions If sales of the first album are good (at least 200,000 units), you may want to run a TV campaign. In this case you would like to deduct the cost of 20% of this from the band's royalties.

5   Advances Since advances are normally non-repayable, you'd prefer to offer a relatively modest one on the first album (say $120,000) and promise higher ones on later albums once the band is established.

6   Territory As you'll be spending a substantial amount of time and money on promoting The Penitents, you require total 'universal rights' to sell their music globally.

7   Touring With a band like The Penitents touring is a key part of building a fan-base. The band is particularly strong live and you would like to capitalise on that. You'd expect them to tour for at least six months in their first year. Your preferred schedule would be: release two singles, record the first album and do the tour. You'd want 70% of the revenue from ticket sales but will pay for hotels, coach travel, clothes and food while on tour.

8 Songwriting The standard songwriter-music publisher split on fees for airplay on radio and TV is 50:50. You're quite happy with this arrangement as long as you retain the rights (see item 2).

02 EXCHANGING INFORMATION

Making things clear

1	American	6	Italian
2	Russian	7	British
3	German	8	Chinese
4	Brazilian	9	Indian
5	French	10	Japanese

CASE STUDY: THE SKY'S THE LIMIT

Group B

Here are the results of your research into the overall market potential for travel and tourism in India:

Medium-term growth prospects:

India GDP	▲ 9.6% p.a.
Domestic air travel	▲ 20-25% p.a.
International air travel	▲ 18% p.a.
Travel & tourism	▲ 8.8% over next 10yrs

Foreign Direct Investment (FDI) in India:

- US FDI up by $50bn over next 5yrs
- Up to 49% foreign ownership of airlines permitted
- Up to 100% foreign ownership of airports permitted
- Modernisation of airports already in progress
- Greenfield development of private airports e.g. Bangalore

Constraints on the LCC Sector:

- a general shortage of airport facilities in India
- out of 454 airports fewer than 100 offer more than one daily service
- top five airports handle 70% of all domestic passenger traffic but cater mostly for FSCs
- secondary airports often have only basic landing strips with few parking bays, takeoff or landing slots

CASE STUDY: THE FUTURE'S UNWRITTEN

According to intercultural guru Geert Hofstede, the cultures can be divided thus (he prefers to talk about uncertainty-avoidance rather than risk-taking):

RISK-TAKERS	RISK-AVOIDERS
Denmark (23)	Japan (95)
Hong Kong (29)	Poland (94)
China (32)	France (86)
UK (35)	Turkey (85)
USA (46)	Brazil (76)
	Italy (76)
	Germany (65)

Source: *Culture's Consequences*

The numbers in brackets give a more accurate evaluation of the level of risk avoidance. The higher the number the less willing people are to take risks and live with uncertainty.

Conclusions and recommendations

- India's economic prospects remain strong with domestic air travel predicted to grow even faster than international travel – we're clearly in the right market segment.

- Considerable FDI should lead to an increase in both the number of major airports and the standard of facilities at existing airports. Longer term, the prospects for LCCs should improve.

- Acquisition of or investment in a number of private airports might be another way of overcoming the problem of poor facilities for LCCs as well as increasing the number of routes and flights we can offer. Demand is certainly growing – we need to be able to handle a greater volume of passengers.

- Alternatively, if Eastern Promise went upmarket and offered a slightly more expensive but better quality service, it could gain access to the top five airports.

- There is obviously an element of risk in investing further in Indian domestic airlines. But, since we are already in partnership with Eastern Promise and the market is growing, this may be the direction we have to take. As media mogul Sumner Redstone once put it: 'In order to succeed, you have to live dangerously... as long as the danger is rationally accepted and as long as the rewards far outweigh the risk'. In our opinion, the rewards do far outweigh the risk. There are currently a lot of new players entering the market, but a period of consolidation is bound to follow as carriers merge and make strategic acquisitions.

CASE STUDY: THE SKY'S THE LIMIT

Group C

Here are the results of your customer survey and research into the possible fit between NMI's current portfolio of businesses and a re-launched and repositioned Eastern Promise:

NMI's Business Portfolio:

- Meridian Records (independent US record label)
- Cult TV (satellite channel showing reruns of classic series)
- Paper Tiger (25% stake in Bollywood movie studio)
- Joo-C (38% stake in Dutch energy drinks company)
- Athletix (90% stake in French sports goods retail chain)
- Eastern Promise (currently a low-cost Indian airline)

Suraj Kapoor:

- Has a number of business interests: restaurants, hotels, casinos and nightclubs throughout India
- A regular panellist on business-related reality TV show *Swimming with the Sharks*

India's demographics:

- By 2020 84% of Indians will be under the age of 50
- The highest percentage of airline users is likely to be young professionals in the 20-35yr age group

Customer survey results:

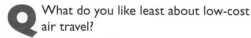 What do you like least about low-cost air travel?

Lack of room	70%
Missed connections	68%
Having a middle seat	61%
Flight delays	55%
Baggage fees	51%
Long queues	41%
Being seated next to noisy children and babies	40%
Lost luggage	37%
Restrictions on liquids in hand luggage	36%
Boredom on longer flights	35%
Overbooked flights	32%
Poor quality, overpriced food and drink	30%
Being treated like a commodity	28%
Environmental damage due to fuel emissions	19%
Inability to use mobile phone during flight	11%

Conclusions and recommendations

- Kapoor's original idea of 'a people's airline for the ordinary traveller' may need rethinking. Most air travellers in India are young professionals – the kind of people many of NMI's other companies target. There should be an opportunity for some synergy here.

- There is clearly a lot of untapped potential for cross-over from our other business interests and Eastern Promise. Kapoor's media presence in India has also been under-utilised.

- The company could be rebranded as a 'lifestyle airline' catering to India's young upwardly mobile professional elite, whilst continuing to represent good value for money. A change of name might be advisable to reflect a more glamorous, aspirational brand.

- Although it is hard to persuade customers that better service is worth paying for, Eastern Promise should be trying to address some of the most common complaints about low-cost air travel without pushing up costs significantly. We need to be creative here!

- The relaunch of Eastern Promise requires a strong advertising campaign. Alongside conventional media, we must increase our presence online and consider strategies such as viral marketing to create buzz amongst our target market.

15 FIRST AMONG EQUALS

The role of leadership

1 Answer b. 'To be smarter, focus on what you already do well,' says Karlin Sloan, executive coach and author of *Smarter, Faster, Better: Strategies for Effective, Enduring, and Fulfilled Leadership*, on which this quiz is based. 'Most people think getting smarter is all about mastering things you're bad at. Instead, look at your strengths, and build on them.'

2 Answer a. 'Surround yourself with experts,' suggests Sloan. 'Brainstorm with colleagues - and also with mentors and friends. The smartest people are those who know that others may be even smarter. Ask lots of questions.'

3 Answer c. 'To work faster, slow down,' says Sloan. 'Take naps. Take vacations. Don't work on weekends. Work shouldn't feel hard. If it is, you're doing too much, moving too fast, and not replenishing your energy - which means it will take you longer to accomplish tasks.' Resolving to work around the clock (a) is a recipe for burnout and, while asking your boss for more time (b) works occasionally, it won't help your career in the long run.

4 Answer b. Recent brain research shows that multitasking reduces the brainpower available for either task and actually slows you down as it takes time for your brain to switch from one task to another, says Sloan. If you're really swamped, choice (c) may be an option, but don't make a habit of it (see answer to question No. 3).

5 Answer a. Perfectionists usually think the right answer is choice (b). But 'perfectionism is enormously consuming of time and energy,' explains Sloan. 'It results in dreadful 'paralysis by analysis' that is the enemy of good decision-making.' Delegating the decision to someone else (c) is chickening out.

6 Answer c. 'If you want to strengthen your team's work ethic, create a 'play' ethic,' Sloan suggests. 'Commit to making work more fun.' Why? The happier employees are at work, the more energy they have for projects, she says. If that sounds counterintuitive, think back to your own career when you had great ideas and put in extra effort. It wasn't when you were slogging through a chore; it was when you were working on something that was fun for you. Trying to fix everything yourself (b) will burn you out and everyone around you too.

7 Answer a. 'Embracing differences forms bonds,' says Sloan. 'To build a cohesive team, find differences in age, culture, thinking styles, experience, and skills - and build on them. Each offers an opportunity for a smarter team.' Ignoring the differences (b) or taking the time to learn the legal issues a diverse workforce presents (c) are fine, but they're not likely to get you to the higher level of performance that true diversity can generate.

8 Answer b. 'To be more profitable, give it away,' says Sloan. 'Managers and companies that are philanthropic, and focused on making their community and the world a better place, attract supporters and fans - not to mention loyal customers, clients, and colleagues.' Spending a day fixing up a local park or refurbishing a homeless shelter can be a bonding experience for your team, too.

Now work out your percentage score. 60% and over shows promise. Over 80% and you're a natural-born leader!

15 FIRST AMONG EQUALS

The mystery leader game

Congratulations! You've just hired …

Applicant 1: Jeff Bezos, founder and head of Amazon.

Applicant 2: Carly Fiorina, ex-CEO of Hewlett-Packard.

Applicant 3: Meg Whitman, ex-CEO of eBay.

Applicant 4: Ricardo Semler, president of Semco S/A.

Applicant 5: Jorma Ollila, ex-CEO of Nokia.

Applicant 6: Indra Nooyi, CEO of PepsiCo.

Applicant 7: Xie Qihua, CEO of Shanghai Baosteel Group Corporation.

Applicant 8: Jack Welch, ex-chairman and CEO of General Electric.

CASE STUDY: HEAD TO HEAD

THE BLACK KNIGHT STRIKES AGAIN

Sir Anthony Black, mastermind of a hundred hostile takeovers, this week makes a bid to topple Clark Brubaker and the board of Chester Electrical, Penn. In a private interview, Sir Anthony responded to accusations of asset-stripping by saying that 'the inevitable job losses at CE are, of course, regrettable, but we have to face the fact that this company is now stone-cold dead. I didn't commit the murder, but I saw it happen, and I want to make sure, the people who supported and cared for this proud company throughout its life – the stockholders – get their proper inheritance, which is to say, a decent return on their investment. I am currently in talks with several parties interested in purchasing some or all of CE, should our motion be passed at the AGM'…

BRUBAKER DIGS IN

Clark Brubaker, new CEO of embattled wire and cable manufacturer, Chester Electric, today brushed off claims that his company was about to be torn away from him by CE's largest stockholder Black Investments. 'CE' says Brubaker 'is at the moment in talks with the Pennsylvania state government about being awarded tax breaks in an effort to save it from closure and the loss of a thousand jobs in an area of high unemployment. Although I've only been with the company a relatively short time, I already feel a huge responsibility to the loyal employees who have stuck with us through the worst period in our history and are now starting to see the green shoots of growth and renewal'. Brubaker remains confident that stockholders will reject the motion to replace the CE board at their AGM next Friday…

OUR WIRELESS FUTURE?

It's the dream of techies everywhere – a world without wires, a world in which data can be wirelessly networked between PCs, laptops and smart phones anytime, anyplace. We have the technology, but are we any nearer the reality? Currently, wireless services are both expensive and unreliable. When cellular signals fade and batteries fail, the safest thing may well be to plug it in! This must come as some consolation to shareholders in companies like Chester Electrical…

JUMP-STARTING THE AUTO INDUSTRY

A new US government stimulus package to save auto manufacturers from bankruptcy won't just protect jobs in cities like Detroit. Auto-parts manufacturers as far away as Chester, Pennsylvania could also feel the benefit. Francine Bryant, head of HR at Chester Electrical, a company facing possible closure if a vote at tomorrow's AGM goes the wrong way, is reported as saying: 'This new government initiative may have come just in the nick of time. Hopefully, it will persuade CE stockholders that their stock is worth holding on to a little while longer'.

DARK FORCES AT WORK?

Allegations of corruption are flying tonight as Susan Cameron, CFO at Chester Electrical, accuses Black Investments, CE's biggest stockholder, of interfering in recent negotiations between the wire and cable manufacturer and the Pennsylvania Department of Transport. A contract to supply cable for a massive highways reconstruction program had almost been agreed, when someone leaked the news to the Penn DoT that CE was about to go up for sale. Sir Anthony Black, head of Black Investments refused to comment beyond saying that his company had absolutely nothing to do with the leak.

04 VOICE AND VISUALS

Giving feedback

Speaker B: Presenter

You work for a major management consultancy and have just given a presentation to an important Taiwanese client. The presentation didn't go very well and unfortunately your boss was in the audience.

You are meeting your boss now, and are not expecting very good feedback. Make it clear that the disaster wasn't entirely your fault. Defend yourself using the following information, and assure your boss that this will never happen again.

- You've been asking your boss for a new laptop for ages – the one you've got just can't handle PowerPoint properly.
- You've been on the road for four weeks and are completely exhausted – this is your tenth major presentation. To make matters worse, the laundry ruined your best suit and left you with virtually nothing to wear.
- You've no excuse for the poor handouts. It was obviously a printer problem and you forgot to check them.
- Nobody told you your Taiwanese audience hardly spoke any English – by the time you realised you were halfway through your talk.
- Some of your jokes may not have translated very well, but you were just trying to break the ice.
- You're sure the video you were going to use was stolen from your hotel bedroom.
- No one checked the microphone: the amplifier was turned down much too low.

> **Useful language**
>
> How was I supposed to know ...?
>
> It's not my fault. You should have ...
>
> Somebody should have ...
>
> It might have helped if ...
>
> Look, I'm not trying to make excuses, but ...
>
> I can hardly be blamed for ...ing, can I?
>
> Rest assured, it won't happen again.

CASE STUDY: HEAD TO HEAD

Dear Mr Brubaker

With the Chester Electrical AGM fast approaching, I have decided to end months of speculation and publicly confirm that Black Investments has, to date, bought a 24% stake in CE. The purpose of this private e-mail is to make sure you are the first to know, although I'm sure you'd already guessed. Of course, we would have liked our percentage of the stock to be higher, but we have of late experienced some reluctance to sell from the shareholders we've approached. Many of them are under the impression that they will be offered higher annual dividends to hold on to their shares. I assume I have you and your team to thank for this piece of disinformation. No matter.

As the single largest shareholder in CE, I have to say that we are not at all happy with the way the company is currently being managed. The wire and cable division is not only losing vast amounts of money, the market itself is in decline. You have a sizeable share of a shrinking market, Mr Brubaker. In fact, I would go so far as to say that many, if not most, of CE's products are uncompetitive and, in the light of recent technological developments, may soon be obsolete.

Fortunately, the company shares were well worth what I paid for them. No need to thank me for the recent rise in CE stock. If we do a quick bit of mental arithmetic, we can work out that CE has $84,000,000 of assets. Divide that by the four million outstanding shares and we see that each share is actually worth $21. Not bad when you consider that I bought most of my holdings for $11.44 a share just a few months ago. And this doesn't even take account of your much more profitable heating and plumbing divisions. We estimate that these could be worth another $40m at least. Although these divisions are doing well, one is operating in a very small and uninteresting market and the other, though there's a large market for it, has a pitifully low market share. Liquidation of all three divisions clearly makes the most sense if we are to maximise shareholder value.

In order to push the proposed sale of CE through at the AGM, we shall be tabling the motion that the present board of directors be replaced with one appointed by Black Investments and with a mandate to sell off Chester Electrical in its entirety.

I have asked for this motion to be added to the agenda.

Best regards

Sir Anthony Black CBE

01 BUSINESS OR PLEASURE?

 1.01

Speaker 1 OK, well, now, we don't know a lot about what the group might be interested in. Anyway, there are going to be about fifteen of them – a dozen men or so and three or four women plus their partners, so it would be difficult to choose something they'll all like. But, since this is the first visit to Britain for some of them, I suggest we go for something, you know, quintessentially British. The main thing is to make sure nothing can go wrong. I know this is the summer we're talking about, but we don't want to be relying on the weather too much. And we definitely need to provide a bit more than just an expensive dinner. We're looking to create a really memorable occasion. What about something cultural?

Speaker 2 Hm, I think culture can be tricky – too much a matter of taste. We don't want half the group bored out of their minds. Besides, we need to be able to socialise. So, it's no good taking them to a musical or an opera or a ballet or anything like that. In any case, I should imagine they've seen enough ballet in Russia to last them a lifetime! And theatre in a foreign language is asking a bit much. No, we just need a really nice setting, good views of the city – somewhere we can relax, enjoy decent wine and food and talk about business. I know we have to be careful about different diets and things – some of them may not drink – but I still think that's the safest bet.

Speaker 3 Hang on. We'll have plenty of time to talk business in the meetings. This is about making sure we show them a good time. Russians are very people-oriented. This is an opportunity for us to build a good working relationship with them, you know, a bit of team spirit. In some ways it could even be a team-building kind of thing. And, let me tell you, Russians certainly like to wine and dine – and I don't think you'll have too many vegetarians and teetotallers! So top-quality catering, sure, but let's offer them something a bit special as well. And keep business out of it!

Speaker 4 OK, look, I can see the direction this is going in. Can I just point out that cost *is* an issue here? Yes, this is a very important project for us and could be the first of many, but I'd like to see us work within some kind of budget if possible. It's not as if we're trying to sweeten a potential customer or anything like that. We're simply trying to get this project off to a good start. Let's be honest, this hasn't been our best year financially and I don't think the Russians are going to be impressed to see us throwing money around like it's going out of fashion! Surely, we can come up with a perfectly enjoyable event that allows us all to get to know each other better without it costing the earth!

Speaker 5 Yes, well, I take your point about the cost. I mean, we shouldn't go mad, no, but we're not talking about a very large group here, are we? In real terms the cost is negligible, surely? I think the main thing is to make the visit as personal as possible. I mean, we could spend a fortune on attending some big event, but that's not very personal, is it? In fact, spending a little less on the event might mean you could afford to do something extra for the team members – I'm not necessarily talking gifts, but something. And, by the way, I happen to know that their project leader, Yuri, spent a year studying in London, so we might think about taking them somewhere else. That means travel expenses, of course, but I'm sure we can keep those within reason.

 1.02

Conversation 1

A Hi, mind if I join you?

B Er, not at all. Be my guest.

A Only if I have to sit through 'Rule Britannia' by the Band of the Royal Scots Dragoon Guards once more, I think I'll scream.

B And I thought you Americans were supposed to like all that traditional British stuff.

A Yeah, well, you can have too much of a good thing. Thought I'd come out here and enjoy the view. I must say, though, it was an excellent lunch. Fabulous ship too.

B Yes, isn't it? I'm James McRae, by the way. BP, engineering division.

A Hello, James. I'm ...

B Helen Keating. Exxon Mobil.

A Yes, how did you ... oh ... ? Have we met somewhere before?

B We have indeed, but I obviously failed to make much of an impression.

A Wait a minute. It's not like me to forget a face. I know – Riyadh. The Petrochemicals Conference. I thought I recognised you.

B As matter of fact, we had dinner together.

A You're kidding! Now, I think I would have remembered that.

B Well, there were rather a lot of us in the group. At least forty. I don't think we actually spoke.

A Aha. OK. Yes, it's all coming back to me now. I seem to remember spending most of the evening fighting off some creepy little guy called Alan.

B Alan Sullivan. My boss.

A Oops! I'm sorry. I didn't mean to ...

B No problem. He's not my favourite person either. Anyway, Helen, looks like we've got the best part of the Royal Yacht to ourselves this afternoon. How about another drink?

A OK. Why not? I'll have another Armagnac.

B Sure. I'll be right back.

 1.03

Conversation 2

A So, Mr Ishida, let me freshen your glass.

B Thank you. I'm fine.

A Some more strawberries, then, perhaps?

B Er, not at the moment, thank you.

A I am sorry about this weather. Typical English summer, I'm afraid. The forecast did say we might have showers. But I'm sure it'll blow over in half an hour or so. So, how are you enjoying the match?

B Ah, very entertaining, I'm sure ...

A Good. Splendid ... So, tell me, have you been to one of these big tournaments before? The American Open perhaps?

B Ah, no, I haven't.

A Ah. But **I hear** you're quite a tennis fan, though.

B Er, not really. In fact, I never watch tennis normally.

A Oh, ... I see. My marketing people must have made a mistake.

B Maybe they meant table tennis. I used to play for my university in Tokyo – many years ago.

A Table tennis! Ah, yes. **I understand** the Japanese are world table tennis champions, isn't that right?

B As a matter of fact, that's the Chinese.

A Ah, yes, of course ... Erm, so, do you still play?

B Not any more. Much too old for running around now.

A Oh, I'm sure that's not true.

B I assure you it is true, Mr Thompson. Bad heart, you see. Doctor's orders.

A Oh, right. Sorry. Erm, ... **I see** the Nikkei's looking strong. That must be good news for you.

B Not especially. For Japan, economic recovery is still a long way off.

A Oh? I read somewhere that things were improving. Or am I mistaken?

B Over-optimism, I'm afraid.

A Ah, well, I suppose, er ... Oh, look, the rain's stopped! Yes, the players are coming back on. Excellent. So, shall we return to our seats?

C Quiet, please. Nadal to serve. Nadal leads by three games to two and by two sets to love.

 1.04

Conversation 1

A Alistair, we've been here nearly three hours! Can't we just make our excuses and go? You know how I hate these things.

B Look, Fiona, I'm not enjoying myself any more than you are, but this is business. Besides, I need to speak to Julian about this Internet advertising idea of his.

A Oh, all right. Where is Julian, anyway? We haven't seen him all evening ...

C Hello! You must be Julian's guests. I don't think we've met. I'm Dan Wilson, Creative Director at JJK Advertising. I work with Julian.

B Ah, pleased to meet you, Mr Wilson. No, we've not met. Julian's mentioned your name, of course. Alistair Hamilton. And this is my wife, Fiona.

C A pleasure to meet you both at last. And please call me Dan.

A We were just wondering what this pile of dirty laundry was doing in the middle of an art gallery.

B Fiona!

C So, you're not a fan of contemporary art then, Fiona – you don't mind me calling you Fiona, do you? Actually, this, er, 'dirty laundry', as you call it, came second in this year's Turner Prize, believe it or not.

A Doesn't surprise me in the least, but, er, still just looks like dirty laundry to me, I'm afraid.

C Well, yes, but I don't think that's what the artist would call it.

A What does he call it, then?

C Erm, I'm not sure. I'll check the catalogue for you... Here we are – erm, exhibit 12, oh, 'Dirty Laundry'.

A What did I tell you?

C Yes, quite. Erm, Alistair, I wonder if we could have a word? Julian tells me you're not very happy with the new Internet campaign.

B Er, yes. **Would you excuse us a moment**, Fiona? Dan and I need to talk.

A Oh, don't mind me. There's a heap of broken glass in the room next door I'm just dying to see.

B Er, right. **Well, I'll catch you later, then** ... Now, look, Dan, the thing is...

 1.05

Conversation 2

A Ricardo! Glad you could make it.

B Hello, Tom. I wouldn't have missed it for the world. It's not every day I get invited to something like this. I hear Massa's out, so it should be a good race.

A Yes, it certainly evens things up a bit with Ferrari down to one car. **Talking of** races, how's the South African bid going? I heard it was just between you and Swedish Steel now.

B Hm, yes, the negotiations are still going on, but we're hopeful. I don't think the Swedes can beat us on price.

A Well, let me know how it goes. We'd be happy to organise the transportation if you need it. We'd do you a good deal.

B Sure, I'll certainly keep you in mind if we win the contract.

A Great ... Ricardo, **there's someone I'd like you to meet.**

B Oh, really?

A Yes, but first let me get you something to drink. Can't have you standing there with an empty glass. What are you on? Champagne?

B Just mineral water for now, thanks.

A Oh, dear ... Here you go.

B Thanks. So, who's this person you wanted me to meet?

A Ah, yes ... Oh, here she is now. Élise, this is Ricardo Piquet. Ricardo, Élise de Cadenet. Élise is ...

C Hello, Ricardo. Long time no see. What is it, five

years?

B Hello, Élise. Must be five at least. You haven't changed a bit.

C Neither have you. Charming as ever.

A Ah, I see you two know each other already.

C Ricardo and I go back a long way, Tom. A very long way.

B Yes, actually, we first met in Monaco – at the Grand Prix, funnily enough ... So, Élise, **last I heard** you were getting married again.

C And divorced again. I'm between husbands at the moment. Far too busy setting up this new business in Biarritz.

A Er, well, **I'll leave you two to chat. See you later.** Don't forget the race starts at three.

B Yes, see you later, Tom. So, Élise, how about a drink?

C Mm, sounds good. I'll have whatever you're having.

B Er, waiter, two champagnes, please.

02 EXCHANGING INFORMATION

 1.06

A OK, people. Let's get the ball rolling. Well, you've all seen the latest figures and I don't need to tell you they're not good. Now, we're not here to run a blamestorming session. But it's clearly time for a reality check, ladies and gentlemen. This division is about to go under if we don't change our attitude and fast. What we need is a complete change of mindset. We need to synergise and take a much more proactive approach to product development. The same tired old ideas simply won't work any more. If we always do what we've always done, then we'll always get what we've always got. And what got us where we are won't get us where we're going.

B I'm sorry?

A What I mean is we need to be thinking outside the box, maximising our creativity. Yes, that's right. I'm talking about nothing less than a complete paradigm shift in the management of this company.

B What's he talking about?

C I don't know.

A OK, the bottom line is: if we don't figure out how to turn this operation around, we have no future in this business. So, let's look at the big picture and then see if we can drill down to the details.

D Can I just say something, Daryl?

A Fire away, Kelly.

D Erm, I don't think we're quite with you.

A Ah, right. No, that's OK. I was expecting a certain amount of push-back to begin with. But it's very important I get your buy-in on this. So let me put it simply. What we have to do is scope out the competition, establish what our core competencies are and then benchmark ourselves against the current market leader.

B But I thought we were trying to be different from the competition, Daryl?

A That's the long game, Tim.

B The long game?

A Yes, that's our long-term objective.

B Oh, I see.

A But right now we're struggling just to compete. If we can only learn from our competitors, then we'll be able to upskill our own people, ramp up product development, become more customer-centric and start to take this company to the next level.

C Erm, and you really want our input on this?

A Yes, Nigel. Change begins at the grassroots in an organisation. Empowerment – that's what this is all about.

D Daryl?

A Yes, Kelly.

D Have you ever played buzzword bingo?

 1.07

A Right. That brings us on to our main business this morning – the new Quasar Online Gaming System. As you already know, the news is not particularly good. In spite of a considerable investment in design and marketing, I'm sorry to report that the project has not been a complete success.

B Not a complete success? What you mean is it's failed – dismally!

A Now let's not overreact, Alan. Certainly, it's failed to meet our original expectations. And, yes, technically speaking, we have run into negative profit ...

B Negative profit! What do you mean negative profit? You mean we've made a loss – an enormous loss if these figures are anything to go by!

C Can we come back to the figures later, Alan, if that's OK? First, let's consider why sales are so disappointing. Now, in my view, it's not the product, but the market. I think there's a general lack of consumer confidence.

B In other words, sales are falling. Look, I'm sorry, Hannah, but you're just looking for excuses. It's obvious that Quasar is simply not innovative enough for today's market.

A Alan, we leave innovation to companies like Sony and Nintendo. What we do is clone the technology and do it cheaper.

C Alan, you know we've always been a market-driven organisation ...

B Market-driven? What you really mean is we've never had an original idea. I say we need to be developing an innovative new product line ...

A What, when the market's so massively oversupplied? I don't think so. Now is not the time to expand, but to consolidate.

B So what you're saying is let's do nothing.

A No, I'm saying let's consolidate.

B I see. And what will this 'consolidation' mean in terms of our staff? Redundancies, I suppose.

C Well, obviously, there will have to be some restructuring of the department.

B You mean people are going to lose their jobs.

C It's a possibility, yes. And we may also have to consider outsourcing production to cut costs.

B In other words, our assembly plant may be closed down too. I can't believe I'm hearing this!

A Of course, we won't be able to finalise anything today.

B You mean we'll have to hold another meeting! If we've all still got a job by then, that is.

A Yes, well, I'm glad you raised that point, Alan.

B What do you mean?

 1.08

a

A Right, I'm allowing an hour and a half for this meeting. Kate is going to fill us in on how the appraisals went. That'll take about a quarter of an hour or so. So that only gives us 45 minutes to deal with everything else. We'd better get started.

B Sorry, I thought we had an hour and a half.

A What? Oh, yeah, sorry. We've got 75 minutes, haven't we? Still, there's a lot to get through.

b

A Look, it's no good going on about pay rises. We pay nearly twice what most of our competitors do. And I really don't see how people can expect another salary increase this year, when they're already earning three times the average rate.

B Hang on a second. You said we pay twice as much, not three times.

A Hm? Oh, all right, twice as much, then. It's still a lot more than everybody else.

c

A You know as well as I do that this project was supposed to take sixteen weeks. And this isn't the

first time we've run over budget, is it? I mean a 20% overspend is pretty serious. And surely three months was sufficient time to complete the project.

B Just a minute. I thought you said sixteen weeks, not three months.

A OK, OK, that's four months, then. But you've taken nearly six.

d

A Frankly, with the Asian economic situation the way it is and the euro getting stronger, we're not doing well in the Far East. Southern Europe is where we should be concentrating our efforts. As a matter of fact, Spain is now our second biggest market after China.

B Hold on. Didn't you just say we're not doing well in the Far East?

A Well, I meant apart from China, obviously! China's always been a huge market for tobacco products.

e

A I'm sorry, but I don't want us bringing in people from outside the company to sort this problem out. There's a lot of highly confidential information on our intranet. And we should really be able to deal with this ourselves. There's a guy I play golf with who runs his own consultancy. He's offered to help us out.

B Wait a moment. You just said you didn't want to bring in people from outside the company.

A Erm, well, what I mean is I don't want just anybody. This guy's different. I've known him for years.

 1.09

A OK, everyone. It's bad news, I'm afraid. As you may have heard, the latest European sales figures are looking extremely disappointing.

B **Are you saying they've fallen short of projections again?**

A I'm afraid so. In fact, we may be 30% down. Now, this will be the third quarter in a row we've missed our targets and, frankly, unless things pick up considerably next quarter, we may have to rethink our whole pricing strategy.

C **Are you suggesting we introduce price cuts?**

A If we still can, Anna. Certainly if we'd done that a year ago, it might have stimulated demand. But do it now and we may end up running at a loss. As you know, we're barely breaking even on some of our product lines as it is.

D **Surely you're not saying it's time to phase them out!**

A No, no, of course not. At least, not yet. But what I am saying is that we need to keep production costs down somehow if we want to remain competitive.

B **Does this mean we should be investing more in new technology?**

A If only it was that simple, Erik. But right now we're not really in a position to invest in anything, even if we wanted to. No, I'm afraid the situation calls for more drastic action. It's clearly time for a major restructuring.

D **Are you telling us there could be layoffs?**

A I don't see how we can avoid it, James – unless, of course, we can get some of our people to accept reduced hours.

C **You mean some kind of job-share scheme?**

A Yes, either that or introduce a four-day week – providing the unions don't oppose it. Of course, it's not just a question of costs. It's also a question of product. The fact is, better products are coming onto the market all the time.

D **So you're saying we should be spending more on R&D.**

A As I've said, capital investment is no longer an option for us. Pour any more money into R&D and we'll simply slide further into debt. And then there are all the problems we've been having with our overseas distributors.

B **Does this mean you're thinking of centralising distribution?**

A Well, that's one option, yes. But even if we decided to do that, and it's a big if, it would take time to implement – time we simply don't have. As you know, our share price has fallen to an all-time low of just 85 cents. And I wouldn't be surprised if, by our next meeting, it's fallen even further. The fact is, we're selling old products at inflated prices in a volatile market through inefficient distributors.

D I hope you're not suggesting the situation is hopeless.

A Well, let's put it this way: we've cancelled the Christmas party!

 1.10

a

A Right. Basically, **the position is this** the contract is ours if we want it.

B But **we're not in a position to** take on another project right now, are we?

A I know. Jan, **what's your position on** this?

b

A Look, **it's not just a question of** software, Alessandro.

B Of course not. **It's also a question of** hardware. The entire system needs upgrading.

A But **that's out of the question**. We can't afford that kind of capital outlay.

c

A Sales are down. **One option would obviously be to** cut our prices.

B **That's no longer an option for us.** We're barely breaking even as it is.

A Well, then **we've no option but to** rethink our whole marketing strategy.

d

A Well, **there's no easy answer to this, but** how about voluntary redundancy?

B **I don't think that's the answer,** but maybe we could reduce people's hours.

A **That might have been the answer if** we didn't already have a strike on our hands!

e

A Now, **let's not make a problem out of** this. What if we just pulled out of Sudan?

B Well, **I've no problem with** that, but our partners won't be happy.

A No, but **that's not our problem**, is it? The political situation is just too unstable.

f

A **I'll get straight to the point.** We're getting too many customer complaints.

B I agree with you. But **the point is** we don't have the staff to deal with them.

A **That's beside the point.** We shouldn't be getting them in the first place!

g

A **I'm afraid the situation is serious.** And if the press get hold of the story, ...

B Look, **we'll deal with that situation if and when it arises.** Let's not panic just yet.

A You're right. **What this situation calls for is** calm and careful planning.

h

A **The fact is**, we're simply not spending enough on R&D.

B **As a matter of fact**, we've doubled our R&D budget this year.

C That may be so, but **the fact remains** we're losing our technological lead.

03 DO THE RIGHT THING

 1.11

Speaker 1 I think in some ways, America's just catching up with Europe when it comes to CSR, if 'catching up' is the right word. Sustainability's been a buzzword in the EU for over a decade. But we tend to be more focused on the bottom-line here, especially with the economy the way it is right now. We don't like the idea of compromising profitability. So for us, CSR is more a matter of compliance with government regulations – we try not to have too many of those – and doing the minimum, really, to keep things legal. Frankly, I'm pretty sceptical about these big oil and sports goods firms who top the league tables of socially responsible companies every year. Mentioning no names, but how come they seem to be the ones involved in all the legal battles to do with corruption, pollution and working conditions? I read somewhere that 60% of all CSR initiatives are really just public relations. And that figures. If you set up a multi-million dollar charity in Lima, perhaps the media will stop noticing that you're cutting down rainforests in the Amazon. And compared with the cost of advertising, let's face it, CSR works out pretty cheap.

 1.12

Speaker 2 I think it's fair to say that Scandinavia is right at the forefront of CSR. Sweden has actually passed a law to shut down its nuclear reactors and explore alternative energy production. Denmark was the first country in the world to use wind power as a significant contributor to its national electricity grid. In Iceland, Shell opened the world's first hydrogen fuel station. And here in Norway the government has now ordered firms to make sure that at least 40% of its board members are women. All quite impressive. However, Scandinavians haven't such a good record further from home. A few years ago, IKEA had problems with child labour in some of the factories it was outsourcing to and they weren't the only ones, of course. That was a wake-up call for us all. And, in my opinion, we still haven't gone far enough with CSR. The word 'sustainability' always sounds to me very modest. As if our main aim was just to stop things getting too much worse. But can't we do better than that? After all, what we do now will affect generations to come. I think we should keep the words of the famous American medical researcher very much in mind. 'Our greatest responsibility' he said, 'is to be good ancestors'.

 1.13

Speaker 3 Ah, I think in China CSR is still something very new. For us, the focus is more on volunteering and charity work than on changing the way we do business. That's partly cultural, partly economic. In Asia, taking care of your community is important. That's why much CSR addresses local concerns. In China that would be HIV, SARS and the condition of roads, which is very bad – many accidents every year! But we know that the success of China is our competitive labour costs, so any CSR must be cost-effective. We are always aware of the cost of changing our behaviour. And if the cost is too high, we won't do it. But I read recently a report by the Economist Intelligence Unit which shows that companies which pay attention to sustainability issues, they see profits rise more than twice as much as companies which have a poor CSR record. You have the expression in the US: 'Good guys finish last!' But maybe this is not true! I think the world is very insecure right now. And maybe to be a company you can trust is a good thing for business!

 1.14

January OK, so now we come to the main item on our agenda for this, the first of our monthly meetings. As you know, we've just completed the annual audits of our Asian plants. Generally, the results are a great improvement on our last audit, but I'm afraid that working conditions there are still far from ideal. There's also a question mark over the age of some of the machine operators and the number of hours they're expected to work. Now, we are taking steps to bring standards in line with our factories over here, but this will take time. The question is do we publish this audit to show that we have nothing to hide or keep it confidential at this stage?

 1.15

February Right, well, this is a rather delicate issue, but you've probably heard reports of several of our junior and middle managers in the New York office being found to have drug-related problems, which, in some cases, have affected their work. Unfortunately, the press managed to get hold of the story and made the situation look even worse than it is. The HR department's proposal is that drug testing now be made a condition of employment and that random drug tests be carried out periodically on all levels of personnel below board level. Many companies now have a similar policy and we don't want to be seen to be condoning illegal substance abuse. So, shall we give HR the go-ahead?

 1.16

March Item three: minority-owned businesses. As you've probably heard, there's a new initiative by the government to promote diversity in the SME sector in favour of small and medium-sized businesses launched by minorities, particularly in areas of high unemployment and ethnic tension. We're being asked to commit to a certain percentage of our suppliers being sourced from this minority-owned group. Clearly, this could affect our bottom line, but we can keep the percentage fairly low if we want. So, your thoughts? Are we going to agree to quotas or not?

 1.17

April Now, finally, I'm sorry to report that the latest figures prove that our manufacturing plant in Venezuela is no longer economically viable. Closure is, unfortunately, our only option. What we must try to do is minimise the impact on the local community and economy. We are, of course, currently the biggest employer in the region and many other local businesses depend on the presence of the factory and its workers. So what, if anything, should we do?

 1.18

May OK, now I know we've discussed this before, but the issue has come up again. Several of our younger managers have requested paid leave to pursue short-term voluntary work, which they are claiming will be beneficial to their personal and professional development. Now, there's absolutely no provision for this in their employment contracts, but it is common practice as some of our competitor firms. If restricted to, say, one percent of our management level employees, the costs would be bearable, but there would obviously be some disruption to the smooth running of certain departments. Anyway, I'd like to hear your reactions to the idea.

 1.19

June Those of you who have dealings with the production department know that some of our manufacturing processes fall outside the proposed government guidelines in terms of safety. Now, whilst these guidelines will probably not come into legal force for at least three years, health and safety groups are calling for all socially responsible companies to phase out the existing procedures before then. Clearly, we are not legally obliged to do so, but would it create better relations with our staff and the public at large if we complied with their wishes?

 1.20

July Just to update everyone on where we are with the proposed storage facility outside London. We have located a suitable brownfield site in East London, which means it can be cleared for new building to commence. We've put in a bid for the site, which we believe will be higher than competing bids. So what's the problem? Well, I was contacted earlier in the week by a Ms Hughes, whose organisation is one of the other bidders for the site. Apparently, she runs an animal welfare organisation which is hoping to use the area to build a sanctuary and veterinary hospital for abandoned animals and she's asking us to withdraw our bid, to enable her to go ahead and purchase the site. Now, I know what you're thinking: why should we care? Well, perhaps we shouldn't, except that Ms Hughes is also a prominent local councillor and, as you know, we are currently seeking council approval for major extensions to all our London-based production facilities.

1.21

August I've just received the results of our internal report into waste management. It seems that a lot of the raw materials we buy in are sitting in storage so long, they are going past their use-by date and then being thrown away. Some of the more toxic chemicals are also starting to leak and present a health hazard. Now, we got through the last health and safety check OK, and we're not due another official check for two years, so the question is: should we review our purchasing and storage procedures now or wait until next year? Obviously, the present system is inefficient and is losing us money. But perhaps it is not yet a priority.

1.22

September I've been asked to add an important item to our agenda, which is the question of our employee pension fund. As you know, we have to disclose by law to what extent our fund takes account of the environmental, ethical and social impact of our investments. Our trade union representative has brought it to our attention that historically our fund has not taken sufficient account of these issues and that this is both socially irresponsible and, in the light of the current CSR programme, somewhat hypocritical. I have to say I agree with her on this last point if nothing else. However, I'm not convinced that ethical investment offers the same long-term returns. To date our pension fund has performed well. So what should we do?

1.23

October If you read the international newspapers this morning, you'll know that the bribery scandal surrounding our distributor in Kazakhstan has now become public. It's true that a final verdict has not yet been reached by the authorities, but I don't think anyone here doubts what the final outcome will be. Now, the question is: do we stand by our distributor until the result of the legal proceedings is officially known or pull out now and avoid the bad publicity which is sure to come? I don't need to remind you that we have so far been unable to locate another suitable distributor in the region.

1.24

November In view of the seriousness of the final item on our agenda, I've asked for this meeting to be extended to give us sufficient time to consider the implications of the decision we must make. After a long internal investigation, commissioned by us in collaboration with an international arms reduction organisation, we have discovered that Colbert Inc., one of our major customers is using some of the components we supply to build weapons. Now, we've known for some time that a small part of Colbert's business has been legally manufacturing weapons for the ministry of defence, but we have always insisted that our components are not put to this use. That's in our sales contract. More worrying still, there are rumours that some of Colbert's products are finding their way onto the open market, supplying the usual assortment of terrorists and military dictators with state-of-the-art weaponry. This is, I'm sure you'll agree, very disturbing news. And I think our decision in this case would be clear, were it not for the fact that Colbert is our second biggest customer and has been for fifteen years. Losing their business would have a catastrophic effect on our sales revenue and would certainly lead to mass redundancies and, who knows, perhaps the collapse of this company.

1.25

December OK, first of all, thank you all for coming in at such short notice. As chairman of the board, I'd like to be able to congratulate everyone on a successful first year. But you know I haven't called you away from your friends, families and holiday festivities to hand out congratulations. Ladies and gentlemen, we have a serious crisis on our hands and we must act fast. In the early hours of this morning, an accident between two vehicles in one of the loading bays at our main facility in Portland caused an explosion that ignited flammable chemicals which were incorrectly stored. You may remember we've had storage problems before – perhaps we should have dealt with them sooner. Anyway, in spite of our best efforts to contain the damage, it's looking as though certain contaminants may have been released into the atmosphere. We won't know for sure until our chemical experts have conducted tests, but if this is the case, the health threat to the local community could be severe. Some preliminary estimates of the possible consequences are in the reports in front of you. We could be talking a major evacuation of the area and a fortune in compensation which our insurance may not fully cover. Television crews from the major news channels are already filming and reporting on the fire, but are so far unaware of the danger of chemical poisoning. I'm counting on you to come up with a crisis management plan before the end of this meeting. So let's get to it!

CASE STUDY: CASH OR CONSCIENCE?

1.26

A Malcolm, can we keep this short? Only I'm due at the studio in just over an hour. I'm having problems with my program editor and the next show goes out in three days.

B Take a seat, Ruth.

A Ah. Why do I get the feeling this *isn't* going to be a short meeting?

B I assume you've read your advance copy of the programming report?

A Not in detail, no. Why? Is this about our viewing figures again?

B Of course it's about our viewing figures, Ruth. This is a television station.

A Malcolm, we've been through this. So, we're a little down on the last two series. So what? We're still pulling in fifteen million viewers, aren't we? We're still number one in the nine o'clock slot. When we start to slip in the ratings, then I'll worry.

B I'm *already* worried. Look at this. In the middle of the last series we peaked at 22.4 million viewers. So far this series we've dropped to 13.1 million and my analysts are saying that trend is going to continue.

A We've had a few disappointing months, that's all.

B The numbers don't lie, Ruth. For series two and three our advertising revenues were 190 and 193 million dollars. Look at ad revenue now. We're projecting it'll be down to 110 million by series-end. For heaven's sake, it was 140 in series *one*!

A Now, take it easy, Malcolm. A program always loses momentum a little after three series.

B We're losing touch with our audience, Ruth. Have you seen the latest audience breakdown figures? More than a third of our audience are in the twenty to thirty age bracket. I called in an independent market research team. Here you can read it for yourself. Twenty to thirty: 34%. Thirty to forty: 26%. Forty to fifty: 22%. Fifty to sixty: 12%. Over sixty: well, who cares, but it's, er, 6%.

A We've always attracted a young professional audience. What's your point, Malcolm?

B My point is: that our audience is not the *old* young professional audience, the money-grabbing generation. They're the *new* young professional audience, Generation Y, Millennials. And they don't like the direction the program is going in.

A Generation Y, Millennials! Now don't start all that marketing-speak with me, Malcolm. We offer business-themed entertainment by getting mega-rich venture capitalists to tear struggling entrepreneurs to pieces on prime-time television … and occasionally give them a half million bucks for their trouble!

B Exactly. And that's what our audience doesn't like any more. They're tired of the egos and the greed and the sarcasm. We ran a survey and 64% said they wanted the show to feature more socially responsible businesses.

A Oh, my god. You want to change the program formula mid-series?

B That's not all. 19% would like to see more female-managed ventures. At the moment, less than one in five of our contestants is a woman. That's disgraceful, as a matter of fact. 11% want more contestants to come from developing countries, especially Africa. I agree with them. And 6% are fed up with the aggressive way the lions treat the contestants. It's not amusing any more.

A But that's what the whole program is about! They're supposed to be lions, for god's sake, not pussy-cats. You want a save-the-world show, go ahead. But that's not *this* show!

B Ruth, I'm not saying we have to change the whole formula. But can't we make it greener? Tame the lions a bit? Give the show a conscience?

A What if I say no?

B Well, I was hoping it wouldn't come to that. But, if we keep sliding in the ratings, we may have to reschedule the show for off-peak viewing.

A Whoa! Now wait a minute …

1.27

Presenter Good evening and welcome to *The Lion's Share*. Here in the den the lions are always on the lookout for a business they can grow into something huge. Have our entrepreneurs got one for them tonight? First up from Argentina is SojaGen …

Cristina Hello. I'm Cristina Artaza and this is my business partner Francisco Michetti. We are the founders and joint-CEOs of SojaGen. And we're looking to raise half a million dollars to take our new and exciting enterprise to the next level.

Argentina has three key resources that make it a real magnet for venture capital: inexpensive land, relatively cheap labour and massive production of … soy beans! These three resources are the foundation of our business model. No, we're not talking about soy-milk or vegetarian meat substitutes. We're talking about a biodiesel micro-refinery, tapping into the fuel of the future.

Francisco The global biofuel market is worth around fifteen billion dollars and expected to triple in the next five years. In Argentina, the government has just passed a law requiring that 5% of all domestic fuel consumed must be biofuel. The famous Hungarian financier and philanthropist George Soros has already invested a quarter billion dollars in biofuel development in Argentina. So the timing couldn't be better. And Cristina and I have masters degrees in geology and engineering and twelve years' experience between us in the oil industry at Exxon and Amoco.

Cristina Biodiesel is a remarkably inexpensive form of renewable energy, made from refining oil from plants like soy beans. The most profitable niche is for commercial vehicles and this is the sector we aim to target selling mostly to agribusinesses. Local farmers actually account for 75% of the diesel market in Argentina.

Francisco Just to be clear, we're not talking about setting up a fifty-million dollar refinery with a hundred staff. There are plenty of large-scale biofuel refineries already in Argentina. But we, along with many clean-tech experts, believe the market is open to smaller players like ourselves to better serve the smaller customer. Off-the-shelf technology is now available which can lower plant construction costs to as little as a hundred fifty thousand dollars for a micro-refinery which can produce a hundred thirty thousand gallons a year.

Cristina We're looking initially to establish three micro-refineries in northern Argentina, where we have good contacts with the local farming community. Many of them are themselves soy bean producers, so by sourcing our soy from them and selling the biodiesel back to them to fuel their machinery and delivery trucks we create a virtuous circle. We need a half a million dollars to add to the half a million we've already raised to continue with our construction plans and we're offering in return a 65% stake in our business.

Presenter OK, thank you, SojaGen. That's your two minutes. Lions?

Lion 1 OK, so as I understand it, you've run out of money, right?

Cristina Well, erm, I wouldn't put it that way. Our first refinery is already in operation, but to achieve economies of scale we need to bring the other two on-stream and that requires a further injection of capital at this stage.

Lion 2 It seems to me that the biofuel market in Argentina is already overcrowded. There appear to be a lot of big investors moving in. You admit as much yourselves. Why should we back a tiny organisation like yours?

Francisco Our business model is based on setting up low-cost micro-refineries in rural areas to serve the local community. We can sell the fuel for two-thirds the cost of diesel. And that means …

Lion 3 Wait a minute! Wait a minute! We're not asking you how you compete with conventional diesel refineries. That's clear. We're asking you how you compete with bigger biodiesel producers.

Cristina The big biofuel refineries largely cater for the cities and for export. We've established a relationship with rural farming communities who can get their biodiesel quicker and cheaper from us. We confidently expect to move into profit within five years and then maybe sell to one of the larger refineries.

Lion 4 OK, you've clearly done your homework. You have the right connections and background, but what's to stop other small start-ups from copying your idea?

Presenter I'm sorry lions. Time's up. Thank you, SojaGen.

Cristina and Francisco Thank you.

Presenter Lions, it's time to confer…

 1.28

Presenter Our second team of contestants tonight comes from Russia. They call their business Elita.

Vladimir Hello. My name is Vladimir Chernoy and this is Boris Goussinsky. I'll get straight to the point, ladies and gentlemen. It is common knowledge that we live in the world of Web 2.0 technology. Social networking is particularly prevalent with websites such as Facebook, MySpace and LinkedIn. In fact, Boris and I were instrumental in the introduction of LinkedIn to Russia some years ago.

But now we see that there is a huge demand in Russia for an elite social networking website for top executives and entrepreneurs and this is the vision of our company, Elita. Boris …

Boris Thank you, Vladimir. Ladies and gentlemen, Russia is a very status-conscious society. The Russian economy may be slowing, but it remains, with China, India and Brazil, one of the emerging super-economies, predicted, in fact, to be the world's sixth largest economy by 2050. The upper class in Russia is still reaping the benefits of the oil boom of the 1990s. You may be surprised to learn that Moscow has the highest concentration of billionaires of any capital city. There are over a hundred thousand millionaires in Russia and their number grows by

about 17% annually. Yet the new super-rich continue to enjoy subsidised housing and relatively low taxes. This means they have huge disposable incomes of which many in the West can only dream.

Vladimir And this is where Elita comes in. Networking in Russia is not so straightforward as it is in the West. Because of a certain amount of – shall we say, unconventional business practices? – it is not easy to build good professional relationships. Doing business is also more complex. There is low credit card penetration and the postal service is mostly unreliable. Russia is not friendly to e-commerce. Flickr and LinkedIn have already been cloned by Russian companies, but what does not yet exist is a social networking site for the wealthiest 10%. We believe the time is right for an online network through which selected members can do business with like-minded professionals and buy everything from a Porsche to a Picasso!

Boris The important thing is to keep membership fairly exclusive. The key, we believe, is to hire a handful of wealthy socialites and business leaders and promote the site through word-of-mouth and viral marketing. It is essential, however, to be the first-mover, to be the first into this market. The second one in will be, er, dead meat, as you say in the States.

Vladimir We're looking for half a million dollars to develop and market the Elita site and we will offer one half of our business for this investment.

Presenter Thank you Elita. Lions, do you have any questions?

Lion 1 So, your website doesn't yet exist?

Boris That's right. We require the seed capital to finance its development.

Lion 1 And what's that going to cost?

Boris Web designers are very plentiful in Russia. And salaries relatively low, say about forty thousand US dollars per year for a good developer. Payroll will not be expensive in the early stages.

Lion 2 OK, finding talent may not be a problem, but how much market research have you done? Seems to me like this would be a very risky venture.

Vladimir There is, of course, an element of risk. But we are sure of our market. In our survey, which we can supply you with a copy of, we had a 60% positive response rate. There is nothing like this in Russia at the moment and Russia is undoubtedly the best market for this kind of service.

Lion 3 Is it just me or does anyone else have a problem with putting a half million dollars into a business that is little more than a social tool for Russian millionaires?

Vladimir I believe you yourselves are all worth many, many millions. I thought the objective here was to create highly profitable new businesses or am I mistaken? Our exit strategy, by the way, is to sell to one of the big US social networking sites within three years. Interest has already been expressed by one large company I cannot name at this stage.

Presenter OK. That's it guys. Lions, it's time to consider Elita's pitch, as we go into the break. Don't go away. We'll be right back.

 1.29

Presenter Welcome back. Before the break we saw pitches from two teams of start-up business owners battling to get their hands on the half million-dollar lion's share of venture capital on offer tonight. Now it's the turn of US-South African entrepreneurs who call themselves The Ulundi Township Confectionery Company.

Angela Hi, I'm Diana Rider and these are my business partners N'namdi Jabavu and Angelina Sithebe. Together we form the management team of The Ulundi Township Confectionery Company. Ulundi Township is in the KwaZulu Natal region of South Africa.

I myself spent five years on Wall Street launching multimillion-dollar funds before going to Durban to do my MBA. It had always been a dream of mine to go to Africa, and it was while I was there that I visited

some of the townships that surround the city. It seemed to me that here were poor areas that needn't be poor. The climate is suitable for many kinds of agricultural and recreational activity, but there's a massive skills shortage, particularly amongst the women. So, with my business partners, who I met on the MBA course, I decided to change that. I gave up my job on Wall Street and we formed the company.

N'namdi The Ulundi Township Confectionery Company currently employs ten women in Ulundi to bake cookies and cakes to local recipes to sell to nearby cafes and hotels. Just last month we won our first order to supply a domestic airline. We've been in business now for two years, funding our operations mostly ourselves, but in the last few months we have started to move into profit. Our business model is simple: we don't employ people to bake cookies; we bake cookies to employ people. There's no lack of talent in poor areas, only a lack of training. And I don't need to tell you that there's no lack of poor areas to draw that talent from. By the way, did I mention that our cookies are probably the best in the world?

Angelina We are definitely not out to save the world, by the way, but we do believe it's possible to create social change and real businesses at the same time. Networking is crucial to the smooth running of our company. In the early stages, we were fortunate enough to find a local food company prepared to donate our first ovens. And more recently Diana has used some of her contacts in New York to put us on the verge of winning a large export contract with the help of a friendly advertising agency to promote our brand.

Diana All this means we need to expand into other townships in the region to increase production. We see no reason why a successful business model cannot be replicated in any number of similar townships. We're from the land of the lion and we're certainly interested in winning the lion's share tonight for a 40% stake in our business. But, in fact, even a hundred thousand dollars would enable us to get things started in at least three other townships. So we hope you have your cheque books open! In the meantime, you may like to try some of our delicious products. Thank you very much.

Presenter Thank you, The Ulundi Township Confectionery Company. Lions?

Lion 1 Well, you certainly have an interesting business proposition, but I'm wondering, how do just ten women manage to produce cookies in commercial quantities?

Angelina We work very hard!

Lion 1 Well, I'm sure you do, and this idea of yours: we don't employ people to bake, we bake to employ people. I mean that's all very noble, I'm sure, but we are not offering micro-loans here. We're looking to invest in a business.

Diana And you couldn't do better than to invest in ours. We don't see anything micro about our future.

Lion 2 I'm impressed that you've invested your own money as well as time and effort in this business. I think the branding of your product is going to be crucial, though, to successfully export and you'll certainly need to grow fast to keep up with demand if it all works out.

N'namdi We want to grow, obviously, but we want to control that. By targeting just specialist food-stores and cafes in the States and Europe, rather than the big supermarkets, we hope to gradually build our market presence.

Lion 3 What about an exit strategy? I have to tell you, we generally don't want to hang on to our business interests too long!

Diana We don't have an exit strategy. We anticipate being able to pay back those who wish to cash in on their investment in us within three to five years and earn them a healthy profit. But we want to continue to run the business along ethical lines.

Presenter That's it, lions. Time to confer.

1.30

Presenter Our final contestants this evening come from a country we've not seen on *The Lion's Share* before – Libya. They call themselves Libu Tours.

Andrew Hello, I'm Andrew Collins and these are my colleagues, Ali Mustapha BenAlashhar and Lamia BintHalim. We're here this evening to persuade you to put aside any preconceptions you may have about the country our business is based in and make the perhaps soundest investment on offer tonight.

Ali Thanks, Andrew. Libya, ladies and gentlemen, is at a crossroads of history, continents and ancient empires. It is home to the Mediterranean's richest store of Greek and Roman cities and eleven hundred miles of undeveloped beachfront. Cosmopolitan Tripoli has many attractions. This year Libya expects one million tourists, four times more than four years ago.

Lamia Since the US restored diplomatic relations with Libya in 2006, we have been welcoming both holidaymakers and entrepreneurs to our beautiful country. Italy has built several hotel chains already. France's ClubMed is also planning to set up here. But in global terms, Libya is still virgin territory and the opportunities for early investors are exceptional. Libu Tours offers an authentic Libyan experience to tourists in search of quiet, culture and a sunny climate.

Andrew I'm obviously British and I bring twenty years' experience in the European hotels and tourism business to the venture. But to succeed in Libya at this point in its development, it is essential to have local contacts. Ali and Lamia have been running a highly successful domestic holiday firm for many years. They have all the right connections with hotels, coach operators, museums and sites of architectural and archaeological interest. Because of the many regulatory agencies in Libya and obstacles to foreign-ownership within the country, their contribution to the business is crucial.

We're looking for five hundred thousand dollars for a 35% stake in our business, largely to market our tours throughout Europe and North America. The business itself is already running successfully, but on a smaller scale than we plan. The market sector we target is the over-35s, professionals, interested in culture and new experiences, and we don't intend to change that. Authenticity is the hallmark of our service. In this way, we differentiate ourselves from the majority of tour operators in places like Greece and Turkey. It's very difficult to find high-quality tour operators in Europe these days. Generally, you have to go to the Caribbean or other exotic island paradises to get that kind of service. We intend to change that in a country most people have never thought of visiting until now.

Ali Thank you very much. We are ready to take questions.

Presenter Thank you, Libu Tours. Over to you, lions.

Lion 1 Why Libu?

Ali Libu is the ancient name of Libya. Classical culture is a key feature of our tours.

Lion 1 I see. I must confess I hadn't thought of Libya myself as a holiday destination. What makes you so sure there's a market?

Lamia Well, as we said, there's a lot of interest in Libya right now. After years of isolation from the West, we really are almost a new country, one ripe to discover.

Lion 2 Hm. I'm worried about all the regulations you mentioned. I know you have an existing business, but what if the political situation should change in Libya? Seems to me there's a considerable risk.

Andrew Libya is politically stable. The regulatory barriers are a normal precaution when a country finds itself suddenly drawing thousands of entrepreneurs eager to set up in business. You find the same thing in Central and Eastern Europe. We are a bi-national organisation and respected in the industry. I don't think the risk is as considerable as you believe.

Lion 3 Just one thing. I understand Libya is a dry country. And I don't mean arid. Isn't alcohol prohibited?

Ali That is correct. Alcohol is officially banned in Libya, although there are government moves to sell it through selected outlets for tourists. I think this will happen soon.

Lion 3 But so far, it's illegal.

Ali Yes … I have to say for most of our clients, alcohol is not an issue. We are not catering to the young beach- and bar-lover. And there are plenty of delicious non-alcoholic alternatives. So it is not a great disadvantage.

Lion 3 It would be for me. On holiday and no gin and tonic?

Presenter Well, we're out of time. Thank you to all our contestants for four excellent pitches. Now, lions, it's up to you. Who, if anyone, gets the lion's share tonight? We'll take another break now and be right back with the lions' verdict …

04 VOICE AND VISUALS

 1.31

Hello, this is Cheng Jing from Nanogen Taiwan. I just wanted to let you know that your presentation this morning was a tremendous success with everyone here. What a brilliant idea to do the whole thing in such a casual, low-budget and alternative way! Very clever. The board certainly got the message.

I hope we didn't seem unappreciative as an audience. Quite the contrary. You must understand that not all our vice-presidents have the benefit of my Harvard education. And some of them don't speak English very well. But they really liked your calm, quiet approach. So please pass on my congratulations to your excellent presenter.

Oh, by the way, the joke about Beijing was greatly enjoyed – even in translation. So, see you at the next strategy meeting. Goodbye now.

 1.32

a There's a whole market in Eastern Europe just there for the taking.

b Quite frankly, the results we've been getting are absolutely incredible.

c Now, I'm sure I don't need to tell you just how crucial this is.

d Net profits are up ninety-seven per cent – yes, ninety-seven per cent.

e Would you believe that so far we've not been able to sell a single unit?

f Miss this deadline and we'll lose the biggest client this company's ever had.

 1.33

a There's a whole <u>market</u> | in Eastern <u>Europe</u> | just <u>there</u> for the <u>taking</u>.

b <u>Net profits</u> | are up <u>ninety-seven</u> per <u>cent</u> | – <u>yes</u>, | <u>ninety</u>- | <u>seven</u> | per <u>cent</u>.

 1.34

a There's a whole <u>market</u> | in Eastern <u>Europe</u> | just <u>there</u> for the <u>taking</u>.

b Quite <u>frankly</u>, | the <u>results</u> we've been <u>getting</u> | are <u>absolutely</u> | <u>incredible</u>.

c Now, I'm <u>sure</u> | I don't need to <u>tell</u> you | just how <u>crucial</u> | this <u>is</u>.

d <u>Net profits</u> | are up <u>ninety-seven</u> per <u>cent</u> | – <u>yes</u>, | <u>ninety</u>- | <u>seven</u> | per <u>cent</u>.

e Would you <u>believe</u> | that <u>so</u> far | we've <u>not</u> been <u>able</u> to <u>sell</u> | a <u>single</u> <u>unit</u>?

f <u>Miss</u> | <u>this</u> | <u>deadline</u> | and we'll <u>lose</u> the biggest <u>client</u> | this <u>company's</u> <u>ever</u> <u>had</u>.

 1.35

A Welcome back to CBN Business. To be or not to be? That is the question for an increasing number of companies putting their staff through drama courses in an attempt to turn them into better public speakers. Jon Heller meets a group of British managers making their theatrical debut.

B 'Next time you are about to make a presentation, take a deep breath and imagine yourself walking on stage – about to give the performance of your life.' That's the advice of William Freeman of Cambridge Associates, one of a new wave of management trainers who believe that presenting is less about PowerPoint and more about acting the part.

At Prospero, a company with a similar aims, Tina Packer and Michael Lame have taken the idea one step further and put Shakespeare on the programme. After all, who better to teach managers how to speak effectively and relate to an audience than classically trained actors? Whether you're a platform speaker at the annual conference, a salesperson pitching to a client or just chairing your weekly staff meeting, actors have powerful communication techniques you can learn from. Prospero is certainly in demand, regularly running courses at Columbia Business School, Harvard and MIT.

So what is it that makes someone a brilliant speaker? Richard Olivier, Royal Shakespeare Company director, creative management consultant and son of acting legend Sir Laurence Olivier, thinks it's 'self-belief'. According to Olivier, 'Much of leadership is acting. Not faking it, but taking on a role. Paradoxically, the acting makes it real.'

But what do the trainees think? We questioned a few who'd taken a course in acting like leaders.

C I thought my boss had gone mad at first. I mean, Shakespeare? No way! But, in fact, it's been really inspiring. And a lot of fun!

D Frankly, I was terrified. Me, acting on stage? I don't think so. But I've learned a lot of stuff I never got on those boring presentation courses.

E Well, the actors have been fun to work with. We've had a lot of laughs. I'm not so sure how useful it all is – you know, in a business context. But, hey, it got us out of the office for a couple of days, so I'm not complaining.

F Well, this really isn't my thing at all. I mean, public speaking just frightens the life out of me, without getting up and acting in front of an audience. Frankly, it was hell. Never again!

G Best course I've ever done – by far. Just totally brilliant. I never realised the true power of the voice and the confidence it gives you when you can make it work for you. I'd definitely recommend this kind of training.

B So, there we have it. Time to shut down your laptop, brush up your Shakespeare and learn how to wow an audience with the professionals.

05 PROBLEMS ON THE PHONE

 2.03

B Hello?

A Dan?

B Speaking.

A It's George. George Chatterton.

B Ah, George … How are you?

A Couldn't be better, mate, couldn't be better! Someone happened to mention they'd bumped into you the other day. So I just thought I'd give you a call. See how you're doing.

B Oh, right. … yes … er, George …

A So how's it going, mate? Just been promoted, so I hear.

B Er, yes, that's right.

A Glad to see they've finally started appreciating you.

B Er, yes, thanks. So, George, what can I do for you?

A Bit more money too, I imagine.

B Hm? Oh, a bit, yeah. Well, George, **I expect you're calling about** that project …

A And how's that lovely wife of yours?

B Suzanne? Oh, she's fine.

A Splendid, splendid. And the kids?

B They're fine too. Look, George, I am rather busy right now. I've just got back from holiday, actually, and you know what it's like. Was there something you wanted to talk to me about?

A Of course, how silly of me! You've just been on that safari you were planning last time we spoke, haven't you?

B Yes, and what with the new job and everything, there's a bit of catching up …

A Kenya, wasn't it?

B What?

A The holiday – Kenya.

B Yes. Listen. George …

A You know, I've always wanted to go to Kenya …

B Well, now, George, I mustn't keep you.

A What's that?

B I'll let you get on. I'm sure you've got things to do, busy guy like you. **It's been great talking to you, though**.

A Yeah, likewise.

B We must get together soon.

A Yeah, yeah. As a matter of fact, I'm going to be in London for a few days next month.

B Oh, god.

A Sorry?

B I said 'Oh, good.' Perhaps we can meet up for a beer.

A Yeah, that'd be great.

B But, erm, **I'll have to let you go now**, George. Someone's just this minute stepped into the office.

A Oh, right, I see.

B And it looks like I've got an international call just come in on the other line as well. Yes.

A No worries. I'll call you back in half an hour, then. I haven't told you my good news yet. Wait till you hear it!

B What? Er, no. Erm, George? George?

🔘 2.04

A Hello. Thank you for calling the iDeals customer service line. All our customer service advisers are busy right now. Please hold and your enquiry will be dealt with shortly … This is the iDeals customer service line. Thank you for holding. All our customer service advisers are busy right now. Please hold and your enquiry will be dealt with shortly …

B Oh, come on, come on!

C Good morning. Lisa speaking. How can I help you?

B Oh, hello. At last! I was just about to ring off.

C I am sorry about that. The waiting system is a bit frustrating, isn't it? It's the only way we can offer our 24-hour service, you see.

B Yeah, yeah. Look, it's about the computer I bought off you two weeks ago …

C Yes? What seems to be the problem?

B Well, I was transferring my files to it from my zip drive and it's lost the lot. Everything!

C OK, now don't worry. I'm sure we can sort something out. First, can you give me a few details? The computer has lost all your data, you say?

B Yes. But, you don't understand. It's wiped everything off the zip drive as well! My whole life, my whole life was in those files.

C Oh, my goodness! Are you sure? Sounds like the problem's with your zip drive.

B Of course I'm sure! And there's nothing wrong with my zip drive. I've had it years!

C OK. I can understand how upset you must be. Now, I don't think we can deal with this on the phone, so I'm going to send a service engineer to see if they can retrieve your data. Can you give me your product reference number?

B Hm? Er, yes. It's … here it is … it's SF11–003.

C Thank you.

B I'll be expecting a total refund and compensation if this can't be fixed!

C Unfortunately, we're not authorised to give refunds, but what I can do is send you a brand-new computer. How would that be?

B This is supposed to be a brand-new computer. You think I want another one of these, after what the last one did to my files?

C Well, let's see what our engineer can do. Hopefully, it's not quite as bad as you think. Now, I've got your address here in your customer file. Oxford OX2 6BJ, right?

B Yeah, right.

C And it's Mr Harris, isn't it?

B Yes.

C Right, Mr Harris. We'll have an engineer with you this afternoon. And I'll ask him to bring a new hard disk with him. Is that all OK for you?

B Er, well, I suppose …

C Good. Glad to be of assistance. Is there anything else I can help you with?

B Hm? Oh, no, no.

C Well, best of luck this afternoon. I hope we can solve the problem for you.

B Well, thanks. Erm, goodbye.

C Goodbye, Mr Harris.

🔘 2.05

B Hello?

A

B Yeah, speaking. Is that you, Piotr? Aren't you supposed to be at the Trade Fair in Krakow?

A

B What?

A

B You haven't got a stand? Well, how did that happen?

A

B Maybe it's the CD player you're using.

A

B Well, what happened to our CD player?

A

B Damn carriers. That's the last time we use them! I'll play hell with them when I speak to them.

A

B Where's Liesl?

A

B This just gets worse, doesn't it?

A

B What's gone wrong with the brochures?

A

B Portuguese! Oh, no …

A

B That may be because I forgot to phone Tony. You remember we were going to attend the Lisbon Trade Fair originally.

A

B It completely slipped my mind. Oh, I'm really sorry, Piotr.

A

B Well, we're snowed under at the moment trying to get things ready for the Midas launch, but, look, don't worry. I'll sort something out. Can I call you back in an hour?

A

🔘 2.06

B Hello?

A Graham?

B Yeah, speaking. Is that you, Piotr? Aren't you supposed to be at the Trade Fair in Krakow?

A I am at the Trade Fair in Krakow, Graham. I'm just about the only thing that arrived here in one piece!

B What?

A Well, the stand got badly damaged in transit, so I've basically just got a table here, a few chairs and a

couple of posters with nothing to attach them to! It's a complete disaster!

B You haven't got a stand? Well, how did that happen?

A Don't ask. Look, it's not just that. I've just tried out three of the promotional CDs and two were defective – wouldn't play at all. I don't know how many more are like that.

B Maybe it's the CD player you're using.

A Wouldn't surprise me. I had to borrow it from another exhibitor.

B Well, what happened to our CD player?

A I'll give you three guesses.

B Damn carriers. That's the last time we use them! I'll play hell with them when I speak to them.

A Yes, well, never mind that now. You've got to do something, Graham. I'm working flat out on my own here.

B Where's Liesl?

A She's come down with some sort of virus. I left her at the hotel.

B This just gets worse, doesn't it?

A Wait till you hear about the brochures …

B What's gone wrong with the brochures?

A The English ones are OK. The others are all in Portuguese.

B Portuguese! Oh, no …

A What?

B That may be because I forgot to phone Tony. You remember we were going to attend the Lisbon Trade Fair originally.

A And you didn't tell Tony about the change of plan?

B It completely slipped my mind. Oh, I'm really sorry, Piotr.

A Graham, you've got to get me out of this mess.

B Well, we're snowed under at the moment trying to get things ready for the Midas launch, but, look, don't worry. I'll sort something out. Can I call you back in an hour?

A OK, I'll be waiting to hear from you.

🔘 2.07

A Hello?

B Hello, Piotr.

A Graham! You said an hour.

B Sorry. I got held up.

A What's happening, then?

B Right. I've been on to the carriers and they're sending a new stand out on the next plane. You should have that by tomorrow morning.

A Well, at least that's something.

B Can you get hold of the organisers and tell them we'll set up tomorrow at 7?

A Yeah, sure. I don't suppose you remembered to put another CD player in with the stand?

B I've sent two – just in case.

A Oh, right. Good. Thanks.

B And do you happen to have a phone number for the promotions people? Because if those CDs are defective, I'll get them to send more by courier.

A I've got it somewhere. Graham, is there any chance of sending someone else out here? Kim, for instance.

B Piotr, you know how short-staffed we are here right now.

A What's this exhibition costing us, Graham? $18,000?

B You're right. I'll check with Liz and see if she can spare Kim for a few days.

A Thanks. It's murder here.

B Well, I'll see what I can do, but I can't promise anything.

A Hm. And would you mind getting some brochures to me in Polish, seeing as I'm in Poland?

B Yes, we're having a few problems with that – seem to have run out. Is there any point in sending the ones we've got in Russian?

A No, Graham, not a great idea. Send the German ones, if that's all we've got. But are you absolutely sure we didn't order a reprint of the Polish ones?

B I'll look into it the minute I get off the phone.

A OK, but could I ask you to hurry that up a bit, please? It is pretty important.

B I know, I know. Would it help if we got a local Polish interpreter in? I know you speak Polish, but it might help you out a bit.

A Well, I wouldn't have much time to brief them on the product, but yeah, anything's better than nothing.

B OK, I'll get on to that right away. Leave it to me.

A I did leave it to you and look what happened!

B Yeah, well. You're doing a great job Piotr. I owe you one!

06 LEADING MEETINGS

 2.08

A Coming up on CBN Business: an interview with media king and head of News Corporation Rupert Murdoch, stock market report and Katy Alexander with the week's business news round-up. But first, suffering from boardroom blues? Tired of taking minutes at meetings that take hours? Tess Liebowitz may have the solution …

B According to diplomat and economist JK Galbraith, 'Meetings are indispensable when you don't want to do anything.' Therefore, logically, if you really do want to do something, it's the meetings you must dispense with. But can you dispense with meetings altogether? And what would take their place? At several well-known companies they think they've found the answer.

At high-profile UK advertising agency St. Luke's, meetings are simply considered 'a ceremonial and rude interruption to people's working day'. So they've introduced meetings-on-the-move. Any member of staff can hold a meeting anytime, anywhere – in the elevator, in a local café or just sitting cross-legged on the floor. Anywhere, that is, but in a boardroom!

At Internet company another.com they've gone one step further by building a 'park area' right in the middle of the building. Staff can go sit on the park bench amongst the flowers or even play on the swings while they hold meetings! They used to have real grass too, but watering it became a problem.

At media strategy company, Michaelides & Bednash they've come up with a different solution. All employees, irrespective of status, work around one enormous central table. Meetings become unnecessary when everyone in the company is sitting just across the table from you the whole time. The working day is a constant meeting!

At the Xerox Corporation a more down-to-earth approach has proved successful. All staff, from junior management upwards, are trained in chairing skills and get an equal opportunity to use them. This breaks up hierarchies in the workplace, creating democratised meetings, where everyone can practise their leadership skills.

Finally, at Federal Express, they've been experimenting with technology. Using specially designed software, people sit around a large U-shaped table at workstations connected over a local area network. Meetings stick strictly to the agenda, are highly focused and more or less silent. Items instantly appear on the participants' screens and people simply key in their views rather than voice them. The software allows you to attach further comments and to see graphically how your position differs from the consensus. The only problem is the price – $35,000 for the fully functional system!

 2.09

Extract 1

A OK, thanks for coming, everybody. Erm, has anybody seen Lance, by the way? He was supposed to be here.

B Oh, yeah, he phoned to say his flight in from Chicago had a two-hour delay. He said to go ahead and start without him.

A Oh, I wanted his input on this one. OK, never mind, let's get started, then, shall we? Erm, so, as I said in my e-mail, the purpose of this meeting is to review last week's talks with the people from timeofyourlife. com and, secondly, to decide if we're interested in taking things further. **Pieter is going to fill us in on the background**. Pieter?

C Yeah, thanks, Ross. Well, now, timeofyourlife is a really exciting business proposition. Basically, the idea is that ordinary people can buy a kind of timeshare in various luxury goods that they could never afford to buy outright. What happens is you buy points online at the timeofyourlife website and you can use these points to buy, like, a Ferrari for a day, a Rolex Oyster for a weekend or a Jean-Paul Gaultier original for an evening! Neat, huh? I just love this proposal …

D Er, sorry to interrupt, but is this going to take long, Pieter? Only I have an appointment at eleven and we have all read the summary on this company already.

A Jack, could Pieter just finish what he was saying? We're looking at twenty million dollars in seed capital here. I don't want us rushing into anything. But **perhaps we could speed things up a little**, Pieter. We are short of time and by the end of this meeting I'd like some kind of decision on this.

 2.10

Extract 2

C So, as you can see, the advance publicity alone is attracting half a million visitors to the timeofyourlife website every day.

A Sorry, Pieter, but we seem to be getting side-tracked here. This is all very interesting, but **can we go back to what we were discussing earlier**?

C Oh, OK. Sure.

A Perhaps we can come back to this later. Tell us about their logistics.

D Can I just say something here?

A Hold on a minute, Jack – you'll get your chance in a moment.

D It's just that I thought we'd agreed we weren't investing in any more dot.coms.

B No, Jack. That's what you wanted. But nobody actually agreed.

D Tania, we've been through this.

B Wait a minute. Who was it that said …?

A OK, OK! **Let's all just calm down, shall we**? We're here to talk about this proposal we have on the table. Tania, **what's your position on this**?

B Well, I agree with Pieter that it's a great business plan. Like you, I'm a little concerned about the logistics, though. The procurement and delivery system for a business like this would be extremely complex. And the insurance costs could be prohibitive.

C Now, hold on a second! This is all covered in the proposal, Tania. What are you saying? I thought you were with me on this one.

A Pieter, I think what Tania is trying to say is she likes the idea but the figures don't quite add up.

B Exactly.

A OK, **maybe we should take a short break at this point**, grab a coffee and meet back here in fifteen minutes.

 2.11

Extract 3

A OK, so just to summarise what we've said so far. Basically, we like the timeofyourlife idea. At least most of us do. We're aware of the risks involved in a major investment in an e-business, but we think the concept has great potential. We need to make another appointment with these people because we have some doubts about their logistics. Pieter, **can I leave that one with you**?

C Sure. I'll get right on to it.

A We're also a little concerned about the amount of insurance a business like this would need. Tania, **can you get back to me on that**?

B No problem, Ross.

A Great. **I think that's about as far as we can go at this stage**. Thanks, everybody. **I'm afraid we'll have to stop it there.**

E Hi, guys. Sorry I'm late. Tania told you the story, right? Say, did I miss anything here?

07 GAMES WITHOUT FRONTIERS

 2.12

Speaker 1 Like many Spaniards, I am a big fan of football. And, for me, one of the best lessons I have learned from football is the victory of the Spanish team in the Euro2008 championship. For us, this was a great moment, because Spain had not won a major competition since 1964 and people ask how can it be that a country with so many famous and successful teams – as Barcelona and Real Madrid, for example – how can it be that Spain never win any European or World Cups? And the reason, I think, is because Spain is very regional. The Castilians, the Catalans, the Galicians, the Andalusians, the Basques – we are all very different people. We have our own ways and there is some conflict sometimes. We are not a team. So after the disaster at the Euro Cup in 2004, Spain has a new coach, Aragonés. Now, Aragonés had some tough decisions. Some players, he will not give a place to them, because they can play, but they have no team spirit. There were big arguments, but, you know, Aragonés is a master of conflict resolution. And, most important of all, he gives the players confidence they can win. And already by the World Cup of 2006 you can see Spain plays much better. Aragonés has invented a new word – 'teamness'. He says he wants 'teamness'. For him, it doesn't matter if you play in the match or you sit on the reserve bench, if you score a goal or you don't score a goal. You are part of the team. Before Euro2008, he took the new team to meet the team of 1964, who were European champions. And this, it can, er, boost morale for the young players. They believe now they are The Red Fury, La Furia Roja, we say. And, as you know, in the final we beat Germany one-nil!

 2.13

Speaker 2 Erm, well, for me, the most important part of building an effective team is maximising the potential of its members. To get the best out of people you obviously want them doing what they are best at. And you certainly don't want them all to be good at the same thing! The writer Stephen Covey says 'strength lies in differences, not in similarities', which is quite a good way of putting it. There are many management models for this. The most well-known is probably Belbin's in his book *Team Roles at Work*. Belbin divides team members into nine types, but, basically there are just three roles they need to take on: action-oriented roles, the people who get the job done; people-oriented roles, the people who facilitate communication between the members; and what he calls cerebral roles, the people who do the creative or analytical work that makes it all

possible. Now, of course, you never have nine people of different types in the team. Some people may play two or three roles. And there's usually some overlap. But, at least in theory, you can make sure you have a balanced team. This doesn't mean that you will always have the right interpersonal relationships for success, however. After all, a team is a social group. And there can be in-fighting and conflict – especially if you have too many 'hotshots' competing with each other. Then it's like a Hollywood movie with too many superstars in it. And you don't want that. As the film director Lindsay Anderson says, 'Eighty per cent of a successful production is in the casting'.

🔘 2.14

Speaker 3 For me, a source of inspiration when working with teams has always been the Apollo 13 rescue mission. Perhaps you remember the movie with Tom Hanks? This was the third manned mission by NASA to land on the moon, but a technical malfunction caused the lunar landing to be aborted. The command module was damaged and so the crew had to try to return to Earth in the tiny lunar module, which was really not built for the journey. Two famous catchphrases people may know are 'Houston, we have a problem' and 'Failure is not an option'. And it is this can-do attitude that I especially admire. I think it is one thing we Germans and the Americans perhaps have in common. Gene Kranz was the flight controller for the Apollo 13 mission and he has spoken about how important it is in a successful team to have the right chemistry as well as technical expertise. This was not easy because the teams he was leading were full of the best young engineering graduates, ace test pilots – a lot of ego problems! In the case of Apollo 13, they put their differences to one side and came up with the brilliant idea of getting the lunar module to rotate, rather like a barbecue, something it was not designed to do. This equalised its exposure to the sun and stopped it burning up. But the NASA team also had a 500-step checklist of procedures and protocols, which it stuck to under pressure and it worked. I think this shows that, whilst flexibility is vital at certain stages in a project, so is having faith in your plans and the courage to do things by the book.

🔘 2.15

Speaker 4 I used to work for Lockheed Martin in Maryland in what is now called ADP, Advanced Development Programs. It wasn't called that when I worked there. It was affectionately known as Skunk Works, a term now in general use in a lot of hi-tech industries, and we were responsible for many state-of-the-art military aircraft designs, which were years ahead of their time. In fact, some of the designs we worked on twenty or thirty years ago are still in production today. The thing about the Skunk Works teams was that we were given a lot of autonomy. And we didn't have to deal with the usual bureaucracy. Most of the projects we worked on were highly confidential, so, at the end of the day, I guess we were still accountable to senior management. But if you want innovative solutions to complex problems, there comes a point where you've got to let the creative guys just get on with it. I think that's key with high-technology teams – management shouldn't interfere. The engineers need to be given some latitude to try out new things or you'll simply kill off their creativity. That's the secret of leading teams – knowing when to let go.

🔘 2.16

Speaker 5 These days we hear a lot about Emotional Intelligence. In fact, it's become a bit of a cliché. But, er, with teamwork playing a bigger and bigger part in business, what we're finding is the teams we've put through some EI training really do get better results. It's like the venture capitalist John Doerr says, 'in the world today there's plenty of technology, plenty of entrepreneurs, plenty of

money. What's in short supply is great teams'. And he should know. He's been involved in the start-up of companies like Genentech, Compaq and Netscape. If you think about it, it makes sense. Human beings are natural team players. It was our ability to develop complex social relationships that brought us out the caves in the first place! It's never been survival of the fittest so much as survival of the most collaborative. The buzzword nowadays is intellectual capital – the combined know-how we carry around in our heads. The Harvard professor Howard Gardner says it best: 'my intelligence does not stop at my skin'. He's right. It also includes all the databases, friends and colleagues within your network. But, for me, emotional intelligence shouldn't just be directed within the team. It's also got to be used outside the team, because you really need people who can act as ambassadors for the project, get buy-in from senior management and, ultimately, sell the idea to the world.

🔘 2.17

Speaker 6 Recently, I have been involved in a joint venture with an American firm. And, I have to say, it wasn't so easy at the start. There were a lot of cultural barriers to overcome. Erm, we just didn't seem to have the same idea about what a team is and how it should work. I had heard, of course, that the Americans were a rather more individualistic culture than the French, but at times this didn't seem to be the case. Then a colleague lent me a book about cultural metaphors by a guy called Martin Gannon and everything fell into place. Gannon has the idea that you can learn a lot about different cultures by utilising a central metaphor for them. For the British, for example, it is the house – you know, strong foundations, a little rigid. For the Germans it is the symphony – lots of co-ordination, discipline. For the French, predictably, the metaphor is wine! Tradition, perfectionism, good taste. You get the idea. Not very scientific, perhaps, but an intriguing concept. Anyway, it seems that for Americans the metaphor Gannon uses is football, American football – a game, I have to say, about which I knew absolutely nothing six months ago. Now, if I have to describe the American football, for me it is short periods of extreme violence between individuals followed by some sort of committee meeting with all the players standing in a circle deciding what to do next. A strange sport! But that is the American attitude to teamwork precisely. They love their meetings. For them business is a sport, so it really is a team effort – but a team of individuals, all trying to out-perform their team-mates if they get the chance. They will commit to a group, sure, but only for a fixed period of time. And within the team you have much competition. Quite fascinating!

🔘 2.18

Meeting 1
The Americans

A Is it me or was that just the worst meeting we've ever had?

B Nope, that was the worst all right. Complete waste of time! You know, I don't know why we have these joint planning sessions if the Osaka team are just going to sit there looking bored. Were they out on the town last night or something?

A I don't think so. Why?

B Looked like two of them were asleep by the end.

A I don't think they were actually asleep, Jim. Maybe they were just concentrating. English is a foreign language for them, you know.

B Hey, there's nothing wrong with their English. Kenichi got his masters at Stanford, for heaven's sake! And I couldn't stop the other two talking when we took them out for a beer last time they were over.

A Oh, yeah, I remember. That was a quite an evening! Well, maybe it's jet lag.

B Jet lag? If you ask me, they hated the proposal. The Japanese don't like coming right out and saying they disagree, but did you see Akio's face when we didn't have that data he wanted?

A Hm. And why do they keep breaking off to have a conversation in Japanese? I mean, what's all the secrecy? We're supposed to be on the same team, for god's sakes!

B Oh, yeah. I hate when that happens. Do you think there's something they're not telling us?

A I don't know. It's been like this ever since we got the green light. Remember the kick-off meeting?

B Will I ever forget? Well, I guess it's just as well we keep coming up with the ideas because they sure as heck aren't going to! …

The Japanese

A These meetings are so exhausting! Did you understand a word of that?

B Well, it's a little difficult when everybody speaks at the same time! Kenichi, your English is best. What were they saying?

C I'm not sure – something about missing 'the first milestone' of the project.

A First milestone?

C The first stage, you know?

A Ah! Yes. Milestone. Why do Americans use all this slang?

C Well, it's not exactly slang, Akio. Actually, it's quite a common term …

A Simple English would be much better. And I need to see the data before I can make up my mind. We don't come all the way from Japan to listen to some crazy new idea, which was not on the agenda. I'm not surprised Americans always want an immediate decision. That's so we don't notice that they don't have all the figures yet!

B And why all the shouting and arguing? It sounded like they couldn't agree on their own proposal. Aren't we all supposed to be working on the same team?

A Yes, they seemed like nice guys when we went out last time, you remember?

B Ah, yes!

A But now they become really aggressive about this proposal they have, which I still don't understand!

C Akio, that's not aggression. That's just how Americans show enthusiasm!

A Enthusiasm? I will never understand this country! …

🔘 2.19

Meeting 2
The British

A Well, I must say, that didn't quite go as I expected!

B No, I don't know what happened there. I thought we were just about ready to execute and then, suddenly, it's like we're right back to square one.

A I mean, if they had all these objections, why didn't they raise them before?

B Well, exactly. And what about Tabor? I thought he was going to have a heart attack! I've never seen him so upset. Who'd have thought he felt so strongly about manufacturing the components in Hungary?

A Well, I did my best to calm him down. You know, tried to make a bit of a joke of the whole thing.

B Yes, I thought you handled it very well. Fortunately, I think he could see the funny side. I mean it was his idea to outsource to Taiwan in the first place.

A Yes, well, exactly. The thing is he's usually very charming, but we certainly got on the wrong side of him this afternoon. In fact, they were all going bananas in there. I could hardly hear myself think! Why do they all have to talk over each other? You can't get a word in.

B Hm. It looks to me as though they just can't stick to a decision once it's made. And there's all this emotion flying about. We're going to have to watch that.

A Anyway, the main thing is it all ended amicably. Erzsébet tried to smooth things over. And Tabor was very apologetic, afterwards. So no real harm done. It was definitely a good idea to defer any final decision until the next meeting.

A   Well, yes. No point rushing them if they're not ready. We've got to have buy-in from them first …

The Hungarians

A   Well, I think we got our point across – finally! Component manufacture has to stay in Hungary.

B   Yes, they certainly got the message, Tabor. In fact, perhaps we overdid it a little.

A   Overdid it? What do you mean?

B   Well, you know what the British are like. They hate making a scene. I think you may have shocked them a little with your … erm, outburst.

A   Well, somebody had to say it. Otherwise, we'd just have spent the whole afternoon in small talk. I mean Brian is a very nice guy, but he can never get to the point. What is it with the British, Erzsébet? Why don't they just say what's on their mind? They seemed to think we were ready to proceed with the whole project. If that was the case, why would we be having a meeting? It's not a social visit. And if they think we're going to give the go-ahead to this at the next meeting, they can think again! There are a dozen things we need to discuss first. Not that they wanted to discuss them. In fact, they hardly said a word.

B   No, I noticed that. And when they do say something, it's all a bit vague. Anyway, I think it was all right in the end.

A   Yes, Brian's quite an amusing guy, when he wants to be. I liked his story about Taiwan. I don't have a problem with him. It's just that we need to spend much more time on this. There's a lot of risk attached.

B   Hm. I'll call him tomorrow and have a little chat.

A   Good idea …

 2.20

Meeting 3
The French

A   You know, Philippe, I can never come out of these meetings with the German team without a headache. My god, there must have been two hundred slides in Christian's presentation. And just you wait, there'll be a hundred-page report on the same subject waiting in our e-mail when we get home – in case we missed something!

B   Well, you know how they like their detail, Jean-Claude. I'm afraid I just switch off when it all gets too boring. What I don't understand is why they have to keep going over every point again and again. Do they think we are stupid?

A   I know. I mean I thought we were almost ready to sign off on this project. The last deliverables have been shipped. We have our instructions from head office. What else is there to discuss?

B   I think they call it consultation. They just want to be sure everything has gone according to plan before finalising things.

A   Consultation? If head office is happy, why aren't we happy? It's not our place to question how the project went. I could see Monique getting more and more frustrated.

B   Perhaps they didn't realise she had been sent from head office. I felt like they were ignoring her and, well, I mean she's the boss really.

A   Quite. And if they wanted a proper consultation why weren't we allowed to speak for more than two minutes at a time? These things have to be worked through, debated, the arguments weighed against each other. You can't just drown us all in data and say 'there you are, this is what we must do'!

B   Well, at least we're about ready to complete this project. It's been a lot of hard work. So, where are they sending you next, Jean-Claude?

A   Bremen!

B   You know, I have a good book on doing business with the Germans I could let you borrow, not that it's helped me much …

The Germans

A   Well, Inge, I think that went rather well.

B   Yes, I think so. Perhaps the French needed a bit more persuading that these final stages of the project require some modification, but, all in all, a successful meeting.

A   You think I should have shown them the figures from the Munich study?

B   No, no. I don't think that was necessary. As a matter of fact, I don't know how well prepared they were. They seemed a little confused during the last part of your presentation.

A   Oh, do you think so? But Jean-Claude had such a lot to say about it afterwards. In fact, I could hardly stop him, but he takes so long to get to the point sometimes, I'm quite lost by the end.

B   I know what you mean. But I think it's better just to let him make his little speech and then we can always get back to the main business later. You have to show a little more cultural sensitivity, Christian!

A   Yes, I know.

B   What did surprise me was they didn't seem to want to question our original plan at all. And they didn't appear to be very interested in your proposal.

A   Yes, I noticed that too. But couldn't they see how much better our idea was? I thought the figures spoke for themselves.

B   And the woman they brought with them this time didn't say very much, did she?

A   Monique? No, she seemed very unhappy about something. I think they said she came from their head office, but I couldn't really see what her role was. All very mysterious.

B   Well, anyway. Let's make sure we put all the information in writing and e-mail it to them as soon as possible. That will give them a chance to read it all through.

A   Yes, I've already got someone working on that.

B   Splendid. So, let's call it a day …

08 PROMOTING YOUR IDEAS

 2.21

1   Erm, well, to tell you the truth, there's a part of me that's still scared I might just dry up completely. I mean, you know, your mind goes completely blank? Makes me sweat just thinking about it. I have this nightmare where the audience has gone deadly quiet, and everybody in the room's just staring at me and I haven't got a clue what to say next! It's only ever happened to me once, thank god, but I still lose sleep over it in case it ever happens again.

2   Technology. Well, it's Sod's Law, isn't it? If anything can go wrong, it will. About a year ago, I had not one, but two projectors break down on me. And then my mike went funny as well. I sounded like Darth Vader out of Star Wars for about half an hour until they fixed it. Completely ruined my whole presentation, obviously. I went mad with the technicians afterwards. But what can you do?

3   I always seem to run out of time and then have to rush the end of the talk or, even worse, run over schedule. Audiences hate that. I've had people tell me I overprepare, but it doesn't seem to matter what I do, I always have at least twenty minutes too much material. So, for me, every talk's a race against the clock!

4   Well, some people, older people especially, have told me that I move around too much when I speak in public – you know, that I pace up and down and wave my arms about. They say it's distracting. They can't concentrate on what I'm saying. But for me, as an Italian, you know, it's quite normal for us to jump around, be rather dramatic. So, now I worry about trying to stand still. And that just makes me feel tense and uncomfortable.

5   What was it Franklin D. Roosevelt said? The only thing to fear is fear itself? That's the thing I'm afraid of, still, after all these years in business – fear. Ridiculous, isn't it? But fear's an absolute killer in a presentation. Your mouth goes dry. Your heart speeds up. Your legs turn to jelly. In my experience, the first two minutes are usually the worst. Survive those and you're in with a chance.

 2.22

1   Er, well, I think the most important thing to remember is that people expect you to be an expert in your field of business. I mean a real expert. That means you should have all the technical information at your fingertips. Which is not to say they won't want to see it all in print after the presentation as well. And if you don't cover every detail in your pitch – costings, cashflow projections, everything – believe me, they won't be slow to interrupt you to ask for it. People here seem to like PowerPoint, the whole technology thing, you know. A word of warning, though: forget the jokes. If you try to be a comedian, they just won't take you seriously.

 2.23

2   Erm, I think the main thing here is to give your presentation the personal touch. That's what they value above everything else. You see, they're judging you as much as, if not more than, what you're actually talking about. But, erm, I think too many presenters worry about offending the local culture and then they end up sounding much too conservative. Don't. Be loud, be lively, be eloquent. They love all that. It's true that attention spans do tend to be a bit short sometimes and you'll get loads of interruptions, but just go with the flow. In any case, people will probably want to talk to you about everything all over again later.

2.24

3   Well, it's almost a cliché, but the hard sell does actually work here. And, believe me, you really can't be too assertive. In fact, they want you to impress them and expect you to work hard to maintain their interest. So, be fast, be slick, make sure you have a few gimmicks up your sleeve. They like all that stuff. And you can say as many nasty things about your competitors as you like – especially if they're funny. Humour's nearly always appreciated, and, er, you don't need to be too subtle with that. They don't want dark sarcasm, though – so nothing too negative. Wisecracks, clever remarks – that's what they tend to go for.

2.25

4   Erm, my main piece of advice here is: don't overwhelm them with your enthusiasm. Of course, they expect you to be highly competent and confident, but quietly confident. People will probably have read through all the paperwork beforehand, but they'll want you to go through all the main points again. For the sake of formality and politeness, they'll want to hear it directly from you. But don't get so carried away talking about your own ideas that you forget to point out why it is their company you especially want to do business with. That's very important – creating a sense of harmony and compatibility between you and them. Oh, and a long-term commitment for them, by the way, is 20 to 25 years, not three to five, as it is in the States.

2.26

5   I suppose having a sense of humour's the main thing. In fact, you can't do without it really. Certainly, if you haven't made them laugh even once within the first five minutes, you probably won't be very popular. People may even switch off altogether. Speakers are kind of expected to be fairly entertaining as well as knowledgeable about their product or service. You don't actually have to crack jokes the whole time, but anecdotes and amusing stories seem to go down well. Making jokes at your

own expense, especially, seems to help build rapport with an audience that can otherwise seem a bit cold and unfriendly. And don't try to wow them too much with technology. Be too techno and people'll just think you're showing off.

 2.27

6   Being stylish seems to be what matters here – both in terms of your personal appearance and how you actually come across as a person. It's true that you do have to keep up a certain formality and your talk should always be logical and well-organised, but within those constraints you can be as imaginative and innovative as you like. In fact, unless you are offering something pretty special, something 'sexy', something unique that they haven't seen before, you'll find them very difficult to persuade. Obviously, knowing exactly who you're presenting to is always important, but here it really is essential that you do your homework. And, er, don't be surprised if the questions you get asked seem quite hostile. Tough questioning is all part of the business culture here.

 2.28

Extract 1

A   Good morning, everybody. Thanks for coming. I'm Rachel Weissmuller, area manager for the north-west division, and this is Brad Kennedy, head of our physiological research unit.

B   Hi.

A   As some of you already know, Brad and I have been working on a project of our own for some time now – a project, which we think you're going to be as excited about as we are. Brad?

B   Thanks, Rachel. Well, now, as the USA's leading chain of health clubs with over 1,000 centres in 35 states, we pride ourselves on providing the best in fitness training programs, on getting nearly a quarter million Americans off the couch and into the gym. For us, staying in shape is not just a business. It's a way of life. There's just one problem – the majority of Americans don't seem to be getting the message. According to the National Center for Health Statistics, seven out of ten of us don't take regular exercise. Four out of ten are not physically active at all! Figures recently published by the Surgeon General show that 61% of Americans are now seriously overweight. That's 122 million people! A disgraceful statistic. But, you have to admit, a tremendous marketing opportunity! The question is, how do we reach that market with something totally new?

 2.29

Extract 2

A   A recent report claims that a mere 13% of Americans are satisfied with their physical appearance. And a staggering 92% are dissatisfied with their current level of fitness. So, why aren't they doing something about it? We did a nationwide survey of people who had previously shown an interest in joining a MaxOut club and then changed their minds. Full details are in the report in front of you, but this chart highlights our main findings. As you can see, 15% of respondents said joining a gym was simply too expensive. 53% said they'd love to join if they weren't so busy. And, interestingly, 32%, almost a third, admitted they were just too embarrassed to join a health club in their present physical condition. They wanted to get fit first! So, what does all this mean? We think the implications are clear. There's obviously a huge market for an inexpensive alternative to going to the gym for people who are conscious of their appearance but short of time. And this represents a golden opportunity to stretch the MaxOut brand and develop a new product that perfectly complements our existing business.

 2.30

Extract 3

B   And here it is! The MaxOut Micro-GYM! 40% of our project budget went into constructing the prototype. And it's taken 18 months to get this far with the design. But isn't this just the coolest thing? I'll pass it round in a moment. Ladies and gentlemen, what you're looking at is the world's smallest full-body workout system – ever. It's the ultimate go-anywhere exercise machine. And, we believe, it could be a significant part of this company's future. With its sleek, lightweight design, the Micro-GYM weighs just over a pound, or 450 grams. That's less than most quality cameras. Disassembled, it fits easily into a coat pocket. The assembly itself is child's play. You can be ready to exercise in under 45 seconds. Now, I know what you're thinking. Can something so small possibly work? Yes, it can. The Micro-GYM offers 35 different exercises for upper body, lower body and mid-section. It can be adjusted from the five-kilo setting for gentle exercise right up to the 18-kilo setting for a real workout. In fact, it can do just about anything that much bulkier and more expensive equipment can. When you can't get to the gym, the Micro-GYM comes to you. You can get fit at home, on vacation, at the office, even in-flight!

 2.31

Extract 4

A   You'll have to excuse Brad. He gets a little carried away sometimes. But we do think the Micro-GYM could be an enormously successful sideline to our main business. OK, to wrap things up. The Micro-GYM has been fully costed – a complete breakdown is included in the report. Estimated costs of manufacturing, packaging and advertising are all itemised. Product testing is still being carried out, but we would obviously need the go-ahead from you before we proceed further with that. The Micro-GYM would probably be priced at around $35: well within the reach of most people. It has been suggested that exercise demonstrations could be recorded on video and that the product might easily be sold online. Both these suggestions would incur extra costs, but are currently being considered. The prospects for Micro-GYM are exciting. What we hope you'll give us today is the authorisation to move on to the next stage. Thank you very much.

B   Thank you, Rachel. OK, we'd like to throw this session open now for questions and suggestions. Feel free to try out the Micro-GYM for yourself. But, sorry, you can't take it home. It's the only one we have at the moment!

09 RELATIONSHIP-BUILDING

 2.32

Extract 1   Yes, well, it's easy to say don't judge by appearances, but, I mean, we all do it, don't we? You take one look at somebody and you're already weighing them up, deciding how friendly they are, how confident, how interesting… um, how attractive. It's automatic. And then two minutes talking to them and you've got them labelled – successful, intelligent, pushy, funny, boring, potentially useful contact … or not.

You know, I read somewhere that we actually evaluate people within ten seconds of meeting them. And apparently that's it! Could then take ten or twenty more meetings with that person to alter our first impression of them. I'm not so sure that's true, but I do think you can tell a lot about a person on first meeting them. It's the little things – a classy watch, a sharp suit, a nice smile, a nervous gesture, an ugly tie. Bitten fingernails are a no-no for me. Or a limp handshake. The wet fish! Absolute turn-off.

Actually, I think a good firm handshake is really important. I'm working in Germany at the moment. You know the Germans shake hands practically before every meeting? Even if they've already met you!

Extract 2   Actually, I think it's last impressions that we sometimes overlook. I mean, it's the impression you leave people with that counts. If you're meeting a lot of people all at the same event, it's easy just to drift around from group to group and never really make contact, like some kind of social butterfly.

I think you've got to be good at listening and drawing people out, investing some time in them and then making sure you close the conversation in a positive way. The old 'Oops, gotta go. Been great talking to you' thing is really bad. Or 'Here's my card. Give me a call.' Way too impersonal. You have to be careful how you end the conversation because that's what people are going to remember. And there's no point having the conversation in the first place if you're not going to try and make that person feel like it's been really worthwhile.

Extract 3   I think a good sense of humour is essential. At least, in Britain and America, it is. Humour's very much how we build relationships over here. On the other hand, have you ever done business in Finland? I have. Very different situation. You can forget the humour. They don't even really like small talk all that much. They'll strip off with you in the sauna, no problem! But they don't give much away personally. Just not part of the business culture there.

Of course, it may be that they just don't understand our humour. I mean, humour's very cultural, isn't it? You watch a comedy on a foreign TV channel and it's hard to see what on earth they're laughing at. They probably think the same about our jokes.

But then I think jokes are usually a mistake, anyway, unless you know the other people very well. But you don't have to tell jokes to be humorous. Better just to make a few amusing observations. The worst thing is telling a long complicated joke and nobody laughs. Agony! Don't do it!

Extract 4   I was thinking about a meal we had with some business people from Toulouse the other evening. Good clients of ours, actually. We had a great time. Didn't pack them off to their hotel till about two in the morning! And, you know, it struck me that what we were really doing pretty much all night was just telling stories. One of us would tell a story about somewhere we'd been, something we'd done or someone we'd met and then that would remind someone else of a similar story and so on and so on. Jean-Luc told a slightly naughty story about a Belgian supplier of his at a wine-tasting session, but I'd better not repeat it!

But, you know, I reckon if you've got a few good stories you can tell, that's all you need really. One story leads into another and, I mean it helps if they're a bit funny, but as long as they're true, I think stories really connect.

Extract 5   A   Of course, now that we live in the so-called 'network economy', everyone makes a big deal about networking. But it depends who you're networking with. Take the Russians. I mean, they'll have a serious conversation with you on any subject you care to name, but small talk is not really their thing. Same with the Germans, the Swiss, the Swedes – generally very good English, happy to talk about work, but not really keen on the social chit-chat.

I mean, go out with a group of Russians after work for a few beers and something to eat and they really let their hair down! In that sense they're a bit like the Chinese. They like a big sit-down meal, plenty to eat and drink. What they don't like is the mingling, the wandering around chatting to people.

Basically, it's the British, the French, the Latins and the Americans who are into the schmoozing thing. Americans, especially, have made an art of it. I mean, they're always easy to talk to. It doesn't get very deep usually, but they'll come right up to you and start a conversation and, actually, I quite like that. Working the room, they call it, and that's what it is for them – work.

2.33

Conversation 1

A Alessandro!

B Hello, Jeanine! How are you? **I didn't expect to see you here!**

A No, I don't normally come to these things. But a colleague couldn't make it, so I stepped in at the last minute.

B How long has it been?

A Oh, ages. A year, at least. **You're looking very well.**

B Just got back from holiday. St. Lucia.

A Lucky you! Look, Alessandro, I was just on my way to an appointment.

B Oh, OK. No problem. Don't let me keep you. Perhaps I'll catch you later.

A I hope so. As a matter of fact, I should be free in about an hour or so. Will you still be around then?

B Oh, yes. It's just me on the stand this year, I'm afraid.

A Oh, well, in that case, why don't I meet you back here when I'm done and perhaps we can go out for a drink – or grab a bite to eat if you're free. I've lots of news to tell you. And I want to find out all about your holiday!

B Great. No, I've no plans for this evening. See you later, then.

 2.34

Conversation 2

A Ms Mendoza?

B Yes.

A How do you do? **I don't think we've been introduced.** I'm Martin, Martin Shaw, the new assistant sales manager for our Central American division. First week here, as a matter of fact.

B Oh, pleased to meet you. Welcome to Mexico!

A Thanks!

B So you're working with Richard, no?

A That's right.

B I head up the biotech team at Zantis here in Tampico. **Perhaps Richard has mentioned me.**

A Yes, of course. He told me all about your set-up here. Actually, Richard's just been detained for a moment. But I'm sure he'll be joining us shortly. Can I get you anything to drink, Ms Mendoza?

B No, I'm fine, thanks. And please, call me Victoria.

A Right, Victoria, well, you don't mind if I …?

B No, no, of course not! Do you drink tequila, Martin?

A Well, I, er, think I tried it once, back when I was a student. Seem to remember being carried home afterwards!

B Oh dear. Well, there's tequila and there's tequila. Why don't I order something typically Mexican for you?

A Sure, why not?

B Por favor!

 2.35

Conversation 3

A This is really very interesting, Mr Toth. I'm sure we could provide just the sort of hydraulic systems you'd need for a project like this and we'd be able to do you a very good price … Oh, my goodness! Is that the time? I've got a taxi coming in ten minutes to take me to the airport.

B Oh, you're leaving this evening, are you?

A Only flight I could get, I'm afraid. What a nuisance! I'd have liked to discuss this further with you.

B Not to worry. Here is my card. Why don't you give me yours, and I'll give you a call when I get back to the office?

A Of course. Here you are. **I'm really very sorry to have to rush off like this.**

B No problem. **It's been interesting chatting to you. Perhaps we can meet up again** to discuss things in more depth.

A Absolutely, absolutely. A pleasure meeting you, Mr Toth.

B Likewise.

A Goodbye now.

B Goodbye.

 2.36

Conversation 4

A Hello, Jake. **Long time no see!**

B Duncan! Hello! Yes, I'd forgotten your Anthony's a pupil here too.

A Just started this year.

B Of course. How time flies! Last time I saw him he was at junior school.

A That's right. And how's Ian doing? Must be off to university soon.

B Yes, Oxford in the autumn. He's reading medicine.

A Oh, congratulations! You must be very proud of him.

B Cleverer, than his old dad, that's for sure!

A So, how's retirement treating you? I expect you're never off the golf course, are you?

B Well, it gets me out of the house. And out from under Helen's feet!

A How is Helen?

B Very well, very well. As a matter of fact, we were just talking about you and Anne the other day, saying what a long time it was since we'd seen you.

A Yes, it's been too long. **We really must get together soon.** Oh, hang on, I think Anthony's in this race. Better go and cheer him on. Catch you later.

B Yes. See you later on.

 2.37

Conversation 5

A Good morning. Ms Vatland?

B That's right.

A We haven't met. I'm Daniel Crane. Ana Lindstrom gave me your name. **She might have mentioned me?**

B Ah, Mr Crane! Yes, Ana said you'd be stopping by. Can I offer you anything? A coffee, mineral water, fruit juice, perhaps?

A Thank you, a mineral water would be very nice.

B OK. … There you go. So how are you enjoying the Fair?

A Well, this is all new to me, but I'm hoping to make some useful contacts. It's certainly been an eye-opener so far. I'd no idea the industry was so developed here.

B Oh, yes. There's a lot of interest right now. I understand from Ana that you're looking for agents in Scandinavia, is that right?

A Yes, that's right. We're also looking for a good business lawyer with local knowledge to work with over here. I don't know if you happen to know of anybody?

B Well, I can think of several people who might be able to help you there. And, as far as agents are concerned, I can certainly put you in touch with some very professional operations.

A That would really be very helpful, Ms Vatland.

B Please. Lena.

A Lena. Ana said you were the person to talk to and I can see that she was right.

 3.01

Extract 1

A Stella! Max! You're just in time to join us in a little pre-match drink.

B Hi, Craig. Hi, Karen. Oh, is that malt whisky? I don't know if I should. I mean, I just had breakfast!

A Nonsense! It's just the thing to warm us up. Max, you'll have one, won't you?

C Of course, thank you.

A There you go. Stella?

B Well, OK, just a drop. It is a little chilly this morning. Beautiful day, though.

A Isn't it? Well, now, we should probably be thinking of making a move quite soon. Unfortunately, we can't count on the weather staying fine at this time of year. Max, you're partnering Karen. And Stella, you're stuck with me, I'm afraid. Now, I've arranged for us to have lunch at the clubhouse – they've got an excellent restaurant there. So I thought we'd start at the tenth and just play the last nine holes, if that's OK with you. That way we should be able to get round the course in a couple of hours or so.

B Sounds perfect.

A And, Max, I think you'll find my game's improved a little since we last played.

C Splendid! I always like a challenge, Craig. You know that …

 3.02

Extract 2

A Damn! I don't know what's the matter with my game today. I just can't seem to keep the ball straight. Sorry, Stella. You must be wishing you'd been teamed up with Max.

B Well, you have been in two sand-traps and a lake, Craig! And this is only our third hole!

A I know, I know. Your shot, Max …

B Craig, **I've been meaning to have a word with you about** this disposal operation of ours.

A Ah, I was wondering when you'd get round to mentioning that. Look, Stella, you know my position on that …

B Now, Craig, listen to me. You know I want that oil platform disposed of at sea. It's by far the most cost-effective method. Oh, sorry, Max. Not trying to put you off your game. Oh, great shot! Wow, that's almost all the way to the flag! Craig, you didn't tell me Max was such a fantastic player.

A No, I, er, look, Stella, this oil platform – disposing of it at sea. Don't you think that's a bit risky? I know it's technically possible. But there must be 130 tonnes of highly toxic and radioactive substances on that platform!

B Craig, you're starting to sound like a Greenpeace activist, for goodness' sake! … By the way, I understand you've applied for the top job here in Scotland.

A Yeah, so?

B So's Max.

A What?

B Yeah. And the way it's looking he may well get it. Seems the board like his competitive spirit.

A I see.

B Of course, I could probably put in a word for you. Let's talk later. For the time being, I'd like you to concentrate on your game! I'm not a good loser, Craig!

 3.03

Extract 1

A Magda!

B Hello, Anne. Brrr! It's a bit nasty out there tonight.

A Horrible, isn't it? Come on in. Let me take your coat. **You managed to find us OK, then?**

B Well, I got a bit lost coming off the ring road, as usual. Sorry I'm a bit late.

A Oh, don't worry. Martin's still slaving away in the kitchen. Actually, he had a bit of a crisis with the starter just half an hour ago. You should have heard the language! Probably just as well you weren't here.

B Oh, right. So Martin's cooking, is he?

A Mm. He's quite an expert in the kitchen – fortunately for me. I can't boil an egg myself!

B Oh, I brought you this. I wasn't sure what you liked, but apparently it's meant to be quite a good year.

A Oh, thanks. You shouldn't have. Lovely. I'll put it in the fridge. Come on through.

3.04

Extract 2

B Oh, what a fabulous apartment!

A Thanks. We like it.

B Have you been here long?

A Um … about two years now. The whole place was an absolute wreck when we moved in. We had to do just about everything to it. Now, what can I get you to drink? How about a gin and tonic? That's what I'm having.

B Yes, that'd be great.

A Ice and lemon?

B Please.

A OK. I'll be right back. Make yourself at home.

C Hi, Magda. I'm Martin. **I don't think we've met**.

B Hello, Martin. Pleased to meet you. You're the chef, I understand.

C Oh, yes. Doing a good job of setting fire to the kitchen at the moment. I had to rescue the starter.

B So I heard.

A Ah, so you two have met. Good. There we are, Magda. Let me know if you want more ice in that.

B Thanks.

A Are we nearly ready, then, darling?

C Er, yes, I'm just waiting for the sauce. In fact, I'd better go and check on it. I don't trust that new cooker.

A Oh, OK.

3.05

Extract 3

B I was just looking at some of your oil paintings, Anne. You've got quite a collection, haven't you?

A Mm, yes. Dutch mostly. Eighteenth century. They're Martin's, really.

B And I love the way you've done the fireplace. Was that here when you moved in?

A Yes, it's the original. We had to have it restored, obviously.

B And what beautiful chairs. I could do with some of those for my place. French, aren't they?

A Italian, actually. We bought them at an auction in Milan.

B Oh, really? And, wow! Look at that view!

A Good, isn't it?

B You can see practically the whole city from here.

C Dinner's ready when you are.

C Right, Magda, sit wherever you like. Now, we're having duck in a port sauce.

B Mm, smells delicious!

C So, I thought we'd have a nice Spanish red, something with a bit of body in it. Or do you prefer white?

B No, red's fine, thanks.

3.06

Extract 4

C Now, there's more duck if you want it. And help yourself to vegetables.

B Mm, this is absolutely delicious.

A It's one of Martin's specialities.

B Mm, it's really good. The duck's all crispy on the outside and juicy on the inside.

C I'm glad you like it.

B You must let me have the recipe.

C Oh, it's very simple, really. You just need the right ingredients.

A A little more wine, Magda?

B I shouldn't really. I'm driving.

A Oh, go on. You've only had one.

B Oh, all right, just a drop, then.

A Magda, **I've been meaning to talk to you about** this business in Poland.

B Oh, yes, that.

A Do you know what's going on there? Because no one seems to be able to tell me anything.

C Right, well, excuse me a moment. If you two are going to talk business, I'll go and see to the dessert.

B Well, **I ought to be making a move soon**. Early start tomorrow.

C Oh, you don't have to rush off just yet, do you? How about some more coffee?

B OK, just half a cup. And then I really must be going.

B Well, thank you both for a lovely evening. Martin, you're a brilliant cook.

C I know. There's no point denying it.

B Next time you must come to my place, although I can't promise you such a fabulous meal.

A Bye, Magda. Take care now. See you tomorrow.

10 TAKING DECISIONS

 3.07

1 Don't even think about jumping from a moving vehicle. At 70 miles per hour the chances of surviving are remote. And crashing into the mountainside at this speed will almost certainly send you straight through the windscreen. So, even though you may be scared of going over the cliff, your best chance of slowing the car down is to repeatedly run it against the crash barriers. After all, that's what they're there for.

3.08

2 Resist the temptation to run. You cannot outrun or outclimb a mountain lion. And put any ideas of playing dead out of your mind. Whilst it may work with grizzly bears, to a mountain lion you'll just look like a free lunch. Your best bet is to shout and flap your coat at the animal to make yourself look bigger and fiercer than you really are. Mountain lions are not proud. If you look like more trouble than you're worth, there's a fifty-fifty chance they'll back away.

3.09

3 Water transfers heat away from the body 25 times faster than air. So trying to keep warm is more or less futile. And while you're staying calm and conserving energy, the chances are you're dying. You have to get out. Turn in the direction you fell and use your elbows to lift yourself onto the edge of the ice. Reach forward as far as possible and kick your feet as if you were swimming. Once you are back on the ice, crawl to shore. Do not in any circumstances try to stand up.

 3.10

4 When landing a light aircraft, make sure that the nose of the plane is six inches below the horizon. As you approach the runway the plane should be flying at an altitude of about 100 feet. If you're higher, you'll overshoot the runway completely. The optimum speed on landing is about 60 miles per hour. Go faster and you may take off again. Go slower and you'll drop like a stone. Upon landing, it's a good idea to brake as soon as you've gained control of the steering. By reducing your groundspeed by 50% you triple your chances of survival.

3.11

5 The current world record for the long jump is just under nine metres, but most people can barely manage three or four. The chances are you can't either. To clear four and a half metres in conditions that are far from ideal you'd need a 20 to 30 metre run-up, perfect timing and a great deal of luck. Frankly, your chances are slim. The truck is a much

better idea and it is quite possible to fall from the sixth floor and live. But don't jump out from the building unless there are balconies in the way. You'll be carried forward and miss the truck completely. Drop vertically and take care to land on your back to avoid breaking it.

3.12

6 The taxi could take anything from a few minutes to just a few seconds to sink. But there's not much point trying to force the door open because the water pressure will make this almost impossible. If the car does sink there'll be little or no air left anyway, so forget about trapping air inside. By far the most sensible thing to do is to open the window and actually let more water in. Even if you can't escape through the window, once the water pressure inside and outside the car are equalised, there's a fair chance you'll be able to open the door and save yourself – and maybe the driver too!

3.13

7 It's very unusual for both parachutes to fail, so by struggling with the emergency chute there's an outside chance you'll get it to work. But don't bet on it. You may just be wasting precious time. If you can share one of your friends' parachutes you're in with a chance, but just grabbing the nearest person is not a smart move. The G-force when the parachute opens will throw you apart. At 14,000 feet and falling at your terminal velocity of 120 miles per hour you've got about 75 seconds before your appointment with Mother Earth. So firmly attach yourself to the chest straps of another parachutist. You don't stand a chance unless you do.

3.14

8 You are 30 times more likely to be struck by lightning than to be attacked by a shark, but this is little comfort in your present position. Splashing around and making a noise will simply give the shark the idea you're in distress and easy meat. It's a common mistake to think the shark's nose is the best area to target. Punch it there and you are liable to lose a hand or arm – depending on the size of the shark. You'd do much better to strike at its eyes or gills since these are a shark's most vulnerable points

3.15

1

A Right, as you know, our last offer to the union was a three per cent pay rise and a two-hour reduction in the working week to be gradually phased in over the next 18 months. The ball is now firmly in their court. Ragnar, do you have any idea which way they'll vote?

B The word is they'll turn it down. In fact, they might even be considering taking industrial action.

A A strike?

B I don't know, Dan. It's a possibility.

A With the current backlog of orders a strike's the last thing we need!

C Now, let's not jump to conclusions. They haven't announced the result of the vote yet.

B My sources are usually accurate, Per.

A Look, time is short. If the vote goes against us, I want us to be able to come straight back with an improved offer. So **let's put our heads together and see what we can come up with**.

3.16

2

A **OK, we've weighed up the various pros and cons**. Now it's time to reach a decision and stick to it. Our latest information is that the political situation in Somalia is worsening. In fact, it may only be a matter of days before the country is plunged into civil war. The proposal is that we should pull our people out of there immediately.

B Now, wait a minute, Richard. **I don't want us rushing into anything**. This whole issue requires long and careful consideration. This is our biggest production plant in North Africa and we're talking about closing it down here.

A I'm well aware of that, Hans. But **I take it we're all in agreement that** our first priority is to safeguard the well-being of our personnel.

B Of course.

A Well, then, **I don't see we have any option but to** give this proposal our full backing.

C Aren't we overlooking something here? I mean it's all very well talking about flying our management team home and closing the plant, but what about our factory workers? They'll all be out of a job.

A I'm afraid our responsibility to local workers is different, Andrea. When it comes to the crunch, we have to look after our European staff first …

 3.17

3

A OK, you've all seen the results of the road tests. It looks like the two-litre model has some kind of a steering problem and we may have to authorise a total product recall while we conduct further tests.

B Isn't that a bit drastic, Simon? I mean, it's only a slight steering problem, isn't it? And it doesn't seem to be affecting the smaller-engined models.

A Well, that's what we're here to discuss, Matt. With a safety issue like this I don't think we should take any chances, but **I'd like your input on this** before committing us to any definite course of action. Laura?

C Hm, **I'm in two minds about it**. I mean, I agree with you that the safety of our customers must come first. But if we take the whole series off the market, I dread to think what the newspapers will do with the story. At this stage **I think we should keep our options open**. And these test results aren't conclusive, are they?

A Well, no, but I don't think we can just sit on the fence here. In the long run, failing to act quickly could do us a lot of harm.

B So what do you suggest?

A Well, in the absence of more reliable data, **I think I'm going to have to go with my gut instinct on this** one. I'm just not prepared to put our customers' lives at risk …

 3.18

Step 1

The mighty Coca-Cola has been the world's number one brand for so long, it's hard to imagine anything threatening its position of global dominance. One of the company's own publicity brochures proudly declares: 'A billion hours ago human life appeared on Earth; a billion minutes ago Christianity emerged; a billion seconds ago the Beatles performed on the Ed Sullivan Show – a billion servings of Coca-Cola ago was yesterday morning.' Quite a claim. And one that makes a loss of consumer confidence unthinkable.

But take yourself back to May 1999. The unthinkable has just happened. Hundreds of people in Belgium and France have become ill after drinking what they claim is contaminated Coke. And when the cause of the problem cannot quickly be established, the famous soft drink is officially banned in both countries as well as Luxembourg and the Netherlands. The price you pay for being the brand leader is that customers expect quality, as Coca-Cola's CEO is the first to admit. 'For 113 years,' he says, 'our success has been based on the trust that consumers have in that quality.' Now that trust is shaken.

In fact, the four countries banning Coke only represent two per cent of the company's $18.8 billion in annual sales. But within a week consignments exported from Belgium to other countries as far apart as Germany and the Ivory Coast have also been seized by officials. Though no definite proof of contamination has yet been found, the panic is starting to spread …

 3.19

Step 2

1999 is not a good year for soft drinks companies. Though the Dow is up 25%, both Coke and Pepsi, normally well ahead of the market, are down by around 13%. Coca-Cola is not going to rush into a highly expensive product recall.

In any case, early examinations of the Belgian bottling plants find nothing unusual and an official toxicologist's report concludes that the 200 cases of sickness are probably psychosomatic.

But while Coca-Cola is deliberating over what action to take, rivals Pepsi and Virgin Cola are quick to fill the gaps left on the supermarket shelves. And Coke's refusal to react until it has conducted a thorough investigation is starting to look like a denial of responsibility …

 3.20

Step 5

This is how Coca-Cola actually handled the problem. Initially, full-page advertisements were taken out in European newspapers to reassure the public that the quality of Coke was 'irreproachable'. This was not totally successful as the public at that time could still remember a similar contamination scare at Perrier some years before and all the talk was of pesticides on fruit and mad cow disease.

But, fortunately, the source of the Coke contamination was eventually traced to a strange fungicide on cans shipped from Dunkirk and poor carbon dioxide at Coca-Cola's bottling plant in Antwerp which makes the Coke taste a little different but does no real harm. It wasn't the Coke itself but the cans that were contaminated.

Coke took the necessary measures and, at enormous cost to the company, all 17 million cases of Coke were withdrawn. Finally, in a spectacular public relations coup, and as an apology to the Belgians who had been ill, Coca-Cola offered a free one-and-a-half litre bottle of Coke to each and every one of Belgium's ten million citizens! Coke was immediately back in the stores.

11 SIMPLY THE BEST

 3.21

A OK, thanks for coming, everyone. You all know the situation. So let's hear your thoughts.

B Well, I'd say we need to **come up with** some ideas for new products and fast!

A So it's a question of **product innovation**.

B Well, I'd like to see us **producing** some fresh ideas at least!

C Hold on. First, we need to know exactly how we **measure up to** the competition.

A You're talking about **benchmarking**, right?

C Precisely. It's standard practice. We need to know how our business processes **compare with** theirs.

D In my opinion, we need to **look after** our best clients. They give us the most business.

A So you're saying it's a matter of **customer service**.

D Well, we get 80% of our business from 20% of our customers, so shouldn't we be **taking care of** them first?

E No, we need to **break into** smaller more specialist markets. They're the future.

A We should be looking at **niche marketing**?

E Yeah. Mass marketing is dead. We need to be **penetrating** those niche markets.

F We need to **speed up** our delivery processing. That's how we're losing orders.

A So the real problem is **lead times**?

F Yes, **accelerate** delivery processing and we'd pick up 20% more business tomorrow.

G Well, you know, I think we need to **bring out** a much wider range of products.

A So what you're saying is **diversification**.

G Yeah, we should be **launching** products in all sectors of the market, not just the top end.

H In my view, we simply need to **bring down** our overheads. They are way too high.

A So it's just a matter of **cost-cutting**, then?

H Well, if you look at the balance sheet it's clear they need to be **reduced** significantly.

I No, look. What we really need to do is **stand out from** the competition more.

A In other words, we're talking **differentiation**, right?

I Differentiation, sure. But it's not just that. We really need to **be different from** the competition in our whole approach.

J If you ask me, we need to **look at** how we could use our name on other products.

A So you're suggesting **brand-stretching**?

J Yes, I think it's something we should **investigate**.

 3.22

Welcome to the In Company Business Podcast. You're listening to *Business Breakthroughs*. This week's episode: *Out of the Blue, the Cirque du Soleil Story, Part 1*.

Music blasts from loudspeakers as trapeze artists swing from chandeliers. A bungee jumper performs an aerial ballet. Masked clowns kidnap members of the audience and invite them on stage. Angels fly through the air in an explosion of fireworks. The lights suddenly go out and a snowstorm fills the darkness. This is certainly not circus as we know it. This can only be Cirque du Soleil.

The history of Canada's most famous export is as dramatic as any of its spectacular performances. Founded in 1984 by penniless street performer Guy Laliberté, Cirque du Soleil now employs over two thousand people and its thirteen resident and travelling shows have a turnover of $600 million a year. About 120 million of that is profit, giving an exceptional profit margin of 20%. Over the last twenty years it has grown at an annual rate of 20–30% to become the world's leading circus.

Based in a developing district of Montreal, Cirque's travelling circuses have now been seen by over 40 million people in 90 countries. Joint ventures with Las Vegas casinos, MGM and Disney provide permanent venues for some of the shows. In Interbrand's 2004 survey of the brands with the most global impact, Cirque du Soleil ranked 22nd, ahead of McDonald's, Microsoft and Volkswagen. With a personal net worth of $1.5 billion, in 2007 Laliberté won the Ernst and Young Entrepreneur of the Year Award.

How has the company been able to achieve such phenomenal success in the space of just two decades? In the 1980s the circus industry was in sharp decline with rising costs and a shrinking market. Other forms of family entertainment were proving more popular and ethical questions about the use of animals were also affecting ticket sales. Laliberté's stroke of genius was to reverse that model. Rather than benchmarking himself against other circuses, he saw that it was useless to measure himself against them. By dropping the animal acts altogether, he both cut costs significantly and solved the moral dilemma. At the same time, by adding several key value innovations – theatrical sets, specially commissioned music, atmospheric lighting, dramatic storylines and intelligent humour – he effectively repositioned the circus, not as a family night out, but as sophisticated grown-up entertainment. And this also meant that he could charge his target market – well-educated, middle class professionals – several times more than the traditional circus. Low-cost structure and premium prices – it has been a magic formula, but one which Cirque's competitors have not been slow to copy.

Cirque's biggest competitor, Feld Entertainment, the company that owns Disney on Ice, Ringling Brothers and the hundred-year-old Barnum & Bailey's circus, once advertised as 'The Greatest Show on Earth', represents the circus at its most traditional. But it has recently started to incorporate more drama and music into its performances in a very Cirque-like way. A number of other circuses with exotically costumed performers and glamorous-sounding names, such as Cirque Eos and Cirque Éloize, have also emerged in recent years. And, perhaps most threateningly of all, two of Cirque's own key creative directors, Slava Polunin and Franco Dragone, left the company to set up their own highly successful rival shows.

Whilst the Cirque du Soleil brand is firmly embedded in the public mind, it is certainly no longer the only show in town. In an increasingly crowded market, and with the recent economic downturn, how long can it hang on to its own unique identity? Find out in Part 2 of *Out of the Blue, the Cirque du Soleil Story*.

 3.23

Welcome to the In Company Business Podcast. You're listening to *Business Breakthroughs*. This week's episode: *Out of the Blue, the Cirque du Soleil Story, Part 2*.

Guy Laliberté has taken Cirque du Soleil from a tiny troupe of amateur performers scratching a living in the streets of Montreal to a multi-billion dollar global industry in the space of just twenty years. But with success has come increased competition from 'copycat' circuses and stage shows. How is the company dealing with that?

In a recent interview, Cirque's chief marketing officer, Mario D'Amico, was asked this question and his answer was a surprising one:

'*We don't really deal with it. We think our product speaks for itself. We will react if people are copying us. But other circuses that have been inspired by what we do – you know what? – more power to them! Great. We think that is actually good for the category of what we'll call the more modern circus.*'

Nevertheless, the company has diversified. Cirque is already offering 3-D entertainment at iMax cinemas, it has its own TV and record companies and there has been talk of stretching the brand to include hotels, spas and theme restaurants. But, perhaps deterred by the failure of similar ventures like Planet Hollywood, and concerned not to stretch the Cirque brand too far, some of these projects have been put on hold in order to concentrate on Cirque's core competencies as an entertainment company.

As Cirque CEO Daniel Lamarre points out, there has been some repositioning:

'*We don't see ourselves any longer as a circus company. It's a blend between circus and dance and music and a lot of different disciplines. And so what we're trying to do is, more and more, be a totally integrated content provider. And we have been very successful lately in Las Vegas, for instance – we have five different shows in Las Vegas right now and each show is very distinctive.*'

Part of that success has come through strategic collaboration. Teaming up with Paul McCartney, Ringo Starr, Yoko Ono and Olivia Harrison to develop the Beatles-themed show LOVE led to a smash hit. A similar venture is planned with the Elvis Presley estate and the Luxor casino in Las Vegas. Another new departure has been magic shows with sensational street illusionist Criss Angel, the man who can apparently walk on water, fly through the air and cut himself in half!

To broaden its customer base, Cirque has a special department called The New Tendencies Group, which tracks new trends in fashion, design, music, art, architecture and counter-culture. And it is these new trends they then build into their shows.

Will this be enough to maintain market leadership? To answer that question, perhaps we need only look to the success of Cirque's biggest partner, Disney. Like Cirque, Disney was the first into the blue ocean of family theme parks. And, though theme parks have proliferated since then, the Disney brand remains by far the strongest. If Cirque can get its own strategy as spectacularly right as Disney, it will have built its own 'magic kingdom'.

CASE STUDY: THE SKY'S THE LIMIT

 3.24

A Come in.

B Gabrielle. I'm glad I caught you. Do you have a minute?

A Well, actually, I was about to call it a day, Piet. It's late … and I'm tired. Can't it wait until tomorrow?

B I just wanted to check you were OK.

A I'm OK.

B Good, good. And no hard feelings about the way the decision went?

A Hard feelings? Piet, I think I made myself pretty clear at the meeting. And I certainly don't want to go over it all again now. The decision has been taken and that's that. Let's move on.

B Well, I'm glad you see it that way.

A What I can't understand, Piet, is why you sided with Herman on this. I would have thought you were the last person to take such a ridiculous risk. Part ownership of an Indian airline? It's completely crazy!

B Now, Gabrielle, you know we've done a lot of due diligence on this. It makes good strategic sense. India's a rapidly expanding economy with over a billion people. That's a market we certainly want a part of! And, as I said at the meeting, this is an opportunity to get into a high-growth industry at the ground level.

A This is another one of Herman's ego trips, that's what it is! Do you know, Piet, airlines are just about the world's least profitable industry? And I should know. I spent six years in the business!

B Exactly. And that's why you're so essential to the success of this venture, Gabrielle. I know Herman's counting on you.

A Piet, let me tell you about the airline industry. First of all, competition is intense. I mean really intense. Basically, you're competing solely on price. There's almost no role for marketing because it's virtually impossible to differentiate your service. You have no idea what we have got ourselves into.

B But, Gabrielle, this is exactly the kind of business NMI targets. We're a highly diversified company. Why not airlines? Did you know that Delhi airport alone is expecting exponential growth – 100 million passengers by 2050!

A 2050! That's science fiction, Piet. We don't have a 40-year marketing plan!

B You know what I mean.

A I know that just about anybody can start an airline. Lease a plane, book a gate, fly a route and you're in business. I know that in the airline market there are practically no barriers to entry. And India's new 'open skies' policy is only going to make that worse.

B A bit of healthy competition's not a problem, Gabrielle. That's the whole point of starting up in India. Look, you know it's mostly the middle classes who fly. And since 2000 the number of middle class families has increased eightfold over there. Eightfold! With their combined income equivalent to the EU, there's huge potential.

A No, there isn't, Piet. Airlines don't make any money. They're under constant pressure from suppliers. Fuel costs fluctuate wildly. In fact, it's the suppliers who make the real money. Airbus, Rolls-Royce, BP – they turn the profits.

B I know that. But you're forgetting tourism. India has the highest tourism growth rate in the world. Three and a half million tourists! That's where we'll make our profit. Look, Eastern Promise already has a solid 8% market share. It just needs capital. Capital we happen to have right now.

A Oh, Piet. If only you'd listened to me. Well, it's too late now. Let's just hope we don't have to face industrial disputes. God knows, the industry's so highly unionised, one pilot's strike could shut us down.

B Gabrielle, I think you may be overreacting. This is a good move for NMI.

A Well, I hope you're right, Piet. I hope you're right …

 3.25

A Come in, Gabrielle.

B Herman. You wanted to see me?

A Yes, it's about the Eastern Promise situation.

B I guessed it would be.

A Yes, well, I know you were against this venture in the first place. And it looks like you were right, after all. In fact, things have now got worse – a whole lot worse. Take a seat … I've just come out of a videoconference with Suraj Kapoor and it seems that, even with a reduced service, more than half of Eastern Promise's flights are running at just 30% capacity. That's a massive loss. Kapoor's talking about sharing flights with other LCCs.

B Sharing our market share with other failing carriers – well, that makes sense!

A Yes, well, it's not much of a market share any more with us down to 5%.

B Quite. Of course, you know why this is, don't you? Eastern Promise is just too expensive to compete as an LCC. And it's too low quality to attract business travellers. It's an elementary law of marketing, Herman. We're stuck in the middle with an airline that would be dead already if Kapoor didn't keep pouring his own money into it. We either step in now or sell off our share in the company.

A Gabrielle, you have to remember that Kapoor still has a controlling 51% stake and his reputation in India is on the line. It's a delicate situation. Any changes we want to make will have to be approved by him. And we're locked into the partnership for another 27 months … I'm sending you and your team out there to find out what's going on.

B Me? Why me?

A You never wanted this deal with Eastern Promise. So I know you'll give me straight answers. Plus, you've worked in airlines before.

B And I got out as soon as I could.

A Still, you have the right experience, Gabrielle. And I'm losing confidence in Kapoor. He seems to think everything can be solved by publicity stunts and ticket giveaways. But we're not going to climb out of this mess with slick advertising or price-cutting. We need a brand-new marketing strategy and you're the one I'm relying on to come up with it. Decide who you're taking with you and we'll hold a briefing meeting the day before you fly out.

B OK, OK, I'll see what I can do.

A Good … Oh, and thanks, Gabrielle.

B For what?

A For not saying 'I told you so!'

 3.26

Welcome to the In Company Business Podcast. You're listening to *Business Breakthroughs*. This week's episode: *Flying High, Kingfisher Airlines*.

Outside his native India, Vijay Mallya is not exactly a household name. Amongst serial entrepreneurs he's not yet up there with the likes of Rupert Murdoch and Richard Branson. But all that may be about to change. Known throughout the subcontinent as 'the king of good times' and host of a hundred lavish business launch parties, the charismatic billionaire tycoon is about to go global.

At the tender age of 27, Dr Mallya inherited the massive conglomerate United Breweries, currently worth $5 billion, and immediately set about streamlining the family business and, most significantly, creating the Kingfisher brand. Internationally, Kingfisher is most commonly associated with the distinctive beer of the same name, but since 2005 it has also been the name of the most successful airline in India, a wholly owned subsidiary of the UB Group.

Right from the start Mallya had big plans for Kingfisher Airlines. Seeing a split in the market between premium-priced full service carriers and the poor, almost bus service, quality of low-cost carriers, he decided to carve out a new niche with a value-added budget airline. With prices lower than economy class on the FSCs and only slightly higher than the LCCs, he purchased brand-new planes and equipped them with state-of-the-art in-flight entertainment systems and tastefully designed cabins. Under the slogan 'Fly the good times', he stretched a brand already familiar to millions of Indians and introduced the Kingfisher 'funliner', a true travel experience for India's rapidly expanding young professional class.

In spite of winning the Best New Airline Award in 2005, it wasn't, however, an easy journey. Between 2005 and 2006 new entrants crowded into the domestic airline market. And things really started to hot up when market leader Jet Airways acquired Sahara and slashed its prices to better compete with Kingfisher. Kingfisher had, controversially, gone for a single Kingfisher class, rather than separate business and economy classes. With strength both at the top and bottom end of the market, Jet-Sahara now represented a significant threat. But Mallya refused to be put off by either the fierce competition or elusive profits, and remained confident that, after a period of consolidation, a smaller number of profitable players would emerge from the price war.

He was proved spectacularly right. In 2007 Kingfisher acquired the biggest low-cost carrier Deccan, rebranding it as Kingfisher Red. This placed the company in the top two Indian private airlines, cut down operational costs and accelerated its progress towards profitability. And in 2009 it shocked the industry by pushing through an alliance with its old rival Jet Airways. Kingfisher and Jet now code-share flights, and points awarded on their frequent flier programmes can be redeemed at either airline. Talk about sleeping with the enemy!

Throughout the history of the company, it has been Mallya's willingness to break rules, buck trends and seek out fresh markets that has kept him ahead. He makes no secret of his aim to make Kingfisher the undisputed number one Indian airline. His latest venture is into international flights, for which he has just taken delivery of five Airbus A380s. It's a high-risk strategy, with questions about the reliability of the super jumbos and the global airline industry in freefall, but who can doubt that the king of good times won't fly through the current economic turbulence and steer his unique airline into serious profit?

12 E-MAILING

 3.27

Welcome to the *In Company* Business Podcast Career Spot.

Forget about spelling, switch off your grammar-check, and you just might e-mail your way to the top of the corporate ladder. According to research by Professor David Owens of Vanderbilt University into what your e-mail says about your career prospects, sloppy, hastily written e-mails are a clear sign of leadership potential. 'High-status people in a company' he says, 'send short messages and they have the worst grammar and spelling in the firm. This isn't because they are the least educated. They just don't have time to waste on the small stuff.'

Owens's study shows that high-fliers invest more time in 'face-mail', face-to-face meetings with those they need to liaise with or persuade. This leaves them just a few brief moments during the day to dash off e-mails confirming what was decided, making last-minute changes and tying up any loose ends. Frequently the e-mails of natural-born leaders are no more than a phrase: 'Fine by me', 'Let's do it!', 'OK, see you at the meeting'.

The neatly paragraphed 300-word e-mail with a 5Mb attachment, on the other hand, is strictly for corporate losers. The message it sends is: my job is so undemanding and lacking in challenge or responsibility, I have hours to craft this e-mail into a work of art. 'Reply to all' usually indicates a time-waster, whilst anyone who uses the 'blank carbon copy' to secretly involve the boss in e-mails to colleagues, is a poor player of office politics and definitely not to be trusted.

Owens's research also reveals that anyone who has a habit of forwarding jokes or sending animated electronic greetings cards is destined never to reach the level of senior management. An overuse of smileys and other more elaborate emoticons further undermines professionalism and guarantees you won't be taken seriously. According to Owens, office jokers play an important social role – they boost morale and are unlikely to be fired, but they don't very often get promoted.

But is it really true that bad e-mail is good? A study attributed to Cambridge University and widely circulated on the internet, claims that bad spelling, at least, is not much of a barrier to communication. And surveys suggest that when native English speakers receive e-mails from non-natives, the last thing they care about is the grammar. So, if you want to stay on the executive fast-track, don't waste your time on e-mail – you're supposed to be much too busy!

 3.28

A This week on CyberReport Terry Lancaster takes a look at some of the biggest e-mail blunders ever made.

B In April 2000 millions of computer users received an unexpected e-mail. The subject line was intriguing. It said 'I love you.' Those whose curiosity got the better of them opened the message and unleashed what later became known as the Love Bug – a virus so lethal it has so far infected 45 million PCs and caused $8.7 billion worth of damage to computer networks worldwide.

Computer viruses like the Love Bug sound like every company's worst nightmare. But the real danger these days is not so much what can get into your e-mail system as what can get out. You just never know where that e-mail you now regret sending may end up.

The first high-profile blunder occurred in 1997 when employees at the Norwich Union insurance company started spreading a rumour about a competitor on their internal e-mail system. Western Provident, they said, was about to go bankrupt. Western Provident was not about to go bankrupt, and when the e-mails suggesting it was came into their possession, it sued. The case was eventually settled out of court for a cool £450,000.

Three years later, Londoner Claire Swire briefly became a celebrity when sexually explicit e-mails she sent to her boyfriend were forwarded to mailboxes right across the world. It might not have been so bad, had Swire's boyfriend not worked for Norton Rose, a company which gives specialist advice to businesses on effective electronic communications.

Understandably, then, when Dow Chemical discovered hundreds of X-rated e-mails being exchanged between members of staff, the company took no chances. It fired 74 employees and suspended a further 435.

But disciplining your staff electronically isn't always a good idea, as the CEO of Cerner, Neal Patterson, found out to his cost. When Patterson reprimanded 400 managers by e-mail, his criticisms somehow found their way onto the Yahoo! website – for all the world to see. Cerner stock fell by 28% within the week.

And at Merrill Lynch in 2002, the company ended up paying out $100 million when Henry Blodget, an Internet stock analyst, strongly recommended buying stock in a company he had previously described, in what he thought was a private e-mail, as 'a piece of crap'.

But perhaps the most famous business e-mails in history came to light during the Microsoft antitrust trials. Netscape CEO Jim Barksdale claimed his company never wanted to collaborate with Microsoft in the Internet browser market – until, that is, Microsoft lawyers unearthed an e-mail from Netscape president Jim Clark to a senior executive at Microsoft stating clearly: 'We do not want to compete with you.' And Microsoft, for its part, denied any attempt to push Netscape out of the market – until an e-mail from Bill Gates to AOL executives was submitted as evidence. The e-mail read 'How much do we need to pay you to screw Netscape?' Oh, dear!

So the message is clear. With e-mail, honesty is not always the best policy. And if you must tell the truth, think twice before clicking that send button.

A That was Terry Lancaster talking about the biggest e-mail blunders ever made. And now a sneak preview of the latest in wireless technology ...

13 MAKING AN IMPACT

 3.29

1 **Did you know that** of the world's one hundred biggest economies only 49 are actually countries? That's right, 49. The other 51 are companies! In fact, if companies were allowed to join the G7 group of the world's richest countries, Microsoft would take the place of Canada! I think it's getting a little scary, don't you, when a corporation can outperform a nation? And maybe it's time to stop and ask ourselves: should business really be that powerful?

2 You know, the joke books of the world are probably full of more lawyer jokes than just about anything else. **One of my favourite lawyer jokes is:** this guy's having a quiet drink in a bar when a drunk starts shouting 'All lawyers are dirty criminals!' The man jumps to his feet and cries 'I resent that remark!' 'Why?' says the drunk. 'Are you a lawyer?' 'No' says the man, 'I'm a criminal!' But I'm here to tell you that not all lawyers are corrupt. It's just 99% of them who give the others a bad name.

3 Good morning. Erm, **I'd like to start off by** thanking Dr Jensen, Dr Tan and, er, Dr Martinez, of the faculty of cybernetic engineering for inviting me to speak today. Our company has a long history of collaboration with this university and it's always a great pleasure to address the robotics experts of the future. Erm, yes, before I begin, perhaps I could just take a moment or two to introduce you to the rest of my team, who are here with me this morning ...

4 **I think it was** Thomas Edison **who said:** 'I have not failed. I've just found 10,000 ways that don't work.' Of course, Edison was an inventor, but he could just as easily have been talking about sales. In sales, our success rate is nowhere near as bad as one in 10,000. At least, it better not be! But we have to go through an awful lot of 'no sales' to make one sale. And the ability to deal with failure is the single most important characteristic of the successful sales professional. **Could you just raise your hand if** you failed to make a sale yesterday? ... Just about everybody, right? Well, congratulations! You're obviously on the right track!

5 **I was** looking through the appointments pages **the other day** – don't we all? – **and came across** this unusual job advertisement. Here it is: 'Good hours, excellent pay, fun place to work, paid training, mean boss! Oh, well, four out of five isn't bad.' Wouldn't you like to be interviewed by that boss who admits he's mean? How powerful that little touch of honesty is. And that's exactly what I want to talk to you about this morning: honesty in advertising. And how you get people's attention when you simply tell the truth ...

6 Whenever I'm asked about Total Quality, I think of the story of the American steel magnate, Andrew Carnegie. It seems Carnegie was doing a factory tour one day, when he stopped to speak to one of the machine operators – a grey-haired old guy obviously coming up to retirement. 'Wilson,' he said, reading the man's name badge, 'how many years exactly have you been working for me now?' 'Thirty-nine, sir,'

Wilson replied with a proud smile. 'And may I add that in all those years I made only one very small mistake.' 'Good work,' mumbled Carnegie, 'but from now on, please try to be more careful.'

3.30

Extract 1 In the long history of the world, only a few generations have been granted the role of defending freedom in its hour of maximum danger. I do not shrink from this responsibility – I welcome it. I do not believe that any of us would exchange places with any other people or any other generation. The energy, the faith, the devotion, which we bring to this endeavour will light our country and all who serve it – and the glow from that fire can truly light the world. And so, my fellow Americans, ask not what your country can do for you – ask what you can do for your country. My fellow citizens of the world, ask not what America will do for you – but what together we can do for the freedom of man.

(John F. Kennedy, Washington DC, 20.1.61)

3.31

Extract 2 I say to you today, my friends ... so even though we face the difficulties of today and tomorrow, I still have a dream. It is a dream deeply rooted in the American dream. I have a dream that one day this nation will rise up and live out the true meaning of its creed: 'We hold these truths to be self-evident; that all men are created equal.' I have a dream that one day on the red hills of Georgia the sons of former slaves and the sons of former slave owners will be able to sit down together at the table of brotherhood. I have a dream that one day even the state of Mississippi, a state sweltering with the heat of injustice, sweltering with the heat of oppression, will be transformed into an oasis of freedom and justice. I have a dream that my four little children will one day live in a nation where they will not be judged by the colour of their skin but by the content of their character. I have a dream today.

(Martin Luther King, Washington DC, 28.8.63)

3.32

Extract 3 These are the two great challenges of our time – the moral and political challenge, and the economic challenge. They have to be faced together and we have to master them both. What are our chances of success? It depends on what kind of people we are. What kind of people are we? We are the people that in the past made Great Britain the workshop of the world, the people who persuaded others to buy British, not by begging them to do so, but because it was best. We are a people who have received more Nobel prizes than any other nation except America, and head for head we have done better than America, twice as well in fact. We are the people who, among other things, invented the computer, the refrigerator, the electric motor, the stethoscope, rayon, the steam turbine, stainless steel, the tank, television, penicillin, radar, the jet engine, hovercraft, float glass, carbon fibres, et cetera – and the best half of Concorde.

(Margaret Thatcher, Blackpool, 10.10.75)

3.33

Extract 4 We are both humbled and elevated by the honour and privilege that you, the people of South Africa, have bestowed on us, as the first president of a united, democratic, non-racial and non-sexist South Africa, to lead our country out of the valley of darkness. We understand it still that there is no easy road to freedom. We know it well that none of us acting alone can achieve success. We must therefore act together as a united people, for national reconciliation, for nation building, for the birth of a new world. Let there be justice for all. Let there be peace for all. Let there be work, bread, water and salt for all. Let each know that for each the body, the mind and the soul have been freed to fulfil themselves. Never, never and never again shall it

be that this beautiful land will again experience the oppression of one by another ...

(Nelson Mandela, Pretoria, 10.5.94)

3.34

a What's the main problem we're facing? The main problem is cash flow.

b It's so risky, so problematic, and yet so critical to our success.

c It's faster, cheaper and easier to use. But, above all, it's more reliable.

d Even if we can never again be the biggest, we can still be the best.

e The point is, more and more graduates are fighting over fewer and fewer jobs.

f Not only are we number one in Brazil. We're now number one in Latin America.

g In this market, no company has outperformed us, not one – ever!

h Not once, in over thirty years of business, have we ever had a complaint – not a single one!

3.35

1 Ladies and gentlemen, we are truly on the brink of a revolution in bio-technology. **I'm reminded of the words of** futurist and science fiction writer Arthur C. Clarke: 'People go through four stages' he said, 'before any revolutionary development. Stage one: it's nonsense, don't waste my time. Stage two: it's interesting, but not important. Stage three: I always said it was a good idea. And stage four: I thought of it first.' In gene therapy we're about to enter stage four. And I'd like this company to honestly be able to say 'We thought of it first.' Thank you.

2 Uh-oh. Sorry. Looks like we've run out of time. Erm, so I'm going to have to cut it short. Er, yeah, I was hoping to show you some of the figures in our comparative study. But, erm, never mind. I think you'll find all the main points are covered in the handout. So I'll, er, I'll just leave copies here and you can pick one up on your way out. OK. So, sorry about that. That's it. Thanks.

3 Well, **that just about brings me to the end of my presentation, except to say** that the future of this company is now in your hands. For if there's one central message I'd like to get across to you this morning it's this· that this consultancy is no more and no less than the consultants who represent it. And whilst our reputation as a firm may have been damaged by the recent unfortunate events, our expertise as a team is in no way diminished. I want to see each and every one of you raising this company to new heights. I know you can. We built our reputation on crisis management, and it would be ironic indeed if we were unable to successfully manage this crisis of our own – and come out on top. Thank you very much.

4 **So, how do you sum up** the new Spearing Silhouette ocean cruiser? I could tell you that it has won just about every boat show in the USA and Europe this year, that the orders for it are coming in so fast we already have a five-year waiting list; that the first three names on that waiting list, though strictly confidential, include a famous Hollywood actor, a member of the Saudi Royal Family and one of the world's greatest sporting legends. I could also mention that, so impressed are they with our award-winning design, the directors of the Museum of Modern Art are actually proposing to place a full-size model on permanent exhibition. But all that would fail to do it justice. For the fact is that the Silhouette is in a class of its own. It is a masterpiece of marine engineering. It is, quite simply, the most stunningly beautiful boat ever built. Ladies and gentlemen, I give you ... the Spearing Silhouette!

14 OUT AND ABOUT

4.02

1: Emma

A So Emma, what's your worst flying experience?

B Well, I think the worst one's probably flying back from Bangladesh to Heathrow. It's quite a few years ago now, but I can still remember it. We were at the gate, ready to taxi to the runway, and suddenly there was this terrible hammering noise from outside the plane.

A A hammering noise?

B Yes, and the strange thing was that the cabin crew just seemed to be ignoring it. But all you could hear was this bang, bang, bang on the fuselage. After a while, some of the passengers were starting to get nervous, me included.

A **I'm not surprised**.

B Anyway, eventually, after we'd been sitting there for about ten minutes with no announcement and the plane still not moving, I said something to one of the stewards and they went and opened the door to see what was going on.

A **And what happened?**

B The pilot got in!

A **You're joking**!

B No, they'd locked him out. **Seems quite funny now, but it didn't at the time.**

2: Enrique

A Enrique, what's the worst flight you've ever been on?

C Definitely the time I was flying from Malaga to Stansted in the UK. **This was around the time of the terrible attack on the World Trade Center in 2001 and people were still very nervous about flying.**

A Oh, yes, of course.

C I was travelling on business, but most of the passengers were British tourists.

A Uh huh.

C Anyway, we were cruising at 30,000 feet and I looked out of the window and saw this French air force fighter plane flying alongside us.

A What? Oh, yes, I read about this. Didn't they think the plane had been hijacked or something?

C Well, apparently, air traffic control had lost radio contact with our plane, so they weren't sure what was going on and they weren't taking any chances. I mean this French jet was armed with missiles and everything.

A **Sounds terrifying!**

C It was.

A **So, what happened?**

C Well, the jet was there for about ten minutes checking us out. Fortunately, the captain of our plane managed to keep everybody calm. And **anyway, to cut a long story short**, everything turned out OK. We even landed on schedule!

A But I bet you were glad to be back on the ground, weren't you?

C You can say that again!

3: Joe

A Joe, have you had any bad experiences on planes?

D Oh, yes, several. One flight I was on, I couldn't understand why they were making us go through the lifejacket drill for landing on water.

A But don't they always do that?

D What, on a domestic flight from Manchester to London?

A Oh, right. **I see what you mean**.

D I'm not sure which flight path they were planning to take but it goes nowhere near the sea. But that's nothing compared to one of my recent trips to Frankfurt.

A What happened there, then?

D Well, we didn't land in Frankfurt.

A You were diverted?

D No, no, the pilot just landed in completely the wrong country!

A What, you mean he didn't know?

D Hadn't got a clue. Just about everybody on the plane was looking out the windows and saying 'Er, look, I'm sorry to be a nuisance, but this isn't Frankfurt.'

A So where did you land?

D Luxembourg.

A Oh, my god! **I don't believe it!**

4: Selina

A Selina, you've flown all over the world. You must have some stories to tell.

E Hm, quite a few. **I'll never forget the time I was** flying in Asia and the cabin crew asked me to sit on the toilet during take-off.

A What?

E Yeah, they wanted my seat next to the emergency exit.

A Doesn't inspire much confidence in the airline, does it?

E Not a lot, no. **And then, to top it all**, I ended up sitting next to a guy with a rattlesnake in a basket!

A Good god!

E Yes, that's what I said. Apparently, he just brought it on as hand luggage. But erm, ... **did I ever tell you about the time** I was working in Nigeria?

A No, I don't think so.

E Well, er, **you're not going to believe this, but** way back in 1985 it was, I was on this internal flight, right? And it was three times overbooked!

A Three times?

E Oh, yeah, that was quite common in those days. But **you should have heard** the arguments at check-in.

A **I can imagine.**

E **Anyway, in the end**, they brought the army in to sort it out.

A The army?

E Yeah. And **you'll never guess** what they did ...

A What?

E They made everyone run round the aircraft twice.

A What on earth for?

E So they could give the seats to the fastest.

A **You can't be serious!**

E It's absolutely true.

A And did you win a seat?

E Certainly did. I came third. I was quite quick in those days!

 4.03

a

A Ugh, isn't it dreadful? And we'd got plans for the weekend as well. Thought we might have some friends round for a barbecue.

B Well, it's always the same, isn't it? You plan anything, it always lets you down. And it was so fabulous yesterday.

C Yes, wasn't it? Never would have thought it could turn so nasty in just 24 hours. But that's Britain for you, I suppose. Heatwave in the morning, a downpour in the afternoon and a howling gale by dinner time. Bloody weather!

b

B I'm not sure this is quite right, is it?

A Hm?

B This. Is it supposed to be like that? Looks a bit soggy to me.

A Hm, yes, it does a bit. It should be all crisp and golden, shouldn't it, the pastry? Not very appetising at all. And there's not a lot of it, is there?

B No, I thought it came with something else. Like a side salad or something ... Ugh! The meat's as tough as old boots as well!

A Oh, dear. I'd tell the waiter to take it back, if I were you ...

c

C Line them up against a wall and shoot the lot of them, that's what I say.

A We can always rely on you for a balanced and mature view, Roger.

C Well, you know what I mean. Interfering in policies that have nothing to do with them. Power-mad they are. And who actually voted for them, that's what I want to know.

B Well, I'm not sure I'd ...

A Actually, Roger has got a point there, even if he is being a bit right-wing about it, as usual. A lot of these Eurocrats are just self-appointed, aren't they? They've never had to go through any kind of democratic election process.

C No, and that's how half of Europe has ended up being governed by a bunch of unelected civil servants in Brussels!

d

B No, it's not my thing at all, I'm afraid.

A Oh, but I thought it was marvellous! And it was so well done. Because it must have been a very difficult adaptation, don't you think?

B Hm, yeah. It went on a bit, though, didn't it? I mean, what was it, two and a half hours?

A Well, I found the whole thing absolutely fantastic. Brilliantly directed. And the special effects were incredible!

B Yes, well, they were good, I'll admit, but they've all got those nowadays, haven't they? I mean it's all just CGI digital animation. Like all those sci-fi, superhero things ...

e

B I'd really appreciate it, because I'm just snowed under at the moment, what with all this backlog to deal with.

A Yes, I'm sorry to have dumped all that on you. Couldn't think of anyone else I could trust. And with the deadline coming up so fast ...

B It's no problem, but if you could let me borrow Kim for a couple of hours, I'm sure that together we could polish the whole thing off that much faster.

C You overworking this poor boy, Suzanne? That's how she lost her last assistant manager, you know, Ian.

A Oh, ignore Roger. I'll speak to Kim about giving you a hand as soon as we get back to the office.

B Thanks.

f

C What on earth is this?

A You don't like it? It's one of my favourites. Lovely bouquet. Fresh and fruity.

C Smells off to me.

A Nonsense! It's fine.

C Like something with a bit more body to it, myself.

B Hm, that's not at all bad.

A See? Ian likes it.

C Hm. All right for lunch, I suppose. But it's still too young, if you ask me. Could do with another couple of years in the bottle.

A Oh, don't be such a wine bore, Roger. Get yourself a glass of something else if you don't like it.

C Think I will ...

15 FIRST AMONG EQUALS

 4.04

The leaders in the photographs have nothing at all in common in terms of background, beliefs, achievements, management style or personal characteristics. Different circumstances also call for different kinds of leader. And leaders rise and fall according to the political, economic and moral climate of the times. So, ultimately, all attempts to define the qualities of leadership are a complete waste of time.

The one thing these, and all other, leaders *do* have in common is this: followers. Every one of them has, or had, people prepared to follow them in one way or another. A leader, therefore, is not what you are, but what other people make you. And whether or not you yourself are a leader is not for you to decide.

 4.05

Speaker 1 In Argentina, er, as in most of Latin America, I guess, the leadership style is quite autocratic. Generally, leaders take an almost military approach, It's very top-down. This does not necessarily mean that it's just a question of following orders from above. Argentinian companies tend to be rather paternalistic. Leaders try to gently persuade subordinates that their way is the best way. So decision-making can be a little slow. But, yes, ultimately, leaders lead and there's not much attempt to reach consensus.

 4.06

Speaker 2 The German promotion system is meritocratic, er, we promote on merit and expertise, and so senior management will usually consist of the most experienced and best-educated people – very often engineers, which is perhaps why German management tends to favour logic and analysis. The standard procedure is that each manager in the hierarchy will guide their immediate subordinate and so on down the corporate pyramid to shopfloor supervisors. However, German managers do prefer to get feedback from their subordinates before adopting a policy and this can slow down the decision-making process.

 4.07

Speaker 3 On the surface, consensus and agreement amongst management is very important in China. We avoid conflict. But behind the scenes, Chinese managers often exercise almost total control. Leaders of all businesses, not only family businesses, act as patriarchs – sometimes benevolent, sometimes not so! Many leaders have communist party connections. Having connections is vital in China if you want to get things done. And so in many ways bosses are like the old warrior-leaders who used to run China. There is a strict code of honour amongst leaders who often have complicated alliances and associations. In China we call this guanxi.

 4.08

Speaker 4 It's interesting. Japanese firms do have a reputation for suppressing individual initiative, for being collectivist, putting group needs first. But this is only partly true. The Confucian system we inherited from China means that we do involve all levels in management to some extent. Proposals must be approved by all concerned. This is the Japanese practice of ringi-sho. And this is the reason why decision-making is extremely slow in Japanese companies. The leader often steps back from the day-to-day running of the company. He is like a very senior politician who must ratify everything before it can be implemented. But once all formalities are completed, we can implement very fast!

4.09

Speaker 5 OK, well, people think that in America it's all about individualism. That's true up to a point. Historically, we've had to be pretty much self-reliant, so there's a certain amount of competition within any work group to be the de facto leader of that group. Teams are fluid. There's rivalry. Meetings are lively. People voice their opinions freely. But there's quite a bit of control imposed from above as well. American managers have to work within fairly tight constraints at times and follow standardized procedures, produce endless reports. Sure, top managers get to be Hollywood heroes – until they screw up. Do that once too often and you simply get fired, so there's little job security. This means there's very little loyalty from employees either. So part of a leader's job in the US is basically motivating and firing up the team and sending them off to get the job done, like, now! Who knows where we'll be tomorrow?

4.10

Speaker 6 Corporate leaders in France tend to belong to a well-trained elite. Intelligence, education and personal charisma count for a great deal with us. In fact, most CEOs come from a relatively small number of top universities. So authority is pretty much vested in the few, who control the many. There is a lot of talk in French meetings, because we value debate and argument, but don't make the mistake of thinking this is how we achieve consensus, because it isn't. The important decisions will already have been made. This means that French companies can act quite quickly, but, on the other, hand, when leaders make the wrong decision, they seldom pay the price. The top jobs are more or less jobs for life.

4.11

Speaker 7 Well, the British attitude to leadership – perhaps I should say English attitude because it's slightly different in Scotland, Wales and Ireland – is fairly casual. Our leaders like to hover just outside the circle of subordinates and, for the most part, let them get on with it. There's a lot of delegation and the leader's job in many ways is to make sure things are running smoothly. We dislike conflict and will always try to seek agreement, rather than impose our ideas. So English leaders try to be tactful, reasonable and expect to compromise on their way to getting the decision they want. And the so-called British sense of humour is really just a clever way of achieving your objectives without offending anyone in the process!

16 TELECONFERENCING

4.12

A Since you're new here, I want you to meet your teams in London, Bangalore and Tokyo. You need to do it right away.

B Oh, I'm really looking forward to meeting them, but it's going to take a week or more to get to all those places.

A Actually, they're right down the hall.

B Oh! … A video conference.

A I wouldn't call it that.

B No?

A I think you'll be pleasantly surprised.

B Wow.

A Hello, everyone. This is Patricia.

C Hello from London. Tania and Owen here.

D I'm Mohan. This is Seema. Greetings from Bangalore.

E And I am Hiro with my colleague Kumi from Tokyo. Hajimemashite!

B I really feel like I'm in the same room with all of you.

Voiceover This isn't the future. It's right now. With Cisco TelePresence you feel like you're sitting across the table from other meeting participants. Seeing them in full life-size images. Making direct eye contact. Hearing them talk left and right … and centre. Making everyone sound like they're in the same room. TelePresence creates an in-person meeting experience over the network, where the quality's so good, it's as if you took a conference table and just split it in half.

4.13

A Ugh! Who on earth can that be? Where's the … the light switch! Ow! Er … hello?

B Pete, is that you?

A Er, yes. Who is this?

B It's Max.

A Max! … Max, it's … it's two o'clock in the morning!

B I'm sorry, Pete, but this is an emergency.

A Well, it better be, I've got to be up in a few hours.

B I think you'd better get up right now, Pete. All hell's broken loose here. We're going to have to shut down the Hamburg plant immediately.

A What!

B It's the heat exchanger. We've got a leakage between the hydrogenation section and the oil heater. There's nothing we can do but stop all production straightaway. Otherwise, the whole thing could go up!

A But Max, do you have any idea what you're saying? If you authorise a plant shutdown, everything grinds to a halt. We'll have container lorries backed up from Hamburg to Lübeck!

B Pete, do you think I don't know that?

A Tell me this isn't happening. It cost us millions last time … OK, look, I have no idea how long it will take me and Monica to get a flight, but we're on our way.

B I think that's best, Pete.

A I'll phone you to fix up a teleconference once we're airborne. Contact Françoise and Otto right away, will you? There's not a moment to lose …

A Monica? It's Pete. Look, I'm sorry to get you up at this unearthly hour, but there's been a disaster at the Hamburg plant. Yeah. Better get dressed. I'll tell you about it on the way to the airport.

4.14

Extract 1

A OK, so we're just waiting for Otto. Françoise, you told him when to call in, right?

C Yes, I did. Perhaps he's still at the plant or he may just be having problems getting through.

B Pete, where are you and Monica?

A Just left Vancouver about half an hour ago, Max. Should be back in thirteen hours or so.

C Pete, I think we should just start.

B Yes, I think so too.

A OK, we really need to talk to Otto, but **let's go ahead and get the meeting started** and hopefully he'll join us later on … Right, well, as you all know, we've had a serious mechanical failure at the Hamburg plant and, basically, we've had to shut it down. There'll be time for a proper analysis of what went wrong later. Right now we need a rescue plan. Max, could you first of all just fill us in on what's going on? When can we expect to get the plant up and running again?

B Well, Pete, it's difficult to say at the moment. My technicians tell me they can't get a replacement heat exchanger for at least 48 hours. And then it'll have to be fitted, of course. We're probably looking at three days.

D Three days!

A It's worse than I thought. And is that your best estimate? Three days?

B I'm afraid so, Pete.

A Well, that's that, then. But I want us back in production no later than Thursday, Max. OK?

B OK, Pete, I'll see what I can do.

4.15

Extract 2

E Excuse me, Mr Mendel has joined.

A Otto! Thank goodness you got through. Have you been to the plant yet? What's the situation there?

F It's pretty bad Pete. We've had to clear the whole site for the fire service to run safety checks.

A I see. Otto, is there any chance we can rewrite our production plan? I mean, can we make sure our key customers get priority on orders?

F I'm already working on that. The problem is it doesn't look as though we'll be able to meet any of the orders completely.

A What's the stock situation?

F Not good.

A Oh, great. Just what I needed to hear. Don't we keep any stock in reserve for this kind of thing?

F What, for a complete plant shutdown? No, Pete, we don't.

A OK, OK. Well, what about transferring stock from one of our other European plants?

F It'd take too long. And, besides, they're already overstretched as it is.

A Right … Monica, is there any point in us buying in traded goods from another supplier to cover the shortfall? Just for the time being.

D You mean buy product from our competitors to keep the customers happy?

A Just for the time being.

D Pete, you know how I feel about buying from the competition. How are we supposed to build a reputation with our customers if we end up selling them other people's products instead of our own?

A It's not as if we haven't done it before, Monica. And what alternative do we have?

4.16

Extract 3

A OK, now, we've got to make up this backlog of orders somehow. How about Handelsmann?

C Er, can I come in on that?

A Go ahead, Françoise.

C Well, I've already been on to Handelsmann. They owe us a favour, actually. We helped them out a few years ago when they were in a similar situation, if you remember. Anyway, it looks like they may be able to do something, but probably not until tomorrow morning.

A Well, at least that's something, I suppose. OK, get back to them and see if we can hurry things up a bit. And get somebody in after-sales to ring round all our biggest customers and smooth things over with them.

C OK, I'll see to it now.

A Now, Max. Are you sure this thing can't just be fixed? I mean, if I gave your technical people, say, 24 hours … Max, you still there?

B Still here. I've just been told the leakage area has now been made secure.

A Well, thank god for that. Anyway, OK, that's it for now. We're going to try and get some sleep. I suggest we schedule another conference call for midnight European Time. But, Otto, keep me posted if there's any change in the situation, won't you?

F Will do, Pete.

A OK, thanks everyone …

17 NEGOTIATING DEALS

4.17

The activity you just did is designed to demonstrate the critical importance in the negotiating process of relationship-building.

In your first negotiation you probably didn't think much about your opponent's interests. And why should you? After all, it was just a stranger who you'd never meet again. But by concentrating on only one objective, you reduced the whole encounter to a single-issue negotiation with little room for manoeuvre. This made it a simple zero-sum game – if I get what I want, you don't, and vice-versa.

In order to win at all costs, perhaps you became hostile and tried to pre-empt negotiation altogether by just grabbing the box off the other person. Or maybe you gave in completely, deciding it simply wasn't worth the hassle. Many professional negotiators act the same way if they think they are negotiating a one-off deal. As the negotiation ended in deadlock, perhaps you became desperate and resorted to emotional blackmail, inventing all sorts of reasons why your kid was more deserving than the other kid.

In the second negotiation, on the other hand, there was a long-term relationship you wanted to maintain. The circumstances were exactly the same, but the prospect of one of you 'losing' was no longer an option. By accepting the need to reach some kind of compromise, you were able to turn a head-on conflict into a problem-solving meeting. Now your main objective was to generate options in the hope that you could create a win-win situation, where you both got something you wanted.

4.18

Extract 1

A OK, so, **do I take it we're in agreement on** volume?

B Er, well, just a minute, wouldn't it be a good idea to talk prices before we go any further?

A Yes, of course. But **in principle you're happy about** taking forty cases, right?

B Er, well, in principle, yes, if the product's as good as you say it is ...

A Splendid, that's settled then.

B ... But, **look, getting back to price for a moment**. This would be just a trial order, you understand? Sale or return. Until we see how it sells. So, **can you give us some idea of** what kind of figure you were thinking of?

A €50.

B €50 per case.

A Er, no. Per pack.

B Per pack? **There seems to have been a slight misunderstanding**. A pack is just twelve bottles, right?

A Yes, that's right.

B Is this meant to be some kind of joke or something? €50 per pack? That's over €4 a bottle. By the time we've added a decent margin, you realise we're looking at a retail price of €7 minimum. How am I supposed to sell a one-litre bottle of water for €7, Mr Koivisto?

A Ms Barrett, O-Zone is an innovative, premium product. A pure oxygen-enriched drink. We're not talking about a bottle of Perrier here.

B Well, that's as may be, but €7!

A O-Zone is an exciting opportunity to get in at the start of a new trend in luxury health drinks.

B Well, there's no way on earth I'm paying you €4 for a bottle of oxygenated water, Mr Koivisto. **With respect, your prices are simply not competitive.**

A Ms Barrett, there are no competitors in this market. O-Zone is a unique product and at €4 – well, I'm afraid that really is our absolute bottom line.

B So you're saying it's take it or leave it?

A I'm afraid so.

B Well, then, I think I'll have to leave it ...

A Wha ...? Now, just a minute. You said on the phone you might want 100 cases.

B That was before I knew your water was more expensive than Chardonnay, Mr Koivisto. OK, look, **let's set the price issue to one side for the moment,** shall we? Tell me a bit more about the product ...

 4.19

Extract 2

A OK, I'll tell you what I'll do. If you order 250 units today, I can offer you not our usual five but a six per cent discount, free delivery and **I'll throw in** twelve months' free parts and service as well. Now, **I can't say fairer than that, now can I?** Of course, that's only if you can give me the order today. Can't hold the offer, I'm afraid.

B Well, erm, Robert, isn't it?

A Rob. Call me Rob.

B Well, now, Rob, we appreciate the free service and delivery, but to be honest with you, **what we'd really like to see is a bit more movement on price**. I'm afraid a six per cent discount is not quite what we had in mind. **We were hoping for something a bit closer to** ten.

A Ten per cent? **I don't think I could stretch as far as that.** Not unless this was a substantially bigger order.

C Oh, come on! You'll have to do a lot better than that, Mr Hayes. You're not the only precision tool manufacturer, you know.

B Hold on, Gavin. Let's hear Rob out.

C Well, frankly, I think we're wasting each other's time here. We've already been offered a much better deal by Magnusson's.

B Now, wait a minute, wait a minute. **Surely we can sort something out here.** Rob, **would you be willing to meet us halfway?**

A How do you mean?

B Well, if you were to offer us an eight per cent discount, we might be in a position to increase our order, say, by fifty units. But **we'd need to see a bit more flexibility on** terms of payment. Maybe on installation costs too.

A Erm, well, **I suppose there may be some room for manoeuvre there.** I'd need to check. Can you give me a moment to have another look at the figures?

B Sure. In fact, let's take a short time-out, shall we? And meet back here in, say, half an hour?

A OK, fine.

C I still say we'd be better off going with Magnusson's.

 4.20

Speaker 1 Make your priorities clear before you begin, that's my advice. I always say remember to check your tie. Not the one you wear round your neck, your T-I-E. 'T' stands for 'tradeables'. These are the things you'll take if you can get them, but they're not that important to you and you'll concede them if it helps you to push the negotiation forward. 'I' stands for 'ideals'. These are the things you'd really like to get and will fight to get, but not if it costs you the deal. Finally, and most importantly, 'E' stands for 'essentials'. It's not that these are absolutely non-negotiable. Everything's negotiable. But if it looks like you're not going to get your essentials, then that's the time to start thinking about walking away from the negotiating table.

 4.21

Speaker 2 Well, frankly, I get a bit tired of hearing people go on about win-win negotiating. I mean, let's face it, a lot of negotiations are basically win-lose, and your opponent's interests are the last thing you should be worrying about. Buying a house, a car, double-glazing – all win-lose situations. And you'd be surprised how many business negotiations are basically one-off deals as well. In my opinion, in a win-lose situation the tougher you are – without actually being aggressive – the further you'll get. That's because your opponent takes your attitude as an indication of what's possible and what's not. And the friendlier you seem, the higher their expectations will be. It's like the old saying: give them an inch and they'll take a mile.

 4.22

Speaker 3 'You always know who is going to win a negotiation – it's he who pauses the longest.' I forget who it was who said that but it's pretty good advice – basically, shut up! And remember that silence is very often your best weapon. It's a very difficult argument to counter. Faced with prolonged and uncomfortable silences, your opponent is liable to make another concession or give away their strategy or weaken their own position by becoming defensive. So play your cards close to your chest. Talk less, learn more. There's an old Swedish proverb: 'Talking is silver. But listening is gold.'

4.23

Speaker 4 I think the biggest trap less experienced negotiators fall into is to turn the whole negotiation into a debate, which it isn't. This is sometimes called 'positional negotiating'. Both sides end up arguing the whys and the wherefores, rationalising their position, trying to justify themselves. It's a complete waste of time. You're not there to convince your opponent that you're right. He doesn't care if you're right or not. And neither should you. You're there to explore both sides' interests, generate options and trade concessions – preferably giving away things that mean little to you but a lot to him and receiving the opposite in return. This is 'interest-based negotiation' – discovering the needs, desires and fears behind your opponent's position and working on those. The two phrases you need most of all are: 'If ..., then ...?': If I give you that, then what do I get? And 'What if ...?: What if we looked at this another way? What if we did this instead?

 4.24

Speaker 5 The key skill in negotiating is the ability to ask the right questions – and ask lots of them. In fact, there's an organisation called the Huthwaite Research Group, who recorded hundreds of negotiations and guess what they found? 'Skilled negotiators ask more than twice as many questions as average negotiators.' So, my advice is: phrase as many of your comments as possible as questions. You don't understand something? Don't say you don't understand – you'll look stupid. Ask a question – you'll look intelligent. You strongly disagree? Don't say you strongly disagree – they'll think you're being difficult. Ask a question – they'll think you're trying to be helpful. You have a good idea? Don't say you have a good idea – they'll wish it was their idea. Ask a question. They'll think it was their idea. Keep those questions coming and don't take 'no' for an answer!

4.25

A Tess?

B Mr Logan. It's Kate and Miles to see you.

A Ah, good. Send them right in.

C Hi, Ronnie.

A Kate, good to see you. You're looking great as usual. Miles, come on in. Rough night, huh? Erm, sit anywhere you like. Can I get you a beer?

C It's a little early for me, Ronnie. Do you have an Evian or something?

A No problem. There you go. Miles?

D Er, don't think I could face anything right now, man.

A No, you certainly don't look as though you could. So, you two had quite an evening at the Marquee, so I hear.

D You could say that.

C Ronnie, you have to sign this band. You could hardly move for A&R people last night. If we don't snap them up, someone else will. I saw Jimmy Armstrong from Sony sniffing around.

A Uh huh. Well, he usually is.

C Yeah, and EMI were there as well. This band's hot. You listened to the demo I sent you, right?

A I did.

C And?

A Well, ...

C Oh, come on, Ronnie. These guys are the best thing to come out of Ireland since U2 and you know it.

A I wouldn't go as far as that, Kate. They sound a little inconsistent on the tape. They need to work on a clear musical identity, if you ask me.

C Well, maybe they need a little help in that direction. We can work on that. But you have to admit the lead singer's voice is just amazing. In fact, they're musically really strong all round.

A OK, I'll give you that. Apart from the drummer, that is, who's pretty second-rate. So he'd have to go.

C She.

A She? They have a female drummer? Interesting. Well, anyway, she's no good.

C Could be tricky to fire. She's the lead singer's girlfriend.

A Hm. I'm going off them already.

C Ronnie, believe me, The Penitents are a class act. And I'm not easily impressed, you know that.

A True, you're not. Miles, meet the woman who turned down Oasis.

D Fine by me. I never liked them.

C I thought we weren't going to talk about that any more.

A OK, OK. Well, what do The Penitents look like? No, let me guess. Like they haven't eaten a hot meal for a week and cut their own hair, right?

C Not at all. The lead guitarist looks like Keanu Reeves. The drummer's fabulous even if her drumming's a little off. In fact, they're all pretty glamorous. Ronnie, I have a good feeling about this one.

A OK, call their manager and set something up. But not next week. I'm at the MTV awards.

C OK, I'll do that. Oh, and by the way, you might want to tune in to VH1 at eight this evening. They're being interviewed live.

A They are? Well, why didn't you say so before? Look, give me their manager's number, I might just call him myself this afternoon ...

18 THE SHAPE OF THINGS TO COME

 4.26

Welcome to the In Company Business Podcast. You're listening to *Future World*. This week's sound bite: *Artificial Intelligence: I'll be back.*

We've heard it all before. Ninety per cent of all scientists who have ever lived are alive now. There is more microchip technology in the average family car than there was in the first Apollo spacecraft to take men to the moon. The electronic singing birthday card you can buy at any newsagent is technically superior to all the computers on earth in 1950 put together. Global computing power is now greater than the combined intelligence of every human being on the planet. And, according to Moore's Law, the amount of information you can store on a microchip is doubling every two years. So, at that rate, within a few decades we'll be demoted to world's second most intelligent species. At least, that's the opinion of some of the world's leading scientists at companies like Intel and Microsoft. Perhaps we should be asking the computers what *they* think.

But will computers ever be able to truly think? Isn't artificial intelligence a contradiction in terms? The painter Pablo Picasso summed it up best when he said: 'Computers are useless. They can only give you answers.'

One person who would certainly disagree with that sentiment is Dr Ian Pearson, head of the futurology unit at British Telecom. In fact, some of his predictions sound like science-fiction. In an interview with *The Observer* newspaper, Pearson explained: 'If you draw the timelines, realistically, by 2050 we would expect to be able to download your mind into a machine, so when you die, it's not a major career problem'. According to the applied mathematician and theoretical physicist, poorer people may have to wait until the procedure becomes routine around 2080, but the brain-imaging technology will be in place well before then. 'Forty-five years' he reminds us, 'is a hell of a long time in IT'.

But Pearson's next prediction is even more incredible. 'We're already looking at how you might structure a computer that could possibly become conscious' he reveals. 'There are quite a lot of us who believe it's entirely feasible. Information comes in from the outside world but also from other parts of your brain and each part processes it on an internal sensing basis. Consciousness is just another sense, effectively, and that's what we're trying to design into a computer. Not everyone agrees, but it's my conclusion that it is possible to make a conscious computer with superhuman levels of intelligence by 2020.' Did he say 2020? By his own admission, Pearson is 'in the 30–40% that believes there's really nothing magical about the human brain'. And, anyway, as he's quick to point out, 'part of my job description is to get into trouble ... We're supposed to be thought-leaders.'

But not everyone has Pearson's faith in trends and statistics. In his runaway bestseller *Black Swan*, business professor and ex-derivatives specialist Nassim Taleb points out that most experts know a lot less than they think they do. The book is called *Black Swan* because until the discovery of black swans in Australia in the 18th century, they were regarded as self-evidently

impossible – like flying pigs. Really big changes, says Taleb, are like black swans – random and unpredictable – but once they've happened we rationalise how they did. Humans have a tendency to make far too many assumptions based on what they think they know. If what we imagine will happen makes a good story, we begin to believe it, when the only thing we should really expect is the unexpected.

And trend-spotting can be misleading. Consider this. When Elvis Presley died in 1977, there were just thirty-seven Elvis impersonators in the world. By 1995 there were 48,000, an exponential increase, to be sure. But if that trend had continued, today one in every three people in the world would be an Elvis impersonator! Still, provided you don't mind coming back as a hard disc, the promise of digital immortality is difficult to refuse. In the words of Woody Allen: 'I don't want to achieve immortality through my work. I want to achieve it by not dying'.

CASE STUDY: THE FUTURE'S UNWRITTEN

 4.27

Alison Good morning everyone. Welcome to Futurescape and the wonderful world of management consulting! I'm Alison Fielding, head of training and development. I'll be coaching you through your first six months with the company, which as you know is probational, but we hope and expect that most of you will be staying with us long into the future!

Now, as you know, you were selected for both your business acumen and industry experience, so all I'm going to do this morning is just briefly talk you through the scenario planning procedure that we use here and then set a little exercise for you!

Scenario planning was really pioneered by the oil giant, Royal Dutch Shell, in the early 60s. Using the technique, they were able to foresee the energy crises of 1973 and 1979, the move towards energy conservation in the 80s, the evolution of the global environmental movement in the 90s and even, it seems, the fall of the Berlin Wall and the break-up of the Soviet Union – all years before they actually happened.

Our aims are a little more modest, but only a little. We aim, by putting huge amounts of data into sophisticated computer models and then interpreting that data, to build up different pictures of how the world may look ten, twenty or even thirty years from now and how that world may impact on the way our clients do business. Clem Sunter, head of scenario planning at Anglo American Corporation, said 'scenarios are to organisations what radar is to a pilot' and I think that's a great way of putting it. Most executives are more concerned with the next quarterly report than with the long term, but we take the opposite view. It's our job to see the threats and opportunities for our clients long before they do and alert them to them before it's too late.

One way we do this is by carrying out a STEP analysis. 'STEP' stands for the sociological, technological, economic and political forces that shape our clients' businesses. Here's how it works ... For example, under sociological change we might consider the impact of longer life expectancies and an ageing population. Is youth going to matter any more? Under technological development we could speculate about advances in biotech and virtual reality – would they be a good thing or a bad thing, not in themselves, but for our clients' businesses? Under economic climate we'll want to try and read the cycle of boom and recession and the international flow of capital. And under political factors we'll obviously need to look at things like regulations, taxes and who's going to get elected, but also, these days, environmental pressure groups and terrorist threats.

Now, this STEP analysis is conducted in the context of competitive trends. What are our clients' competitors doing? How might the very structure of the industry change and how would our clients react to that? Would they be able to react? We also need to take account of our clients' customers and their needs. If the customer is king, what is the customer going to be demanding?

Finally, we need to think the unthinkable. Is there anything on the horizon that could really revolutionise or destroy our clients business? Maybe not today or even tomorrow, but sooner than we'd like. We call these issues 'long fuse, big bang' issues. They may not happen for a while, but if and when they do, they could be explosive! For instance, a cure for cancer would obviously save the lives of millions and make billions for the pharmaceutical company that developed it, but would it have such a positive effect on the healthcare industry or the manufacturers of radiotherapy equipment? What if the USA literally went bust? What if China had another revolution?

Now, the best place to begin to look for the future is at the cutting edge of the present, so here's an activity for you to get you thinking along the right lines. Have a look at this chart. This is an overview of an industry analysed according to the factors we've been talking about. It's really like taking an industry snapshot to get the big picture. What I'd like you to take a few minutes to do is to consider the industry you have most experience in and complete the chart, adding, eliminating or changing things whenever you need to. Then turn to people around you and compare your snapshots, discussing how these may affect the outlook for your respective industries. And then we'll pool our ideas. OK, let's take a time-out to do this ...

 4.28

Iván Hi there. It's Iván. I was hoping to catch you before you left the office. Listen, I've got an appointment with an important new client in a few days and I'd like to be able to send them some kind of brief industry report before we meet. You know, a bit of free inside-information, something to get our meeting off to a productive start. It just so happens you have the most experience of the business they're in, which is why I'm asking for your help. Could you and your team sift through some of our general scenario files and decide what might be relevant to them? Put that together with the industry snapshot you produced for us the other day and see if, between you, you can come up with an executive summary of trends and developments that may affect them in the next five to ten years? A couple of hundred words should do it. But, er, you know, make it look good, OK? No dull stuff! That'd be great. Thanks.

Macmillan Education
Between Towns Road, Oxford OX4 3PP
A division of Macmillan Publishers Limited
Companies and representatives throughout the world

ISBN 978-0-230-71722-0

Designed by eMC Design
Illustrated by Julian Mosedale, Martin Sanders, Laszlo Veres and eMC Design
Cover design by Keith Shaw, Threefold Design Ltd
Cover illustration/photograph by STOCKBYTE, PHOTOALTO

Author's acknowledgements: We originally planned to do relatively little to the
old edition of In Company Upper Intermediate, but ended up doing one heck of
a lot, so there's hardly space to acknowledge the enormous amount of work that's
gone into it. Once again, my thanks chiefly go to Darina Richter, Anna Gunn,
John Park, Ian Harker and, this time round, to Kath Kollberg. They know why
I'm thanking them! I think the new book looks, sounds and works a great deal
better than the old one. If only authors could come out in a new edition as well
as books. As it is, my wife Begoña is still stuck with the old edition, which doesn't
look, sound or work any better at all. In that sense, she's been the greatest support
of all.

The publishers would like to thank the following schools and teachers for their
help in developing the second edition: Sylvia Renaudon, Hannah Leloup, Sven
Steph at Transfer, Paris; Nadia Fairbrother at Executive Language services, Paris;
Fiona Delaney at Formalangues, Paris; Paul Chambers, Ruth Maslen at BPL,
Paris; Moira Jansen and teachers at Anglo English School, Hamburg; Patrick
Woulfe and John Ryde at International House, Hamburg; Charles Reid Dick,
Christine Dlugokencky, Petra Mocklinghoff, Marie-Colette Dodd, Orla Mac
Mahon at Eurospeak, Hamburg; Bill Cope at English School of Hamburg;
Slavomir Gibarti, Slovakia; Sylvie Jeanloz, France; Elain Skarsten-Pflieger and
Rick Cervenka at Learning Circle, Munich; teachers at Globus International,
Moscow; teachers at Denis School, Moscow; teachers at Mr English School,
Moscow; teachers at Inlingua, Moscow; teachers at Moscow Institute of
Linguistics, Moscow; teachers at Peoples' Friendship University, Institute of
International Economics and Business, Moscow.
Many thanks to all the teachers around the world who took the time to complete
our In Company online questionnaire.

The author and publishers would like to thank the following for permission
to reproduce their photographs: **Phil Adams** p23 (b); **Alamy**/John Arnold
Images pp7 (br) 147 (b), Alamy/John Crum p4(r), Alamy/Danita Delimont
p69(m);Alamy/Time Harris p138(b), Alamy/Peter Haygarth p138(t), Alamy/I love
images p14, Alamy/Image source Black p42(r), Alamy/ Image Broker p52, Alamy/
Jeff Morgan Environmental Issues p143 (tm), Alamy/Juniors Bildarchiv p22,
Alamy/Jupiter Images/ Comstock p87 (joker), Alamy/Jupiter Images Goodshoot
p8, Alamy/Larry Lilac p81, Alamy/T Payne p72, Alamy/PhotoAlto pp60,137,
Alamy/Photodisc p118, Alamy/Photolibrary inc p6 (th), Alamy/ Pictorial Press
Ltd p110 (Ghandi), Alamy/Science Photos pp2, 133, Alamy/Mark Weidman
photography p50 (b); Courtesy of ©Apple Inc. Use with permission. All rights
reserved. Apple® and the Apple logo are registered trademark of Apple Inc
p80 (Get a Mac (Mac vs. PC) advert); **Bananastock** pp2,3 (Toivo), 17, 18,
55(Toivo), 58, 84 (b), 125; **BMW** p80; **Brain Reserve** p134; **Brand X** pp6(house),
6(trumpet), 6 (plane), 37, 53, 69 (t), 73, 85 (bl); **Car Photo Library** p76(b);
Corbis pp2 (microchip),2 (lab technician), 2 (Magic), 3 (Francois), 3 (Oskar),
6 (employer), 6 (Football), 51, 55 (Francois) 55 (Oskar) 57 (globe), 87 (ladder),
88, 90, 102, 25 (br), 133 (microchip), 133(lab technician), 133 (Magic), Corbis/
Morton Beebe p73, Corbis/ Bettmann p110(Ceaser),Corbis/ Digital Stock
p110 (Buddha), Corbis/ Epa pp110 (Suu Kyi),157, Corbis/ Fritz Hoffmann p24
(b), Corbis/ Steve Lupton p82, Corbis/ Steve Prezant p107, Corbis/ Reuters
p96(br), Corbis/ Nick Wheeler p44; **Digital Vision** p132 (L); **Fancy** pp 3,55
(Carrio); Fotolia pp 77, 86, 87 (smiley), 87 (champagne), 127; Courtesy of
Martin Frey p150 (CabBoots); **Getty Images** pp7(bl), 32, 96 (Thatcher) 110
(Thatcher),129,147(t), Getty Images/Amwell 87(t), Getty Images/Ross Andersen
p105, Getty Images/Michael Blann p27, Getty Images/Paul Bradbury p2 (nervous
man), Getty Images/Paul Bradbury p56(r), Getty Images/Rosemary Calvert
p24(t), Getty Images/Chris Clinton p42(l), Getty Images/Comstock p29(l),
Getty Images/Feingersh pp3,55 (De Silva),Getty Images/Getty Images for RBS
p3 (Jackie Stewart), p54(t), Getty Images/C Hawkins p74, Getty Images/Jon
Feingeresh Photography, Getty Images/John Lund p26, Getty Images/David
Madison p94, Getty Images/Manchan p14, Getty Images/Joe Mcnally p6(tr),
Getty Images/ p39, Getty Images/NBA p116, Getty Images/Photonica p124,
Getty Images/Jeff Rotmann p143(m), Getty Images Dennis Scott p19(r), Getty
Images/Hugh Sitton pp2(African Man),56(l), Getty Images/Janek Skarznski
AFP p28, Getty Images/Zia Soleil p84(t), Getty Images/Chip Somodevilla p25
(tm), Getty Images/Stockbyte p31, Getty Images/Tetra Images p30, Getty Images/
Mark Thompson pp3(crash), 54 (m), Getty Images/Time and Life Pictures
pp2(rocket), 33(1),133(rocket), Getty Images/Wire Image p83(b); **Goodshoot**
p136; **Image Source** pp3 (Giancarlo), 50(t), 76(t), 114, 134, 135; **Image 100**
p85(br); **KPMG International** p23(m); Macmillan Publishers Ltd/Paul Bricknell
pp2, 133(car), **Macmillan Publishers Ltd**/David Tolley p6 (dictionary); J Miele
p97; **Panos Pictures** p99; **PhotoAlto** p6 (family); **Photodisc** pp2 (palette), 3
(Sonia), 6 (classroom), 25(bm), 25 (tr), 55 (Sonia), 133 (palette); **Photolibrary**/
Blend Images p19 (sumo), Photolibrary/Martin Brigdale p69 (b), Photolibrary/
Rosemary Calvert pp2 (swan),133(swan), Photolibrary/Corbis p3 (Fiore),
Photolibrary/Corbis p36, Photolibrary/Corbis p55 (Fiore), Photolibrary/Design

Laguna pp2 (computer face), 133 (computer face), Photolibrary/Rob Elmy
p115, Photolibrary/Tony Pleavin p67, Photolibrary/Jean Baptiste Rabouan p73,
Photolibrary/Lynne Stone p83(t), Photolibrary/Larry Williams p64; Rex Features
pp33(r), 96(tl), 96(tl), Rex Features/Everett Collection p96(tr), Rex Features/
Everett/New Line p110 (Gandalf), Rex Features/Masatoshi Okauchi p110
(gates), Rex Features/Paramount/Everett p110 (Kirk), Rex Features/Sipa Press pp2
(Dilbert),132(t), 143(t); **Robert Harding**/John Miller pp121, 122; **Rubberball**
pp2 (Elvis),133 (Elvis); **Peter Sablis** p112; **Stockbyte** p66; **Superstock** pp 3
(Moretti), 54(b), 95, 110 (Washington), 110 (Queen Elizabeth), 143(bm);
Thinkstock p25 (l); Courtesy of **Brad Trent** p23(t); Courtesy of **University of
Edinburgh/Entrepreneurship Club** p116 (George Mackintosh); Courtesy of
Frag Woodall p154 (Everglade collapsible bicycle).

The authors and publishers would like to thank the following for permission
to use copyright material: Extract from 'Breaking the Glass Ceiling' by Linda
Lowen, copyright © Linda Lowen, reprinted by permission of the publisher,
About.com; John Adair for extracts from 'Effective Decision-Making' by John
Adair (Pan Books, 1985); Material from 'The Accidental Tourist' by Anne Tyler,
copyright © Anne Tyler 1995, reprinted by permission of A.M.Heath & Co.
Ltd., and Random House Group Limited; Adapted material from article 'Coke
Products Banned in Belgium' copyright © Associated Press, first appeared on
Portsmouth Herald website 1999, reprinted by permission of the publisher;
Francis Beckett for extracts from 'Creative way to better management' by Francis
Beckett first published in Financial Times 08.11.99, copyright © Francis
Beckett 1999; Fast Company for extracts from 'You have to start meeting like
this!' by Gina Imperato first published in Fast company April 1999 Issue 23
(www.fastcompany.com); Adapted extract from article 'Jet Lag Hater's Guide
to Business Travel' by John Cassy, copyright © John Cassy 1999, first appeared
in The Guardian 14.09.99, reprinted by permission of the publisher; Adapted
extract from article '2050 – and inmmortality is within our grasp' by David Smith,
copyright © David Smith 2005, first appeared in The Guardian 22.05.05,
reprinted by permission of the publisher; Sandra Harris for extracts from 'Deliver
us from e-mail', copyright © Sandra Harris 2000, first published in Business
Life Magazine September 2000; Quotation by Tim Sanders: 'What are the
biggest Email Mistakes?' copyright © Tim Sanders first appeared on Better Life
Coaches Group on You Tube, http://www.youtube.com/user/BetterLifeCoaches,
reprinted by permission of the author; Extract from 'The Ultimate Business
Presentation Book' by Andrew Leigh (www.maynardleigh.co.uk), copyright
© Andrew Leigh 1999, reprinted by permission of the author; Extract from
Speech at the Conservative Party Conference 10th October 1975 'These are the
two great challenges of our time.....' by Margaret Thatcher, reprinted by kind
permission of the Margaret Thatcher Foundation; Extract from Inauguration
Speech 10 May 1994 'We are both humbled and elevated by the honour and
priviledge....' by President of South Africa, Nelson Mandela, reprinted by kind
permission of Nelson Mandela Foundation; N I Syndication for material from
'Should genetic tests decide job prospects?' by Margaret Cole, copyright ©
Times Newspapers Limited 1999, first published in The Sunday Times 24.01.99,
reprinted by permission of the publisher; Quirk Books for extracts from 'the
Worst-Case Scenario Survival Column' by David Borgenicht taken from www.
worstcasescenarios.com/mainpage.htm; Material from 'The Essential Guide
to Email for Office and Home' copyright © David Shipley and Will Schwalbe
2007, used by permission of Alfred A.Knopf, a division of Random House,
Inc.; Adapted material from 'Contemporary Public Speaking' by Courtland L.
Bovee, copyright © Courtland L. Bovee, reprinted by permission of Rowman
& Littlefield Publishers, Inc.; Tribune Media Services International for extracts
from 'In a High-Tech World, It's a Cinch for Employers to Spy on Workers' by
Liz Stevens, first published in Knight Ridder Newspapers 12.06.02, copyright
© Knight Ridder/Tribune Media Services International 2003; 'I Have a Dream'
reprinted by arrangement with The Heirs to the Estate of Martin Luther King
Jr., c/o Writers House as agent for the proprietor New York, NY. Copyright ©
1963 Dr. Martin Luther King Jr; copyright renewed 1991 Coretta Scott King;
Extract from Inaugural Speech 20 January 1961 'Ask not what your country
can do for you....' by President John F. Kennedy, Washington D.C.; Adapted
material from website www.intrapreneur.com, reprinted by permission of Gifford
and Elizabeth Pinchot; Adapted material from Business Benefits 'Reinventing
the Way you Collaborate and Communicate' from website www.cisco.com,
used by permission of Cisco. Inc.; Extract adapted from 'Corporate Social
Responsibility in a Recession' by Jack and Suzy Welch. Reprinted from May
2009 issue of BusinessWeek by special permission, copyright © 2009 by The
McGraw-Hill Companies, Inc.; A transcript extract by Lord Michael Hastings,
Global Head of Citizenship and Diversity, KPMG, published on http://www.
youtube.com/watch?v=TNKn93VViUc, reproduced by permission of KPMG;
An extract from 'Green Talk', by Brendan May shown on http://www.green.tv/
green_talk_brendan_may_1, reproduced by permission of Planet 2050; A quiz
adapted from Smarter, Faster, Better: Strategies for Effective, Enduring, and
Fulfilled Leadership by Karlin Sloan, as published by Fortune on http://money.
cnn.com/quizzes/2007/fortune/leadership_annie/, copyright © John Wiley &
Sons, Inc.; A transcript extract by Trompenaars Hampden Turner, published
on http://www.youtube.com/user/THTconsulting, reproduced by permission of
Trompenaars Hampden Turner; Details about Faith Popcorn adapted from www.
faithpopcorn.com. Reprinted by permission of BrainReserve, Inc. copyright ©
2009 BrainReserve, Inc. All Rights Reserved.

Printed in Thailand

2015 2014 2013 2012
10 9 8 7 6 5 4